ERICH MÜHSAM

LIBERATING SOCIETY FROM THE STATE

AND OTHER WRITINGS
A POLITICAL READER

Edited and Translated by Gabriel Kuhn

Liberating Society from the State and Other Writings: A Political Reader
Erich Mühsam
Edited and translated by Gabriel Kuhn

ISBN: 978-1-60486-055-9

LCCN: 2010927794

PM Press
PO Box 23912
Oakland, CA 94623
www.pmpress.org

Cover by John Yates/stealworks.com
Layout based on design by Daniel Meltzer

Printed by the Employee Owners of Thomson-Shore in Dexter, Michigan.
www.thomsonshore.com

Published in the EU by The Merlin Press Ltd.
6 Crane Street Chambers, Crane Street, Pontypool NP4 6ND, Wales
www.merlinpress.co.uk
ISBN: 978-0-85036-683-9

TABLE OF CONTENTS

1918–1919: Munich III, Revolution and Council Republic

1919–1924: Imprisonment

1924–1933: Berlin

Liberating Society from the State: What Is Communist Anarchism?

Appendix I

Appendix II

Bibliography

EDITOR'S NOTE

NEXT TO GUSTAV LANDAUER, ERICH MÜHSAM HAS BEEN Germany's most influential anarchist. Johann Most and Rudolf Rocker had a bigger international impact, but Landauer and Mühsam have left the biggest mark on anarchist history in the country itself. Mühsam's *Die Befreiung der Gesellschaft vom Staat. Was ist kommunistischer Anarchismus?*, included in this volume as *Liberating Society from State: What Is Communist Anarchism?*, is arguably the most widely read anarchist text in Germany.

Die Befreiung der Gesellschaft vom Staat was the programmatic summary of Mühsam's political beliefs, penned one year before his death. It is presented in this book alongside numerous essays, letters, and diary entries, documenting the life of a unique personality straddling the lines between bohemia and proletarian organizing. The volume's selection contains Mühsam's best-known and most frequently reprinted essays, such as "Bohemia" and "Bismarxism," as well as texts chosen particularly with an English readership in mind, such as his articles on Sacco and Vanzetti. With few exceptions, the texts appear in chronological order, hopefully providing a comprehensive overview of the intersections of Mühsam's life, thought, and politics. The order of the chapters follows the structure of the Introduction. Two appendixes provide additional material: the first contains supplementary diary entries and letters; the second documents the fate of Erich's wife, Kreszentia "Zenzl" Mühsam, who spent twenty years imprisoned and exiled in the Soviet Union after her husband's death—a horrendous tale of Stalinist persecution.

Apart from political essays and articles, Mühsam wrote plays and hundreds of poems. Both his work as a playwright and as a poet deserve detailed study, which has been conducted by some scholars, even in English.[1] This volume, however, focuses on Mühsam as a political thinker and activist, reflecting both the editor's and the publisher's main interest and providing an addition to the Gustav Landauer reader, *Revolution and Other Writings*, published by PM Press in 2010.

All of the texts in this volume are published in print in English for the first time and have been translated by Gabriel Kuhn, with the translation of *Die Befreiung der Gesellschaft vom Staat* borrowing elements from the online translation made available by Chris Edmonston on *erichinenglish.org* in 2008.[2]

Translating Erich Mühsam

Translating texts that are roughly a hundred years old poses certain challenges. Mühsam's German is antiquated and many sentences extremely long-winded. They are not always easy to read, even for native German speakers. However, readability was a priority in the translation process in order to make this book relevant for a contemporary English-speaking audience. In cases where this demanded that the original text be treated in a liberal rather than a literal way, that was the chosen path. Needless to say, no liberties were taken that, in the translator's judgment, would have jeopardized the intentions or contents of the original.

The number of untranslated German terms has been kept to a minimum. Where it seemed important or inevitable to retain the original terms, explanations are provided in footnotes. Sometimes, the original German term, German name, or essay or book title follows the translation in parentheses. English translations of German names and titles follow in square brackets.

There are some terms frequently used by Mühsam that ought to be introduced with an explanation:

Geist–spirit: *Geist* is a notoriously difficult German term to translate. "Spirit" is the most common English translation, and I have adapted to this. However, the philosophical notion of *Geist*–for example in Hegel–lies somewhere between "intellect" and "soul;" as such, it can apply to an individual (in which case it might also be understood as an individual's "essence") as well as to a community, a people, an era, even a place; it defines individual or collective identity beyond its mere physicality (hence the major attacks on the term by materialists). Mühsam uses *Geist* much in this sense, being strongly influenced by Gustav Landauer, who offered the following explanation in a speech shortly before his death: "Geist is when knowledge, emotion, and will unite and become an active force."[3] In a less philosophical context, *Geist* can also be a close equivalent to "mind" or "reason." On the few occasions Mühsam uses the term in this sense, it has been translated accordingly. "Ghost," another meaning of *Geist*, plays no role in Mühsam's usage.

Philister–philistine: Mühsam makes frequent use of the term *Philister*, popularized as a pejorative for bourgeois scholars by Friedrich Nietzsche. As "philistine" (or "cultural philistine") has been the most common translation of the Nietzschean term, it will be used here too. It must be understood as a term for scholars bereft of soul and spirit, however, and not as a term indicating mere lack of education, culture, or taste.

Mühsam's language—like that of all German writers at the time, male and female—was marked by an inclusive use of male terms. Given the many problematic implications of a "modern cleansing" of Mühsam's language, this has been reproduced in the translations.

Acknowledgments

As always, it is impossible to thank everyone who has helped in the course of compiling this book, so I will limit myself to naming the following projects and organizations without which independent scholarly research would be near impossible:

Lausanne's *Centre International de Recherches sur l'Anarchisme* [International Center for Anarchist Research] (CIRA) and the wonderful Marianne Enckell.

The *International Institute for Social History* (IISH) in Amsterdam and its extremely accommodating staff.

Stockholm's *Arbetarrörelsens arkiv, Kungliga biblioteket*, and their many generous volunteers and employees.

Berlin's *Bibliothek der Freien* [Library of the Free], including computer wizard Sven-Oliver Buchwald and anarchist historian extraordinaire Wolfgang Eckhardt.

Lübeck's *Erich-Mühsam-Gesellschaft* [Erich Mühsam Society], under the longtime guidance of Johann-Wolfgang Goette and Sabine Kruse.

Special thanks also to Michael Ryan and Gregory Nipper for precious copyediting, to Chris Edmonston, the host of *erichinenglish.com*, for vital editorial assistance, to Chris Hirte for providing crucial information, and to Siegbert Wolf for steadfast support!

1. See the bibliography at the end of the book.
2. Edmonston's translation is an excellent rendition. The reason for using an altered version in this book is to keep the style and the terminology consistent throughout the volume.
3. "Der Krieg und die Revolution" [The War and the Revolution], in *Gustav Landauer und die Revolutionszeit 1918–1919* [Gustav Landauer and the Revolutionary Period of 1918–1919], edited by Ulrich Linse (Berlin: Karin Kramer, 1974), 98.

INTRODUCTION

Childhood and Youth

ERICH MÜHSAM WAS BORN INTO A RELIGIOUS JEWISH FAMILY ON April 6, 1878, in Berlin. His father, Siegfried, was a pharmacist, his mother, Rosalie Seligmann, born Cohn, a housewife. Erich had three siblings: Elisabeth Margarethe, born 1875, Hans Günther, born 1876, Charlotte Adelheid, born 1881.

When Erich was one year old, the family moved to Lübeck. Erich spent his childhood there. He was expelled from school at age sixteen for "socialist agitation." On January 16, 1896, the school's principle wrote the following letter:

> On December 10, we had a rare disciplinary problem in our school that involved the mathematics teacher. Several students had to be expelled. Erich Mühsam was not involved. However, Mühsam listened to the report I delivered to the entire school on the occasion of our Christmas celebration. He has admitted that he already planned to make use of this at the time. He reproduced my speech from memory and handed it to the editor of the social democratic *Volksbote* [Messenger for the People], who had expressed interest in it. As a consequence, the journal published a scandalous and disgraceful article about our school and a reprint of my speech, shortened, distorted, ridiculed, and with sardonic commentary—in truth, both the content and the form of the speech were noble, warm, and well measured. With this deceitful betrayal, Mühsam has placed himself beyond the school's boundaries and severed all ties with it.[1]

Following his father's wishes, Erich became a pharmacist apprentice.

In 1899, Rosalie, Erich's mother, "the only human being close to him as a child," died.[2] One year later, Erich moved to Berlin. According to Gerd W. Jungblut, he "remained the 'black sheep' of the family, receiving respect on an exclusively moral level for his selflessness and kindness."[3] As several documents included in the book will illustrate, Erich's relationship with Siegfried, his father, remained particularly strained. The relationship with his siblings appears to have been amicable, but distant. All of his siblings emigrated to Palestine in the early 1930s. Charlotte was the last one to die there, in 1972.

1900–1904: Literary and Anarchist Awakening

After moving to Berlin, Erich continued to work as a pharmacist, but was soon spending a lot of time among the *Friedrichshagener Dichterkreis*, a circle of writers with a progressive orientation.[4] He was particularly inspired by the eccentric poet Peter Hille.[5] Some historians have also stressed the influence of expressionism on the young Mühsam.[6]

Some months after his arrival, it came to a fateful meeting with Heinrich Hart,[7] who encouraged Mühsam to follow his true passion, writing, even if this disappointed his father. According to Rudolf Rocker, Hart spoke the words: "If you are not afraid of a little hunger and some missteps, then go ahead and do what you have to do! How can one discourage a man from doing what he wants to?"[8] Mühsam, who later claimed, "I think I rhymed before I knew how to read and write," followed the advice.[9] The deep rupture this created in the relationship with his father was never resolved.

Through acquaintances in the Friedrichshagener Dichterkreis, Mühsam joined the *Neue Gemeinschaft* [New Community], a spiritual-communitarian group founded by the brothers Heinrich and Julius Hart. It was there that he met his longtime friend, comrade, and mentor Gustav Landauer, whom Mühsam would later also call his "teacher."[10] Both soon became disillusioned with the Neue Gemeinschaft, however. In Mühsam's words:

> Eventually, the entire idea of a new community ended in a compromise that turned the bohemian plan of a free and self-determined life beyond bourgeois conventions into a caricature. No land was ever purchased. Instead, a children's home was rented in Schlachtensee.[11] Its rooms were distributed among the families according to how much rent they could pay. Class differences were supposedly overcome by the use of a common kitchen.[12]

Mühsam and Landauer remained close friends throughout their lives, although Landauer always behaved as an elder toward Mühsam, often criticizing him harshly. In a letter dated May 3, 1907, Landauer commented on some of Mühsam's writing with the following words:

> I was not impressed. The style lacks refinement and clarity. The contents lack rigor and strength. I wish we could sit down together and go through it all sentence by sentence. You would have to concede—like you have had to previously—that I am right when I speak of playful and unabashed superficiality. Nonetheless, you would do it all over again the next time...[13]

In general, Mühsam accepted Landauer's advice and always held him in high regard. After Landauer's death at the hands of right-wing soldiers who had overthrown the Bavarian Council Republic in 1919, Mühsam called him "one of the noblest minds of our time."[14]

Still, there were a few points of contention. The most important concerned matters of family life and sexuality. Landauer, who saw the nuclear family as the social core of mutual aid and solidarity, repeatedly drew the ire of Mühsam, who was a strong believer in free love and sexual experimentation.[15] The conflict came to a head in 1910 over the publication of Landauer's article "Tarnowska,"[16] a biting critique of free love, which Landauer saw as a mere pretext for moral and social degeneration.[17] For a while, Mühsam even saw the friendship threatened, but the two soon managed to work out their differences.[18]

Landauer and Mühsam also differed in their assessment of the proletariat's role in the revolution. Even though Mühsam was heavily influenced by Landauer's ideas of a "socialist spirit" as the basis for liberation,[19] he always tried to reconcile this with a notion of class-based communist anarchism. The vision of a "united proletariat" was one that Mühsam pursued his entire life. At times, not least during the Bavarian Revolution,[20] this brought him closer to communist allies, even the *Kommunistische Partei Deutschlands* [Communist Party of Germany] (KPD),[21] than Landauer would have ever felt comfortable with.

Other disagreements were of a more trivial kind. In "Unpolitische Erinnerungen" [Non-political Memoirs], a series of texts that Mühsam published between 1927 and 1929 in the longstanding and popular liberal *Vossische Zeitung*,[22] he recalls sharing a kitchen with Landauer in the Neue Gemeinschaft: "Landauer soon took permission from me...and made all the meals himself, only because I had once used the entire supply of milk and eggs for omelets that didn't turn out right—I had added plaster instead of flour."[23]

Of the two, Landauer has often been regarded as the "scholar" and "philosopher," with Mühsam seen as the "bohemian" and "activist." Needless to say, such categories are simplistic, but they contain some truth. In the words of Chris Hirte, one of Germany's most renowned Mühsam scholars: "To sit in a chamber and to dream of anarchist settlements, as Landauer did, was not Mühsam's way. He had to be in the midst of life; he had to be where life was at its most colorful, where things fermented and brewed."[24]

Landauer and Mühsam were not only lifelong friends, they also collaborated on several projects.[25] Mühsam was one of the founding members of the Socialist Bund, initiated by Landauer in 1908,[26] and he contributed regularly to Landauer's "Third" *Sozialist*, also providing a poem for the first issue.[27] Finally, both were very close during the Bavarian Revolution and were the driving force behind the proclamation of the Bavarian Council Republic on April 7, 1919.[28]

Internationally, the two were perceived as such close companions that mix-ups were frequent. In 1923, after being named an "honorary soldier" by the Soviet government, Mühsam noted in his diary: "Once again, they have used Landauer's picture instead of mine. ...But this repeated confusion with my best friend, whom I was so close to in life and in thought, moves me and urges me to keep on fighting!"[29]

Ironically, both were outsiders within the German anarchist movement: neither Landauer's "mystical anarchism" nor Mühsam's eclecticism fit into the rather rigid blend of proletarianism and moral purity embraced by most anarchists at the time.

After Mühsam and Landauer left the Neue Gemeinschaft in 1901, Mühsam started writing for anarchist journals. He published some texts in *Der freie Arbeiter* [The Free Worker], a journal closely connected to the *Anarchistische Föderation Deutschlands* [Anarchist Federation of Germany],[30] and he coedited the short-lived revival of *Der arme Teufel* [The Poor Devil], which had been edited as a German-language journal in Detroit from 1884 until 1900 by Robert Reitzel.[31]

In 1903, Mühsam's pamphlet "Die Homosexualität" [Homosexuality] was published with curious consequences. In the pamphlet, Mühsam defended the rights of homosexuals based on the theories of the German physician and gay rights activist Magnus Hirschfeld, who had studied homosexuality as an inborn quality. Before the pamphlet was even returned from the printers, Mühsam distanced himself from it, arguing that a purely genetic interpretation of homosexuality undermined the ideal of "erotic friendship," which he now saw as the noblest form of same-sex relationships.[32] He publicly renounced his pamphlet in an "open letter" to *Der freie Arbeiter*, which drew a response by Hirschfeld in the next issue. Translations of both letters are included in this book.

At around the same time, the publication of Mühsam's poetry began to increase dramatically. His first collection of poems, *Die Wüste* [The Desert], appeared in 1904. Over the years, several more volumes followed, and hundreds of poems were published in various journals. According to Chris Hirte, Mühsam laid the foundation "for a socialist poetry linked to the proletarian class struggle."[33] In the opinion of the famed anarchist historian Max Nettlau, Mühsam was "the only German anarchist poet to emerge after Mackay's *Sturm*[34]—handling the weapon of irreverence masterfully and finding the natural tone of the folk song like no other before him."[35]

Never nearly as prolific an illustrator as he was a writer, Mühsam did, however, draw throughout his lifetime. His most famous collection of drawings is *Bilder und Verse für Zenzl [Drawings and Poems for Zenzl]*, published posthumously in 1974.

Socially, Mühsam mainly moved in Berlin's bohemian circles, where he gained some notoriety. Chris Hirte writes:

> He liked to frequent the bohemian bars in Berlin's western districts, whose clientele he invigorated with his passion for debate, his sarcastic humor, and his spiritedness. A lean youth in old-fashioned attire, with restless eyes, wild hair, cigar, pince-nez, and cane, Mühsam turned his public appearance into a show. He enjoyed the attention. While he shocked the bourgeoisie, others embraced him as a bizarre but delightful embodiment of bohemia. Even before cabaret became popular, Mühsam recited frivolous verses in early morning hours, improvised rhymes, and made fun of the Kaiser and the Reich. When it was time to pay the bill, he passed his hat around.[36]

1904–1909: Traveling Years

In 1904, Mühsam and his close friend—and, as some suggest, lover—Johannes Nohl[37] decided to leave Berlin and to travel around Europe to satisfy personal wanderlust and to search for bohemian circles and utopian communities.

Mühsam moved around for four years, sometimes with Nohl, sometimes by himself. His most regular points of call were Vienna, Lausanne, Ascona, Paris, Zurich, Bern, and Munich. He described these years thus:

> The years from 1904 to 1909 I call my "wandering years," as it is entirely impossible for me to recall any experiences, meetings, journeys, or homes in chronological order. When I think that something happened in Munich at a certain time, I often realize that I could have only been in Vienna—or no, maybe in Zurich—or, wait, maybe in Ascona… In other words, it is best not to make any claims and to avoid contradictions that anyone can point out who looks through my mail. In any case, I never spent more than half a year in the same place, and I think I only stayed in Zurich for that long; maybe also in Berlin and Munich, the two places I eventually always wanted to return to, no matter where I was. …I do not regret anything that I did to see new things and to make the most of life. Sometimes we were incredibly hungry, and it is true that we ended up in terrible situations, but we always found a way out. Then we shook things off like a wet poodle shakes off water and laughed about what we had experienced. We headed out into the world with no other plan than to travel as far as our money would take us, and we only concerned ourselves with matters of food and accommodation when

they became urgent. Had we not been that carefree, then I would now be fifty years old and would have never seen Florence or Paris. In other words, I would long for a youth that I missed because of the bourgeois fear of some hunger pangs and bedbugs in some Italian hostel.[38]

Apart from insightful letters, Mühsam's account "Ascona," which describes the utopian-settlement-turned-sanatorium Monte Verità and the community of colorful characters that had gathered in the Ascona surroundings, provides the most vivid image of Mühsam's traveling period. Long excerpts are included in this book. In his writing, Mühsam concentrated on poetry during these years.

1909–1914: Munich I, Socialist Bund and *Kain*

In 1909, Mühsam moved to Munich, a town he had taken a liking to during his travels. He particularly enjoyed the bohemian suburb of Schwabing.[39]

Shortly after arriving, Mühsam formed the group *Anarchist*, soon renamed *Tat* [Deed]. It was a member group of the Socialist Bund (*Sozialistischer Bund*), initiated by Landauer in 1908. Mühsam was one of the founding members. For some months, Mühsam, who one scholar has called an "unbending advocate for society's downtrodden," concentrated his efforts on winning the lumpenproletariat over to the anarchist cause.[40] Eventually, this led to a charge of "conspiracy" and a court case. Three of Mühsam's essays chronicling these events are included in this book.

Mühsam was acquitted, but the bourgeois press, whose author fees Mühsam was dependent on, refused to publish his poems and articles. Despite the protest from renowned writers such as Heinrich and Thomas Mann and Frank Wedekind, Mühsam continued to be boycotted. Some have called this a blessing in disguise, as it led Mühsam to found the first of the two periodicals his name remains associated with to this day: the monthly *Kain–Zeitschrift für Menschlichkeit* [Cain–Journal for Humanity], whose first issue appeared in April 1911. Mühsam opened his editorial with the words: "This journal has been founded without capital. Not because of any principle, but because there was no capital."[41] Nonetheless, *Kain*, basically a "one-man journal,"[42] sold well enough to guarantee Mühsam a modest living until he was forced to suspend publication at the outbreak of World War I.

As in Berlin, Mühsam was a well-known figure in bohemian circles. Nonetheless, he became increasingly upset if people concluded that he was not serious about the proletariat's liberation. In "Unpolitische Erinnerungen" he writes:

> For a long time, I have been called the "prototype of a coffeehouse writer," yet it was always known to people that I moved in proletarian circles, that I did tedious political work like distributing leaflets and going door-to-door,

and that I gave lectures at group meetings and speeches at large gatherings. I stood before judges in political trials, just as I roamed with artists, recited satirical poems, and frequented licentious locations in Berlin, Munich, Zurich, Geneva, Florence, Paris, and Vienna; there I would sit with a girl on my lap and bad jokes on my lips, and I would drink away entire nights with bohemian dreamers, like the wonderful Friedrich von Schennis.[43] Everyone knew that I was friends with many famous people who I used to hit up for money—and not always for myself! Frank Wedekind once said to me, "You always ride on two horses that pull in different directions. One day, they will tear your legs off!" I answered, "If I let go of one, I will lose my balance and break my neck."[44]

1914–1918: Munich II, The War

The outbreak of World War I marks one of the most troublesome incidents in Mühsam's political life. When Mühsam published a statement explaining the suspension of *Kain*, he ended with the lines: "I am united with all Germans in the wish that we can keep foreign hordes away from our women and children, away from our towns and fields."

Mühsam later explained that he added the sentence after acquaintances who he had met on the way to the printers urged him to. He said that the words were written "under the pressure of anxiety, fear, mental strain, and emotional turmoil," and he omitted the sentence in later publications of the statement.[45] Mühsam seemed unhappy in general with the terminology he had used during the earliest phase of the war. Chris Hirte, the editor of Mühsam's diaries, noted that Mühsam later corrected the personal pronoun "we" in early World War I commentary on German troops.[46]

In July 1915, Mühsam's personal life was shaken by the death of his father. Bitterness had defined their relationship ever since Mühsam abandoned his career as a pharmacist for the life of a writer, bohemian, and political activist, but Erich had still counted on inheriting enough to feel financially secure. He received far less than expected, and noted in his diary: "Now the whole misery starts anew—the only difference being that I will no longer be able to borrow money in the name of an impending inheritance!"[47]

In September 1915, Mühsam married Kreszentia "Zenzl" Elfinger, the daughter of a Bavarian innkeeper. Despite Mühsam's ongoing promiscuity and related problems with Zenzl, she remained his lifelong companion. In a diary entry on December 24, 1914, Mühsam remarked: "This morning, when she sat at my bed, I realized how dear she is to me. She comes close to what I most long for in a lover: a substitute for my mother. I can put my head in her lap and let her caress me quietly for hours. I don't feel the same with anyone else. Her love is extremely important to me, and I have to thank her more in these hard times than I sometimes realize myself. Maybe I can return some of this one day!"[48]

The years of World War I were a trying time for its opponents. Mühsam desperately tried to organize coordinated resistance, but, like others, failed.[49] From April 24 to October 31, 1918, he was banished to the small Bavarian town of Traunstein, about one hundred kilometers east of Munich. Everything changed dramatically, though, with the end of the war and the German Revolution of November 1918.

1918–1919: Munich III, Revolution and Council Republic

The German Revolution was initiated by the rebellion of navy soldiers in Wilhelmshaven who refused to board their ships for a final desperate defense against the allied forces. The rebellion spread from Wilhelmshaven to Kiel, from soldiers to workers, from the military to the government, and only ten days later, on November 9, the social democrat Philipp Scheidemann—against the explicit will of some Social Democratic Party leaders—proclaimed Germany a republic, effectively ending the Kaiserreich. On the very same day, Karl Liebknecht, the only steadfast SPD opponent of the war and the cofounder of the *Spartakusbund* [Spartacus League],[50] declared Germany a "socialist republic." These parallel announcements marked a divide between moderate and radical forces within the German Revolution that would come to define a period of severe infighting with disastrous consequences.[51]

In Bavaria, the leader of the *Unabhängige Sozialdemokratische Partei Deutschlands* [Independent Social Democratic Party of Germany] (USPD),[52] Kurt Eisner, had already proclaimed Bavaria a republic on November 7. Mühsam, allowed to return to Munich, was critical of Eisner's "bourgeois-democratic politics,"[53] but excited about the opportunity to work in a revolutionary climate. In order to comment on the revolutionary developments, he even revived *Kain* from November 1918 to April 1919. Meanwhile, Eisner had called Gustav Landauer to Munich, asking him to "advance the transformation of souls as a speaker."[54]

As part of his socialist vision, Eisner supported the establishment of several councils, mainly workers' and peasants' councils. However, the legislative powers of the councils were limited and they were to be controlled by a cabinet and a national assembly of elected party representatives. Mühsam and other radicals opposed this concession to parliamentarism but supported Eisner in his efforts to keep counterrevolutionary forces at bay. Hence, they were deeply troubled when the USPD experienced a crushing defeat in the Bavarian election of January 12, 1919, heaving the SPD into power with the support of conservative parties. When Eisner was shot dead by a right-wing student on February 21, Mühsam and his comrades decided to take matters into their own hands. Fearing the revolution's defeat, and inspired by the Russian example (Mühsam failed to see the authoritarian tendencies in Bolshevism for years), they deposed the cabinet and the national assembly and proclaimed Bavaria a council republic on April 7.

The SPD-led government fled to the northern Bavarian town of Bamberg. One week later, they sent troops to Munich to overthrow the council republicans. The Communist Party's Red Army repelled the attack after Mühsam and some other leading figures were arrested and transported to Ebrach Prison, near Bamberg. This might have saved Mühsam's life. It was only two weeks later that the central German government in Berlin sent troops to Bavaria, supported by reactionary Free Corps soldiers.[55] Despite spirited resistance, Munich was taken by force, Landauer lynched on May 2, and Leviné, the leader of the Communist Party, executed on July 5. The same month, Mühsam was sentenced to fifteen years of confinement in a fortress. A few weeks later, the Weimar Republic was established, giving Germany a parliamentarian constitution.[56] The short dream of a socialist revolution was over.

1919–1924: Imprisonment

Mühsam remained incarcerated for five years. Being confined in a fortress–a sentence usually reserved for political dissidents–meant certain privileges compared to the general prison population, most notably the opening of cells for communal meetings and activities during the day, but it also meant increased harassment, reaching from the confiscation of papers and diaries to punishments like isolation and food deprivation. Mühsam's health deteriorated drastically during those years.

Mühsam continued to idealize the Russian Revolution. He called Lenin a "Bakuninist"[57] and continued to propagate a non-party version of the "dictatorship of the proletariat."[58] When he wrote his "Eye-Witness Report" of the Bavarian Council Republic, "Von Eisner bis Leviné" [From Eisner to Leviné][59]–the only first-hand account of the events from an anarchist perspective[60]–it was addressed "to the attention of comrade Lenin." It was only in 1925, after Mühsam was released from confinement and had better access to news from Russia, that he finally broke with Bolshevism.[61]

In 1919, Mühsam briefly joined the KPD, explaining in a letter to his Danish friend Martin Andersen Nexø:[62] "I recently joined the Communist Party–of course not to follow the party line, but to be able to work against it from the inside."[63] Mühsam was desperately looking for ways to unite the proletariat, at the time believing that "the only organization that can bring this unity is the KPD."[64] It only took a few months for Mühsam to become disillusioned, however. He left the party again in November after the party congress's decision to run in general elections.[65]

Mühsam's desire to unite the proletariat was a lifelong effort. At times, this meant opening himself up to left-wing factions of the SPD,[66] at times even to nationalist forces, like the expelled "left wing" of the NSDAP[67] under Otto Strasser.[68] While these efforts were certainly based on honorable intentions, they also rested on ill-fated idealism. Ulrich Linse notes: "Mühsam lacked a particular talent for organizing; his many ideas rarely allowed him to properly focus on one thing. His political naïveté prevented him from acknowledging the deep, unbridgeable oppositions between groups that he wanted to bring together for common action."[69] Rudolf Rocker draws a similar picture, albeit with a more conciliatory tone:

> There was something child-like and unconstrained, something joyful in this man; something that no personal sorrow, no misery could erase. With an almost lyrical passion, he believed in the proletariat's natural desire for freedom, and whenever I challenged this assumption, it deeply upset him. His soul was filled by the same convictions that had once filled the souls of Russia's youth—those who "went to the people," following Bakunin's call. Mühsam was a believer. His belief could move mountains. He was a poet to whom there was no clear difference between the reality of life and his dreams.[70]

Mühsam made an impression on almost everyone he met. His kindness—the characteristic that also earned him the lifelong respect of his siblings, although they did not maintain close personal ties and did not share his politics—has been commented on by many. In Augustin Souchy's description, Mühsam had "a fascinating personality; he was spiritual, imaginative, witty, funny, and possessed a great sense of irony—at the same time he was kind, helpful, and emphatic. …Erich had his heart in his hand, and comradeship in his blood."[71] Rudolf Rocker wrote: "As a human being, Mühsam was one of the most beautiful people I have ever met. He belonged to no party, which means that the humanity in him had not been destroyed, as in so many others. He was always noble in his conduct, a loyal and dedicated friend, and an enormously thoughtful and entertaining host."[72]

Mühsam was freed by an amnesty for political prisoners in December 1924. Ironically, the amnesty was declared to free Hitler and his co-conspirators after their 1923 coup attempt.[73]

1924–1933: Berlin

After Mühsam was released from confinement on December 20, 1924, he returned to Berlin. Zenzl had moved there a few months earlier. Upon arrival, Mühsam was greeted by an assembly of workers, who were attacked by the police.[74] The journalist Bruno Frei described the scene thus:

> Thanks to my press card I was able to get past the police barriers. Helmet-wearing security forces, both on foot and on horses, had sealed off the

station. On the square in front of it, there were several hundred, maybe a thousand workers and youths with flags and banners. Their republican deed: to greet Erich Mühsam! When the express train from Munich arrived, a few youngsters managed to make their way into the arrival hall. Mühsam stepped out of the train in obvious pain, accompanied by his wife Zenzl. The young workers lifted him on their shoulders. …Mühsam fought back tears and thanked the comrades. Someone started to sing "The Internationale." At that very moment, the helmet-wearing mob attacked the people who had gathered around Mühsam. They yelled at them, pushed them, and hit them with batons. The comrades resisted courageously, though, protected Mühsam, and led him outside. Unfortunately, the police had already begun to chase the workers from the square. …Many were arrested and wounded.[75]

Mühsam was instantly engaged in political work again. In Souchy's estimation, "there was no left-wing or progressive movement in the Weimar Republic that he was not a part of."[76] The focus of Mühsam's work was prisoner support. According to Souchy, this constituted "more than half of his daily work."[77] He became very active in the *Rote Hilfe Deutschlands* [Red Aid of Germany], the German branch of the International Red Aid network, commonly known by its Russian acronym MOPR.[78] The Rote Hilfe was officially a non-party organization, but always closely tied to the KPD.[79]

Mühsam also pursued his old dream of uniting the working class, trying to establish an "Einheitsfront des revolutionären Proletariats" [United Front of the Revolutionary Proletariat]. The attempt failed, due both to the sectarianism of many anarchists and to the authoritarianism of the Marxists.[80]

Mühsam's relationship with a large faction of German anarchists, mainly organized in the *Föderation Kommunistischer Anarchisten Deutschlands* [Federation of Communist Anarchists of Germany] (FKAD),[81] which had sent Mühsam monthly financial aid during his imprisonment,[82] became increasingly strained. A major point of contention was Mühsam's work with the Rote Hilfe and other KPD-linked groups like *Roter Frontkämpferbund* [Association of Red Front Fighters] and *Roter Jungsturm/Rote Jungfront* [Red Youth Storm/Red Youth Front].[83] In 1925, the FKAD released a declaration in which it accused Mühsam of "open propaganda in the interests the Communist Party," of activities that were "not compatible with fundamental anarchist principles," and of receiving pay for talks at Rote Hilfe events that "indirectly undermined anarchists and the anarchist movement." The declaration ended with the words:

> We ask our comrades to no longer provide Erich Mühsam with the platforms that he uses to hurt our movement. It does not matter whether or not Mühsam still calls himself an anarchist. We are taking this opportunity to clearly state that Mühsam's activity for "non-party" organizations under

the thumb of the KPD is non-anarchistic, and that we no longer see him as an anarchist.[84]

The Austrian anarchist Pierre Ramus even saw an "agent of Bolshevism" in him.[85] This is particularly ironic given Mühsam's reaction to an offer he received from the Bolshevik government at the time: it invited him to visit the Soviet Union. Mühsam said that he would gladly come if he was allowed to bring an exiled Russian anarchist with him as a guide—otherwise, he would not be able to get a fair impression of the country. Unsurprisingly, the Bolsheviks declined.[86]

Another conflict with the FKAD derived from its strong non-violence stance. Mühsam was particularly irate over the organization's attempt to claim Gustav Landauer as a pacifist.[87]

Finally, Mühsam's persistent defense of the council system caused opposition within anarchist ranks, as it was deemed too close to the council communist tradition, which, albeit libertarian, was largely influenced by Marxist theory.[88]

In 1926, announcing the publication of the journal *Fanal*, Mühsam declared: "The editor calls himself an anarchist without always agreeing with the ideology and tactics of the majority of German anarchists."[89] For a number of historians, though, Mühsam's unorthodox anarchism made it the most interesting of the Weimar period. Ulrich Linse writes that "Mühsam became the protagonist of a non-dogmatic, open anarchist politics," while Heinz Hug states: "The incorporation of the council system into the body of anarchist social philosophy was Mühsam's most original move. ... It marks the attempt to merge anarchist, anarcho-syndicalist, and Marxist beliefs."[90] Augustin Souchy described Mühsam's "special role"[91] within German anarchism thus: "He could not fully embrace the syndicalists because he considered revolutionary councils more important than union organizing. He was separated from the individualists by his proletarian sympathies. And he was alienated from the FKAD because of his hostility toward frozen dogmatism and because of personal differences."[92]

Among the anarchist groups that Mühsam worked with, the most important was the *Anarchistische Vereinigung Berlin* [Anarchist Association of Berlin], which had split from the FKAD in 1923.[93] Mühsam also kept good relations with the anarcho-syndicalist *Freie Arbeiter-Union Deutschlands* [Free Workers' Union of Germany] (FAUD), although he only became an official member in 1933, just after the Nazis had seized power and shortly before the organization disbanded.[94] Rudolf Rocker was active in both groups and a close friend of Mühsam during this time. In his memoirs he writes that he saw Mühsam "almost every day," while living in Berlin in the 1920s.[95]

In 1926, Mühsam founded the second of his renowned periodicals, the above-mentioned *Fanal*. Although it never reached the readership and relative financial success of *Kain*, it found a fairly wide audience and remains an essential chapter in the history of radical German publishing. Kurt Kreiler has called the fifty-nine issues of *Fanal* that appeared between 1926 and 1931 "a fulminating anti-chronicle of the Weimar Republic's end."[96]

The first volume of *Fanal* was exclusively written by Mühsam. In the first issue from October 1926, he declared categorically: "There will be no contributions from others. I was in Bavarian captivity for almost six years and practically prohibited from presenting my thoughts to a wider public. ...People ought to grant me the modest sixteen pages I intend to fill every month, so that finally I can propagate ideas that no one else will print."

With the second volume, Mühsam started to include texts by others. Rudolf Rocker was one of the most prominent contributors, and during certain periods, *Fanal* effectively served as the publishing outlet for the Anarchistische Vereinigung.[97]

Mühsam's financial situation remained dire; not least, because he always shared the little he had. Augustin Souchy stated: "His own material needs came last for him. ...Himself poor and living in misery, he once spent days collecting money to enable a proletarian comrade suffering from tuberculosis to go to a mountain retreat. Frequently, he borrowed money to travel to far-away prisons so he could visit proletarian inmates."[98]

From September 1927 to April 1929, Mühsam published his "Unpolitische Erinnerungen" [Non-political Memoirs] in twenty-five installments in the *Vossische Zeitung*.[99] The texts tell anecdotes from his bohemian and literary life and allow an insight into his personal development. The decision to publish in a mainstream journal was hardly random. Mühsam always tried to reach wider audiences, and agitation was a crucial part of his political work. According to Ulrich Linse, he was "the only German anarchist during the Weimar Republic who realized the significance of broadcasting and made propaganda for anarchism on radio shows."[100] Many have lauded his qualities as a public speaker. In the words of the socialist writer and editor Fritz Erpenbeck, "he was able to capture the masses. He spoke with real passion and appealed to the people's feelings. ...He described events with such involvement that it felt real—people believed him."[101]

It was in the late 1920s that Mühsam received his greatest recognition as a dramatist. *Staatsräson. Ein Denkmal für Sacco and Vanzetti* was produced by the popular socialist stage director Erwin Piscator in 1929.[102] Mühsam had already had success with *Die Freivermählten. Polemisches Schauspiel in drei Aufzügen* [The Freely Married: Polemical Drama in Three Acts], a play about free love completed in 1914, and *Judas. Ein Arbeiterdrama in fünf Akten*, written in prison in 1920.[103] Mühsam's last play, *Alle Wetter! Volksstück mit Gesang und Tanz*, an ominous portrayal of society under fascist rule, was written in 1931.[104]

Mühsam believed strongly in the political significance of theatre and of the arts in general. In his programmatic essay, "Kunst und Proletariat" [The Arts and the Proletariat], published in the May 1930 issue of *Fanal*, he declared:

Agitational art is good and necessary. It is needed by the proletariat both in revolutionary times and in the present. But it has to be *art*, skilled, spirited, and glittering. All arts have agitational potential, but none more than drama. In the theatre, living people present living passion. Here, more than anywhere else, true art can communicate true conviction. Here, the idea of a revolutionary worker can be materialized. ... Arts must inspire people, and inspiration comes from the spirit. It is not our task to *teach* the minds of the workers with the help of the arts—it is our task to *bring spirit* to the minds of the workers with the help of the arts, as the spirit of the arts knows no limits. Neither dialectics nor historical materialism have anything to do with this; the only art that can enthuse and enflame the proletariat is the one that derives its richness and its fire from the spirit of freedom.

In 1929, the ever-increasing influence of the Communist Party on the Rote Hilfe caused Mühsam to finally leave the organization.[105] Two years later, *Fanal* was prohibited by the authorities. The ban was limited to four months, but Mühsam was not able to resume publication due to financial difficulties, so it essentially marked the end of the publication.

Mühsam continued to send occasional calls and manifestos to the former *Fanal* readers, and also published his political literary legacy, *Die Befreiung der Gesellschaft vom Staat*, under the *Fanal* banner in 1933. The booklet, the only longer programmatic text published by Mühsam, summed up the key issues of the social and political vision that he had pursued over thirty years: free love; a "spiritual," anti-Marxist understanding of socialism in the sense of Gustav Landauer; an outspoken commitment to the workers' struggle and the worker's revolution; a continued defense of a non-party interpretation of the "dictatorship of the proletariat;" and his affinity for the council system.

Only a few months after the publication of *Die Befreiung der Gesellschaft vom Staat*, the Nazis took power in Germany. Mühsam—anarchist, council republican, Jew—was an obvious target. He further incited the Nazis' fury by tirelessly campaigning against them. Mühsam's safety became ever more threatened when Nazi journals blamed him for the shooting of right-wing *Thule-Gesellschaft* [Thule Society] members during the final days of the Bavarian Council Republic[106]—by which time Mühsam had already been imprisoned. Friends encouraged him to leave the country, but for months he refused. Finally, in February 1934, he bought train tickets to Prague. The night before his planned departure on February 28, he was arrested at his home in the early morning hours. It was the night of the Reichstag Fire, a crucial event in the Nazis' quest to establish totalitarian rule.[107] Souchy reports that Mühsam had visited him on the evening of the twenty-seventh. "We urged him to stay the night, as we considered it safer for him than returning home. But he declined, saying that he did not want his wife to worry."[108]

Mühsam spent the next seventeen months in various prisons and concentration camps, tortured and humiliated. The following is an account of a fellow prisoner:

> One evening the iron gate to our ward was opened. "Achtung!" Everyone jumped up. Two wardens appeared. "Mühsam, step up!" One of the wardens, a big fellow with broad shoulders, held an issue of *Arbeitertum* [The Workers][109] in his hands. "Mühsam, here is an article about you." Then he turned to us: "You have an important figure among you!" Back to Mühsam: "Mühsam, where were you in Munich in 1919? Weren't you some kind of minister?" Erich Mühsam calmly looked at the warden and said, "In 1919, I was on the Executive Council of the Bavarian Council Republic." The warden: "And what did you do?" Mühsam: "We tried to realize the proletarian revolution." "Bullshit," yelled the warden and hit Erich in the face. The other warden added a blow. "You pig, you ordered twenty-two hostages to be shot!"[110] Erich staggered, tripped over a bank, and fell on some straw mattresses. The wardens jumped after him, striking more blows. We stood still, clenching our fists and grinding our teeth, condemned to watch. We knew from experience that the slightest sign of resistance would send us to the hole for fourteen days or straight to the medical ward. Finally, the wardens pulled Erich up again and taunted him: "Hey, don't give in right away!" Then the big warden yelled, "So, what did you do in Munich?" One of Erich's eyes was bloodshot. His voice was trembling. He said, "When the twenty-two hostages were shot in Munich, the social democratic government had already put me in prison." The warden raised his hand: "What are you saying, you pig? They put you in prison? You put yourself in prison, because you were afraid and you knew that you were safe from bullets there. You masterminded the revolution, you Jewish pig!" They hit Erich again with their fists. He fell back onto the straw mattresses, the wardens followed and continued to hit and kick him.[111]

Mühsam also had his thumbs broken to prevent him from writing, and he had lost his hearing almost completely due to the repeated beatings. His fate did not go unnoticed internationally. Alexander Berkman commented:

> I received a note from Germany yesterday. Erich Mühsam, the idealist, revolutionary, and Jew, represents everything that Hitler and his followers hate. They are attempting to destroy cultural and progressive life in Germany by destroying him. Mühsam became a particular object of Hitler's scorn because of his outstanding role in the Munich Revolution, alongside men like Landauer, Leviné, and Toller.[112]

Defying repeated demands that he kill himself, Mühsam was finally found hanged in the Concentration Camp Oranienburg on the morning of July 10, 1934. His death was officially declared a suicide, yet eyewitness reports and later investigations suggest that he was murdered by SA soldiers from Bavaria. This is the account of John Stone, an Oranienburg inmate at the time:

> In the evening, Mühsam was ordered to see the camp's commanders. When he returned, he said, "They want me to hang myself—but I will not do them the favor." We went to bed at 8 p.m., as usual. At 9 p.m., they called Mühsam from his cell. This was the last time we saw him alive. It was clear that something out of the ordinary was happening. We were not allowed to go to the latrines in the yard that night. The next morning, we understood why: we found Mühsam's battered corpse there, dangling from a rope tied to a wooden bar. Obviously, the scene was supposed to look like a suicide. But it wasn't. If a man hangs himself, his legs are stretched because of the weight, and his tongue sticks out of his mouth. Mühsam's body didn't show any of these signs. His legs were bent. Furthermore, the rope was attached to the bar by an advanced bowline knot. Mühsam knew nothing about these things and would have been unable to tie it. Finally, the body showed clear indications of recent abuse. Mühsam had been beaten to death before he was hanged.[113]

On July 16, Mühsam was buried at Waldfriedhof [Forest Cemetery] Dahlem in Berlin. The German writer Susanne Leonhard was present at the funeral: "In the chapel, there were fourteen people. At the gravesite another half dozen joined. Not more. Only this small group of people dared to show sympathy for the dead poet. Not a single prominent writer was among them."[114] Zenzl Mühsam was advised not to attend for her own safety. She had left Berlin for Prague on July 14. Her fate is documented in an appendix to this book.

Legacy

During his lifetime, Erich Mühsam was known and respected internationally as an uncompromising revolutionary. A number of texts by and about him were published in Italian, French, and Russian.[115] After his death, the *Press Service of the International Workers' Association* (IWA) published a Special Issue (no. 181) on August 8, 1934. It included obituaries from newspapers in Prague, Paris, and other European cities. The *New York Times*, which had already reported on Mühsam leaving the Rote Hilfe in 1929, also ran an article. Several English-language texts about Mühsam were published during the 1930s in *Man!: A Journal of the Anarchist Idea and Movement*. The tireless Augustin Souchy published a Spanish booklet about Mühsam, *Erich Mühsam: su vida—su obra—su martirio*, in 1934.[116] During the Spanish Revolution, German and Scandinavian volunteers formed a small unit called *Centuria Erich Mühsam*.[117]

As a result of World War II, the overall demise of anarchism, and the fact that Mühsam's papers were locked away in Moscow—a fact that the appendix about Zenzl Mühsam's fate will address in more detail—very little research on Mühsam was conducted for decades afterwards. There was some awareness in East Germany, where copies of his papers arrived in the late 1950s, but the GDR's official portrayal of Mühsam was ideologically limited: he was lauded for his anti-fascism and communist leanings, but chastised for his "immature" anarchism. International articles, like the one in the August 1965 issue of the British *Anarchy* journal, were few and far between.

Only with the collapse of East European state socialism, the resultant access to the Mühsam archives, and the foundation of the Erich-Mühsam-Gesellschaft [Erich Mühsam Society] in Lübeck in 1989 did scholarly work on Mühsam begin to thrive again. There have been numerous German publications over the last twenty years, and new translations have appeared in French and, particularly, in Italian.

In English, only a handful of short Mühsam texts had been available for a long time. Luckily, Chris Edmonston has recently made a number of excellent translations available on the website *erichinenglish.org*, which I highly recommend as a companion to this book, not least because it includes translations of the Mühsam plays *Judas* and *Staatsräson*. The translation and setting to music of Mühsam poems by Gary Bachlund are also highly recommended.[118]

There are two notable studies of Mühsam's work available in English: Lawrence Baron's *The Eclectic Anarchism of Erich Mühsam*, published in 1976, provides a general overview of his life and work, while David A. Shepherd's *From Bohemia to the Barricades: Erich Mühsam and the Development of a Revolutionary Drama*, released in 1993, focuses on Mühsam the political dramatist. I can only hope that this volume helps to instigate further research into a unique and remarkable figure of anarchist thought and praxis.

1. Letter by Prof. Dr. Schubring, quoted from Chris Hirte, *Wege zu Erich Mühsam* [Ways to Erich Mühsam] (Lübeck: Schriften der Erich-Mühsam-Gesellschaft, 1989), 16–17.
2. Chris Hirte, Nachwort [Afterword] in Erich Mühsam, *Tagebücher 1910–1924* [Diary 1910–1924], edited by Chris Hirte (München: dtv, 1994), 366.
3. Gerd W. Jungblut, Einleitung [Introduction] in Erich Mühsam, *In meiner Posaune muss ein Sandkorn sein. Briefe 1900–1934* [There Must Be a Grain of Sand in My Trombone: Letters 1900–1934], edited by Gerd W. Jungblut (Vaduz: Topos, 1984), XVII.
4. Literally, "Circle of Poets of Friedrichshagen." For a description Mühsam's of Friedrichshagen, a suburb in the southeast of Berlin, see Erich Mühsam, "Unpolitische Erinnerungen" [Non-political Memoirs], in *Publizistik–Unpolitische Erinnerungen. Ausgewählte Werke Band 2* [Journalism–Non-political Memoirs: Collected Works, vol. 2] (Berlin: Volk und Welt 1978), 505–513.
5. See, for example, Mühsam's article "Peter Hille" in *Kampf*, April 1904.
6. Ulrich Linse, *Organisierter Anarchismus im deutschen Kaiserreich von 1871* [Organized Anarchism in the German Kaiserreich of 1871], Berlin: Duncker & Humblot, 1969, 104–105.

7. Heinrich Hart (1855–1906), brother of Julius Hart (1859–1930), social reformers and founders of the *Neue Gemeinschaft* [New Community]–see below.

8. Rudolf Rocker, *Aus den Memoiren eines deutschen Anarchisten* [From the Memoirs of a German Anarchist] (Frankfurt am Main: Suhrkamp, 1974), 353.

9. Mühsam, "Unpolitische Erinnerungen," 485–486.

10. Ibid., 502.

11. A lake in the southwest of Berlin, where the Hart brothers established a sanatorium. It closed in 1904, marking the end of the Neue Gemeinschaft.

12. Mühsam, "Unpolitische Erinnerungen", 495.

13. *Gustav Landauer. Sein Lebensgang in Briefen* [Gustav Landauer: His Life in Letters], 2 volumes (Frankfurt am Main: Rütten und Loening, 1929), 1: 313–316.

14. Mühsam, "Gustav Landauer und die bayrische Revolution," *Der Abend*, August 19, 1920.

15. See, for example, Mühsam, "Unpolitische Erinnerungen," 666–667, and diary entry from August 28, 1910, 14, in Mühsam, *Tagebücher 1910–1924*.

16. *Der Sozialist*, April 15, 1910.

17. Mühsam, *Tagebücher 1910–1924*, 14.

18. Cf. Christoph Knüppel, Einleitung [Introduction] in *"Sei tapfer und wachse dich aus." Gustav Landauer im Dialog mit Erich Mühsam–Briefe und Aufsätze* ["Be Brave, Develop, and Mature!" Gustav Landauer and Erich Mühsam–Letters and Essays], edited by Christoph Knüppel (Lübeck: Erich-Mühsam-Gesellschaft, 2004), 8.

19. Cf. Gustav Landauer, *Revolution and Other Writings*, ed. and trans. Gabriel Kuhn (Oakland: PM Press, 2010). See also Mühsam, *Tagebücher 1910–1924*, 29.

20. Cf. Erich Mühsam, "Von Eisner bis Leviné. Die Entstehung der bayerischen Räterepublik" [From Eisner to Leviné: The Emergence of the Bavarian Council Republic] (Berlin: Fanal-Verlag, 1929; written by Mühsam in prison in 1920), 57.

21. The KPD was founded on January 1, 1919, as a conglomeration of various radical left-wing groups and organizations, of which the *Spartakusbund* [Spartacus League] (see footnote 50) was the most prominent.

22. Published in Berlin under different names from 1617 to 1934.

23. Mühsam, "Unpolitische Erinnerungen," 493.

24. Hirte, Nachwort in Mühsam, *Tagebücher 1910–1924*, 366.

25. A good overview is provided by Siegbert Wolf's essay "'Wir sind imstande, wir selbst zu werden durch die Revolution': Zur Freundschaft zwischen Erich Mühsam und Gustav Landauer" ['We Are Able to Become Ourselves through the Revolution': On the Friendship between Erich Mühsam and Gustav Landauer], *mühsam-magazin*, no. 2, January 1991.

26. The Socialist Bund existed from 1908 until the outbreak of World War I in 1914. It consisted of several autonomous groups in Germany and Switzerland that subscribed to the Socialist Bund principles, which were based on spiritual development, free association, and the establishment of self-sufficient communities. See the first version (June 1908) of "The Twelve Articles of the Socialist Bund" in Gustav Landauer, *For Socialism*, trans. David J. Parent (St. Louis: Telos Press, 1978), and the second (January 1912) in Landauer, *Revolution and Other Writings*, 215–216.

27. "Zum Beginn" [For the Beginning], *Der Sozialist*, January 15, 1909.

28. Cf. Mühsam, "Von Eisner bis Leviné," 45–46.

29. Diary entry from May 7, 1923, in Mühsam, *Tagebücher 1910–1924*, 328.

30. The *Anarchistische Föderation Deutschlands* (AFD) was founded in 1903 by "proletarian anarchists," many of whom had left the *Sozialist* collective in the 1890s to found their own journal, *Neues Leben* [New Life], renamed *Der freie Arbeiter* in 1903. The AFD was the successor to the *Föderation revolutionärer Arbeiter* [Federation of Revolutionary Workers], founded in 1900, and existed until the outbreak of World War I in 1914. *Der freie Arbeiter* was Germany's most important proletarian anarchist journal up until 1932. Mühsam had an ambiguous relationship with *Der freie Arbeiter* but maintained a closer relationship with it than Gustav Landauer did.

31. Robert Reitzel (1849–1898) was a German-born anarchist who emigrated to the United States in 1870.

32. The ensuing exchange between him and Hirschfeld is documented in this volume.

33. Dieter Schiller, Nachwort in Mühsam, *Publizistik–Unpolitische Erinnerungen*, 681.

34. *Sturm* [Storm] was a collection of poetry published by the Scottish-born German individualist anarchist John Henry Mackay (1864–1933) in 1888.

35. Max Nettlau, *Geschichte der Anarchie* [The History of Anarchy], vol. V (Vaduz: Topos, 1984), 249.

36. Hirte, Nachwort in Mühsam, *Tagebücher 1910–1924*, 365.

37. Johannes Nohl (1882–1963) was a German bohemian, writer, and lifelong socialist; after the division of Germany in 1945, he moved to the Soviet-controlled Eastern Zone, which became the German Democratic Republic (GDR) in 1949.

38. Mühsam, "Unpolitische Erinnerungen," 545–549.

39. Cf. Mühsam, "Unpolitische Erinnerungen," 563–564.

40. Hans-Joachim Heydorn, "Vorwort" [Preface], in Gustav Landauer, *Aufruf zum Sozialismus* [For Socialism], Frankfurt am Main: Europäische Verlagsanstalt, 1967, 11.

41. *Kain*, April 1911.

42. Schiller, Nachwort in Mühsam, *Publizistik–Unpolitische Erinnerungen*, 704.

43. Friedrich von Schennis (1851–1918), German artist.

44. Mühsam, "Unpolitische Erinnerungen," 480–481. Some early thoughts on the bohemia phenomenon can be found in Mühsam's 1904 essay of the same name, included in this volume.

45. Kurt Kreiler, "Längerer Leitsatz" [Longer Introduction] in Mühsam, *Fanal. Aufsätze und Gedichte 1905–1932* (Berlin: Wagenbach, 1977), 41. See also Mühsam's diary entry from August 24, 1914, in Mühsam, *Tagebücher 1910–1924*, 112–113.

46. Hirte, Nachwort in Mühsam, *Tagebücher 1910–1924*, 369–370. See also Mühsam diary entries from January 1914, in Mühsam, *Tagebücher 1910–1924*, 136–139. For a summary of the affair, see Linse, *Organisierter Anarchismus im deutschen Kaiserreich von 1871*, 313–317.

47. Diary entry July 29, 1915, in Mühsam, *Tagebücher 1910–1924*, 155.

48. Diary entry December 24, 1914, in Mühsam, *Tagebücher 1910–1924*, 134.

49. For an extensive summary of Mühsam's activities during the war, see Linse, *Organisierter Anarchismus im deutschen Kaiserreich von 1871*, 330–346.

50. The *Spartakusbund* was formed in 1916, when a group of radical social democrats with internationalist leanings declared their opposition to the war in an illegal publication called *Spartakusbriefe* [Spartacus Letters]. The most prominent members of the *Spartakusbund* were Karl Liebknecht (1871–1919) and Rosa Luxemburg (1871–1919). The group became best known for initiating the *Spartakusaufstand* [Spartacus Uprising] in Berlin in January 1919, which led to the deaths of Liebknecht and Luxemburg at the hands of right-wing soldiers.

51. This conflict will be documented in *All Power to the Councils! A Documentary Reader of the German Revolution of 1918–1919*, edited by Gabriel Kuhn, Oakland: PM Press, 2012.

52. The USPD was founded by a renegade faction of the SPD which opposed the party's ongoing support for the war.

53. Mühsam, "Von Eisner bis Leviné," 15.

54. *Gustav Landauer. Sein Lebensgang in Briefen*, 2: 296.

55. The German Free Corps (*Freikorps*) were used by the government following the end of World War I in order to bolster its military power. The vast majority of the Free Corps soldiers were monarchist and conservative military war personnel. Effectively, the Free Corps acted as independent right-wing militias.

56. The Weimar Republic was named after Weimar in Thuringia—the home of Johann Wolfgang von Goethe (1749–1832) and Friedrich Schiller (1759–1805)—where the constitution was drafted.

57. Letter to Albert Reitze, dated October 14, 1919, in Andreas W. Mytze, ed., *Erich Mühsam zum 40. Todestag* [On the Fortieth Anniversary of Erich Mühsam's Death] (Berlin: Europäische Ideen, 1974), 65.

58. He did so throughout his lifetime—see also *Liberating Society from the State* in this volume.

59. Eugen Leviné (1883–1919) was a Russian-born German communist. In March 1919, he was appointed by the KPD to lead the Munich chapter. He called for the defense against the first government attack on the Bavarian Council Republic on April 13 and defended it until its eventual overthrow on May 1. He was executed on July 5, 1919.

60. Mühsam was particularly bitter about the accusation, formulated by many KPD members and historians, that the council republic had been the product of "literary dreamers" with no understanding of politics. "Coffeehouse republic" was used as a derogatory term by many party communists.

61. Kreiler, "Längerer Leitsatz," 39–40.

62. Martin Andersen Nexø (1869–1954), Danish socialist writer.

63. Letter to Martin Andersen Nexø, October 27, 1919, in *Mühsam, In meiner Posaune muss ein Sandkorn sein. Briefe 1900–1934*, 365.

64. Quoted from Mühsam, *In meiner Posaune muss ein Sandkorn sein. Briefe 1900–1934*, 348.

65. See Mühsam's declaration in *Der freie Arbeiter*, yr. 12, no. 22, 1919, and his letter to Karl Franz Kocmata from November 30, 1919, in Mühsam, *In meiner Posaune muss ein Sandkorn sein. Briefe 1900–1934*, 369.

66. Linse, *Organisierter Anarchismus im deutschen Kaiserreich von 1871*, 340.

67. *Nationalsozialisische Deutsche Arbeiterpartei* [National Socialist German Workers' Party], commonly referred to in English as the "Nazi Party."

68. Linse, *Organisierter Anarchismus im deutschen Kaiserreich von 1871*, 375–376.

69. Ibid., 340–341.

70. Rocker, *Aus den Memoiren eines deutschen Anarchisten*, 354.

71. Interview with Augustin Souchy, quoted from Mytze, ed., *Erich Mühsam zum 40. Todestag*, 46.

72. Quoted from *Pressedienst der Internationalen Arbeiter-Assoziation* [Press Service of the International Workers' Association], Special Issue, no. 181, August 8, 1934.

73. The so-called Beer Hall Putsch (*Hitler-Putsch*) took place on November 8, 1923, when Hitler and armed stormtroopers disrupted a meeting of the Bavarian government in a beer hall and Hitler declared himself the new leader of Germany. The coup failed; Hitler was arrested a few days later and sentenced to five years in prison. Mühsam comments on the events in a diary entry on February 28, 1924, included in this volume under "Hitler and the Fledgling Nazi Movement."

74. Hirte, Nachwort in Mühsam, *Tagebücher 1910–1924*, 372.

75. Bruno Frei, "Mühsams Ankunft in Berlin 1924" [Mühsam's Arrival in Berlin 1924], in Mytze, ed., *Erich Mühsam zum 40. Todestag*, 29.

76. Augustin Souchy, *Erich Mühsam: sein Leben, sein Werk, sein Martyrium* [Erich Mühsam: His Life, His Work, His Martyrdom] (Reutlingen: Trotzdem, 1994), 50. Originally published in Spanish as *Erich Mühsam: su vida—su obra—su martirio* (Barcelona: Guilda de amigos del libro, 1934).

77. Ibid., 53.

78. The International Red Aid network, a social service organization with a strong focus on the support of socialist prisoners, was established in 1922; its influence waned in the late 1930s and it officially disbanded in 1941. The *Rote Hilfe Deutschlands* existed from 1924 to 1936. The modern-day *Rote Hilfe e.V.* was founded in 1970.

79. Mühsam was already active in prisoner support work while still incarcerated himself. See for example the letter to Maximilian Harden from December 15, 1919, on behalf of Martin Gnad, who was the head of a gang that had committed a number of warehouse robberies in Munich in support of revolutionary activities (Mühsam, *In meiner Posaune muss ein Sandkorn sein. Briefe 1900–1934*, 376–378).

80. Kreiler, "Längerer Leitsatz," 41.

81. The *Föderation Kommunistischer Anarchisten Deutschlands* (FKAD) was founded in 1919 as a successor to the *Anarchistische Föderation Deutschlands* (see footnote 30), which had disbanded at the beginning of World War I in 1914.

82. Erich Mühsam, *Revolution: Kampf-, Marsch- und Spottlieder* [Revolution: Songs of Struggle, Marches, and Satirical Verses] (Berlin: Der freie Arbeiter, 1925), 9. Mühsam donated the income of the volume to the FKAD's Prisoner Support Fund.

83. *Roter Frontkämpferbund*, an association of militias sponsored by the Communist Party in the 1920s; the *Rote Jungsturm*, later *Rote Jungfront*, were the *Rote Frontkämpferbund's* youth chapters.

84. "Ein entscheidendes Wort in Sachen Mühsam" [A Decisive Word on Mühsam], in *Der freie Arbeiter*, no. 18, 1925.

85. Letter from Pierre Ramus to Rudolf Oestreich, March 29, 1927, quoted from Heinz Hug, *Erich Mühsam. Untersuchungen zu Leben und Werk* [Erich Mühsam: Studies of His Life and Work] (Glashütten im Taunus: Verlag Detlev Auvermann KG, 1974), 169.

86. Mytze, ed., *Erich Mühsam zum 40. Todestag*, 48.

87. See, for example, Mühsam, *Tagebücher 1910–1924*, 265–267.

88. Hug, *Erich Mühsam. Untersuchungen zu Leben und Werk*, 169.

89. Mühsam's "Mitteilung" [Notification] was sent out to announce *Fanal*.

90. Linse, *Organisierter Anarchismus im deutschen Kaiserreich von 1871*, 374; Hug, *Erich Mühsam. Untersuchungen zu Leben und Werk*, 195.

91. Souchy, *Erich Mühsam: sein Leben, sein Werk, sein Martyrium*, 164. Rudolf Rocker writes: "Although Mühsam always called himself an anarchist, he was never a typical representative of the German anarchist movement; he always stood for a special direction both ideologically and in political activism" (*Aus den Memoiren eines deutschen Anarchisten*, 385).

92. Souchy, *Erich Mühsam: sein Leben, sein Werk, sein Martyrium*, 56–57.

93. Linse, *Organisierter Anarchismus im deutschen Kaiserreich von 1871*, 374.

94. Mühsam, *In meiner Posaune muss ein Sandkorn sein. Briefe 1900–1934*, 816. For a general overview of the relations of Mühsam to the FAUD see Helge Döhring, "Syndikalist aus Überzeugung: Erich Mühsams Entscheidung erfolgte nach gründlicher Abwägung zugunsten der FAUD" [A Syndicalist of Conviction: Erich Mühsam Voted for the FAUD After Much Reflection], in FAU-Bremen, ed., *Syndikalismus–Geschichte und Perspektiven* [*Syndicalism–History and Perspectives*] (Bremen: FAU–MAT, 2005). The FAUD was revived in 1977 as the *Freie Arbeiter-Union*, today *Freie Arbeiterinnen- und Arbeiter-Union* (FAU).

95. Rocker, *Aus den Memoiren eines deutschen Anarchisten*, 356.

96. Kreiler, "Längerer Leitsatz," 40.

97. Jungblut, Einleitung in Mühsam, *In meiner Posaune muss ein Sandkorn sein. Briefe 1900–1934*, XII–XIV.

98. Souchy, *Erich Mühsam: sein Leben, sein Werk, sein Martyrium*, 54.

99. Published in Berlin under different names from 1617 to 1934.

100. Linse, *Organisierter Anarchismus im deutschen Kaiserreich von 1871*, 330.

101. Interview with Fritz Erpenbeck, quoted from Mytze, ed., *Erich Mühsam zum 40. Todestag*, 43.

102. Accessible in English as *Reasons of State: A Memorial for Sacco and Vanzetti* at erichinenglish.org.

103. Accessible in English as *Judas: A Workers' Drama in Five Acts* at erichinenglish.org.

104. Available in English as *Thunderation! Folk Play with Song and Dance*, translated, edited, and introduced by David A. Shepherd (Lewisburg, PA: Bucknell University Press, 2001).

105. For a summary of Mühsam's relationship with the KPD see Hug, *Erich Mühsam. Untersuchungen zu Leben und Werk*, 176–178.

106. Souchy, *Erich Mühsam: sein Leben, sein Werk, sein Martyrium*, 71.

107. The fire was allegedly set by communist activists. The Dutch worker Marinus van der Lubbe (1909–1934) was arrested at the site, sentenced to death, and executed. However, the exact circumstances of the Reichstag Fire remain unresolved to this day. In any case, the event gave the Nazis a welcome pretext for increasing the repression of their political opponents and for

accelerating the process of *Gleichschaltung* (roughly, "bringing everything in line"), a term used to describe the abolition of parliamentary democracy and the establishment of totalitarian Nazi rule.

108. Souchy, *Erich Mühsam: sein Leben, sein Werk, sein Martyrium*, 72.

109. A Nazi propaganda journal.

110. This refers to the above-mentioned shooting of *Thule-Gesellschaft* members. The incident became known as the "hostage murder" (*Geiselmord*). "Twenty-two" is an exaggerated number.

111. Quoted from *Pressedienst der Internationalen Arbeiter-Assoziation*, August 8, 1934.

112. Quoted from Kreiler, "Längerer Leitsatz," 41. Ernst Toller (1893–1939), German socialist playwright.

113. Quoted from Souchy, *Erich Mühsam: sein Leben, sein Werk, sein Martyrium*, 80–81.

114. Susanne Leonhard, *Gestohlenes Leben. Schicksal einer politischen Emigrantin in der Sowjetunion* [Stolen Life: The Fate of a Political Emigrant in the Soviet Union] (Frankfurt am Main: Europäische Verlagsanstalt, 1956), 72.

115. For bibliographical details of all of the following publications, please see the bibliography at *erichinenglish.org*.

116. The book was finally made available in German in 1984 in a revised version entitled *Erich Mühsam: sein Leben, sein Werk, sein Martyrium*, published by Trotzdem Verlag.

117. See the personal account by Rudolph "Michel" Michaelis, *Mit der Centuria "Erich Mühsam" vor Huesca: Erinnerungen eines Spanienkämpfer* [With the Centuria Erich Mühsam at Huesca: Memories of a Volunteer in Spain], Berlin: Oppo-Verlag, 1995.

118. See *www.bachlund.org*.

CHILDHOOD AND YOUTH

AUTOBIOGRAPHY

Mühsam's short "Selbstbiographie" [Autobiography], mainly kept in note form, was written in 1919, but only published decades later. Mühsam made two short additions in 1920 and 1927, listing details of his life at the time that added little to the original version, which is included here.

I
T IS NOT THE EXTERNAL FACTS THAT DETERMINE A PERSON'S LIFE; IT is the internal changes that a person goes through. They define the impact of a person on his or her surroundings. The events in the life of an individual are only of interest in the context of life's events in general. Individuals whose personal lives have never had any relevance for social life might be very interesting to study for those interested in the human soul, but they are of no relevance for the community.

If I was completely defined by my poetry, and if my poetry was all that I had to offer to the people, then I could write an autobiography that satisfies the simple needs of literary historians for classification:

Born on April 6, 1878, in Berlin. Childhood, youth, high school in Lübeck. Teachers who did not understand this particular child, and who did not see his special traits. No one else did either. Rebellion, laziness, and the occupation with "strange" things as a logical outcome. Early attempts at poetry with no support from school or parents. Poetry was seen as a distraction from duty and had to be pursued in secrecy. Involved in many pranks, and, as a high school freshman, passed on a report about internal school affairs to the social democratic paper, with the consequence of being expelled for "socialist activities." One year as a high school sophomore in Parchim, Mecklenburg, then back to Lübeck as an apprentice in a pharmacy. Worked in different pharmacies and moved to Berlin in 1900. Joined the Hart brothers' Neue Gemeinschaft as an independent writer.[1] Acquaintance with many public figures and friendships with Gustav Landauer, Peter Hille, Paul Scheerbart, and others.[2] Bohemian life. Travels to Switzerland, Italy, Austria, France. Finally, settled in Munich in 1909. Cabaret[3] and work as a theater critic. A lot of writing, mostly polemical essays. Friendly interaction with Frank Wedekind[4] and many other poets and artists. Publication of three volumes of poetry and of four plays. From 1911 to 1914, editor of the literary and revolutionary monthly *Kain–Zeitschrift für Menschlichkeit*, published as a journal focusing on the German Revolution from November 1918 to April 1919. Since then, I have been in the hands of the counterrevolutionary Bavarian state.

Again, if my life was defined by my literary achievements alone, then this information would suffice. However, I see my work as a writer, especially my poetry, only as an archive of my soul, only as a partial expression of who I am. A human being's personality is the result of all the outside impressions gathered by mind and heart. My personality is a revolutionary one. In my personal development and in my activities I have always resisted everything that was imposed on me, both in private and in social life. I have done so since my early childhood.

Even at a young age, I realized that the state apparatus determined the injustice of all social institutions. To fight the state and the forms in which it expresses itself—capitalism, imperialism, militarism, class domination, political judiciary, and oppression of any kind—has always been the motivation for my actions. I was an anarchist before I knew what anarchism was. I became a socialist and communist when I began to understand the origins of injustice in the social fabric. I owe the clarification of my views to Gustav Landauer: he was my teacher until the white guards, called in by the social democratic government to crush the Bavarian Revolution, murdered him.

My revolutionary activity has often brought me in conflict with the state. In 1910, I stood in front of a judge because I had attempted to raise socialist consciousness among the so-called lumpenproletariat.[5] During the war, I actively opposed those who were determining Germany's fate. I was detained in Traunstein because I refused to serve the fatherland as a medical orderly. I stayed there until the "Great Time" ended in defeat and collapse.[6]

The revolution found me at my post from the first hour. I was a member of the Revolutionary Workers' Council. I fought against Eisner's politics of concession. I participated in the proclamation of the Bavarian Council Republic. I was sentenced to fifteen years of confinement in a fortress by a drumhead court-martial.

1. For more information on the Neue Gemeinschaft, see "1900–1904: Literary and Anarchist Awakening" in the Introduction.
2. Peter Hille (1854–1904), German libertarian poet; Paul Scheerbart (1863–1915), German fantasy artist.
3. German *Kabarett* has a strong focus on satire, stand-up comedy, and political commentary, with fewer dance and theater elements than *cabaret* in the English-speaking world.
4. Frank Wedekind (1864–1918) was a renowned German libertarian playwright.
5. See the essays "New Friends," "The Fifth Estate," and "My Secret Society" in the chapter "1908–1914: Munich I, Sozialistischer Bund and *Kain*."
6. Propaganda term for the German Kaiserreich.

"FATHER'S 72ND BIRTHDAY"

Diary entry Château d'Oex, Friday, September 2, 1910.

T
ODAY IS MY FATHER'S SEVENTY-SECOND BIRTHDAY. THE DATE evokes emotions that have little to do with childlike happiness and celebration. I retain some warm feelings for my father, I respect many traits of his character, I have sympathy for him (which probably lies in my blood), I feel sorry for his many worries (even for those for which he holds me responsible), but I have completely lost the supposedly natural feeling of gratitude felt for a parent. When I ask myself what I have to thank my father for, I cannot think of a single thing other than his having fathered me. All of my other thoughts are so bitter that I am inclined to cite Franz Moor.[1]

Truly! That my father has raised me doesn't elevate him above others; certainly not above poor day laborers who protect their children from hunger and who care for them with love. The fact that my father had to raise me caused him no hardship. Yes, he sent me to school—at least until I left in disgust. But there is no reason to sing songs of praise because of this. He did not send me to school so that I could do and become what I wanted, what I was destined to do and become; in short, what I *was*.

How about the way in which he raised me? I feel something akin to hatred when I recall all the terrible beatings intended to deprive me of my natural inclinations. My desire to read was well known. I never got any books. When my parents realized that I was getting up secretly in the middle of the night to fetch the works of Kleist, Goethe, Wieland, and Jean Paul[2] from their shelf, they locked the books into a cupboard, robbing me of the only opportunity available for satisfying my yearning.

I never got any money either. When I lied, claiming that I needed money for notebooks, pencils, etc., I was beaten in the most gruesome manner. I think with true horror of the days when I tiptoed around the house, waiting for an announced beating. For a crime as terrible as "embezzling" (my father loved to express himself in legal terms on such occasions) twenty or thirty pfennige,[3] I was given three beatings, meaning that I had to call in for my punishment three days in a row. No more outrageous and beastly cruelty could be conceived. I was probably twelve, thirteen years old at the time, full of childlike awakening, with a longing and feeling that was much deeper than that of other boys.

In school I was incredibly lazy. It never occurred to anyone that I, whose cleverness and intellectual capacity anyone should have noticed, was being treated in the wrong way. Had I had teachers—maybe private teachers—who understood me, I would have learned with dedication and pleasure. But all I knew was punishment. And not only physically—I was also banned from expeditions or from the other pleasures that my siblings engaged in, I was punished by neglect and by other more cultivated means of damaging a child's soul.

My father, of course, always took pride in his education. It was the pride of a man unable to realize that not all of his children were the same, that three turned out as he wished—dutiful, diligent, and obedient—but that I was different. He always claimed that he did everything with the best of intentions, and that he only wished the best for me. Meanwhile, I continuously gave him reason for more punishment and admonishment, thanks to jolly pranks and every possible kind of mischief. I became disgusted with studying and weary of life. But still, I always knew who I was. I always felt that there was something special about me, that I was chosen for big things.

Once, when I was around fifteen, I confessed to my mother—only in hints, really—how ambitious I was, and it seemed that she understood and believed me. But she was a weak woman, and my father had complete control over family affairs. He was an absolute authority to her. She never interfered when he mistreated me, in keeping with his terrible educational masterplan.

When I was in junior high school, a decision was made that I should receive a musical education. I was allowed to choose the instrument, and I chose the cello. I got lessons for a few months, but then I brought home a bad report from school, and my parents claimed that the music was keeping me from studying. As a result, I was no longer allowed to have cello lessons and cannot play an instrument to this day. I was punished for my entire life because of one bad report.

My God, when I remember the days after the prank that led to my expulsion![4] I was ostracized. Once, during the holidays, I returned from a *Lachswehrkonzert*[5] at a quarter past ten, and my father opened the door and welcomed me with a resounding slap in the face because I was a quarter of an hour late—I was eighteen years old! My face still burns today when I think of it!

Oh, and later! I wanted to become a writer, and I confessed to my mother that I thought I could not make it through the pharmacist apprenticeship. Tears, appeasement, panic. In the end, the verdict was: finish your apprenticeship, after that you can become a writer. Then my mother died. To avoid adding to my father's grief, I vowed to my sister Margarethe that I would abstain from literature and everything that interested me until the end of my apprenticeship. I kept my promise. It is impossible for anyone to understand what this cost me.

Nine months later I did what I both wanted and had to do. I moved to Berlin, where I soon gave up the work in pharmacies altogether and escaped into the Neue Gemeinschaft. Finally, I was a writer. My father was frantic. I received no support. He literally wanted me to starve. Thank God, I was stronger. To this day, I am victorious in this struggle; a struggle that has already lasted ten years.

My father now gives me one hundred marks every month. *Gives* them to me? Well, after he has taken five or six times that much from me! When I reached legal age, he made me sign an official paper, waiving my claims to the interest of my grandfather's inheritance because my father had deemed it unjust that this inheritance was going to his children and not to himself. When I signed that paper, how could I know the misery that it would bring me? Needless to say, I above all have myself to blame. If I were like others, without any consideration for my father, I would have gone to court and demanded my rightful part. It is true, I will one day inherit from my father, and even if it will be no more than my legal portion, it will be more than what all of my friends have. Still, the best years of my life will have been spent in poverty, and a lot of precious time will have been wasted. I am thirty-two years old, and I still have to live from hand to mouth. I do not have an apartment of my own, and no hope that my situation will improve.

Should I wish for my father's death? I don't know. My feelings would not stop me from doing so. My life seems ruined, but I am still young and there are still many things I can do. There is still plenty of work for me were I freed from misery and need. My father's life, however, lies behind him. He is old and he has a weak heart. So far, he has managed to stay alive. I wish for him to enjoy a quiet and serene end, but it need not be dragged out. Maybe, in a clear moment before he goes, he will realize how much punishment–punishment under which I suffered so cruelly–he deserves for his education.

৵

1. Franz Moor is one of the main characters in Friedrich Schiller's play *The Robbers* (1781); he is deeply estranged from his father.
2. Heinrich von Kleist (1777–1811), Christoph Martin Wieland (1733–1813), Jean Paul (1763–1825, born Johann Paul Friedrich Richter), renowned German writers.
3. 100 pfennige to 1 German mark.
4. See "Childhood and Youth" in the Introduction.
5. An annual festival in Lübeck–literally "Salmon Weir Concert."

1900–1904: LITERARY AND ANARCHIST AWAKENING

THE "HOMOSEXUALITY" PAMPHLET

IN LATE 1903, ERICH MÜHSAM PUBLISHED THE PAMPHLET "DIE Homosexualität. Ein Beitrag zur Sittengeschichte unserer Zeit" [Homosexuality: A Contribution to the History of Morality in Our Times] with M. Lilienthal Verlag in Berlin. It was the pamphlet no. 5 in a series entitled "Zur Psychologie unserer Zeit" [Psychology in Our Times], edited by Dr. Veriphantor, a pseudonym of the dermatologist Iwan Bloch (1872–1922). Other topics included erotic spanking, fetishism, masochism, and sadism.

In the pamphlet, Mühsam argued passionately against §175, a provision in the German criminal code that outlawed homosexual encounters (the paragraph survived in revised form until 1994). Mühsam built his arguments on the theories of physician, sexual researcher, and gay rights activist Magnus Hirschfeld (1868–1935), who saw homosexuality as an inborn desire and who argued for the acceptance of a "third gender" called *Urning*, based on the theories of nineteenth-century scholar Karl Heinz Ulrichs (1825–1895).[1]

Before the pamphlet was even back from the printers, Mühsam distanced himself from it. In an "Open Letter," published in January 1904 in *Der arme Teufel* [The Poor Devil],[2] he reiterated his opposition to §175, but juxtaposed genetic predisposition with the higher ideal of "erotic friendship." Magnus Hirschfeld replied in the subsequent issue with an "Open Letter" of his own. Both of these letters are included here.

There has been a lot of open speculation about Mühsam's own homosexual encounters, especially in relation to his close friend Johannes Nohl, who features prominently in the section "1904–1909: Traveling Years."[3]

Open Letter, Erich Mühsam, January 1904

Dear Weidner,[4]

I am asking you to publish this letter in Der arme Teufel, because I no longer have the option of adding a critical afterword to my pamphlet "Die Homosexualität," which was recently published by M. Lilienthal. I wish to publicly state that I have fundamentally revised my thoughts, and that I no longer agree with the theories on the origins and the nature of homosexuality presented in the pamphlet.

The only aspect of the publication I still defend is my uncompromising opposition to the nonsensical, unjust, and offensive paragraph that punishes sexual encounters between men.

It is inadmissible that I have confused socio-ethical reasons, which alone justify the abolition of §175, with scientific and historical reflections that might be of some interest to physicians and historians, but that are of no relevance to the struggle for human rights. We have no "knowledge" in these fields; we only have opinions opposed to other opinions.

I also fell into a trap that I myself argue against in the text: I have named as examples of Urninge[5] some celebrities who embrace an ideal of friendship that should have kept me from portraying them as freaks. They would be freaks, if they—as I claimed in the pamphlet—were Urninge in Hirschfeld's sense, i.e., degenerated human beings of a third gender (what a contradiction!). Alas, one usually only realizes mistakes after they have been made. It required the unabashed criticism of friends for me to realize that it was only the fanatical zeal of Dr. Hirschfeld and of his followers that has led to the incredible nonsense of putting humans who are attached to one another in a friendship that has been elevated to erotic love in the same category as individuals who are biologically inferior due to homosexual desire. I regret that I, without undertaking further study and posing further questions, took Hirschfeld's apodictic and axiomatic declarations as the basis for my work.

As clearly as I remain opposed to §175, I will from now on oppose any trivialization of the best sensation that we know: friendship.

I am not able to sufficiently explain the reasons for my change in opinion here. But I can announce that I will soon publish a pamphlet with my friend Johannes Nohl entitled "Das humanitär-wissenschaftliche Komitee—oder Kultur und Päderastie" [The Humanitarian-Scientific Committee, or Culture and Pederasty].[6]

I regret that I have written the pamphlet "Die Homosexualität," and I discourage people from buying it!

Erich Mühsam

Open Letter, Magnus Hirschfeld, July 1904.

DEAR MR. WEIDNER!

I am very happy to accept the kind offer to respond to the "Open Letter" published by Erich Mühsam in *Der arme Teufel*. I will not say anything about Mühsam disclaiming his pamphlet so soon after its publication or about him discouraging people from buying it. I am puzzled, however, that a free thinker like himself would use "Hirschfeld's apodictic and axiomatic declarations as the basis" for his work without *his own* investigation.

If I understand the case of Mühsam vs. Mühsam correctly—which, admittedly, I am not sure I do—then this year in January he understands homosexual attraction as a cultural phenomenon, while last year in November he understood it as a natural phenomenon (as I do). Except for the "unabashed criticism of friends," he does not tell us what caused this sudden shift in opinion; nor does he tell us why he now sees people with homosexual dispositions as "biologically inferior" and as "freaks." The mixture of masculine and feminine characteristics that homosexuals certainly show can never be a sign of inferiority, especially since—regardless of sexual orientation—so many great women show masculine traits, and so many great artists feminine ones.

Mühsam is right in questioning his use of close celebrity friends as examples for *Urninge*. Those who know our *Jahrbuch für sexuelle Zwischenstufen* [Yearbook for Sexual Intermediaries][7] are aware of how carefully we distinguish here, which is both mandatory for the understanding of *Urninge* and for public education in general. We try to establish how these men and women relate to the preservation of their species and to the opposite sex, and we examine how physical and intellectual characteristics of both sexes mix in them to determine whether their relationship with a person of the same sex is more akin to friendship or to love. Of course it is often very difficult to draw exact boundaries between friendship and love. However, the friendship that Mühsam describes as "elevated to erotic love," is certainly not friendship, but love, precisely *because* it is elevated to "erotic love," as he himself says.

For the readers of *Der arme Teufel* it is certainly true that socio-ethical reasons are enough to reject §175. For most of them it would probably suffice to say that it is no one's business—and hence not the state's either—what two consenting adults do if no rights of others are violated. However, the great mass of people, educated and uneducated, will only come to a just and reasonable assessment of this matter when they see scientific proof that the homosexual disposition is not cultural or artificial, but an inborn characteristic, inherently tied into the personality of many individuals. This, I believe, is the purpose that my book *Der urnische Mensch* [The Urning] serves.

With regard to the pamphlet that Mühsam is now promising, I would advise him to "fundamentally revise his thoughts" *before* publishing it, so that he will not once again, like Cronus, eat his own children[8]—I would feel sorry not only for Mühsam, the father, but for his children too.

With sincere greetings,
Magnus Hirschfeld

1. The term *Urning* was introduced by Ulrichs, since he considered all previous third-gender terms derogatory. *Urning* comes from Plato's *Symposium*, according to which the Greek Goddess Aphrodite Urania derived from Uranus's genitals after Uranus was castrated by his son Cronus. *Urning* was Ulrichs's term for male homosexuals; *Urninde* was used for female homosexuals. Neither term ever became common in German.

2. *Der arme Teufel* had been published in Detroit from 1884 to 1900, almost the entire time by Robert Reitzel (1849–1898), and was revived by several anarchists in Berlin from 1902 to 1904.

3. See for example Walter Fähnders, "Anarchism and Homosexuality in Wilhelmine Germany: Senna Hoy, Erich Mühsam, John Henry Mackay," *Journal of Homosexuality* 29, no. 2, 1995.

4. Albert Weidner (1871–1948), long-time proletarian activist and publisher, at the time editor of *Der arme Teufel* (see footnote 2).

5. Among others, Mühsam named Michelangelo, Raphael, and Oscar Wilde.

6. As with many other of Mühsam's announced publications, this pamphlet never appeared.

7. Hirschfeld published the *Jahrbuch für sexuelle Zwischenstufen* from 1899 to 1923. It was a unique annual collection of scientific articles on sexual minorities and "deviant" sexual practices.

8. In Greek mythology, the God Cronus, one of the first generation of Titans, devoured his own children after it was prophesized that one of them would dethrone him—Zeus eventually did, after he was saved by his mother Rhea.

1904–1909:
TRAVELING YEARS

"JOHANNES NOHL"

Following are two of Mühsam's most impassioned descriptions of his close friend–and possible lover–Johannes Nohl. The first one is an excerpt from a letter to Julius Bab, dated Lausanne, August 18, 1904.[1] The second is an excerpt from "Ascona," a pamphlet published by Mühsam in 1905–extensive excerpts of "Ascona" follow under the next header.

Letter to Julius Bab–Lausanne, August 18, 1904

[...] Now something about our memorable Italian journey: I was in the company of my friend Johannes Nohl, the most complete and natural Gypsy I have ever met. He's a professor's son from Berlin. For about a year now, we have done everything that you might consider important together. I can no longer separate his name from mine.

In Berlin, we stayed together at Augsburgerstraße.[2] Our extravagant activities ended with my friend spending three months in a sanatorium in the Harz Mountains, me in a sanatorium in Mecklenburg. While our nerves healed, we figured that Berlin had become a little too risky for us, and, for different reasons, we chose Lausanne as our next battleground. Nohl traveled there in April; I arrived in May. At first, we had plenty of money. Apparently, we acted out so much that we soon had undercover police following us, convinced that they would catch us red-handed as impostors.

The international proletariat of Lausanne–Frenchmen, Germans, Swiss, Italians, Russians, and Turks–adored us for our generosity since gin mills and dives were our standard haunts. Every day we caused pure horror among the German students–the most revolting group among the inhabitants of Lausanne–as well as among the guests at our pension, when we, arm in arm with a number of drunken Italian workers, staggered along the Grand Pont, Lausanne's main promenade.

As the first of June approached, we got some more money, but not nearly enough to continue spending the way we had. We decided to get out of town and to move on to Italy, the country we really wanted to see. Equipped with a little backpack, a borrowed Baedeker,[3] and Goethe's weakest book, the *Italienische Reise* [Italian Journey] (from which Baedeker seems to have copied plenty), we rode to Locarno to begin with, then continued on foot along the Lake Maggiore. From Cannóbio, we took the steamboat to Pallanza. We stayed there for three days and lived very, very luxuriously. On the third day, I realized that I had only twenty francs left in my wallet—and we were still a long way from Capri, our aspired destination, where Hanns Heinz Ewers, E. v. Wolzogen, and other acquaintances lived.[4] I didn't dare confess this to my friend, although I didn't expect him to immediately abandon the journey. I assumed that he still had enough money for both of us. Still, I asked several people to send funds, claiming that we were in great despair. I asked for general delivery to Milan, where I ended up going by myself, since my friend could not be torn from a crowd of harmonica players.

The next evening, I was sitting sad and alone with my last two and a half liras in a Milan café, when my friend suddenly appeared at my side, exclaiming, "Oh, that I finally found you! I do not even have five cents left!" While hatching plans, we spent the rest of my money. Then we went to a first class hotel for the night. The next day we received help. Among those who I had asked was a doctor in Berlin who, very much to my surprise, sent 50 liras from the Monte Verità, a vegetarian sanatorium near Ascona at Lake Maggiore. We had passed through Ascona a few days earlier, and the place would soon play an important role for us.[5]

Two days later, we were broke again. However, it was hot and we both suffered "heatstroke"—which got us some more money from relatives. A few friends stepped in as well. I got an advance payment from a journal I worked for, and we got by from day to day without sacrifices; in fact, with a lot of entertainment.

Fourteen days later, we traveled to Genoa with thirty liras. In the evening, the money was gone. Now things had become more difficult. We sent letters, telegrams—nothing. The hotel where we had spent the first night would not give us any further credit. So, we decided to go to the German General Consulate. The staff sent a number of telegrams without success and put us up in a filthy, sordid hostel. We left the next morning, wandered around all day hungry, camped out under a colonnade, and returned to the consulate. This time we were told that nothing more could be done for us. What now? We wandered around with an empty belly and increasing desperation. We bathed in the Tyrrhenian Sea and feasted on salt water. In the evening, I promised my friend I would get some decent food and find some proper sleeping quarters no matter what. Otherwise, so I declared, I would kill myself before his very eyes. He accepted, and I headed out to achieve my goal, a death sentence hanging over my head (and believe me, I would have paid my dues for the eccentricity factor alone!).

At one point, I heard two men speaking German. I approached them, told them that all our money had been stolen (which is what we had told the consulate staff too), and that we were left without means, food, and abode. They recommended a German innkeeper at the port, to whom I explained that it was indeed a human obligation to provide us with food and a place to sleep. He did so, but only under the condition that we would pay the next day. In the morning, we returned to the consulate once more, explaining that it was a shame for the fatherland that two well-educated sons were forced to starve or to become criminals. As a result, we got to meet the consul himself.

The consul held a moralistic speech and told my friend not to keep company with me. Obviously, he had identified me as the culprit and had no qualms about letting me know. Then he sent a consulate clerk to pay our bills at the hotels and to get our things from the hostel. He also gave us five liras each, a letter of reference for the vice consul in Lugano, and the stern advice to stay in good hotels and to eat well because the heat would otherwise get to us. Finally, we received bread, wine, cheese, sausage, and fruit, and, before we even knew it, we were put on a train to Lugano. There we heeded the consul's advice and checked into the best hotel. Unfortunately, the vice consul in Lugano was not as generous as his superior in Genoa, who had spent around one hundred liras on us in total. In Lugano, we only got twenty liras, which we used to return to Locarno. The debts at the hotel we left behind. From Locarno we made our way back to Ascona on foot, and from there to the Monte Verità, where I was allowed stay. My friend found a place at the home of a writer in Ascona, who knew me quite well because I had panned one of his books.

We now had to live as vegetarians, had no alcohol to drink, and nothing to smoke. We had to run around barefoot, bareheaded, and in linen. Eventually, we got some more money, and once I had paid my bills at Monte Verità, we both moved in with a young German woman, Lotte, who lived self-sufficiently on her own property at a mountain slope.[6] Her two-story house consisted of four walls and a ceiling and was only used to store food. We lived and slept outside.

We stayed there until last week. Then we decided to separate for a while. My friend is probably walking around barefoot in Pallanza right now, while I am in Lausanne, from where I will take our modest belongings to Zurich tomorrow. There we will soon reunite.

Excerpt from "Ascona" (1905)

For a few years now, literary circles in Germany have tried to define the essence of bohemia. In the process, some notions of the term have been presented that are utterly ridiculous. Furthermore, as people who have so little to do with those who it originally referred to have claimed the term for themselves, I almost feel ashamed to be associated with it in any way. We have perfumed youngsters who, hidden under bombastic ties and oil-soaked Napoleonic curls, chirp through cafés with castrate voices, indulging in the preposterous self-delusion that idleness, borne of intellectual impotence, renders them representatives of bohemia. Then, there are the artists with nothing to do, who share a tiny studio with their girlfriends, read Murger,[7] and, if they happen to have a taler, buy a bottle of Mosel.[8] At the same time, all they really long for are assignments that will pay for an elegant villa with a park, where they can live happily with their family.

If I am correct then, the bohemian is a human being who, due to great despair—an artist's most genuine characteristic—has never felt close to the masses, who takes risks in life, who experiments with chance, who plays catch with the here and now, who is a sibling to the always present eternity. This means that Johannes Nohl is the most genuine bohemian of all.

We met one and a half years ago in Berlin. We have since shared everything we have been able to share—few material things, but many intellectual treasures. We have seen Switzerland together, visited its different cantons, and we have traveled through Northern Italy, sharing the hardships of everyday life, hunger, and thirst, but also lavish feasts. We dined and dashed, and finally landed in Ascona. Landed? Well, you could say that we got stuck…

Nohl is twenty-three years old. He comes from a professor's family in Berlin. Still, he is already the freest man who I have ever met. Moralistic blabber and prejudice mean nothing to him. He judges every human being, every living creature, according to their individual characteristics. He is only demanding when it comes to himself; he rigorously attempts to follow the principles that derive from his view of the world. One is tempted to revise one's low opinion of the German race when considering that this man is German. But artistic blood is probably international; and Nohl is an artist through and through, not only in his life but also in his poetry. Although not even a syllable of his has been published yet, I dare proclaim that he will soon be a poet held in highest regard by all experts. I give every reader the right to call me on these lines. If my prophecy should not come true, I will look like the greatest of fools and will be accused of having been a delusional friend. But I claim the opposite: it is because I am such a close friend of Nohl that I know his qualities and the direction in which he is headed better than anyone else.[9]

1. Julius Bab (1880–1955) was a dramatist who Mühsam had met in the Neue Gemeinschaft.
2. A street in the Berlin suburb of Schöneberg where Mühsam had rented a room.
3. A German publishing house established in 1827, pioneering modern-day travel guides; it exists to this day.
4. Hanns Heinz Ewers (1871–1943), German writer, artist, and world traveler; Ernst von Wolzogen (1855–1934), Austrian-German writer. Both became Nazi sympathizers.
5. See "Excerpts from 'Ascona'"
6. Lotte Hattemer—see "Excerpts from 'Ascona'"
7. Henri Murger (1822–1862) was the French author of the popular Scènes de la vie de bohème [Stories of Bohemian Life] (1851).
8. A popular German wine region in Rhineland-Palatinate.
9. Nohl's literary success was rather limited.

Excerpts from "Ascona"

In the late nineteenth century, the area around Ascona in Ticino, the Italian-speaking part of Switzerland, had become a favorite place for German vegetarians, naturalists, and utopian socialists. The early commune of Monte Verità–legendary among some pacifist anarchists to this day–soon turned into a sanatorium. Mühsam spent some time in the area in 1904–1905 and wrote about his experiences in a pamphlet entitled "Ascona," first published in 1905.

[...] Ascona is the most enchanting of places. The green lake casts reflections of dark mountain summits, and it is easy to get lost in its beauty. God forgive me if I begin a text about this place with a critique of my compatriots. But whenever a troop of the worst and most stupid kind of German philistines trudges here from Locarno and stares at the wonderful shores of Lake Maggiore, I cannot help but compare them to the great people who call this land their home, Swiss-Italians with dark and open eyes and a joyful embrace of life. And not only that. I am also forced to compare them to some Germans who live very special lives here, and for whom I will put ink to this paper...

If anything reveals a people's character, then it is its workers' movement. Progressive minds that know what goes under that name in Germany must possess enormous generosity if they do not despise the character of the German people as a result. For my part, I have long rejected the so-called workers' movement in Germany, precisely *because* I am for the working class's liberation struggle and for a socialist society. I do not retain even the slightest sympathy for the German masses, who replicate the character of the propertied class. Still, I do not join in the self-satisfied laughter of some individualists when the proletariat lines up at the ballot box and thinks that it helps its cause by sending the Social Democratic Party, backed by three million votes, into sanctioned bureaucratic confines. I continue to struggle for the workers and against the party leaders with angry words. This might very well be the result of an atavistic national consciousness that keeps alive the hope that the hour of revolutionary self-realization will even come to Germany one day.

The psychological cause of the passivity and of the fear of altering the status quo in Germany–even when it is recognized as bad–seems to lie in people's bottomless diligence. This observation is nothing new. In *The House of the Dead*, Dostoyevsky described a fellow sufferer with the words, "He was diligent, like a German." It is by no means true that a pronounced sense of duty—and, related to this, the enjoyment of work—is a general moral trait (and it is not typically Jewish either, as an acquaintance once claimed). It is a typically German trait. Only the German is proud when he works. The Romanic person sees work as a necessary evil and feels ashamed if he has to submit to it. Jews see work as a punishment, resulting from the original sin—and no one is proud of punishments.

There are two sayings that illustrate these differences better than any theoretical reflections. *Arbeit macht das Leben süß* [Work makes life sweet]—this is what every German child learns while still in diapers. *Dolce far niente* [It is sweet not to do anything]—this is what the Italians teach their children. Such sayings truly reveal the voice of the people. The fear of revolution among Germany's social democrats, their blind belief in Marx's theories of development, the very low number of German anarchists—all this can be explained by the sense of loyalty that is deeply entrenched in the German people's character and that guards all duties once they have been accepted. This is also the reason for the intolerance of Germans in moral questions. What is "morality"? Nothing but a set of norms established by certain customs. To the superficial German, everything that the majority does—everything that is convention—becomes duty. Everything that deviates is "immoral." How different, how much more free, how much more beautiful, and how much more endearing is the Italian's approach! *As long as you do not disturb my ways, do as you like!* This is the understanding among people here, at least if they are not caught in the nets of detestable priests who, under the disguise of Christian love, inject the poison of morality into unspoiled minds.

A healthy sensuality is in the blood of every Italian, unhindered by any laws. I don't know if paragraphs like §175, part of the German criminal code,[1] exist in Italy or the Swiss-Italian canton of Ticino. What I do know is that the young workers here dance with one another and kiss one another without ado. And what I know even more clearly is that despite this moral violation, a spirited, strong, and beautiful people, to whom the moralistic drowsiness of German workers is completely alien, is blossoming.

A wild revolutionary hatred for their oppressors rests in the very fiber of these people. If someone explained to them that they should vote one of their own into parliament, they would only laugh! Just as with the priests of the other parties, the likes of Turati and his comrades in the Italian Parliament, and especially the likes of Greulich and his comrades in the Swiss Parliament,[2] are instinctively counted among the reactionaries by the vast majority of workers in Italy and Ticino.

People here know that liberation from the state and the church is only possible as a result of the struggle of every individual and of the refusal to work—in other words, through the departure to the holy mountain. It is unthinkable that something like Schiller's "Lied von der Glocke" [Song of the Bell], this classical document of German squaredom and German bleakness, could become the national sermon from the mount as it did in Germany (and in German-speaking Switzerland as well, since the faceless German character reaches as far as the German tongue). *Where people free themselves, people will not do well!* German proletarians ardently learn such lines by heart. The Italian (including the Swiss-Italian—language plays the same role here) on the other hand, sings a wonderful folk song at night by the open fire celebrating the poor Caserio who avenges his friends Ravachol and Henry.[3] Only eleven years have passed since the fearless deed of this young hothead. The German philistine condemns the "miserable bloodhound," while the German worker whistles the *Vorwärts* song[4] declaring him a mad fanatic. In Italy, however, he is honored by a folk song sung by all classes.

In this part of Ticino, a short way from the Italian border, the population is and feels Italian through and through. Yet, it is unaffected by the police repression in the Italian monarchy. The Swiss republic knows the people in Ticino well and applies the state apparatus very carefully. In the midst of all this, a colony of Germans has settled, including some individuals whose colorfulness and originality provides such a refreshing change to the boring one-dimensional mindset of the fatherland that it is worth paying some attention to them, as individuals, as well as a community and *sub specie aeterni*.[5] [...]

If you walk from Locarno along the western side of Lake Maggiore toward Italy, about halfway between this marvelous town—whose only stain are the German honeymooners, tourists, and business travelers—and the customs station at Brissago you are bound to encounter at least one odd hairy creature. This is Ascona. [...]

Ascona has about one thousand inhabitants. The German colony consists of fifty to one hundred people. One has to make a proper distinction between those who seek recovery from true or imagined sickness by sun bathing and by eating fruits and salads at the sanatorium Monte Verità (a place I still have to introduce) on the one hand, and those who have settled here permanently and who are generally known among the local population as *vegetariani*, no matter whether they indeed eat vegetables or "carcasses," on the other. [...]

Once there were many vineyards in the region, but then the vine fretter came. When the locals saw their only source of income destroyed, many of them left the area and their homes decayed. This explains the ridiculously cheap prices for beautiful properties and the property buying mania among the German settlers. [...]

It should probably be my duty to trace the historical development of this place from a small Ticino town with undisturbed Italian flair to a colony of German weirdos. However, I am unfortunately not very well informed about the beginnings of this development and can say little more than the following.

Some years ago, a number of vegetarians who had met in the Jungborn group in the Harz Mountains[6] moved south and decided to found an ethical-social-vegetarian-communist settlement. I believe that they first settled in Rapallo.[7] Looking for a better location, they found what is today known as Monte Verità. The site was well chosen for its beauty; practicality was a different issue.

The Monte Verità is a high plateau, to which you have to climb for about twenty minutes from Ascona. The ascent is rather steep. Once you are at the top, the view over Lake Maggiore is magnificent. The first settlers built a couple of wood cabins. Apparently, a quite comfortable communist existence developed at first—particularly comfortable for those who joined with empty pockets. The dilettantism of such a beginning is obvious. Communist settlements that are not based on solid revolutionary and socialist ideas will always fail. They cannot survive when the principle that ties the participants together is as irrelevant as vegetabilism.[8] Needless to say, this utopian community could not last long. Costs were rising and people had to think of ways to make money. They opened a sanatorium that slowly but inevitably developed into a purely capitalist venture. Only the official demands for simple living and the religiously practiced vegetabilism serve as a reminder of the place's ethical origins. The simple living will probably soon be gone, though, with the ever-increasing number of spoiled guests.

Abandoning the principles of a social and ethical community necessarily implied the division of the participants. Several moved, leaving the premises to Herr Henri Oedenkoven, the founder of the sanatorium, who is still the owner of Monte Verità. The defectors bought their own properties where they could do as they pleased. Their example found more and more imitators, and this is why there are so many Germans, most of whom are vegetarians, in Ascona and the neighboring villages today.

Monte Verità is no longer of great interest to the socially inclined visitor. It is a sanatorium like any other, with the simple difference that it is vegetarian. However, since German vegetarians are better than average Germans, in the sense that they at least differ from the masses, every now and again you may meet an interesting individual there.

I see several parallels between the transformation of Monte Verità from an idealistic experiment of determined men and women to a capitalist sanatorium frequented by anyone who is able and willing to pay, and the Neue Gemeinschaft of the Hart brothers, which was built on great principles and ideas, before it all ended miserably in the Schlachtensee, the result of fear, which degenerated into a bed and breakfast with an ethical name plate.[9] [...]

It was very similar in the case of Monte Verità. Vegetarianism was sold as an idea that would liberate humankind, and when it became obvious that no socialist dream could be realized on the grounds of such an insignificant ideology, people tried to link an ethical principle to a capitalist enterprise—under all circumstances, a futile venture. As always in such cases, the ethical principle lost out. What is left of the original hopes today is merely laughable: a cheerful owner who lets "colleagues" engage in minor tasks in five-hour shifts, while he relies on an exploited workforce that receives irregular pay for everything else (and I do not mean this as a personal attack against Mr. Oedenkoven). Oh, yes, and there is a list of rules requesting that all guests keep their own cabin in order. Julius Hart also insisted that the Schlachtensee sanatorium formed the basis of a new, enlightened humanity, although it accepted any old bourgeois who was willing to rent a room. [...]

The third and most serious problem that the history of Monte Verità shares with that of the Neue Gemeinschaft concerns the ethical leeches with their spiritualistic, theosophical, occult, and completely exaggerated vegetarian ideas. All who have ever peeked into groups made up of bizarre characters know what I mean. They have seen the pale faces with weak eyes, whose only objective it is to keep their body and their soul in harmony, based on their oh-so-virtuous lifestyle. Almost all of these characters are vegetarians. I have nothing against that per se. If someone could convince me that eating plants, refraining from drinking alcohol, and everything else that is required would be best for my health, and if I was of the opinion that the intensive care of the body was more important than the care of the spirit and of the soul, then I too would probably become a vegetarian. Besides, I am convinced that a recovering patient might benefit from a few months of strict vegetarianism, even on the Monte Verità. But when someone throws moralistic sermons at me, accuses me of eating "carcasses," and acts like a higher moral authority, then I see this as merely pathetic.

Unfortunately, most explain their vegetarianism by making such ridiculous claims. As if they did not take a life with every radish they eat. Of course they eat "carcasses" too! There are many such people at Monte Verità. They wear their linen gowns—which are very useful against sunburn!—like priests sport their robes. Their hair is kept long; not for aesthetic reasons, as in the case of many artists, but for "natural" reasons. It flows around their strained Christ-like faces as if it contained magical force.

It is obvious that people who substitute external adornment for inner substance will not be of much help when it comes to the realization of a serious undertaking. I am convinced that the history of Monte Verità could have taken an entirely different course had these people been kept in the background from the beginning. I got to know the type very well in the Neue Gemeinschaft. I know how they self-importantly portray themselves as "individualities" on the basis of their petty *Weltanschauung*,[10] while, essentially, they are all the same—as if carbon-copied. [...]

Let me now turn to the secessionists of Monte Verità, the co-founders of the original vegetarian community who left when the sanatorium was established. I begin with the most interesting, most sincere, and most important of all of them,

Karl Gräser. This man, once an army officer, lives with his wife, Frau Jenny Gräser, on a fairly large property that together they have turned into an almost completely self-sufficient home by the work of their own hands. It is a source of pride for them to satisfy as many of their needs as possible themselves. This, of course, means that their needs are very basic. They reject participating in monetary exchange on principle.

Gräser is the first human being who I have ever met who really has, with rigid consistency, put his theoretical beliefs into praxis. There exist wonderful stories about how the Gräsers deal with situations that pose a particular challenge to their principles. For example, Frau Gräser once had to go to a dentist. Since she has a beautiful voice, she paid for the service by singing a few songs. If there is anything that the two cannot produce themselves, they take their own fruit to Locarno and Bellinzona and barter with the merchants. Whatever they can somehow produce themselves, they will not get from anyone else. I once met Gräser when he was busy carving an eating spoon out of a piece of wood. On another occasion, he was preparing a pair of sandals. During such efforts, he happily shares general observations and aphorisms about the beauty of nature, about his personal relationship to the universe, and about his many personal insights.

The range of his ideas is rather limited, but the ideas he holds go very deep. His philosophy might be summarized by saying that "everything finds its likeness": good finds good, and bad finds bad; beauty finds beauty, energy finds energy, weakness finds weakness. To Gräser, nature comprises everything that is good, beautiful, strong, and pure. While the weak spirits of the carbon copy vegetarians propagate the slogan *Back to Nature!* without understanding it, Gräser has embraced the notion fully. All of his endeavors, all of his actions, attempt to reflect nature, i.e., ultimate perfection, as completely as possible. [...]

Gräser refuses to study the theoretical musings of others on principle. He would consider this a block to his own natural imagination. All that counts is what derives from his own feelings. This is what he accepts as true and as the only basis for his actions. Acting according to a theoretical program would be unnatural. To live naturally means to act freely and independently, spontaneously and immediately. [...]

The principle of having no principles is of course a contradiction in itself. This is where the foundations of Gräser's theory become shaky. It also seems contradictory that someone who praises spontaneity obviously feels the need to justify everything that he does. However, at least Gräser's philosophy is concrete and his uncompromising ambition to put it into practice is tremendously refreshing in comparison to the dull, lifeless, and abstract maxims that the majority of vegetarians propagate. These people call themselves "free," but do not even consider it necessary to strive for a higher inner freedom. They are caught up to their necks in restrictions of all kinds. Gräser, on the other hand, works continuously to liberate his soul. This alone would lift him far above his surroundings, even were he not the much freer human being that he is.

Every time I visited Gräser I left with a strong impression. He lies in the grass, almost naked, and philosophizes. His eyes say more than his words. In his desire to enlighten his guests with every word and in his effort to never say anything trivial, his speech can become somewhat tedious, but it is delightful to watch the man search for the right word for every single thing he wants to say. [...]

Karl and Jenny Gräser basically use their own terminology when they communicate. She has adapted to his ways so perfectly that the two can hardly be conceived of separately. For a little while now, they have had a child living with them; the four-year-old son of a socialist women's rights activist of their acquaintance, who suddenly converted to Catholicism. [...] The little Habakkuk (this is the name that the Gräsers have given him) is an exceptionally intelligent and beautiful child and enjoys the freest education that one can imagine—that means: none. He has no rules to obey, and nothing is prohibited. He can sleep and eat as much as he likes whenever he wants to, and he can play where he likes for as long as he feels like it. The most beautiful part is that his foster parents show him full respect. He is not trained in the way the children of bourgeois German families are trained. He is not required to behave politely and to utter hypocritical phrases whenever visitors come. Instead, he sits among the adults, and when he has something to say or when someone has a question for him, he receives the same attention as any grown-up.

How disgusting it is when children have to thank people for a gift before they can feel gratitude! I lose all the joy of presenting a child with a gift when he responds with that sort of conventional lie. If children are really happy, it will show in their feelings—in ways that are much more heartfelt and honest than the utterances of a child in Berlin who receives a beating every time a wishful thought escapes his heart and every time his rich fantasy invents precious tales—as if being a child were a mortal sin. The children's minds are corrupted by corrupted educational methods, and all this happens in the name of the parents' best intentions. Compared to this, the education of the little Habakkuk feels like redemption!

Given all the great virtues that Karl Gräser displays in both thought and action, I do not want to make too big a deal out of one flaw I have noticed in him, but I do not want to conceal it either. It is the intolerance he shows for real or alleged weaknesses on the part of others. Intolerance is necessary and appropriate when we are threatened by others in our struggle to bring a liberating idea to humankind. Gräser, however, stresses constantly that he does not fight for anyone's liberation other than his own. Hence, his intolerance is but an indication that he is still a long way from his goal. I have seen him change his interaction with a person he had always been on friendly terms with for no other reason than having seen the person drunk. This reveals a shortsightedness, an inconsistency, an inner limitation. It is shortsighted because Gräser does not to even try to understand the psychological reasons that lead others to use alcohol as a means of liberation during temporary or permanent suffering; it is inconsistent because it passes moral judgment on the lifestyle of others in contradiction to Gräser's claim to only focus on individual perfection; and the shortsightedness and inconsistency derive from an inner limitation, insofar as establishing a universal moral code, and submitting oneself to it, necessarily implies a strong inner dependency.

However, I am totally convinced that Gräser, in the course of a dedicated struggle with himself, will eventually be able to cast off this weakness and to overcome the last obstacle that stands between his thought and his action. He already is by far the most original personality among all the Germans in Ascona, and the one that must be taken most seriously.

* * *

Lotte H., known as "the Lotte," was also among the original founders of Monte Verità who left when things did not turn out as planned. She had tried for a while to work at the sanatorium, where she "allotted servings," as she says ironically. She soon realized, however, that eternal happiness could not be gained in the context of such an enterprise and decided to settle on her own account.

If Gräser is the most original *individual* among the Ascona settlers, then Lotte is definitely the most original *being* in the region. There is a difference between the terms. Lotte's originality borders on the grotesque, the adventurous, and the absurd. When she trolls along the country roads, wrapped in a few pitiful garments that substitute for clothes, some flowers in her hands and in her wild blonde hair, no one would guess that this is the daughter of a high Prussian official. Her property, a quarter of an hour south of Ascona, is situated very nicely. It contains a ramshackle, windowless hut that creates the same impression as its owner: a mixture of romanticism and chaos. Somewhere out in the open lies a blanket and a fascine. This is where Lotte sleeps. Every now and again, one stumbles over a piece of clothing, a pot, or a souvenir from the times when Lotte lived the life of a higher man's daughter. Things are even more colorful in the two-storey hut. There are suitcases, utensils, foodstuffs, books, letters, and rats, and in-between them twine, leather straps, mattresses, logs of wood, and all sorts of other things. A single sandal here or there, something that was once a hat, and pieces of broken glass complete the picture. Everything is in total disarray.

Lotte has been living in this environment for years by herself. Is she happy? She acts like she is; and convincingly, one must say.

Lotte's character is not nearly as apparent as Gräser's, and it is not easy to gain a clearer image of her being; she displays a wide range of contradictory qualities. Besides, I do not want to offend the young girl with indiscreet observations. Still,

I have to talk at least a little about her ways, because her uniqueness can only be explained in the context of her surroundings. She is typical of the influence of extraordinary social conditions on the individuals who are part of communities as peculiar as the one I am describing here.

Two things are of particular importance for the analysis of Lotte. First, her Catholic origin and the mystic tendencies that derive from it. Second, the obvious influence of Gräser on her ideas: she, too, is a very rational person who desires inner independence, while, at the same time, praising nature and mystical union. Her—from what I can tell, subconscious—desire is to understand the hidden forces behind everything, to surrender herself, to find bliss in being a child of God, to worship humbly, and to suffer as a believer; all this, while simultaneously seeing herself as the center of everything, confirming herself as a driving force, following her impulses spontaneously and without any concern. This is the source of all of the contradictions in her being. The constant struggle to reconcile her heterogeneous feelings never allows Lotte to leave a state of almost pathological ecstasy. There is something violent in her behavior. This impression becomes particularly strong, as well as painful to observe, because her misautic nature constantly forces her to display philautic traits that do not seem to arise from her inner nature.[11] This is expressed in a kind of spontaneous radiation of energy. […] On numerous occasions, I have observed how she ostentatiously left a group that was sharing a moment, only to return fifteen minutes later with flowers all over her body. Apparently, a religious mood had suddenly come over her. The mood might be natural, but certainly not the fact that she has to demonstrate it to everyone by drawing attention to herself, first by the grand departure, then by the botanical decoration.[12] […]

It would go too far to portray in depth every single eccentric who lives here. I will content myself with mentioning a few more of the settlers who have exceptionally original traits…

[…] There is one man who lives in Orsolina, a town between Locarno and Ascona, whom I wish to mention. The reason is that he has a particularly funny spleen. This man is not only an eater of raw foods and a teetotaler, he even objects to eating raw grapes because it would interfere with his sexual abstinence. Grapes, he claims, have a strong influence on the genitals. He cites as proof that the ancient Greeks celebrated the festival of Dionysius together with that of Aphrodite. This is just one example of the many follies that are presented to you with utter conviction here every day.

I also want to mention a hypochondriac who almost completely avoids people and always feels sick. I do not know whether it was vegetarianism that turned him into a hypochondriac or hypochondria that turned him into a vegetarian. In any case, his counterpart is an always jolly former worker from Berlin who sings incessantly. His credo is that God is a good man, and that if you only believe in this strongly enough, you will inevitably be rewarded in the long run. Convinced of this, he ceaselessly intones chants in sedulous devotion, directed at the sky. A patient neighbor once counted him singing "Now Thank We All Our God" forty-six times. [...]

I consciously did not elaborate on the interactions of the settlers and on their relationships with the local population. The social control that is so typical of small communities, a complicated web of erotic liaisons and jealousies, as well as spite, intolerance, and distrust—all of this is essentially the same as anywhere else. I have not sensed a single close bond or friendship among the Germans, apart from that between myself and Johannes Nohl. Nor have I met anyone, except for Karl Gräser, whose existence could in any way serve as an inspiring example for others. And still, I find reflecting on the life around Ascona worthwhile, especially with the future in mind. Not because I can see anything in vegetarianism that human culture could benefit from, nor because I see the certainly encouraging phenomenon that most of the marriages here are not sanctioned by the state or by the church as convincing proof of significant social development. Indeed, I see the fact that those who live in free marriage boast so much about it as a weakness. It appears to me that being so excited about something that should be entirely self-evident is a means of acquiescence to a bourgeois conscience that tells you that you have stepped away from the right path. In other words, it reveals that these people's decision was merely based on principle, not on how they feel in their souls. Still, I see future possibilities in this particular constellation of landscape, local population, and settlers. It is true that Ascona and its qualities might be destroyed by mad property speculation and intolerable spa guests. However, other possibilities remain, and it is worthwhile to examine them.

I once believed that Ascona was indeed the appropriate place for a large communist settlement. The attempt to live with a group of people in self-determination based on a primitive communal economy without capitalist means—kind of like what Karl Gräser has already achieved for himself as an individual—would certainly be intriguing. (The idea for this comes from Gustav Landauer, who first mentioned and developed it in a Berlin Zionist meeting.)[13] However, Ascona is not the right place for this. First, better land would be needed. The land that can be bought here is very, very cheap, but it is separated into many small properties, and the soil has not been cultivated in decades—it has so many grapevine shoots, roots, and rocks that it would require an enormous effort to make it fertile again. Second, it cannot be recommended to start an enterprise that demands a lot of optimism and courage in a place where a similar enterprise, even if it was not exactly the same, has previously failed. Every time that the participants' eyes caught a glimpse of Monte Verità, doubts and fears would arise; such sentiments alone guarantee a fiasco. Third, the settlers who have been here for years—in other words, the ones who would be the pioneers of any communal venture—have become so used to individual labor that it would be very difficult for them to organize a common economic system. Gräser, for example, understands property strictly in personal terms: everything that is the result of his own labor is his property—and nothing else. He would never be able to join a workers' cooperative. To him the verses uttered by Faust apply: "Only those earn freedom and life who conquer it every day!" Most others are too caught up in their vegetarian doctrines. They would rank their ethics and their ideology over real life. In short, a socialist settlement in Ascona would be condemned from the start to follow in the footsteps of the Neue Gemeinschaft; the thought of using the situation in Ascona as a springboard for a greater social experiment must be dismissed. [...]

However, Ascona seems to be suited for a much more interesting, even if new and possibly strange, experiment. The number of unconventional people who already reside here, together with the acquiescent and libertarian character of the locals and the relatively weak presence of the state in the canton of Ticino, destine Ascona to be a gathering place for people who, as a result of their individual pre-dispositions, are incapable of ever becoming useful members of a capitalist society.

I am repeating an observation that has been made by many different writers a thousand times when I say that the best people of all nations rot in prisons and jails. I know from my own experience that you can meet individuals in the hostels along Germany's country roads and in Berlin's gin mills who are regarded with contempt and shunned by our "good citizens," but whose hearts make the hearts of all those who approach them beat faster. What happens to the people who break the suffocating chains of the unjust division of property? They are called "criminals" by the bourgeoisie.[14] What happens to them after years in dungeons and behind bars—years that are supposed to render them insane? Do they obey and crawl to the yoke of exploitation? Oh no, because even if the tortures of justice have worn them out and they want to submit and say *Father, I have sinned!*, they will be rejected by those who claim immaculate virtue; after all, they dared rebel against the divine world order of European civilization. This forces them to rebel anew, before being slowly tormented to death as a punishment for keeping a trace of human consciousness. No, people with such a strong sense of individuality will never be useful citizens in today's society. Instead, they will be pioneers of a better, freer, more beautiful society. This can come true if there is a place somewhere, an area of land, where no one looks at them suspiciously and where no one avoids and rejects them as immoral and depraved.

This is why I wish from the depth of my soul that one day Ascona will become a refuge for released and escaped prisoners, for persecuted vagabonds, for all those who are hunted and tortured, for all those who are drifting without direction as victims of the current social order, for all those who have not lost the dream of living in human dignity among people who respect them as fellow human beings. All German Holy Rollers may gasp in chaste horror! However, if some pious souls find this wish all too blasphemous, then a reference to Jesus Christ might be in order. Jesus constantly defended the sinners and demanded that his followers "break bread with them." If Schiller has ever said a good word, then it was, "The earth has enough space for everyone"—even if this is a dream whose realization is still far off. Maybe Ascona will one day contribute to making that dream a reality. Maybe Mother Earth will one day have room for those who rebel against servitude and rape with true human anger.

I will not be able to stay in Ascona. I still have many countries to see and many people to meet. But if I return to Ascona in a few years, and it is inhabited by people who have found a home and happiness after being dragged through prisons and tortured by the propertied class and its executive organs, the state, the police, and the justice system, I will rejoice!

1. A paragraph criminalizing homosexual acts.
2. Filippo Turati (1857–1932), Herman Greulich (1842–1925), socialist parliamentarians.
3. Ravachol, born François Claudius Koeningstein (1859–1892), and Émile Henry (1872–1894) were French protagonists of the "propaganda by the deed;" both were executed by the authorities. In a self-declared act of revenge for their deaths and those of other executed anarchists, Sante Geronimo Caserio (1873–1894) killed Marie François Sadi Carnot (1837–1894), president of the French Republic, on June 24, 1894. Caserio was executed on August 16 of the same year.
4. The social democratic journal *Vorwärts* [Forward] was founded in 1876 and has served as the journal of the SPD, Germany's Social Democratic Party since 1891.
5. Commonly translated as "from the viewpoint of eternity."
6. The *Jungborn Harz* was founded in 1895 by the brothers Adolf Just (1859–1936) and Rudolf Just (1877–1948) as a naturopathic retreat. In 1896, Adolf Just published the popular book *Kehrt zur Natur zurück!* [Return to Nature!].
7. Small Italian town near Genoa.
8. *Vegetabilismus* was a fairly common German term in the early twentieth century, sometimes used for an exclusively plant-based diet, sometimes for a holistic "back to nature" philosophy, sometimes as a mere equivalent to vegetarianism. Mühsam appears to use the term here in the latter sense.
9. See "1900–1904: Literary and Anarchist Awakening" in the Introduction.
10. Literally, "perception/view of life."
11. *Misautisch* and *philautisch* were terms coined by the Austrian philosopher Otto Weiniger (1880–1903); they can roughly be translated as "self-hating" and "self-loving."
12. Lotte Hattemer committed suicide in 1906, two years after Mühsam wrote his text.
13. Mühsam is referring to Landauer's call for the creation of "settlements" (*Siedlungen*). In February 1904, Landauer presented his ideas at a Berlin meeting of the *Zionistische Vereinigung* [Zionist Association], following a talk by the sociologist and political economist Franz Oppenheimer.
14. In German: "*Verbrecher*" [criminals] *nennt die Bürgersprache diese Zerbrecher* [destroyers]. The wordplay cannot be reproduced in English.

Bohemia

Published as "Bohême" [sic] in Karl Kraus' *Die Fackel* [The Torch], no. 202, April 30, 1906.

P HILISTINISM IS THE TENDENCY TO GENERALIZE. TO BE MORE precise, philistinism is the tendency to turn your own moral horizon into a moralistic cordon for humanity. This is confirmed if we look at it from the opposite perspective: the least philistine person is the one whose social conduct is the least determined by the demands and prohibitions that some human beings levy against others. Philistinism is not defined by the mere attempt to live the life of the majority; it is defined by keeping fellow humans from transgressing the philistine horizon and from escaping the confines of moral evaluation and judgment. The most typical characteristic of the philistine is a tremendous fear of moral debauchery among his contemporaries and of the impossibility of controlling them. These sentiments stem from jealousy.

The main philistine weapon is moral indignation: a miscarriage based on fear and megalomania. The books of law, with all their lies, legally protected interests, "public needs," and other abstract fetishes, derive from this—they are the only writings that are truly immoral. The principle of the centralized state, with its generalizations and formulas, allows the moral indignation of the philistine to cause social ostracism and economic ruin for the ethical outsider. The state provides the economic and legal administration preventing the transgression of the philistine horizon. It is inseparably tied to the church, whose duty it is to centralize fear, jealousy, thick-wittedness, and banality. The liberal demand for the separation of state and church is nonsense. Both institutions have developed parallel to one another and each depends on the other. Culture can only develop on a grave they both share.

So, on the one hand, we have the philistines—the bourgeoisie—organized centrally in the state and the church and protected economically by the cunning capitalist order. On the other hand, we have a minority of isolated and poor pariahs who are excluded from bourgeois education and competition. The proletariat provides little hope here, although it should naturally be at the forefront of the struggle against the propertied class (which is identical with the philistines). However, the proletariat (the word has become very distorted) has been completely alienated from the class struggle by social democracy, which is obsessed with a future state, at least in Germany and Austria. The centralized workers' organizations, modeled after the state, have erased the revolutionary core of the union struggle by stamping out individuality; they have turned the worker, the natural vehicle of the social revolution, into a politician making deals with his enemies. Today, the proletariat stands between the bourgeoisie and the outcasts who fight outside of all organizations, together with criminals, vagabonds, whores, and artists.

Philistine morality deals swiftly with the first three of these groups. The criminals, who break the moral code of economic expedience due to anger or desperation, end up in prison. The vagabonds, who refuse to become an exploiter's coolie and to collect meager wages, are sentenced to forced labor. The whores, whose wild laughter holds more sparkle than anything that the "decent citizen" who has bought her for the night will ever experience with his wife in several lifetimes, are confined to pursue their "shameful profession" that is so necessary to the indignant philistine in brothels; they even receive a "control book"[1] to help the horny customer avoid a venereal disease. In all cases, the philistine's moralistic fury finds ways to justify itself.

Problems arise only with the artists. I want to make it clear, though, that by "artists" I only mean those who do not demote their art to business, i.e., those who refuse to produce without artistic inspiration. I see as artists all those who base their lives on artistic impulse, whether or not they produce any works of art. I see the artist essentially as a social outcast; a human being who refuses to submit to the expectations of the philistine horizon and who challenges its limits. What puts the artist in a special position is that every now and again one among them—a poet, a painter, a sculptor, a composer—will be recognized by the authorities, since authorities love the opportunity to prove their apparent admiration of culture to the world. This leads them to celebrate the chosen artist, while letting him starve at the same time. Still, this particular role of the artist makes him hard to persecute. The artist makes the philistine's staggering fear of anything extraordinary most obvious. The philistine approaches the artist with a mixture of respect and panic, which not only reveals a concern about how the artist will behave, but also an instinctive understanding of his superiority. The philistine is worried that his worthlessness will be disclosed.

In the end, certain artists receive a charter for unconventional behavior and are called "bohemian." On the one hand, the decent member of the propertied class, the bourgeois, looks down upon all artistic activity, since it is unprofitable. On the other hand, he likes to see artistic freaks around every once in a while—at least as long as they are not members of his own family, in which case they would be mercilessly ostracized. The problem is that the decent member of the propertied class has no idea about arts. As a result, any child of a millionaire who waves a paintbrush around can become a "bohemian."

The word *bohemian* is, as linguists tell me, not a real word. It should be *bohème*. Still, I will call a representative of the *bohème* a *bohemian*, since I find a terminological distinction between a general category and an individual representative useful.[2]

To define the term "bohemian," we first have to free it from the baggage that it has acquired as an object of sensation for grinning fools who know nothing about art. The craving for recognition among philistines with little talent who somehow end up in the art world does not help either: one day, a potato merchant discovers his voice, trains to become a concert tenor, and from now on considers himself a bohemian; a clerk loses his job, writes poems for his principal's maid, goes to a literary café at night, drinks absinthe, calls himself a "writer," and plays the "bohemian" every Sunday at the table of his uncle, the pottery master; a lazy student seduces an artist, spends all his money, and thereby becomes a member of "bohemia."

Murger's popular novel has added much to the confusion.[3] There are neat parts in the book, but the protagonists are not bohemians. They are dispossessed libertines who are very creative in overcoming the obstacles thrown in their way— but at the end of the book, when all of them have acquired money and fame, they safely join the philistines and leave their "bohemian" period behind.

To define the bohemian in mere materialistic terms is too simple. Even more absurd is the assumption that the bohemian automatically gives up his identity as soon as he can afford to live the life of a philistine. No, "bohemian" is a deeply rooted quality. It is neither earned nor nurtured, and it cannot be lost by a mere change of external circumstances.

Germans have the very unfortunate habit of categorizing each and every human being they meet. This has turned me into a prime example of the bohemian. I am not happy about this, as I reject any characterization that builds on nothing but external factors, may it be my hair or my attire, which, I understand, is not elegant enough for the bourgeoisie.

What truly defines the bohemian is the radical skepticism with which he approaches the world, the radical negation of all conventional values, the nihilistic temperament expressed in Turgenev's *Fathers and Sons* and described by Peter Kropotkin as the characteristic of the Russian nihilists in *Memoirs of a Revolutionary*.

Of course the bohemian's uncompromising rejection of adapting to the uniform life of the philistine is also expressed externally. After all, the self has to be defended against the instincts of mass society. The bohemian will always be an eccentric. It is therefore impossible to define a general pattern for bohemian living. I have basically said everything there is to say about bohemian life in the pamphlet "Ascona," published in 1905. There I described the bohemian as someone "who, due to great despair—an artist's most genuine characteristic—has never felt close to the masses, who takes risks in life, who experiments with chance, who plays catch with the here and now, who is a sibling to the always present eternity."[4]

The bohemian despairs because he cannot bridge the gap between himself and the masses and is angered by society's narrow-minded conventions. This can lead to a conscious rebellion against the ordinary, and in turn to a staunch demonstration of being different. However, I do not agree with the conclusion drawn by Julius Bab in his work on the bohemians of Berlin, namely that the bohemian is "asocial."[5] On the contrary, the uncompromising rejection of the current order in all its forms is usually connected to a longing for a perfect humanity.

What is interesting in Bab's work is the connection that he draws between bohemia and anarchism. The hatred of all centralized organization and the emphasis on self-determination, both central anarchistic features, are essential characteristics of the bohemian. This is the source of the heartfelt solidarity with the so-called fifth estate, the lumpenproletariat; a sentiment that is shared by almost all bohemians.

The outcasts of society are all united by the same longing, whether they have been ostracized by philistine cold-heartedness, or whether they chose to remain separate. The human beings who populate the gin mills and the brothels, the hostels of the road and the shelters of the city, with laughing faces and crying hearts, i.e., the rabble, from which even the representatives of the so-called proletariat distance themselves, are the closest relatives of the artists who are tolerated by the philistines as oddities and as objects onto which they project their own megalomania. Meanwhile, these artists, in their desperate loneliness, present to the world the ideal of a future society they long for.

Criminals, vagabonds, whores, and artists—this is the bohemia that will clear the path for a new culture.

1. *Kontrollbuch*—this was a common German means to enforce regular medical checks on prostitutes.
2. In German, the French term *bohème* is commonly used to refer to the community of bohemians. Since there is no English equivalent, Mühsam's explanation is hardly relevant to English-speakers.
3. See footnote 7 in "Johannes Nohl."
4. See the "Excerpt from 'Ascona'" in "Johannes Nohl."
5. In 1904, Julius Bab (see footnote 1 in "Johannes Nohl"), published a book entitled *Die Berliner Boheme* [Berlin's Bohemia].

1909–1914: MUNICH I, SOCIALIST BUND AND *KAIN*

NEW FRIENDS

Published as "Neue Freunde" in *Der Sozialist*, August 1, 1909. Mühsam describes his efforts to win Munich's lumpenproletariat for the Socialist Bund.

T HERE IS AN OLD SUPERSTITION CLAIMING THAT NO ONE BUT the industrial proletariat desires socialism. This false belief is one of the strongest protective mechanisms of the capitalist state. It leads innumerable people suffering under the economic status quo to accept their fate instead of following their inner rage, which would lead them to rebellion. In other words, it is not suitable for bringing new friends to the anti-capitalist parties and struggles. *The Communist Manifesto* says that the liberation of the working class can only be achieved by the working class. We say that any kind of liberation can only be achieved by those who are oppressed and tortured. But what does it mean to be oppressed and tortured? The criteria are not external means of oppression. It is not enough to be whipped to be oppressed. You need to *feel* the whip to be oppressed. And there are some who feel the whip on someone else's back as strongly as on their own.

What motivates the political actions of the workers educated by social democracy? A general desire for liberation? I doubt it. Liberation itself does not seem to be their goal. They focus so much on their "proletarian class consciousness" (a category that makes sense only within the capitalist state) that they have already allowed a class to form *beneath* them; a class from which they explicitly distance themselves, and which they judge with more contempt than they themselves have ever been judged by the upper ten thousand. They contemptuously call this class the "lumpenproletariat."

Many proletarians today put on their Sunday clothes for May Day and other festivities and, proud of their wage labor status, sing the pretty tune "We, men in shirts…"[1] They have lost any sense of being enslaved and oppressed, and of solidarity with those below them. The longing for liberation has been replaced with a longing for relative comfort, paid for by unabatingly hard mercenary labor. In the difficult, demanding, and long struggle for socialism, we cannot count on many among them. We cannot count on those who no longer feel the whip.

However, there are people who have no interest in compromise, coziness, and security. We find them in shelters, gin mills, sleazy bars, and illegal basements. These people laugh at the "revolutionary" earnestness of the "proletarians" who want to become factory inspectors and "five-cent pensioners" who live off the interest rates of the little capital acquired by other workers. They laugh at the embarrassing respect that the proletarian philistines show for tradition, at their moral rigidity and indignation when it comes to the upper classes' dirt—something the proletarians rally against in their journals with a pathetic glorification of their own supposed righteousness. We find both carefreeness and critical thought, both joy and despair among the vagabonds and the *lumpen*,[2] something they themselves are hardly aware of. This is why I like to call them the "proletarian bohemia." Theoretical education has not yet entered their circles. Up to this point, they have expressed their hatred against the existing economy mainly by breaking its rules, their love for freedom by demonstrating idleness, and their hopes by dreaming wistfully.

Are we not to find our kind among these individuals who have become rebels as a result of their nature and their lives, who are on permanent strike for reasons of their own, who are destroyers due to an unconscious sense for justice? Is it not that their desire for destruction is but a crude expression of a desire to be active in positive ways—a desire which so far has lacked hope and vision? To refuse working for oppressors and exploiters does not mean to refuse all social activity. Many among these people might happily work for themselves and for one another in free communities. Is this not pristine soil which ought to be cultivated by the Socialist Bund?

In Munich, we have already started to make friends with people from the "fifth estate." I will proceed to tell you about the activities of our group, *Tat*, and about how far we have come.[3]

It started with some of us—those of us who are in close contact with them—inviting the vagabonds and all their friends to a discussion about the role of the so-called lumpenproletariat in society overall and in the struggle for liberation specifically. This quickly aroused curiosity, and about twenty lumpen came—more than we had expected. They were of different ages, some very young, some bald, but all showed the signs of a life of misery, full of deprivation and long prison terms. At first, they were a bit reserved and skeptical, but interested in what we had to say. While we were waiting for everyone to gather, we gave them flyers and journals to read. Then I gave a short speech whose contents I will reproduce briefly below. To my joy, the talk relieved their uneasiness. They listened attentively, commented in ways that proved understanding, and became very warm when they realized that they were among people who were sympathetic, who did not care about their shabby clothes, and who talked about useful communal action without compromising personal freedom.

I began my talk with the following words:

> Dear friends! You know who we are and we know who you are. It seems to me that we fit together. We have long wished to come closer to you, because you vagabonds seem to be destined, maybe more so than anyone else, to spread our ideas and to carry them into many countries—and this means *your* ideas, even if you might not be aware of it yet. In the gin mills and on the highways, in the hostels and in the prisons, you have plenty of opportunity for propaganda. We really are talking about *your* ideas! You are the born enemies of oppression and of restrictions on liberty; you would rather live in poverty than accept peanuts from the rich to help them get even richer; you would rather die in prison or on the road than in the their hypocritical "welfare" houses. This is your greatest virtue: your stubborn resolve, your desire for total independence. It is not your fault that it is impossible to fulfill this desire in ways that do no harm to others and particularly to you yourselves! So far, you have only known solidarity among yourselves. Now we want to show you how you can leave this society behind by building a new one.
>
> It is, however, not your fault that you did not come to us earlier. We know how little the masses know about our work. We also know that you do not frequent people's assemblies because you know the reality better than the self-appointed experts who put on an act in front of those they can easily fool.
>
> That you are here today is important for you, and it is important for us. Our ideas justify your anger. We can turn the desire and the urge you feel into consciousness, and this consciousness will be the source of clear and purposeful creation. Once you have realized how important your existence is for the creation of a new society—and how much more important it can get!—will you not live with more joy and more energy? I am sure that some of you think of yourselves as lumpen. When drowning your sorrows in liquor, when going hungry for days, when forced to sleep outdoors, some of you might sigh in resignation and wish that you were like other people who at least have bread and shelter. We, however, assure you that you have always been better than most other people, that you were born as brave and fine individuals to whom we extend our hand.
>
> You refuse to partake in the dominant order—and still you make it through life, based on mutual aid. But how sad are all the obstacles to your independence! You are chained and hunted. You go hungry, you have to sleep in the cold on hard floors, you have torn clothes, some of you might not even

have a shirt, and when you desire a girl, where will you find one who wants to live with you? How many of you fall ill as a result of the circumstances of your life, how many seek escape in disgusting, cheap liquor out of sheer desperation? Sooner or later, you are all going under. What you lack is a backbone, the feeling of self-worth that you can only get by working for a better future. How can you engage in such work? It is obvious that you refuse to work within the capitalist system, even if you cannot justify this theoretically. This is noble and respectable. But are you satisfied with always being miserable? As an individual, there is nothing you can do about this monstrous system. But the courage of a group determined to transform this system is as powerful as dynamite; it can blow the monster to pieces by introducing new ideas and new ways of acting. It is the spirit of community that must take hold of you! It is the spirit of community that will lead you from merely destroying the social order that you detest to creating a new one that you will cherish.

I continued by explaining the principles of the Socialist Bund and its federative organization, and by encouraging the listeners to instigate Socialist Bund groups in their own circles.

As a test of the impact of my talk, we scheduled a subsequent discussion for a later date. We were very pleased when a large number returned. Some have been coming regularly to meetings ever since, and some are now thinking of forming a collective in a small shared apartment, shedding the dependence on shelters. We have reason to hope that the Socialist Bund in Munich will soon have a *Vagabund* [Vagabond] group.

Based on these positive experiences, we have decided to edit a flyer for the lumpen and the vagabonds. We are asking other Socialist Bund groups and all our friends to support us and to contribute to the printing costs. I believe that sensible propaganda among the "fifth estate" can help our cause in many ways. It will bring people to our Bund who have nothing to lose, and who have a strong desire for freedom, a feeling of solidarity, and no attachments to the existing social order. To them, the Socialist Bund will not be some random movement they join, but a matter of the heart, deeply rooted in their own experience.

1. "*Wir Männer in der Bluse*"—old German workers' song.
2. The German term *Lump* (plural *Lumpen*), which *lumpenproletariat* derives from, refers to an unreliable, mischievous person; it combines connotations of "loser," "bum," and "crook."
3. See "1909–1914: Munich I, Socialist Bund and *Kain*" in the Introduction.

THE FIFTH ESTATE

Published as "Der fünfte Stand" in *Der Sozialist*, July 1, 1910. Mühsam looks back at the attempts to organize Munich's lumpenproletariat after his efforts have earned him a court case for "conspiracy," based on the testimony of a young man who cited Mühsam's influence in connection with a petty firecracker incident.[1] The opening passages refer to the article "New Friends."

S OME TIME AGO, I EXPLAINED IN THIS JOURNAL HOW SOCIAL democracy has created a class of people underneath the "fourth estate;" a class treated with contempt and slandered as the "lumpenproletariat." This was the consequence of social democracy's effort to become a player within the current state system, to be recognized as a cog in its machine. Social democracy began to serve the interests of the workers by turning them into small capitalists. I also explained how those who end up as the "fifth estate" can be awakened from their apathy and how their sad and empty lives can be filled with expressions of human dignity and libertarian ideas. I described how the Socialist Bund could benefit from these people once they have embraced these ideas, and how they can directly work for cultural change, since no capitalist labor holds them back. Finally, I laid out how I had begun to carry the messages of unforced, joyful labor, of mutual aid, of communality, and of socialism to their hearts.

I remain as convinced as ever that I had the right idea. I still believe that many of these "lumpen" have the capacity and the willingness to embrace these ideals and to serve them. If it now appears that my attempt has failed, this does not mean that the members of the fifth estate cannot do many great and useful things if their qualities are channeled appropriately. The fiasco that I've experienced only proves that my tactics were incorrect. Today, when reflecting upon my agitation among the vagabonds, I believe that my biggest mistake was to underestimate the differences in character, age, experience, and intelligence among my listeners.

I never had any doubt that there would be people at my talks who would always, without any hesitation, do whatever promised the biggest momentary advantage. I was prepared to speak before a disproportionate number of informers, and I knew that the any one of the majority of our guests might become a Judas at any time; a few cents would suffice. I would not have been surprised if some of our listeners had lost a watch or a wallet, and sometimes I laughed silently when I realized that someone had only come in hope of a free meal or a pint of beer. These concerns—and some more serious ones—proved to be completely valid. Nonetheless, to this day I am convinced that there were also men with open eyes and ears at these talks; men who were enriched by the things they heard, encouraged in their longing for something better, and ready to follow our path with joy and courage.

If the good Lord had created the world in a way that allowed us to foresee the consequences of our actions, then I would have chosen three or four people after the first two talks and introduced them to the intentions of the Socialist Bund in special meetings. The others I might have gathered for very basic classes focused on general knowledge. Those who had proven incapable of learning anything, I would have eventually kept away altogether. Unfortunately, I only realized that this would have been a good way to proceed when my experiment had already failed.

I was under the illusion that it would be enough to explain the "Twelve Articles of the Socialist Bund" week by week.[2] But I was only judging on the basis of the capabilities of the most mature among my listeners. I did not know how to measure how much of what I talked about was really understood. As a result, the majority hardly understood anything at all—or, they *mis*understood. When I told them that I saw their existence as a result of the existing economic order, that I perceived them as victims of the state system, and that the notion of a "crime" incriminated the society that produced it, this was understood as an encouragement to break the law as often as possible. When I spoke about how a feeling of togetherness is apparent in small gestures, for example the sharing of bread and money among comrades, i.e., the practice of mutual aid in everyday life, then it was later said that I had recommended collective instead of individual thieving. When I encouraged people to value themselves and to develop human consciousness, never accepting poverty, I had apparently justified murder, arson, burglary, and robbery. These misunderstandings seemed particularly common among the youngest of my listeners and were passed on by them to others.

Since I now know what these youngsters said in court, I can see very typical patterns of imaginary associations. In my talks, I considered it useful to provide a term with which the listeners could identify their new ambitions, and so I often spoke of "anarchists." I defined "anarchy" in accordance with the Twelve Articles of the Socialist Bund as "order through voluntary association." I explained the term often and in detail. All to no avail. The association of anarchists with bombs ran so deep that the judge was told that I had spoken of dynamite and assassinations, of time bombs and similar things. As far as I can recall, none of this was ever mentioned at any talk.

I also realized how important it was for these youths to accuse me before the judge. It appeared as if they hoped to win favor that way. I found it remarkable how much more they trusted the tales of a psychopathic liar among their peers who said the most ridiculous things about me, my friends, our talks, and our meetings than anything I had to say.[3] The fellow in question had apparently collected his friends after each one of my talks to tell them what I had said, adding all sorts of adventurous tales, which were then used by the prosecution to blame me for intentions I never had. But it was his fantasy world that occupied everyone's minds, while my actual words seemed entirely irrelevant.

There is a frightening proportion of insane, delusional, and hysterical individuals among the fifth estate. It remains an open question whether this is the reason why these poor men cannot join social life and are left to the misery of the shelters, or whether the dreadfulness of the lumpen life with its police harassment, hunger, and despair causes such confused states.

In any case, I now understand that I was talking to an audience of psychopaths, dimwitted boys, greedy social losers, and a small number of really fabulous men who lived their vagabond lives in conscious rebellion against the dominant order and who approached the ideas presented to them with curiosity, and sometimes even with enthusiasm. One example might illustrate the character of these men. In my very first talk, I had repeatedly used the term *Kunden* for lumpenproletarians.[4] Two men protested afterwards: they were no *Kunden*. *Kunden* were apprentices who traveled from place to place asking for work. "We are vagabonds or lumpen!" they declared with pride. "We do not seek labor, and we refuse to work for any master!" The men who spoke and felt that way were not born sluggards. They longed for work, but only for work that did not compromise their personal honor and independence. They were receptive to my words, and even if they also misunderstood some of them (one must remember how difficult it is to converse with people in educated German who speak nothing but Upper Bavarian dialect), they did grasp the gist of it all, the core of the socialist idea, and they connected "anarchism" with ethos and human value.

I have been asked repeatedly if, given my negative experiences, I have had enough; if it was not my intention to stop working with these people. My response is: *No!* Even if I shipwreck another dozen times—the few people who I can give something to, who feel enriched by what I do, provide me with the courage to try again and again, always careful not to repeat former mistakes. The wandering knight Don Quixote was beaten up by the galley slaves he had freed from their chains because he demanded that they go greet his beloved Dulcinea. Call me a Don Quixote if you want! Even if the ones who I want to liberate are ungrateful galley slaves, their chains still remain a disgrace in my eyes. Besides, the socialist freedom I would ask them to greet is more than just a phantom like the blessed Dulcinea of Toboso.

1. Mühsam writes about the trial in the following essay, "My Secret Society."
2. See footnote 26 in the Introduction.
3. See "My Secret Society."
4. *Kunde* most commonly means "client" or "customer" in German. Mühsam's usage of the term is antiquated.

My Secret Society

In this article, published as "Mein Geheimbund" in *Wiener Neues Journal*, January 1911, Mühsam talks about the aftermath of his attempts to mobilize the "fifth estate," namely a conspiracy trial in Munich.

Dear Editor,

Did you know what you were getting yourself into when you asked me to write an article? Did you know where it might lead when you ask me for a polemic? Did you not know that I am an anarchist? And I am not talking about an anarchist who has lost his fangs and revolutionizes nothing but snobby studios and cafés. I am no *Edelanarchist* or *Salonanarchist*![1]

Well, fine by me. But I want to remind you that only half a year ago I sat in front of a judge in Munich, accused of inciting the "vermin" and the "scum" of society to crimes against life and property, to murder, theft, robbery, arson, and all possible crookedness. In the name of the group *Tat*,[2] a "secret society," I supposedly trained people in the "propaganda by the deed." Obviously, I was acquitted, and it was proven that I never did anything that was against the law. Nonetheless, a dozen shackled people appeared as witnesses, guarded by policemen, and there was a lot of talk about dynamite, bombs, and assassinations.

I and my alleged accomplices were acquitted because publicly announced meetings are hardly characteristic of secret societies, because *Tat* [deed] does not mean *Untat* [misdeed], and because anarchism relates to crime in the same way that factories relate to industrial accidents—no more. I expected that a legal acquittal would put an end to the ridiculous accusations against me. However, once a trial has shaped public opinion, the outcome matters little. In public opinion, I had already been sentenced to contempt and scorn; or, to put it more clearly: to social exclusion and economic boycott.[3]

The trial left little space for explaining the ideas of the group *Tat* and the idealistic—if you will, ideological—intentions of my activities. Many humorous episodes illustrated this. In one case, a witness for the prosecution renounced his former testimony, stating that he had enjoyed telling lies to agitated police officers. Another's motivation for his false accusations was the prospect of a trial: as a witness, he was fed better than usual. A number of witnesses said that the only interest they had taken in our meetings was the free beer.

The youth who was the main trump card in the state prosecutor's hand possessed a truly fantastic imagination. He had told the police officers and the coroner hair-raising stories about me. The allegation that I had incited my listeners to go on robbery sprees was one of the most harmless. He also mentioned dynamite that had been delivered from Switzerland and was hidden in the woods. He claimed that we owned floor plans of the town hall, the main court, and the police headquarters, and that we intended to blow all of them up. He also declared that we chase free-roaming chickens for fun…

When he appeared in court, he stood there, grinned, and rescinded every single sentence he had said. "How dare you come up with such ludicrous accusations?" the court magistrate yelled at one point. The youth said that he had been surrounded by four police officers who insisted that he "knew something." "And so I knew something."

From that point on, there was chaos in the courtroom. However, my co-defendants and I were still looking at a possible two-year sentence. Then another witness, called Hiasl by his friends, appeared.[4] He had just been sentenced to forced labor and was asked what he understood by the term "anarchist" and why he thought that it applied to us. His answer was, "Oh no, these are not anarchists—anarchists are the ones who kill kings!"

The state prosecutor looked more and more desperate with each witness, especially once the witnesses for the defense made it clear that some of those who had attended our meetings were able to say what had actually happened. The prosecutor did not ask any of the witnesses a single question, until a Swiss jurist entered the witness stand, a woman who shared my ideas and had always actively supported my attempts to reach the "fifth estate,"[5] for example giving a talk to a group of prostitutes who we had invited. When the judge asked her about her motivations, and when her warm and beautiful responses seemed to pull the final rug out from underneath the case, the prosecutor finally intervened: "But you support free love, don't you!?" My comrade looked at him and said very carefully: "I believe that there is no love but free love." It was the only time that I have ever heard applause in a German courtroom without the judge calling for order.

I understand that all these episodes were more important for the journalists than the few theoretical reflections that we were able to present (my interrogation took at least four hours). After all, they have to entertain their readers. Still, no one outside the courtroom ever got to know my true role in all this. No one ever answered the question of why an educated man, a poet, the child of a bourgeois family, goes to shelters and gin mills, to cheap bars and brothels, in order to find people for his community. Some thought I must have a criminal instinct and avoided contact. Others thought I must be an impostor, a geek, a loudmouth, a show-off, and they only had scorn and ridicule for me and for everything I have ever done. Some thought that I was perverse and crossed the street when they saw me. The kindest ones simply called me crazy.

Public memory is short-lived. My trial is forgotten. My name is forgotten, too, since the journals that used to print my poems no longer do so lest their papers suffer as a result of my reputation. Psychology, suspicion, and defamation are all quiet. But now I will speak. What did I do? And why did I do it?

About two years ago, the writer Gustav Landauer set out to reorganize the anarchist-socialist movement according to new principles.[6] He deemed the struggles that had so far been led in the name of socialism shortsighted; as mere proletarian struggles they only affected the relations between capital and labor. Social democrats have long been using the socialist demand for a new society based on just economic exchange as a mere catchphrase. Anarchists and anarcho-socialists have been focusing too much on a strike that would only be disruptive.[7] Landauer said that it makes no sense for those who want socialism—i.e., a society in which work and the products of our work are in balance—to regulate the relations of production and consumption within a state, since the state implies an oligarchic privilege when it comes to using the means of labor. However, he said that we must not answer the reformers with a merely negative notion of revolution. Instead, we must stress the creation of a new society, in which the labor of the individual is no longer a capitalist figure but a means to satisfy the needs of all. As a result, coercion and domination will fall, oppression and exploitation will disappear, and order will exist through voluntary association.

Free your forces from wage labor in order to use them for your own needs! This is what the theses of the Socialist Bund teach us[8]—an organization that consists of freely associated groups. Unite with people who share your ideas and who are ready to work. Together, leave the capitalist market behind, use your minds and your hands to serve your own needs, and work in happy communities for your own benefit, with your own means of production and on your own land!

I was the first to say yes to Landauer's ambitions, which stand in the tradition of Proudhon and Kropotkin. I was one of the first to help found voluntary groups. I also instigated a group that formed in Munich. This was where I gave my talks. It is self-evident that such a young movement, with such large goals, can at first only work with the word. In the beginning, it has to bring the idea to the spirit of the people. Who can deny that? However, the daily misery, the attachment to the class struggle, the experience that hunger hurts, and the conviction that a bird in hand is better than two in the bush kept the workers tied to their immediate interests whenever I turned to them. Our group—in the beginning called *Anarchist*—was small and fragile. I soon realized that the passion for a beautiful, free future easily loses out to the immediate concerns of daily life.

This is how I got the idea of turning from the wage laborers to the people who did not have to leave behind a job in order to work for themselves. Thousands, tens of thousands, find themselves outside of the state system for various reasons. The demand for work is always greater than the system can meet, and many have been left behind. Unemployment has condemned them to misery, and misery to crime. They are sons of Cain, whose sacrifice has neither been demanded nor accepted. They became murderers of brothers and now drift through the world as marked ones, unstable and restless. I asked myself: are there not among these work resisters, these criminals, these lumpen, these vagabonds, these lost souls—are not some among them to whom we could provide stability and hope by showing them a new goal? Is not the rejection of work and the temptation to commit crimes only a misguided rebellion against a state system that wants to force drudgery upon those whose natures keep them from obeying? Is it not this defiance that leads them from workhouse to prison, from shelter to homelessness—and worse?

And so I went to them. I looked for listeners in infamous quarters. I collected the poorest of the poor and spoke to them. Not like an apostle of the Salvation Army or a domestic missionary, but like a friend who understands and who motivates others to understand their fate and to free themselves through creative deeds. I tried to evoke human values and to arouse passion and anger by encouraging people to look at their own special qualities. I never wanted to evoke criminal excesses. I knew that this would only lead to new persecution, to new misery, and to new worries. I wanted to evoke activity—socialist, tangible doing. I wanted to evoke the spirit of togetherness and brotherhood and to show these men ways to begin.

Was this so bad? Does it justify those who swim with the tide calling me a scoundrel and a madman? I knew all along that many of these people had neither the capacity nor the desire to understand and follow me. Some only came to find accomplices for a crime. Most came for the free beer. Well, to catch fish you need bait. After all, the people had no idea what to expect. Should I have hoped that my beautiful eyes would incite them to come? If you want to woo privy councilors to contribute to a social cause, you organize a ball. If you want to woo vagabonds, you organize free beer.

I admit that my audience was no selection of top-rate human beings. But I had to speak to all of them if I was to find the few whom I was looking for. Some observers have ridiculed me for my "Don Quixote-like act." To them I can safely say: I have given comfort and courage to quite a few of my listeners. People tortured in prison by police and the state, and who are now living in desperate and miserable conditions, have embraced what I had to say and have found hope and faith in the times to come. I have given something to people who no one ever tried to give anything to.

It was an accident that informed the public about the existence of the group *Tat*. A stupid youngster, who I had never seen, seventeen years old and mentally ill, pulled a prank. In the middle of the night, he detonated a small bullet that he had taken from his workplace in an empty street. (He received a year in prison, by the way, for something that any high school graduate might have done.) However, this happened in the midst of the Ferrer protests, when the police was at their most agitated.[9] Posters went up everywhere in the search for the young man. When he looked for refuge in the *Soller*, the favorite watering hole of my listeners, they told him, "Go to the anarchists! They will help you."

Anarchists and bombs: there you have it! What followed were investigations, surveillance, and interrogations. The police learned about the lecturer Mühsam, and the "secret society trial" was put in place. The loose tongues of young vagabonds combined with the wild imagination of zealous police officers turned the indictment into an insane pulp adventure novel.

I have outlined the results of the trial itself above. As far as my attempts to ease the lives of the unfortunate ones are concerned, they will certainly continue. I will continue to speak to vagabonds and lumpen. If people believe in the phrase, *Tell me who you associate with, and I will tell you who you are*, well, then they are welcome to call me a *lump*[10] as well!

1. *Edelanarchist* literally means "noble anarchist;" *Salonanarchist* roughly means "living room anarchist"–"armchair anarchist" would be a fair translation. Opponents of Mühsam continued to use the terms as pejoratives. See for example the booklet by Richard Förster, *Erich Mühsam, ein "Edelanarchist"* (Berlin: Kulturliga, 1919).
2. See "1909-1914: Munich I, Socialist Bund and *Kain*" in the Introduction.
3. As a consequence of his trial, Mühsam was boycotted by the bourgeois press and could no longer publish his poetry, which had been his only stable source of income.
4. In Bavaria and Austria, *Hiasl* is a common abbreviation for *Matthias*.
5. This refers to Margarethe Faas-Hardegger (1882-1963), a Swiss syndicalist. Faas-Hardegger was involved in the Socialist Bund and romantically involved with Gustav Landauer until opposing views on free love and family life led to alienation. Faas-Hardegger and Mühsam, who shared her ideas in these matters, remained lifelong friends.
6. Reference to the foundation of the Socialist Bund.
7. Reference to Landauer's concept of an *active general strike*, where, parallel to rejecting capitalist wage labor, workers should engage in building alternative economic structures.
8. Reference to the Articles of the Socialist Bund–see footnote 26 in the Introduction.
9. When the libertarian Spanish educator Francisco Ferrer (1859-1909) was arrested and awaiting execution in Spain in 1909, there were widespread protests all over Germany.
10. See footnote 2 in "Neue Freunde."

"Riot in Berlin"

Diary entry, Munich, Thursday, September 29, 1910.

Encouraging news. In Berlin, workers and women have gathered to confront the strikebreakers at the Moabit coal workers' uprising.[1] Shots were fired, and the crowd turned on the police. (Right now, as if to illustrate why I feel so joyous about people taking action, a pompous artillery battalion is passing by my window–an endless line of cannons and horses, whose rattling and trotting makes my writing desk shake. The parade is led by a mounted band. The people just stand and stare. No one seems to think about who is paying for these murderous instruments, and to whose detriment they are employed. Thank God, the disgusting spectacle is gone…)

All right, back to Berlin where true streetfights erupted: a church was stormed, shots rang out from windows, women attacked policemen who entered their homes, one of them throwing a burning oil lamp onto a cop's head. (The police are under the direct command of the notorious superintendent von Jagow: "I'm warning onlookers!")[2]

This is clear proof that even the German proletarian is no longer willing to put up with whatever might occur. It is gruesome to think about the trials that will follow. People will be sentenced to several years in prison. The villainous "liberal" press, such as the *Münchner Neueste Nachrichten* [Munich's Latest News], is already inciting its readers.[3] But no one can take away the inspiration we derive from such events and the trust it builds in the libertarian instincts of the people.

Especially encouraging is the fact that the workers have moved so far from their leaders that they dare create enormous trouble for the despicable Social Democratic Party officials. The whole episode is yet further evidence of something I have known all along: Berlin's workers are the best, the manliest, the most independent, and the most libertarian in Germany. […]

1. On September 19, 1910, 141 workers at the coal merchant's business Ernst Kupfer und Co. began a strike for higher wages and shorter working hours. Strikebreakers were protected by the police. Rioting erupted after an armed strikebreaker wounded a worker at a picket line on September 23. The rebellion was crushed when the police attacked the workers with live ammunition, killing two and wounding 150.

2. Traugott Achatz von Jagow (1865–1941), Berlin's police superintendent from 1906 to 1916, had once famously commented on the announcement of a left-wing demonstration: "The streets are for traffic. I'm warning onlookers!" He was involved in the reactionary Kapp Putsch in 1920 and imprisoned for several years.

3. Popular Munich daily newspaper from 1848 to 1945.

WOMEN'S RIGHTS

Published in *Der Sozialist*, September 15, 1910, as "Frauenrecht." Mühsam strongly argues against opinions expressed by Gustav Landauer in the article "Tarnowska" (*Der Sozialist*, April 15, 1910), a reaction to the highly publicized trial of the Russian aristocrat Maria Tarnowska, who had allegedly incited one of her lovers to murder a rival. Landauer used the story to criticize free love and to defend the family unit. This was an ongoing point of contention in the relationship between Landauer and Mühsam, who was much more libertarian in matters of love and sexuality.

O NE OF THE MOST POPULAR OF THE MANY TOPICS THAT THE liberal and the social democratic press exploit until all content is sucked out of it is the "women's question," i.e., the discussion of women's rights in the present state system as well as in the future society. Of course this is a problem of utmost urgency. However, it has been turned into a tasteless flat cake of pitiful political demands by those with the power to shape public opinion.

Whenever women's rights are discussed, we can hear two sides yelling at one another. One says, "Women belong in public life in the same way that men do, in universities, in businesses, in parliament, and in government!" The other says, "No, no, as they always have, women belong in the kitchens, at the sewing machines, at the washboards, and in their husband's beds!"

It is natural that the second opinion, the war cry of law-abiding conservatives, meets with most women's approval. Putting things in order, cleaning, taking care of the household, and being nurtured by a man is the traditional profession of women. It is neat and tidy. So why change it? It is hence very unnatural that the first opinion, demanding the equality of women in the competition over jobs, ideas, and public influence as an intrinsic aspect of the social ideal, also has many female supporters, that that movement behind it is even led by women today. Those with eyes in their head can see that the participation of women in professional life—as workers, accountants, lawyers, etc.—is based on the misery of our social condition, and those who want women to live in dignity must wish for conditions that guarantee women the freedom to be and to do what their nature demands.

There has been a request to use this journal to advance new ideas on the issue. I am responding to this request. There are many thoughts expressed in Gustav Landauer's article "Tarnowska" that I do not in any way share, and I would consider it very problematic if they were deemed socialist. I want to reiterate what has been said in the article "Vorläufiges zum Neumalthusianismus"[1] [Provisional Remarks on Neo-Malthusianism[2]]: "Socialism…has nothing to do with matters of lust nor with temporary relief of misery; it does not recommend palliatives in the marital bed, nor in free love, nor in law."

Indeed, it can never be the task of socialism to approach sexuality on the basis of Puritan morality. Sexual matters are of a very intimate nature, dependent on the personality and the feeling of the individual, and they can never be defined as depraved and ugly, nor as sick and decadent. Sexual intercourse is connected to sensations of lust. The ambition to reduce all human sexual activity to the purpose of reproduction can never be justified. Those who take such arguments seriously would have to demand that all infertile women be sexually abstinent. Furthermore, when dealing with this very difficult and delicate question, we must never forget that the exchange of physical sensations, the sharing of physical lust between humans is the strongest and most private expression of love. And love exists and expresses itself even when a weak constitution or other compelling reasons do not recommend procreation.

There are many reasons why the movement for socialism should not engage in this complicated issue at all right now. As long as we live in the present state, in a society with unhealthy institutions and values, we cannot predict the ways in which decadence and strength will express themselves in private life under socialist conditions. In particular, we must abstain from judging comrades for their thoughts on matters of love and lust. For good reason, people are most sensitive and bashful when it comes to these matters.

Monogamous marriage has received a lot of praise in this journal. I do not question that it can be a beautiful arrangement and the basis of human culture if it rests on mutual love and on an intimacy undisturbed by unforeseeable events. Yet it would be very bold to base a moral demand for monogamy on the claim that humans—men as well as women—have a monogamous disposition. There are individuals of both sexes whose sexual life focuses on one person—but there are also those who desire variation. It is a completely arbitrary demand that people who are in close relationships should remain "faithful" to one another. The state makes these demands largely in light of inheritance laws—they have nothing at all to do with socialism. Whether socialism will be built on marriages and families is hardly a question that can be answered today, although it has received serious attention from a number of convinced socialists, and not only contemporary ones. In any case, it is wrong to refer to the past. There has hardly ever been a time during which marriage was a truly voluntary institution. In Antiquity, almost all men were allowed to have more than one wife, and to this day, the husband wields absolute power within the institution of marriage, while the woman is left with hardly any rights to speak of. Terrible regulations remain in place, the most scandalous of which denies a mother full control of her children in the name of the holy institutions of marriage and the family—and that is not all: when a married couple separates and the woman is found "guilty," the children are taken from her.

It is certainly true that love is free. However, it is also true that the freedom in the context of love must still be won—especially in the case of women. This makes "free love" very much a woman's right; a right that seems more important than all of the political rights that do not help in any case—look at the men who already have them!

Independence in the most intimate matters. Control over your own body, uninhibited by society's moral codes. Liberation from the public control of virginity. Uncompromising respect of women's humanity. These are women's rights for which we socialists must fight! Whether the increased freedom of women will have any impact on their sexual lives is of no concern to us.

Eduard von Hartmann[3] said it well: "The women's question is a virgin's question." Indeed, the paranoid preservation of virginity, which girls must endure long after reaching the age of sexual activity, is a wicked means devised by men to reduce women to flesh that serves no other purpose than to satisfy men's lust. The deflowering of a woman has been turned into a moral devaluation to keep the woman, in her role as a husband's wife, obedient to one man for her entire life. Those who relate sexual matters to matters of purity must, in my opinion, not overlook this sad reality.

The article "Tarnowska" argues passionately against the efforts to do away with the dominant role of fatherhood in the context of love and family life. The article states that the political circles that demand such things are "controlled by degenerate, uprooted, and wild women."

To me, the right of the mother is a sanctuary of humanity. Hence, I want to respond to the above simply by quoting a few words that Rahel von Varnhagen,[4] Goethe's dignified, prudent, and sensitive friend, wrote in her diary in 1820 (long before the publication of Bachofen's theoretical reflections on *Mutterrecht*[5]):

> Children should have only mothers and they should carry their mothers'
> names. Mothers should administer the family and its wealth. This is what
> nature demands. It is only necessary that nature be made more moral. …
> Nature is cruel in the sense that a woman can be abused and forced to give
> birth to a child against her will. This dreadful situation must be rectified
> through human effort and by human institutions. It also confirms how much
> a child belongs to a woman. Jesus had only a mother. All children should

be allowed to have an imaginary father, and all mothers should be regarded with the same innocence and respect as Mary.

Does a woman who feels that way really deserve to be called "degenerate, uprooted, and wild"? The issue here is that women lack basic rights and that men must become active if they believe that the opposite sex also deserves freedom.

To avoid misunderstanding: I, and those who share my opinion, have nothing in common with the neo-Malthusians. To generally control pregnancies and births is in keeping with the logic of a capitalist society. Of course, in individual cases, it might make life easier for a woman if she has fewer children, especially if she is living in poverty. To fight the law prohibiting abortion and to oppose the gruesome punishment it implies is merely a matter of humanity. However, this has nothing to do with socialism or the liberation of the female gender. To the contrary: to give birth is the holy and natural profession of women. May they give birth to as many children as their motherly hearts desire! May they live lives that allow them to bless the people with strong, healthy, astute, and happy children! And may they choose as a father, as *fathers*, for their children whoever they want! ...Once this is the case, then we can truly speak of women's freedom and of women's rights!

1. Article by Gustav Landauer, *Der Sozialist*, August 15, 1910.
2. A group of theorists who wanted to control population growth by birth control and abortion based on the overpopulation theses of the British scholar Thomas Robert Malthus (1766–1834).
3. Karl Robert Eduard von Hartmann (1842–1906), German philosopher. The quote is from his book *Phänomenologie des sittlichen Bewusstseins* [Phenomenology of Moral Consciousness] (1878).
4. Rahel (von) Varnhagen (1771–1883), German writer of the Romantic period; see also "Culture and the Women's Movement."
5. Johann Jakob Bachofen (1815–1887), Swiss historian who published the book *Das Mutterrecht* [The Right of the Mother] in 1861, which proved highly influential on modern-day theories of matriarchy.

The Moroccan War

Germany first got involved in the colonial power struggle over Morocco in 1890. After two decades of diplomatic gambling, Germany, Spain, and France were ready to divide their interests in 1910. In early 1911, however, French and Spanish troops entered Morocco without informing the German government, which sent a warship to Agadir to oppose the invasion. A diplomatic crisis erupted that was only resolved by the French making concessions to Germany in the division of West Africa. The "Morocco-Congo Treaty" was signed in Berlin on November 4, 1911. Mühsam published this text as "Der marokkanische Krieg" in *Kain*, September 1911, with the crisis still unresolved.

OW MUCH LONGER WILL WE HAVE TO BEAR THIS? How much longer shall millions of strong men and their wives, brothers, friends, lovers, parents, and compatriots be fooled by diplomatic chitchat, while the media makes a game out of cannons and canister shots, out of human blood and human misery? How much longer will the masses accept the role of "It" in a special version of Blind Man's Bluff?

For more than six years, hardened patriots have been talking to us about Morocco, and we are supposed to be excited about the fact that the western part of this land is "ours." Ours? Who are "we"? "We" are the important Herren Mannesmann[1] and their partners in speculation, and "our" enemies are those we are supposed to fight over this, namely the French (who have always been our enemies—or so we are told). But wait: are we really fighting "the French," or rather some French speculators who want to make millions off their compatriots' need for iron ore and mutton?

I admit that I understand nothing about colonial politics. I do not want to understand anything about it either. If domestic politics appear to be mad, then colonial politics seem to be utter and complete—and, let us not forget, inhumane—madness. Who *does* Morocco belong to? The French? The Germans? The Spanish? All of them? My opinion might appear bizarre, but I believe that Morocco belongs to the Moroccans.

The patriotic clamor with regard to Morocco has an ethical advantage over other heated colonial debates. There is much less hypocrisy involved. The interested parties do not hide the economic interests that drive them. Their raids are not sold as moral expeditions and cultural missions. Usually, the story unfolds as follows: warships land at the coast of countries whose inhabitants are called "savage" and "uncultured" because they work together peacefully, know nothing of import and export, and enjoy the abundance that the land has to offer. They know no misery and no exploitation. Now, however, they are given European "culture," namely firewater, guns, and tacky clothes to cover what has so far been natural. In exchange for these generous gifts, the blessed savages only have to surrender their land, their labor, their bodies, their wives and children, their natural resources, their freedom, their customs, and their naïve heathen religion–nothing else. Those who resist are killed, and those who obey become slaves. The moral justification for all this is provided for by the Europeans'"superior culture," proven by their effective modern weaponry. These are the colonial politics we are expected to celebrate as a moral duty.

Why all this perfidy and insanity? Because working the landowners' domestic possessions does not bring as great a profit as the absurd import and export practices that guarantee capital return. In *Fields, Factories, and Workshops*, as well as in *Mutual Aid*, Peter Kropotkin has demonstrated convincingly that every country can satisfy its own demand for food if the land is worked properly. However, this is not the case today. In Germany, there are enormous areas of unused land. While high import taxes have to be paid on even the most essential of goods, the export of grains and cattle is subsidized. Thanks to this, millions of Germans cannot satisfy their most basic needs. Thousands perish in misery, and hundreds of thousands are suffering. Meanwhile, the landowners do not even know what to do with all their riches and look for "markets" in faraway lands.

This is what all the fuss about Morocco is based on! Half a dozen businessmen on this side of the Vosges[2] and half a dozen on the other are quarrelling about this beautiful country, and the national honor of two fatherlands is so affected that both sides wave their swords.

Who will eventually screw over the poor Moors? This will be sorted out in the chambers where the governments involved mix their diplomatic poison. If they do not come up with a concoction that suits all parties, then it is time for the last resort: the national passions of the people will be aroused by alcohol and propaganda until everyone wants to see blood, and then they are let loose against one another with murderous weapons. Now the question arises: Who will do the fighting? The princes? The governments? The parliaments? The stock exchange speculators? No. It will be the soldiers. And who are the soldiers? The sons of the princes, of the ministers, of the parliamentarians, of the stock exchange speculators? No. The ranks of the soldiers are almost exclusively made up of workers and peasants. These are the people who will pay the price for possible victory. These are the people who are torn from the arms of their loved ones. These are the people who are taken from the workshops and fields, handed guns and sabers, forced to leave their homes, grouped in battalions and regiments, and sent against battalions and regiments that are made up of equally peaceful human beings. Then they will be ordered to strike and shoot these strangers who are just like them, and to kill as many of them as possible. They will also be told that it is heroic to be struck and shot, and that they will be more useful to the fatherland (how many of them own even one square meter of it?) if grenades tear them apart than if they provide for their children and their parents, than if they were a man to their lovers and a friend to their companions.

The masses which comprise the armies have no influence on the decisions made by those in power. The opportunity for the masses to take power themselves by determined economic struggle has been lost over the course of forty years of fruitless parliamentarian bickering—at least in Germany. All of their energy has been wasted on the ridiculous bugaboo of electoral politics and vote counting. This has proven to be entirely useless. As a result, the masses are helpless and are condemned to wait for the outcome of secretive diplomatic bargains.

If there is to be a war, we cannot count on the passive resistance of the soldiers. We cannot recommend such tactics either: the few who took them up would probably end up dead. Once war has been declared, everyone will be marching, and there will be nothing that can be done. It is different, however, as long as war is only a looming danger. Then the question is: do the masses have effective means of acting against organized mass murder?

When the Socialist Congress met last year in Copenhagen, the French and the English proposed a resolution that demanded that socialists of all countries respond to the danger of war by proclaiming a general strike. The effect such an action would have is evident. A country where transport comes to a halt for just three days, where no goods are circulating, where no trains are running, where no lights are shining, where no chimneys are smoking, where the sick are not nursed, where the dead are not buried, where no mail is sent or delivered, where the poison of the newspapers disappears—such a country cannot breathe, and it will need its most powerful force, i.e., its people, for more important things than providing cannon fodder at its borders.

England, the most industrialized of all countries, is not yet contaminated by social democratic cacklers of the Marxist persuasion. Have we not recently seen in England what even a partial strike can do?[3] It started with the seamen, spread to the waggoners, and eventually to the railway workers, and the most peaceful of all governments lost its head and intervened using the clumsiest means of all, i.e., military might, in a struggle in which not a drop of blood would have been shed without this savagery. In the end, the workers' demands were met. These demands were not very important in and of themselves, but the workers had forced the government to dance to their tune. And this in England, a country which all capitalists applaud for its exemplary economic institutions; but it was the economic structure of the class struggle that suddenly overcame all social democratic sophistry and allowed the true socialist idea to shine and inspire solidarity, determination, and truthfulness of such force that all of our hearts beat faster. If England were now called to war, could it even go? It will take a long time before everything in the country will again function according to the capitalists' wishes.

Back to the Socialist Congress in Copenhagen: as a result of German opposition, the motion of the English and the French did not pass. One of their most radical, most clever, and most honest representatives, Mr. Ledebour,[4] declared that German social democrats had to refuse the resolution, because it would make their domestic position too difficult. This means that calling for a general strike in Germany is pointless. The workers would not respond, because they have been blinded for decades by party propaganda; they can no longer see the necessary actions.

Those of us who want peace in Germany can expect nothing from the German workers. Their demonstrations and all-important declarations would not even cause a dog to leave the negotiating tables and money vaults. We have to look to France for help! The French have Hervé, Griffuelhes, Yvetot[5]—men of a radical nature, full of passion and love for the people, men whose fire ignites the masses and whose words the masses heed. In France, the government does not know what will happen if it calls the workers and peasants to war. There, the will of the people stands clear, strong, and tall against the deceptive tactics of the technocrats. Furthermore, a factor comes into play that causes only shame and nostalgic envy among us Germans: there exists a common spirit among the French, a people whose poets and artists still serve the cause of humanity.

There is no German Anatole France.[6] Those who should represent the common spirit of Germany are fast asleep. German poets and artists, do you not finally want to blow the trumpet? Is it not blood of your blood that shall flow for Morocco? Do you not want to wake up at last and unite with the people, without whom your work is nothing but hot air? The spirit and the people must be united! May the day come soon when they will be united in Germany as well, united against the noblemen and against the stock exchange, against the diplomats and the priests and the hatemongering journalists!

1. Big German corporation founded in 1890 by the brothers Reinhard Mannesmann (1856–1922) and Max Mannesmann (1857–1915).
2. Mountain range in eastern France, near the German border.
3. Probably a reference to the 1911 Liverpool general transport strike.
4. Georg Ledebour (1850–1947), prominent German social democrat.
5. Gustave Hervé (1871–1944), Victor Griffuelhes (1874–1922), Georges Yvetot (1868–1942), radical French socialists—Hervé later displayed nationalist and fascist leanings.
6. Anatole France (1844–1924), humanist French writer who received the Nobel Prize for Literature in 1921.

ANARCHY

Published as "Anarchie" in the *Kain-Kalendar für das Jahr 1912* [Kain Calendar 1912].

A NARCHY MEANS FREEDOM FROM DOMINATION. THOSE FOR whom it means nothing but chaos have the sensory perception of a horse.

Anarchy is freedom from coercion, violence, servitude, law, centralization, and the state. An anarchic society rests on voluntariness, communication, contract, agreement, alliance, and people.

Humans demand to be controlled, because they cannot control themselves. They kiss the robes of priests and the boots of princes, because they lack self-respect and must find an object of adoration outside of themselves. They call for the police, because they cannot protect themselves against the bestiality of their own instincts. In making decisions, they trust others to represent them (the German language is very subtle[1]), because they lack the courage necessary to trust their own opinions.

To continue with the horse analogy: the political life of the civilized peoples remains limited to conceiving ever more perfect reins, saddles, shafts, curbs, and whips. The working human being only distinguishes himself from the working horse by helping the master to develop ever better tools of bondage and by adjusting to them voluntarily. Both share the trust in iron mountings and accept blinders to prevent these from being used properly.

Scientific studies have revealed how the capitalist system robs human beings of the profits of their labor. They are exploited, and they know it. They also know the route to socialism: the redistribution of land and the means of production from the hands of the privileged to the hands of the people. They have known this for half a century, but they have not taken a single step in the right direction up to this day.

The means to change conditions that you know are dreadful is action. But the people of our times are lazy. As an excuse for their lack of action, they have developed the theory that history follows materialistic necessity: time changes things automatically. Meanwhile, the working people wait, repair and wash their dishes, complain, and vote. These provisional activities have become their habit, their need, their purpose in life. In fact, they have forgotten what they were waiting for. And if anyone dares to remind them, that person better watch out!

Anarchy is the society of humans as brothers. Its economic alliance is called socialism. Humans who are brothers exist. Anarchy is alive whenever they come together. They need no domination. However, they still have to create socialism. This demands labor. Those who refuse to help *create* and to engage in socialist labor in brotherly communion, those who want to wait until things change without themselves lifting a finger, they may go on repairing and washing their dishes, they may go on complaining and voting—but they must not call themselves socialists! In particular, they must not speak of anarchy! Anarchy is a matter of the heart, and they know nothing of that.

1. Mühsam uses the word *vertreten* for "represent;" in a more literal sense, the term can also mean "to kick [someone/something] away." The wordplay cannot be reproduced in English.

THE SUFFRAGETTE AMAZONS

Published as "Stimmrechts-Amazonen" in *Kain*, March 1912.

T HE POINT HAS COME WHERE IT SEEMS NECESSARY TO CRITICIZE the foolish scorn directed at the activities of the English suffragettes and at their attempts to achieve their goal. The facts that these women are indeed *fighters* and that they reveal honest passion—a very uncharacteristic trait in women—are reason enough to show them respect and support. Tens of thousands of women, from all social milieus, have realized that they not only have duties to fulfill, but also rights to demand. Since their duties are the same as those of men, they also demand the same rights, the first one being the right to vote. They began with declarations, petitions, and resolutions. These have all been ignored. Those in power thought they could simply shrug off the women's wishes. This got the reaction it deserved: since the attempt to discuss things went nowhere, the women decided to make themselves heard in other ways. In order to counter the ignorance of the men in charge, they started a movement that makes the entire public a witness to their demands. Huge numbers of them gather for street demonstrations in London, they walk defiantly and rebelliously, they break windows, and they wave their small fists menacingly at the strong male muscles that run the state. It requires a lot of stupefying arrogance, stemming from a culture that assumes the superiority of men, to question the genuine will of these women. It also reveals the embarrassing level of men's moral capacities that women have to go to prison and be separated from their husbands and children to make men understand that they are serious about their demands.

As far as the demand for voting rights is concerned in general, my readers know that I do not consider this a cultural achievement. The fact that women are not allowed to vote is certainly ridiculous and unjust, since parliamentarism is hailed as an expression of freedom. One might wish, though, that the determined women activists would put their energies into more important things than gaining the "rights" of men. The exclusion from the political realm is the most insignificant of all injustices that women must suffer. If women want to breathe freedom, their efforts should first go into securing dignity in their personal lives. As long as the personal lives of women are under the control of men; as long as chastity is expected from girls and seen as a virtue; as long as women's sexual activity outside of state-sanctioned marriage is considered debauched and immoral—as long as these realities remain in place, women will be subordinate to men and should not bother to make equality on a formal level their primary objective. A woman who is ashamed to be the mother of an illegitimate child can hardly claim entitlement to public office, for which spiritedness, independence, and responsibility are demanded. Women must first free themselves from the prejudices of a prudish morality and follow their own will in personal affairs, rather than the expectations of others. This is the safest way to demand respect from men, and it will also strengthen their political cause—especially in England.

CULTURE AND THE WOMEN'S MOVEMENT

Published as "Kultur und Frauenbewegung" in *Kain*, December 1913. The text indicates a change in Mühsam's perception of women's contributions to public affairs.

T HE MOST SHAMEFUL ACCUSATION THAT MUST BE MADE against the undignified culture–or lack of culture–of an era obsessed with mechanical inventions is related to the treatment of the female half of the population. Needless to say, the enormous historical changes that humankind has experienced on all levels of society have also had a huge impact on the relations between the sexes and the status of women. However, the traditional right of men to exclusively control public affairs remains in place, and women still have to fight ferociously for even the smallest influence over social life.

The industrialization of the national economy and the expansion of capitalism forced women out of the kitchens and the nurseries, out of their existence as housewives, and into the mechanisms of wage labor. Economic necessity placed them in competition with men who they slowly–after overcoming numerous obstacles–began to challenge in almost all fields of work. Today, women are so omnipresent in manual as well as in intellectual labor that the bigotry of die-hard chauvinists who want to see the "soft gender" reduced to pots, washboards, and the marital bed is disproved by mere facts. We must not overlook, however, that the use of women's labor to satisfy our basic needs is not part of the natural organization of the world. The substitution of female labor for the work of men is one of the most scandalous developments of our time–a time characterized by many scandalous developments. It is repulsive to think that the majority of women in the civilized countries have to pay for the opportunity to have children, and to nurture and to educate them, by wasting their energy on wage labor; in fact, innumerable women basically lose the right to be mothers as a result of this insanity, established and administered by men.

All this means that women have every right in the world to demand to participate in public affairs, not only in economic production! The doubt that they are capable of doing so, still common among men, is outrageous! Let us only recall the Romantics and names like Charlotte von Kalb, Bettina von Arnim, and Rahel.[1] This alone confirms how stupid it is to deny that women have intellectual ability. In fact, we can assume, almost with certainty, that the practical influence of women on social life would be the fastest and most effective way to rectify the damage done to humanity by the fact that there are neglected and malnourished children growing in the wombs of toiling mothers. Once their passion has been aroused, women usually pursue their goals much more directly than men; they do not waste much time on petty details. Most recently, the women of the Russian people's rebellion have proven this by forming the most active unit of the whole revolution.[2] Right now the suffragettes in England are proving the same thing: they show no fear of prison, or even of death, while trying to force their will upon the country by terrorist means.[3]

The scornful comments in the newspapers about the "*Wahlrechts-Weiber*" are dumb, cheap, and embarrassing.[4] These women fight for something that will benefit everyone. We could only wish that the heroes sitting behind editorial desks had an ounce of the courage and dedication of these women. Following the example provided by men—namely, to pursue their cause with pure violence—they fight for their convictions, they sit in prison for months, and they go on hunger strikes with a willpower reflecting true revolutionary spirit—by employing such means of passive resistance, they render the muscle power that the police are using against them utterly useless.

Of course there is something pathetic in all acts of violence, and when such acts are committed without a clear and obvious purpose, the demonstration of anger loses its power of conviction. However, it can hardly be said that the actions of the suffragette Amazons in London have so far lacked reason or thoughtfulness. Apart from the fact that arrests and prison sentences in the context of civil rights struggles never fail to have strong propaganda value, the suffragettes have also found very successful ways to strengthen their cause. Street parades are impressive events for the wider public, people's meetings are useful to persuade undecided minds, and the attack on the (empty) apartment of the minister responsible for the government's hard line against the suffragettes can hardly be misinterpreted. I also believe that the message of bombs put in letter boxes is tangible enough: if women want to prove that they can positively contribute to trade and transport by demonstrating their ability to disrupt it, it is not a bad campaign. Inexcusable, however, are the attacks of some women on orchid and flower greenhouses. Women who destroy flowers? That is ugly. It offends all womanhood.

My strongest criticism of today's women's movement, as it is currently seen in London, is the lack of radicalism expressed in its goals and purposes. The relative insignificance of the rights that these women demand stands in no proportion to the passion, courage, and sacrifice that go into their campaigns. By limiting themselves to the issue of certain political rights, women lower their struggle to the level of freethinkers, pacifists, land reformers, and vegetarians. They stop fighting for true cultural change. Exactly one year ago, I wrote the following lines in this journal:[5]

> The fact that women are not allowed to vote is certainly ridiculous and unjust, since parliamentarism is hailed as an expression of freedom. One might wish, though, that the determined women activists would put their energies into more important things than gaining the "rights" of men. The exclusion from the political realm is the most insignificant of all injustices that women must suffer. If women want to breathe freedom, their efforts should first go into first securing dignity in their personal lives. As long as the personal lives of women are under the control of men; as long as chastity is expected from girls and seen as a virtue; as long as women's sexual activity outside of state-sanctioned marriage is considered debauched and immoral— as long as these realities remain in place, women will be subordinate to men and should not bother to make equality on a formal level their primary objective. A woman who is ashamed to be the mother of an illegitimate child can hardly claim entitlement to public office, for which spiritedness, independence, and responsibility are demanded. Women must first free themselves from the prejudices of a prudish morality and follow their own will in personal affairs, rather than the expectations of others. This is the safest way to demand respect from men, and it will also strengthen their political cause—especially in England.

A women's movement that is following the correct course can do the most important pioneer work of all for radical cultural transformation. To take away a woman's right to determine her own affairs and those of her children is the most scandalous crime of men's economic system. Cars, cinemas, and airplanes remain a mockery of culture as long as the disgraceful public control of a woman's body and sexuality remains in place, as long as virginity is glorified, as long as deflowering means moral devaluation, and as long as fatherhood remains a central right in the code of law. "The women's question is a virgin's question," said Eduard von Hartmann.[6] The right that women should uncompromisingly fight for is not the right to vote but the right of the mother. Every woman and every girl should memorize the wonderful words that Rahel von Varnhagen wrote in her diary in 1820:

> Children should have only mothers and they should carry their mothers' names. ...This is what nature demands. It is only necessary that nature be made more moral. ...Nature is cruel in the sense that a woman can be abused and forced to give birth to a child against her will. This dreadful situation

must be rectified through human effort and by human institutions. It also confirms how much a child belongs to a woman. Jesus had only a mother. All children should be allowed to have an imaginary father, and all mothers should be regarded with the same innocence and respect as Mary.

1. Charlotte von Kalb (1761–1843), Bettina von Arnim (1785–1859), Rahel Varnhagen (1771–1883), German writers of the Romantic period.
2. It is unclear which developments Mühsam is referring to. His impressions might be related to the work of Alexandra Kollontai (1872–1952), who was agitating in Germany at the time.
3. Militant actions of the English suffragettes were at their height in 1912–1913.
4. Literally, "suffrage broads."
5. In "Die Stimmrechts-Amazonen," translated as "The Suffragette Amazons" in this volume.
6. Karl Robert Eduard von Hartmann (1842–1906), German philosopher. The quote is from his book *Phänomenologie des sittlichen Bewusstseins* [Phenomenology of Moral Consciousness] (1878).

THE BLESSING OF CHILDREN

In the September 1913 issue of *Kain*, Mühsam published an article entitled "Kindersegen." The first half addressed debates on neo-Malthusianism[1] and contraception; these were of some significance in Germany at the time, but are of little relevance to contemporary readers. The second half of the article dealt with the question of abortion rights more generally. This part is translated here.

PARAGRAPH 218 OF THE PENAL CODE STATES:

> A pregnant woman who deliberately aborts her fetus or who kills it in her womb will be punished with five years of imprisonment. If mitigating circumstances apply, the sentence can be reduced to six months of imprisonment, but not less. The same applies to those who consensually help a woman to abort or kill her fetus, either by applying the means directly or by providing advice on how to apply them.

In addition, §219 stipulates that midwives—or anyone else—providing means of abortion for payment, are threatened with a prison sentences of up to ten years.

In short, the state forces its female members to give birth even if their pregnancy is unwanted. Today's moral codes treat women as inferior human beings. Women are mere objects of legislation. Men prescribe their behavior, take away their children with the flick of a pen, condemn them if they follow their lust without state-sanctioned papers (marriage certificates or control books[2]), and do not even grant them the right to control their own bodies. Women must give birth even if they have no means of providing for their children, even if their own life is endangered, and even if the father of their child has syphilis. The state *orders* them to give birth, no matter how much they and their children will suffer. The state needs soldiers, and women have to deliver. At the same time, the state makes sure that they are ostracized when fulfilling this duty.

Paragraph 218 is often defended with the emotional argument that abortion equals murder. However, this makes no sense in the context of the state's laws. In the penal code's definition, you have to be born to count as a human being and to be granted certain rights. Hence, an abortion is merely an injury inflicted upon yourself—an act that is not illegal. If we take off our emotional glasses, it becomes clear that §218 has nothing to do with morality. It is all about economics.

Justice and humanity are not the only reasons for demanding the abolition of §218. There are also health reasons. Everyone knows that despite the terrible threat of punishment as many abortions take place in Germany every year as in France, where the well-being of the state is apparently not jeopardized by abortions, since they are legal. Many individuals in Germany help desperate women and girls to procure abortions, some motivated by greed, some merely by sympathy. However, the procedure cannot occur under proper sanitary conditions with professional supervision. The necessary secrecy and the fear of being detected often mean that even the most basic sanitary preparations are neglected—every day we read about a midwife being arrested because a woman she had helped have an abortion died in her arms. Even more dangerous—and also more frequent—are the attempts of women to abort a fetus themselves. All sorts of instruments are used, and very often they cause permanent damage.

If it were possible to entrust the procedure—a very serious and delicate procedure indeed—to qualified doctors, it would mean that the health and well-being of many young women would not be at risk. After all, these women might very well want to become healthy mothers to healthy children one day should their circumstances change. The clandestinity and the fear that are the cause of so much physical and psychological harm would be eliminated, as well as the consequences of being caught, namely imprisonment or, even more commonly, suicide. Instead, there would be proper medical treatment, reducing the cases of death to an absolute minimum.

The paragraphs 218 and 219 are possibly the cruelest of all paragraphs in the penal code, and along with §166 (blasphemy), §184 (distribution of obscene literature), and §175 (sodomy), certainly the most pointless—and that says a lot! It is the duty of everyone with a heart to fight these paragraphs by all possible means. This also applies to the neo-Malthusians, who should fight against such absurd, ghastly, and, not least, hypocritical means of violence—there is no other way to describe denying women the control over their own bodies—if they are really concerned about the well-being of women and children.

The happiness of a people can only come from individual freedom. So far, women have experienced much less of this freedom than have men. Their struggle, which is also the struggle for children's freedom, deserves our support. They must no longer be forced to become mothers against their will. Instead, they must have the right to give birth on the basis of their own judgment and at a point when their motherly nature demands it.

1. See footnote in "Women's Rights."
2. *Kontrollbuch*–this was a common German means to enforce regular medical checks on prostitutes.

Ritual Murder

Mühsam comments on the 1913 court case against the Jewish builder, Mendel Beilis, in Kiev. Beilis was accused of ritually murdering a Christian child to bake matzo with the child's blood. The case received a lot of attention throughout Europe. Gustav Landauer dedicated an entire issue of *Der Sozialist* (November 5, 1913) to the case.[1] This article by Mühsam appeared as "Ritualmord" in *Kain*, November 1913. It is one of Mühsam's few explicit reflections on Judaism.

I WONDER WHAT HAS TO HAPPEN FOR EUROPE'S COMPLACENT masses to become enraged. In Kiev, a poor Jew sits in front of a jury, forced to defend himself against the accusation of ritual murder. Those who accuse him, a Russian state prosecutor at their head, claim that he killed a Christian child to devour his blood with other Jews during a religious ceremony. The accusation is made although it has been known for hundreds of years that the idea of "ritual murder" is mere superstition. Nonetheless, even in Germany, it finds its believers, although it is crystal-clear that the entire Beilis trial is nothing but a maneuver on the part of "true Russians" to justify another pogrom. Yet, hardly anyone seems to care. When people read about hordes of patriotic Christian Russians going from Jewish home to Jewish home, torturing and killing dozens in the most gruesome manner, not even sparing women and girls, it is little more than sordid entertainment to them. People await the outcome of the Beilis trial with complete indifference; their emotional involvement is about the same as if they were playing solitaire: sometimes the cards add up, sometimes they don't. [Addendum: The fact that Beilis has now been acquitted does not change the persistence of the ritual murder myth, nor does it affect the conclusions that need to be drawn.]

In fact, people wonder why this trial should concern us at all. They agree with the anti-Semitic journals claiming that Jews are turning a local Kiev affair into an issue for international Judaism. Please! Of course the Beilis trial is an issue for international Judaism, since the ludicrous accusation of ritual murder concerns each and every Jew. The case would also be an issue for international Christianity if there were even the tiniest trace of truth to the allegations. But all those who have Jewish blood running through their veins know that this is not the case;

they know it with the same certainty as the accused—and his accusers! This is why in moments like these all of us who are Jews have the duty to remember our heritage and our community, and to demand that the accusation levied against Beilis be levied against all of us. In moments like these, the distinctions between orthodox and liberal, religious and secular, Sephardic and Ashkenazi become irrelevant. In moments like these, I feel solidarity with every Galician horse dealer, just as Spinoza or Heinrich Heine would have.[2]

The recurring defamation of Jews as murderers of Christians is a major element in the general persecution of Jews. Anti-Semitism is the most despicable and disreputable movement there is. Peace and well-being for humankind can only be achieved if all peoples unite behind a common aspiration. Anti-Semitism makes this impossible, since it systematically attacks one people that, dispersed among all others, has contributed significantly to many cultures.

The anti-Semitic struggle is rarely honest and rarely fought with clean weapons. It is usually built on slander. It knows no honor.

1. The issue includes Landauer's essay "Der Beilis-Prozeß," which appears in English translation as "The Beilis Trial" in Landauer, *Revolution and Other Writings*, 295–299.
2. Baruch Spinoza (1632–1677), Portuguese-Dutch philosopher; Heinrich Heine (1797–1856), libertarian German poet.

1914–1918: MUNICH II, THE WAR

THE GREAT SLAUGHTER

An ominous anti-war piece published in *Kain*, May 1914, as "Das große Morden."

MANY OF OUR FELLOW HUMAN BEINGS—EVEN SOME WITH intellectual capabilities—repeatedly surprise us with attempts to present serious arguments against the most basic of humanitarian principles. We reiterate repeatedly that it is only natural for humans to help one another and to create a just balance between production and consumption, while enjoying peace, internally as well as externally; and we repeatedly receive an all-knowing, pitying smirk in response from those who defend war, espionage, exploitation, and oppression as "God's will," as "beautiful and noble necessities." It is embarrassing to have to repeatedly stress the moral commonplace that war is bad and ugly, while peace is good, natural, and vital. Yet, we need to continue dismissing the arguments of the warmongers if we do not want to be seen by future generations as people who have given in and surrendered to stupidity and cold hearts.

In these times of refined technological civilization, the human mind cannot think of any higher tasks than the perfection of murderous machines. The ones whose guns and cannons shoot the farthest, load the fastest, and hit the most often win the crown. The ugly and the grotesque go hand in hand in the twentieth century, while insisting that people admire the world's apparent perfection.

This is what contemporary culture looks like: hundreds of thousands of young men who are able to work and procreate are taken from their workplace, put in pathetic uniforms with clean buttons, golden metallic headgear, and numbers on their shoulders. From their hips hang long, sharp knives that are useful both for striking and stabbing. Over their shoulders hangs a gun from which several shots can be fired in rapid succession perforating humans at long range and with a piercing force that can kill two people with a single shot. The handle of the weapon is massive and hard. It can be used to crush human skulls. They have a little bag dangling from their neck that holds many additional bullets, should those in their guns fail to work. They train for years to properly use these instruments when the time comes. In the barrack yards, where hundreds of them have to live together, stand wooden figures representing enemy soldiers. The disciples of war are trained to see them as human beings, as living images of God—and then they have to shoot at them. They are taught blind obedience to people who they have no relationship with in real life. In order to train them, they are made to do entirely senseless exercises. Look, for example, how they pull their knees up to their bellies when they walk together, how they throw their toes forward and stamp their feet down as loud as they can, first the right, then the left, and so on, in never-ending succession. They also have to pay special honor to their superiors, using their guns, their hats, or their pant seams, depending on the situation. To be precise, the greetings are not for the superiors, but for their superiors' clothes, which have even more gold on them than is on their own.

All of this is being paid for by the people, who expend a great deal of labor on it. Taxes are so high that the economic crises have been ongoing for years. The consequences of these crises are unemployment and lower birthrates, and in turn less production and even worse crises; after all, the demands of militarism never decrease, they only grow.

However, the day that war is declared, all the sacrifices, the abandonment of self-will and of people's power, will prove their worth. On that day, jubilation among the people will know no end. Former soldiers will join the ranks of those who are trained in the barracks, and even young ones who have not been trained at all will follow. Young husbands and fathers will be fetched from their homes, leaving their dreams behind. Sons will have to become part of the battlefield's glory. Apprentices and students will have to abandon their education in order to go to war without ever knowing the reasons for it; reasons that have nothing to do with their interests. They do not go out to face danger and death voluntarily; they are forced to do so and are left with no choice. If they refuse, they are signing their own death warrants.

Now the army has set in motion a force of a few million men. The units head for the borders of the nations they are supposed to do battle with. They leave behind sadness and desperation. Mothers, wives, and daughters cry for their husbands and sons. Harvests are ruined by horses and marching troops, production and trade comes to a halt, foodstuffs rot and become unaffordably expensive, diseases spread, and misery engulfs everything.

Shall I illustrate what happens next? I would need several hours to list all the horrible things that define the nature of war. Think of the reports of those who have been on these heroic tours! Think of besieged towns and starving populations, of thousands perishing from hunger, of communities attacked and set aflame, with everyone, children, women, the old, the sick, and the crippled dying–all in the name of the fatherland! Think of soldiers who have not seen a skirt in weeks uncontrollably jumping at women! Think of the inner brutalization of the individual who sees corpses every day and is always in fear for his own life! Who would not turn into a predator under such circumstances, especially when being taught that killing people is a sign of bravery? Furthermore, think of modern warfare! What does any of it have to do with heroism? People fight like machines; there is not a hint of bravery! They fire cannons and machine guns from hidden trenches in the direction they suspect the enemy to be; they are torn apart by shell splinters without ever knowing where the murder came from. The invisible fight the invisible–is there anything that could be more shameful to human dignity?

I know that even among the readers of this journal there will be quite a few who will find my passionate hatred of war silly and childish. These are people who feel no hatred against institutions and customs, because they are "mature" and "know about life." They welcome military drill as good exercise, and it does not occur to them that enforced exercise that pays no regard to an individual's desire can never be healthy for anyone. They say that there are plagues that have caused more victims than the deadliest of wars, and that war is just as natural a means as disease for keeping population size down.[1] How come that the same people applaud every medical advance? If they use the above arguments to defend war, they have no right to celebrate medication against the black plague and cholera or the invention of serum, arsphenamine, and mesothorium as victories of humankind. If it is good enough for humans, it should be good enough for God as well. Either we accept thousands of deaths willingly, because they are sent by fate (in which case it is hypocritical to fight bacteria), or we want to avoid manmade disasters like we would any other plague.

They say that it is economic need that causes war; if a country can no longer feed its people, it must take lands from its neighbor. Lies! For as long as capitalism has ruled the world, almost every war has been led by the rich against the poor. The big guys suck the blood out of the little guys. States act just like individuals. The accumulation of power is not determined by a need–it is a need in itself, just like the accumulation of capital is not useful to the people but a mere end in itself for the modern tycoons. In fact, the accumulation of power by the states, for which wars are waged, is nothing but the accumulation of capital at the hands of individual capitalists. The workers sacrifice life, possessions, labor, hope, and happiness in the same way that the small states sacrifice self-determination, national possession, and customs. Still, the war cannons are loaded in the name of the crucifix, God, justice, and morality.

A primary example of the connection between unscrupulous greed and war is currently provided by the Unites States of North America, represented by the honorable President Wilson, an enlightened professor and author of pacifist make-up, apparently committed to social causes.

Mexico has been in turmoil for years. The horrible land laws of Porfirio Díaz[2] aroused people's passions, and in turbulent struggles that brought the rebels close to victory several times, they were repeatedly forced to turn their weapons against their own leaders; men who had only used the revolution as a means to satisfy personal ambitions. It is hard to say from a distance what kind of leaders the rebel generals Villa and Carranza are.[3] However, accepting the complaisant wink of the United States in their struggle against the democratic despot Huerta[4] does not make them appear very trustworthy. It becomes increasingly obvious what the respectable "friends of the people," Wilson and Bryan, had in mind when becoming friendly with the rebels, causing complete confusion in the country and making it easier to send in their own troops.[5]

The pretext for the Mexican War is as ridiculous as it is scandalous. For days, the most urgent questions in the world were whether Huerta would greet the Yankee fleet with a twenty-one-gun salute, whether Wilson's cannons would answer him, and whether Huerta's demand that the cannons be fired one shot at a time would be accepted. Otherwise, the war would start.

What happened in the end was the intended outcome of all this demoralizing nonsense: the Americans occupied Veracruz, effectively starting the war without needing to declare it. They can now portray themselves merely as disciplinarians. Seldom have such actions involved hypocrisy as blatant as this penal expedition. The North American peace apostles shed tears of desperation about the blood flowing in their name, and Mr. Wilson issued a declaration to the Mexican people assuring them that he was after their president and not after them. At the same time, he appointed himself the master of their towns. That the invasion now meets more resistance than he thought, and that he is therefore inclined to accept the intervention of the South American republics, does not change the fact that this man, who fills European journals with humanitarian manifestos, has marched into a foreign land as a tool of exploitative billionaires to take advantage of social unrest. In his own words, he went there to "establish order." He did this at a time when soldiers in his own country, in the state of Colorado, conduct bloody battles against striking workers and allow women and children to die in agony.[6]

"There you go!" I can hear my military-loving friends cry out contentedly. To them, the events in Colorado only prove how the maintenance of a strong, combat-ready army is incontestably God's will. After all, it is useful even in times of peace, since there is always a domestic enemy!

1. The argument is based on the theories of Thomas Robert Malthus (1766–1834), who wrote in *An Essay on the Principle of Population* in 1798: "The power of population is so superior to the power of the earth to produce subsistence for man, that premature death must in some shape or other visit the human race. The vices of mankind are active and able ministers of depopulation. They are the precursors in the great army of destruction, and often finish the dreadful work themselves." See also footnote 2 in "Women's Rights."

2. Porfirio Díaz (1830–1915) was Mexican president from 1876 to 1880 and from 1884 to 1911. In 1911, he was ousted in a coup by Francisco Madero (1873–1913), a major event in the Mexican Revolution.

3. Pancho Villa (1878–1923, born José Doroteo Arango Arámbula) and Venustiano Carranza (1859–1920) were prominent generals during the Mexican Revolution. Conflict between the two arose in 1914, Carranza eventually becoming president of Mexico. In 1920, army generals instigated his assassination over questions of his successor.

4. Victoriano Huerta (1850–1916), president of Mexico 1913–1914.

5. Huerta overthrew the government of Francisco Madero (see footnote 3) with the help of the U.S. Secretary of State, William Jennings Bryan (1860–1925). However, the U.S. government subsequently refused to recognize Huerta's government.

6. Reference to the brutal repression of the 1913–1914 Colorado Coal Strike.

KAIN LETTER

In August 1914, after the outbreak of World War I, Mühsam published the following letter to explain the suspension of his journal *Kain*. The version published here does not include the original last sentence about "foreign hordes attacking our women and children," which Mühsam later removed, claiming that it was written under pressure and in distress.[1]

Munich, Early August, 1914

To the readers of *Kain*!

The catastrophe that is striking many countries and peoples can no longer be stopped. At this point, it would be useless to point fingers or to cast blame. I founded this journal *for humanity*–the current developments take the feather from my hand.

The readers who have understood my intentions during forty months of publishing will understand and accept my decision now. I only have two choices: to remain silent, or to say what no one can say without putting himself in danger under martial law. There are no other options, since I cannot deny or hide my convictions and as I refuse to turn the journal into a collection of mundane trivialities or into an outlet for art criticism. In this hour, a fateful hour for everyone, there is nothing that a journal dedicated to humanity could address.

This is why I have decided to interrupt the publication of *Kain* for the duration of the war. After that, I will return to help pave the road to peace and happiness. May it be soon!

Erich Mühsam
Munich, early August 1914

1. See "1914–1918: Munich II, The War" in the Introduction.

"The Typical German"

Diary entry Munich, Friday, February 5, 1915.

I HAVE RECENTLY COME CLOSER TO AN EXPLANATION FOR WHY Germans are so incredibly disliked all over the world. I think it is related to their "clerk mentality" (*Beamtencharakter*), to the exaggerated demands for correctness, clarity, and thoroughness in everything they do, to the truly despicable conviction that a German can do no wrong, and to the related belief that Germanness will make the world a better place.

Germans believe in science. For Germans, science understands and explains everything—and whatever it does not understand and explain, for example metaphysics, is simply ignored. As a result, the typical German lacks personality; he is boring, clinical, and pedantic. He *functions*; he does not *live*. That is why he makes such a good soldier. Militarism mechanizes human beings and turns them into machines. It cannot wish for better material than Germans. In their much more relaxed disposition, all other peoples feel threatened by German arrogance, and, consequently, hate the representatives of German self-righteousness who violate their own souls. This is confirmed by all the accusations that have ever been levied against Germany from abroad, as well as by the German belief that all foreign hatred is built on envy.

"DISCHARGED"

Diary entry, Munich, Friday, September 24, 1915

D ISCHARGED! UNFIT FOR SERVICE! NOT EVEN THE MOST
divine music could have sounded nicer in my ears than this
ruling of the medical officer in front of the "Reserve Units'
Commission" yesterday.

Two days earlier, I stood with Zenzl at the corner of Görres Straße
when an older medical officer passed by. I confessed to Zenzl how
nervous such encounters made me. Zenzl, with much concern, tried
to calm me down. I told her that the mere sight of an army doctor was
enough to make me lose my nerve. In an interesting twist of fate, it was
the very same man who yesterday allowed me to live instead of handing
me a death sentence.

I had to be at Room 38 of the recruiting station at half past eight
in the morning. All in all, about 170 men were there, all born within
the years of 1878 to 1881. First, an officer in civilian clothes explained
to us how we would be examined. Then, a lieutenant colonel, calling us
"squads," confirmed that those who were selected would soon be drafted,
probably in October. The mood among the gathered men, who had so
far been declared "permanently unfit," was devastating. It did not make
things better when the first ones returned from their examinations with
bleak faces, complaining that "they touch everything"! One after another
was deemed "useable," and classified as infantryman, pioneer, etc. Those
who were appointed administrative posts had a reason to celebrate
and drew the envy of others. It seemed like only the cripples got away.
I felt terrible for all the poor men who returned from the examination
room, while realizing with horror that my prospects of going free were
very low. I wished that the people's representatives, the Kaisers, kings,
chancellors, and ministers, these "war heroes" welcomed with ringing
bells and staged exultation wherever they go, would be called into Room

38. This would allow them to feel the real sentiments of the people a little better. Among the 170 men assembled yesterday, not one thought about fatherland and glory; every single one was downhearted, and the faces of those selected expressed nothing but despair, i.e., the feeling of having been sentenced to death!

I contemplated the consequences that the selection would have for me and thought about the oath I would be forced to swear: *Loyalty to King and Fatherland!* Everybody knows that these terms are meaningless to me, and that my only relationship to them is my constant struggle against them. To the human being, God is the highest expression of truth, emotion, and holiness. Those who swear an oath on God do it because of the way they feel in their hearts. It is an expression of piety. The state claims God as its patron, the king claims to rule by God's grace. The oaths that people are forced to swear, however, do not come from the heart—they offend the feelings of many. The oaths are the result of extortion, and they are used as weapons against those who swear them. Has there never been a cleric who took notice of this blasphemy, of this outrageous immorality? Sitting there contemplating it, I decided to refuse the oath, no matter the consequences.

Luckily, I was spared making this decision. When I was asked what was wrong with me, I cited bad eyes and a dilation of the heart leading to constant exhaustion. The medical officer suggested claiming problems with my lungs, examined me for a few seconds, and declared me *discharged*! Whether this was thanks to all the cigars, black coffee, alcohol, and women I have enjoyed over fifteen years, or whether it was a conscious decision by the military, I do not dare say. The curious looks of the officers and clerks when I entered their abode in shining nakedness, though, made me believe that they knew who I was and that they had previously talked about me. People might have reached the conclusion that a traitor like myself would do more harm than good if he joined the ranks of the German army. If this is true, then for once the steadfast commitment to my principles paid off. I would never have been a "proud" martyr.

Waiting for my turn in Room 38, sitting in a circle with about ten fellow sufferers, my heart shivering with fear, I understood the situation that war puts you in better than ever. We all sat there wearing only a shirt, naked legs poking out of it: hairy and smooth, crooked and straight, skinny and fat. In this grotesque masquerade, demanded by the fatherland, we had to await a verdict determining our fate—and a tragic fate for some it will be.

"Plans for Anti-War Protests"

Diary entry, Munich, Sunday, October 31, 1915

I AM TOYING WITH THE IDEA OF ORGANIZING PROTESTS AGAINST the war. So far, however, I have no clue how to do this. Public demonstrations are certainly the most effective means and the most feared by the authorities. At this point, a cry for peace and bread would without doubt be received well among the masses. If, for example, during one of the police-protected parades in front of the Wittelsbach Palace,[1] four or five people suddenly shouted from different points, *We want peace and bread!*, then maybe the homage to the emperor would turn into a protest—and maybe even into a proper riot, which would be the most promising way to make those in power understand the urgency of ending the disgrace.

The problem is that the parades always happen when victories are celebrated, i.e., when the mood among the public favors the powerful and not us. Furthermore, the people who usually join these parades are stubborn loyalists (at least on the outside). Finally, I am not sure how to find reliable people willing to take the risk of being beaten and arrested, while I myself remain entirely in the background. It is not that I am afraid. If I was convinced that my participation would help, even years in prison could not stop me. But if my name appears in connection with peace demonstrations, it would ruin everything. The social democrats would instantly point to me and speak of "anarchist provocateurs." This tactic has served them well for a long time. When people in Germany hear the word "provocateur," they only think of *agents provocateurs*.

Maybe I can come up with a plan if I think a little longer—or an opportunity will arise and everything will simply unfold by itself.

1. The Wittelsbach dynasty effectively ruled Bavaria from 1180 to 1918.

"Riot in Munich"

On Sunday, June 18, 1916, a significant riot occurred in Munich over frustration with food distribution during the war. The following is the account from Mühsam's diary, accompanied by subsequent reflections on the event.

Munich, Sunday, June 18, 1916

THE PEOPLE ARE RISING! YESTERDAY, WE SAW THE BEGINNING of the revolution!

At noon, my wife returned with the rumor that something had happened at Marienplatz,[1] a butter riot or something of the kind.

In the evening, we were in the Bunte Vogel.[2] Some guests talked about confrontations that had occurred at Marienplatz at 7 p.m. They said that the square was still filled with people. At 10 p.m., we decided to head over there to see for ourselves.

Indeed, the square was packed. I would guess that there were around ten thousand people, although it is difficult to say, as I had no proper way to measure the number. People were booing and jeering—at the beginning, that was all. Slowly, however, the anger and the noise increased. People started swearing: they expressed anger about their misery, the distribution of food, and the mass killings. Ten mounted policemen guarded the Café Rathaus.[3] At first, they did not move. Customers had apparently poured water on the crowds and thrown bread crumbs out of the windows. In response, some of the windows were smashed.

Eventually, the crowd began to move about. The policemen did the same, telling people to leave, chasing them around the square. Thirteen- or fourteen-year-old boys had climbed halfway up the Mariensäule and threw down the flower pots.[4] When the policemen requested that they step down, one of them said, "My mother has been crying all day, because she is out of bread stamps—give me one, and I'll come down!"

At the Café Rathaus, you could hear more windows being smashed, although most people in the crowd were still more curious than hostile. This changed quickly, however, when the military started descending on Marineplatz from Dienerstraße, bayonets in hand. The soldiers positioned themselves on the east side of the Rathaus. Then, all hell broke loose. People yelled, *Pfui! Pigs! Shame on you! We want bread, and you give us blue beans!*[5] and similar things. Then the soldiers started moving across the square. They arrested a youth at the corner of Rindermarkt.[6] The noise became deafening! We made our way toward the soldiers, who were being taunted and abused: "Shame on you! Attacking your own wives and children! The French would never do that!" The soldiers obviously felt uncomfortable. When addressed personally, they would shrug their shoulders and say, "But we have to…"

Finding themselves facing an incensed crowd, the security forces retreated to the old Town Hall. Rocks and other hard objects were then pelted at the windows of several houses (Hagé und Pölt[7] and others). On Rosenstraße in particular, hundreds of rocks were thrown and first one window was smashed, then another and another, each time drawing thunderous applause from the masses. Only once the Seidlsche Bäckerei[8] got its share did the policemen ride up the street, attempting to get things under control. Meanwhile, we had moved to the western side of the Town Hall, where some windows were smashed as well. Suddenly, we heard wild screams and the clamoring of women. Everyone started to run. The policemen had pulled their sabers and rode across the square, swinging in all directions. You could hear the wounded cry out and anonymous yells of disgust fill the evening air: *Pfui! Pigs! Prussian slaves! You call yourself heroes!? Attacking women and children—very courageous! Pfui! Pfui!*

People had dispersed in all directions and got trapped in the side streets. We ended up on Weinstraße. There, policemen attacked us on foot with weapons drawn. There followed more fleeing and more yelling. We ended up on yet another side street, leading to the Frauenkirche.[9] The heroic saber-swingers even followed us there. A woman who was with us was struck with the dull side of a saber on her back. Eventually, we made it through a crowd of agitated people onto Neuhauserstraße, where emotions were still at a boil, but where we were also safe from the police.

We will never know how many were arrested and wounded, nor to what extent. We will only hear rumors. However, I am certain that this episode was only a beginning. I expect a follow-up as early as today, on Sunday. In the Weinstraße, people said, "See you again tomorrow!" And whether the crowd will return unarmed after this display of state power is questionable.

Yesterday's demonstration had revolutionary features. Cries like *Peace!, Down with War!, Bread!* could be heard everywhere. Afterwards, the judgments ranged from *Right on!* and *This had to happen!* to *It's far from enough!* People are in uproar, and they seem united. The only question is whether the soldiers have enough courage to support them—their own kind!—or whether they will allow their superiors to send them against their relatives, in much the same way as they are being sent against Russians and Frenchmen. Maybe we will find out today…

The trigger for the riot was apparently the following: In the morning, a peasant woman had appeared at Viktualienmarkt with a lot of butter that she wanted to sell.[10] She was offering it cheaply and had many potential customers, but almost none of them had butter stamps left. Everyone agreed to the sale of the butter without any stamps. Then, a policeman arrived and prohibited it. The crying woman was forced to go home with everything she had brought, and the people were left without God's delicious gift. This is the nature of our current wonderful system. When the people turned on the policeman, he drew his weapon. The incident turned into a mass gathering on Marienplatz and into public demands presented outside of Town Hall, lasting all day. I have already described the evening events. It took until midnight before the heroes from Ettstraße took control of the battlefield.[11] The saber attack occurred exactly at twelve o'clock. The Munich police did not want the curfew to be violated.[12]

This riot in Munich was obviously more intense than the preceding riots in Berlin, Hamburg, Leipzig, and other towns. If it was more than just a temporary expression of unhappiness; if it was, as I hope, the first step toward dedicated self-help; if its example spreads to other towns (even, at first, only within Bavaria)—then, the war cannot last much longer. No government can defend itself forever against the conscious and systematic resistance of the people. And I doubt that any army can defend itself forever against its enemy if the soldiers learn—despite the government's disinformation campaigns—that the people at home have declared war on the real enemy.

Munich, Monday, June 19, 1916

An addition regarding Saturday's demonstration at Marienplatz: among the demonstrators were many soldiers in uniform, voicing their anger loudly and openly joining the masses. Others had come in civilian clothes, but wearing their medals. One was carrying the Eiserne Kreuz[13] and said with reference to the saber attack: "I have already lost one arm on the battlefield, I might as well lose the other!" Another one had medals across his entire chest, medals of merit and bravery, and he was among those who railed the loudest.

It is not surprising that the official police report knows only of riffraff and adolescent youths. It describes the incident as nothing serious. However, by 5 a.m., there were posters all over town announcing the distribution of new bread stamps—on a Sunday! In other words: the protest worked!

Yesterday, there were no new demonstrations; probably because the food was distributed so quickly. The Marienplatz was filled with people on their Sunday walks, curiously inspecting the damage. Policemen on foot and on horses were present everywhere, but their hope of seeing some action was in vain. People knew that the police had received orders to act "vigorously" at the very first sign of a new riot. If you saw these scoundrels at work, then you would know what kind of individuals rule over the German people; how ludicrous it is that they dare call the Cossacks bloodthirsty beasts...

Twenty people were arrested. I have not heard any numbers in regard to the wounded, and nothing about the seriousness of their injuries.

Munich, Wednesday, June 21, 1916

Apparently, my humble self once again receives increased attention from the honorable security forces. Yesterday, I met the Feuchtwanger couple at the Kammerspiele.[14] They told me that police officers had inquired about me in the Torggelstube.[15] Apparently, I am suspected of having organized the Saturday riot. As if one could organize something like that! My participation consisted of nothing more than pushing the complaints of the crowd in a certain direction and turning their anger about the lack of bread into an anti-war statement. But people would have probably yelled *Down with War!*, *We want Peace!* etc. anyway. The authorities overestimate my influence on the masses. I wish I was that important...

1. Central square in Munich.
2. Bohemian café/bar.
3. Upper-class café.
4. Marian column in the center of Marienplatz.
5. *Blaue Bohnen* [blue beans] is a German metaphor for bullets.
6. Central market square in Munich.
7. Large department store.
8. Upper-class bakery.
9. Munich's main cathedral.
10. Central market square in Munich.
11. Location of Munich's Police Headquarters to this day.
12. Strict nightly curfews were enforced in Munich during the war.
13. "Iron Cross," one of Germany's highest military decorations.
14. Lion Feuchtwanger (1884–1958), prominent German writer, and Marta Feuchtwanger (1891–1987); the Kammerspiele is one of Munich's most popular theatre houses.
15. Wine tavern and restaurant frequented by artists and intellectuals.

"BERNHARD KÖHLER"

Bernhard Köhler was a Bohemian acquaintance of Mühsam's in Munich. The following is an entry from Mühsam's diary about an encounter with him in August 1916; Köhler was on leave from the front. Mühsam was obviously shaken by his glorification of the war.

Köhler went on to become an active Nazi. When Mühsam was imprisoned in Plötzensee,[1] he asked Carl Georg von Maasen,[2] in a letter dated August 24, 1933, to establish contact with Köhler. Possibly, Mühsam thought his old friend could help in his difficult situation. Maasen forwarded the request. Köhler answered on September 18:

> I FIND MÜHSAM'S LETTER TO YOU RATHER TACTLESS. His nature makes him believe that personal connections can fix everything. He has to realize that his political charades are over. He has no reason to complain. The time in which Jews were allowed to meddle in German politics is past.
>
> Mühsam himself is not dangerous. But the groups he belongs to are. You yourself have sent me observations about them, individuals filled with hostility toward all that is German. Today, the time for struggle has come, and we can make no exceptions for these people, no matter how harmless they are as individuals.
>
> I do feel sorry for his honest and decent wife. But more important things are at stake here. Right now, we cannot even be too concerned with the suffering of those who have fought for Germany—how can we be concerned with the well-being of those who oppose us?

On December 2, 1933, Maasen received another letter from Köhler, which included the following passage:

> I also received a letter from Frau Mühsam. Even though there is nothing I can do about Mühsam's imprisonment—even if I wanted to—I would like to send her a response. There are obvious reasons for Mühsam being in a concentration camp. But his wife, who is so loyal to her husband and such a decent human being, deserves a few lines. Her sender address only reads "Berlin-Britz." Do you know the street and the number?[3]

Munich, Saturday, August 19, 1916

I am still utterly demoralized by the short conversation I had yesterday noon with my old friend Bernhard Köhler. He is an army lieutenant and the commander of a machinegun unit, and is currently on holiday. He was with his unit at Verdun, where some of the worst fighting occurred, and he calls those days the happiest of his life.[4] He praises war for war itself. He says, and these are his precise words, that it is the "lack of inhibition" (*Hemmungslosigkeit*) that makes the war so exciting.

When I responded that what was happening was murder, he readily agreed; he also agreed that his views were barbaric. I asked whether it was not terrible to know that death could come at any moment. No, he said, that was exactly what was so beautiful. "Okay, for you as a volunteer," I ventured, "but can you really claim the right to destroy the lives of others who do not share your views? Can you justify chasing your own men to their possible deaths?" "Yes," he said unperturbed. "No human being can expect another to respect his will to live."

I could not help but say to him, "If I were in your unit, you would not be sitting here!" He only laughed and said that he also had to accept that. Nor did he take offense when I said, "Your views cannot be argued against—there is nothing to do but to make you shut your mouth!"

It seems to me that Köhler's beliefs are the result of the foul aestheticism that was en vogue fifteen years ago, now given a mystical air by him. Under the weight of war, he seems to have gone mad, which is also indicated by a strange flickering in his eyes. I am convinced that it is his work at the machinegun and the killing of Frenchmen for almost two years that has aroused in him an actual lust to kill. Working with his imposing machine, he has gotten so used to seeing dead human bodies slain that he now sees the destruction of human life as a mere game and himself as some kind of athlete—and then he amuses himself by adding aesthetical and philosophical meditations.

I must assume that Köhler will become entirely insane as a result of the war, which will render him one of its victims—in fact, being slain in battle might spare him an even more dreadful fate…

1. A couple of months after his arrest by the Nazis in February 1933, Mühsam spent some weeks in Plötzensee Prison, where his situation was, relatively speaking, better than in the concentration camps. He was allowed to correspond and to keep a diary.
2. Carl Georg von Maasen (1880–1940), German literary critic and historian.
3. It is unknown whether Köhler ever sent a letter.
4. The Battle of Verdun in northeastern France lasted from February to December 1916, resulting in more than seven hundred thousand casualties.

1918–1919: MUNICH III, REVOLUTION AND COUNCIL REPUBLIC

Karl Liebknecht–
Rosa Luxemburg

Although Mühsam was critical of what he considered the Spartacists' "centralism,"[1] he always respected Karl Liebknecht for his uncompromising anti-war stance. On December 3, 1914, he wrote in his diary: "In the Reichstag, all parties agreed, with much blustering, to spend another five billion marks on the war. Only Karl Liebknecht remained seated, which resulted in the most ludicrous attacks against him. His own party intends to put him on trial for heresy and lack of discipline. I applaud the courage of this individual. His act will not be without its influence: it will cause at least some to think!"

The following article was published in *Kain*, January 1919, after the murder of Karl Liebknecht and Rosa Luxemburg on January 15.

A SHAMEFUL AND GRUESOME ACT HAS BEEN COMMITTED. The story of Christ has repeated itself in a horrible manner. All who share their heart and their spirit with the heart and the spirit of Karl Liebknecht and Rosa Luxemburg must be standing with their hair on end, tears in their eyes, and a burning shame when they think of future generations. We have witnessed a crime that disgraces Germany even more deeply and unforgivably than the atrocities which the German people were guilty of during four terrible years of war. During those four years, the people were blinded by lies, persuaded by leaders with heinous ambitions to blame their foreign victims for their own misery; the people were blinded by victories that were sold to them as the triumphs of a just cause; the people were blinded by the delusion that trusting the despots and generals would bring peace as compensation for all the deprivations and ordeals experienced—a peace that would guarantee a safe and undisturbed future. But then the hour of awakening arrived. Frightened and confused, the German people saw their military glory in ruins and realized that the ones who had held the imperialist aspirations of capital and the power-hungriness of the German military responsible for the war's misery had been right, the ones who warned and accused and never tired of calling for a social revolution as the only means to end the misery and to eradicate its roots. Karl Liebknecht and Rosa Luxemburg were at the forefront of these upright visionaries, they were the bravest of them throughout the war, and they were the most hated and persecuted by the capitalists and the militarists.

Karl Liebknecht was the first German member of parliament to refuse to sanction war credits for the Hohenzollern's[2] murderous system and the first to publicly protest against the crimes violating Belgian neutrality.[3] Vilified by the entire nation (there were so few of us who understood and suffered alongside of Liebknecht and Luxemburg at the outbreak of the war!), bullied by his superiors (the feared and hated man was given the lowest of tasks), ostracized by his own party (which was ashamed of this strong man who never lost the belief in socialism and internationalism despite all the betrayal he experienced), physically attacked by the parliamentarian representatives of the bourgeoisie, and handed to the myrmidons of the unforgiving class justice system,[4] he never abandoned his beliefs and, when he was released from prison two and a half years later, he instantly grabbed the red flag to guide and inspire the people who had finally arisen for the revolution.

Rosa Luxemburg was the flame of the revolution. Her enemies knew that. She was immediately incarcerated at the outset of the war. Her frail body was dragged from prison to prison. She bore all the humiliation and sacrifices strongly and bravely, trusting that the day of salvation would arrive, the day when the military economy would collapse and when the people would rise up.

That day came. Liebknecht and Luxemburg were freed, and immediately took the lead in the revolution. Working tirelessly, without concern for their health or fear of their enemies, filled by the vision of socialism and of the freedom of humankind, they did their duty as revolutionaries and as true friends of the people.

Now they are dead, horrifically murdered, lynched by the unbound beast of the counterrevolution. Both were slaughtered on the same day. By who? Noske, Ebert, and Scheidemann will innocently wash their hands.[5] Maybe they will hold the military responsible—after calling on them to protect their pitiful power against socialism and the conscience of the world. The military, however, will blame the mob and say that the two revolutionaries could not be protected against the people's murderous rage in two different places at two different times. Well, the Prussian military has always been strong enough to protect the guilt of his majesty Wilhelm II. No, there are no excuses. They and their "socialist" commanders will have to accept the blame, the most terrible blame that can be borne.

However, the German people, the German workers, are just as guilty if they were not among the supporters of Liebknecht and Luxemburg. It was workers in soldiers' uniforms who led the terrible battle against the defenders of the revolution in the *Vorwärts* building and at the police headquarters.[6] It was workers and their wives who formed the bloodthirsty mob, who brutalized the already arrested Liebknecht, who shot the already unconscious Luxemburg, and who gloated over the corpses of these revolutionaries like wild animals.

And the story does not end there. All over Germany, the two were cursed on the day of their death. Everywhere, people expressed malicious joy over the appalling deed.[7] The German people themselves turned into murderers and traitors to these selfless liberators, the messiahs of their rights and of their future.

The shame is immeasurable. There is only one thing we can do: keep alive the legacy of Karl Liebknecht and Rosa Luxemburg, continue their struggle, and sanctify the revolution by pursuing it until freedom and socialism are won. Let us wrap the bodies of the deceased in red flags and swear over them: *We will fight until the victory of the world revolution! We pledge this to you, our beloved friends and leaders, Karl Liebknecht and Rosa Luxemburg! You will not be forgotten! You have gained immortality!*

1. In his account of the Bavarian Revolution, "Von Eisner bis Leviné," Mühsam writes: "[We were asked to become] a local chapter of the Spartacus League. I refused. [...] I feared that forming a party would have the same consequences that it has always had in Germany: the submission of the proletarian revolutionary will to party interests. Furthermore, I could not agree with the point in the Spartacus League's program that demanded a unified, centralist council republic for all of Germany. Bavaria, and all of southern Germany, only joined the Reich ruled by Prussia fifty years ago, and fought a war for independence from Prussia in 1866. The separatist currents were enormously strong in Bavaria, and the unification that was pursued by the 'democratic' government of the Reich and the social democratic parties therefore extremely unpopular" (16).

2. The House of Hohenzollern was a royal German dynasty of the Kaisers of the German Kaiserreich (1871 to 1918).

3. At the beginning of World War I, Germany invaded Belgium, neutral since gaining its independence in 1830.

4. After leading an anti-militarist demonstration on May 1, 1916, Liebknecht was arrested and sentenced to four years and one month in prison for "high treason." He was released in October 1918 during a general amnesty for political prisoners.

5. Gustav Noske (1868–1946), Friedrich Ebert (1871–1925), Philipp Scheidemann (1865–1939), leading SPD members.

6. The offices of the *Vorwärts*, the journal of the SPD, and Berlin's police headquarters were important sites of confrontation during the Spartacus Uprising (see footnote 50 in the Introduction).

7. Mühsam recalls in a diary entry from March 28, 1923, confined in Niederschönenfeld Fortress: "On January 16, I sat with Landauer and the two Franks in a small wine tavern in Munich when Weigel brought us the terrible news of Liebknecht's and Luxemburg's murder. Grotesquely, right after Weigel, a lieutenant entered with a girl and celebrated with the owner. We paid and left our food on the table. On the streets, people were carrying telegrams, grinning—and not only the bourgeoisie, unfortunately also many proletarians. Lisa Frank cried bitterly. We all knew that this was the beginning of the worst tragedy ever for the German people."–Leonhard Frank (1882–1961), German socialist writer, and Lisa Frank (?–1923); Fritz Weigel (1890–?), communist comrade.

Excerpts from "From Eisner to Leviné"

In September 1920, Erich Mühsam wrote a "personal account" of the Bavarian Council Republic while confined in the Ansbach Fortress. It was written "to inform the creators of the Russian Soviet Republic" and addressed to "Comrade Lenin." The hand-written manuscript was smuggled out of the fortress. A typed copy sent back to Mühsam was confiscated by the prison authorities. Along with all the other papers confiscated during his imprisonment, it was only returned to Mühsam in 1928. The account was published as a pamphlet one year later under the title "Von Eisner bis Leviné." In his preface, Mühsam wrote that a comrade had personally delivered a copy of the account to Lenin in 1921 and that Lenin had read it. This cannot be confirmed. Mühsam also stated that one of the major motivations for writing the text were the distorted accounts of the Bavarian Council Republic presented by Communist Party members, in particular the booklet *Die bayrische Räterepublik. Tatsachen und Kritik* [The Bavarian Council Republic: Facts and Critique] by P. Werner, which ridiculed the Bavarian Council Republic–before the Communist Party took control of it on April 13[1]–as a "sham council republic," initiated by "dubious characters and confused minds."[2]

Mühsam's entire account will be published in the forthcoming PM Press volume *All Power to the Councils! A Documentary Reader of the German Revolution of 1918–1919* (2012). Included here are some excerpts that sketch the events, provide an insight into Mühsam's involvement and motivations, and present his later assessment.

[...] The distinction between the "sham council republic" and the council republic run by the Communist Party (supposedly the only "true" one) was drawn by the KPD to justify to the proletariat its lack of support for the first council republic. The presentation of this nonsense in a published account of the council republic can only be characterized as demagogic historical revisionism. The workers associated with the phrase "dictatorship of the proletariat" the simple notion that the oppressed class throws off the chains of capitalism in a revolutionary uprising in order to exercise self-determination over its own affairs through its councils. This is all they were interested in. They knew nothing about a distinction between the council republic proclaimed on April 7 and a council republic that formed on April 13 under a new administration. They fought for *one and the same* council republic, risking their lives and sacrificing their freedom. They were the comrades who shouted after Eisner's murder (and even before) *Power to the Councils!*, who demanded the proclamation of the council republic in early April, who refused to accept a reactionary bourgeois dictatorship in Bavaria modeled after the one in northern Germany,[3] who forced the ill-prepared events from April 4 to 6, who declared their confidence in the central council of the "sham council republic" on April 11, who stormed Munich's Central Station after the Palm Sunday Coup,[4] and who sacrificed their lives as Red Guards, were executed, or spent years in the dungeons of the vindictive social democratic justice system. [...]

I did not have the means to do a comparative historical study. However, I want to [make] at least one comparative reference, which is very important to me for two reasons: one, the party communists love to hold the anarchists—by which they always mean Gustav Landauer and myself—responsible for the mistakes of the so-called "sham council republic;" two, even many of our anarchist comrades often believe that our undertaking was condemned to fail from the outset due to the power of the Communist Party and its Marxist doctrines. I believe that I can respond to both criticisms with a quote by Friedrich Engels, who, in 1891, in his introduction to Karl Marx's *Der Bürgerkrieg in Frankreich* [The Civil War in France] wrote the following words about the collaboration between Proudhonists and Blanquists in the Paris Commune:

> What was more important [than the previously-criticized failures] were the many things that were accomplished by this commune consisting of both Proudhonists and Blanquists. Of course the Proudhonists were primarily responsible for the economic resolutions (for better or worse), and the Blanquists for the political decrees. However, as it is usually the case when doctrinarians take control, in the end both did the opposite of what their doctrine demanded. Such is the irony of history.

Does this not perfectly sum up the roles of the party communists and of the anarchists in the Bavarian Council Republic? On the crucial night from April 4 to 5, Landauer and I decided, against our usual convictions, that it did not really matter whether or not the proclamation of the council republic happened with the mandate of the factory workers. Furthermore, despite certain concerns, we had decided to participate in a provisional "government," thinking that this was a historical necessity. The party communists, on the other hand, who generally imposed authoritarianism on the masses, criticized our actions because a council republic, so they insisted, could only be built from the bottom up. Nonetheless, on April 13, the pressure of the events forced them to do exactly what we had done a week earlier. Unfortunately, the party egotism of the KPD had prevented collaboration at that decisive moment. Otherwise, some mistakes of the first council republic might have had less fateful consequences, some mistakes of the second might have been avoided, and the many things that had been achieved during both (at least in terms of good will) might have led to real success. [...]

No one even considered the possibility that the KPD might oppose our plans. We all knew how passionately Munich's proletariat demanded the council republic, and so we overlooked the danger implied in the random form of its proclamation as we had planned it. I believed that we had been given an opportunity that was unlikely to repeat itself: a general strike in Augsburg[5] with the clear demand on the part of the proletariat for the immediate proclamation of the council republic; a breach by the bourgeoisie of the agreement it had reached with the councils' congress;[6] the fresh impressions of the events in Hungary;[7] unrest in Braunschweig and Thuringia, with the explicit goal of establishing a Bolshevik council dictatorship; the possibility of building bridges, since the power of the Bauers and Adlers[8] in Austria was expected to crumble if the country was wedged between council republics in Hungary and Bavaria; the possibility of islands in Braunschweig and in central Germany, making our actions the signal for a general German Revolution that would shatter the rule of Ebert-Scheidemann-Noske.[9] These were the reasons why I believed that the proclamation of the council republic in Bavaria was a necessity in the pursuit of the world revolution. [...]

The effect of the KPD's refusal to support the council republic were felt everywhere. The Revolutionary Workers' Council (*Revolutionärer Arbeiterrat*),[10] which had up to that point always been characterized by a strong sense of unity, broke apart, because the KPD demanded that its members resign. Some of them did not comply, which led to major conflicts within the KPD itself. The same thing occurred among the masses. Many KPD members declared their disapproval of the party's official stance and resigned or acted against the orders of their leaders. Similar news arrived from around the country. For example, the KPD chapter in Nuremberg split into two factions. Particularly devastating was that the lack of unity among the revolutionary proletariat had a negative impact on the soldiers. To give an example (I only learned about this later), in Nuremberg the leader of a corps of two thousand men had offered his unconditional services. A day later, he declared that he and his soldiers had to rescind their commitment, given the fact that the KPD opposed the council republic. [...]

Only after a visit from the comrade Axelrod[11] did I realize what a mistake we had made with our rushed proclamation of the council republic. Axelrod explained to me that he had opposed the proclamation because it had happened without sufficient preparation. There was no proper cabinet and no proper outline, and the military was far from effectively organized. However, he insisted, these things needed to be taken care of first. Then one can act, with the exact formalities not really mattering all that much.

If someone had presented these arguments on April 4, I am sure that the disaster that followed could have been avoided. When I asked Axelrod if things could be reversed, he said that it was too late. However, he still did not see this as an obligation for the party communists to get involved.

This conversation, as well as the doubts among the workers, caused by the party communists' accusation that we had established a "sham council republic," made me turn to the proletariat with a proclamation that Landauer released on April 9:

> *Working Men of the World Unite!* The final words of *The Communist Manifesto* have become the rallying cry of the International! Now we direct this appeal to the revolutionary people of our own country: *Workers of Bavaria Unite!*
>
> The unification of the proletariat must, as the glorious example of the Russian people has shown, be based on a single foundation: the council republic!
>
> *Bavaria is a Council Republic!*
>
> Disregarding the differences of their leaders, the working people have united in their will to realize socialism and to realize communism!
>
> The *Landtag* has been chased away.[12] The petty-bourgeois social democratic cabinet no longer exists. A Provisional Council of People's Delegates and a Provisional Revolutionary Central Council are now administering the country's affairs. Since not a single one of the leaders of the war socialists[13] is represented on these bodies, it is guaranteed that these bodies will serve the revolution without considering the interests of the capitalists and the bourgeoisie.
>
> *The Dictatorship of the Proletariat is a Fact!*
>
> *A Red Army Will Be Raised Immediately!*
>
> *Relations with Russia and Hungary Will Be Established at Once!*
>
> There will be no union between the socialist Bavaria and the imperial Germany, no matter its republican façade.
>
> A revolutionary court will punish any attempts at reactionary agitation. The newspapers' freedom to lie will be brought to an end. The socialization of the press secures the true freedom of opinion for the revolutionary people.
>
> The Provisional Central Council will schedule reelections of the factory councils on a revolutionary basis as soon as possible. Based on these elections, the council system will be built from the bottom up. Power will be transferred into the hands of the working people themselves—and *only* the working people! The capitalists will be excluded from participation in the decision-making process.
>
> In the council system, the wealth will finally belong to those who produce it. Socialism will follow. Together with revolutionary Russia and revolutionary Hungary, the new Bavaria will form a revolutionary International, paving the way to the world revolution!
>
> Proletarians! Keep the peace among yourselves! We have only common enemies: the reactionary forces, capitalism, exploitation, and privilege. It is against these enemies that all fighters for freedom and socialism must unite.

Get to Work! Each One to His Post!

Long Live the Free Bavarian People! Long Live the Council Republic!

Erich Mühsam

I added the following explanation to this proclamation:

> The leadership of the KPD Munich does not support the provisional administration of the council republic for reasons of principle. However, we hope to overcome our differences soon, especially once the factory reelections, from which proletarian power shall once and for all emerge, have taken place. As far as I am personally concerned, I declare that I will not accept any official post in the council republic before the unification of the workers has been achieved. It is impossible for me to hold such a post without the approval of the comrades who have so far been my closest allies in the struggle, and with whom I still believe I share a common desire.

April 9, 1919–Erich Mühsam

[…] The next day, I had a longer conversation with Leviné; it was the first and the last time that we spoke in private. Comrade Leviné assured me that he had absolutely no doubt about the sincerity of my actions. However, he sternly rejected my requests that the KPD become actively involved in the council republic. Leviné said that he was personally convinced of the hopelessness of the government's work. When I said, "But we can't just leave the cart stuck in the mud!" he laconically replied, "Then pull it out!" He confirmed, though, that turning the country over to the Hoffmann government was out of the question.[14] I suggested to Leviné that we be forcibly ousted so that the hopeless situation would end and the revolutionary work could be secured. He did not consider the time right for this, but acknowledged that the fighting against the bourgeoisie that had to be expected could only be led by his party. Although we had not found common ground, we parted with a handshake that transcended personal differences and that gave me hope that a political agreement was possible. […]

[On April 13], at 4 a.m., I was arrested in my bedroom by members of the Republican Defense Force, which had assured us of its loyalty only days earlier. I was brought to the Central Station, with another twelve comrades arriving over the course of the morning. Posters had been put up announcing the overthrow of the council government in the name of the military and proclaiming the Hoffmann government as the only legitimate one. Some comrades, among them the people's delegate Soldmann,[15] had been taken from the Wittelsbach Palace,[16] where they had stayed to continue working for the people throughout the night. Others, among them comrade Dr. Wadler,[17] had also been arrested at their homes. Some had been arrested while taking hostages. We stayed in the station until noon, in constant expectation of a proletarian attack to free us. Instead, we were taken away to Northern Bavaria on a special train under heavy military escort.

The attack on the station came a few hours after our departure, ending in a triumphant victory for the workers who reestablished the council government under the leadership of the KPD. [...]

The purpose of this report is to explain our actions psychologically, to defend ourselves against the ludicrous accusation that we, especially Landauer and I (against whom this attack is mainly directed), had wanted to realize an adventure developed in literary musings in cafés, and to explain that many of our actions had been forced upon us by the external conditions. I admit that we made mistakes. However, I plead the following as mitigating circumstances: the demands of the workers on general strike in Augsburg; the breach of agreement by the Hoffmann government; the inspiration of the Hungarian example; the hope of serving as an example for Austria and Northern Germany; and especially the KPD's secret diplomacy: contrary to the former close collaboration with us (especially with me), the party communists did not invite any of us to their debates during the crucial days, they refused, despite repeated invitations, to delegate someone for the most important meeting on the afternoon of April 4, and they finally let strangers present their resolution, employing arguments that were highly dubious. As openly as I confess that in principle the comrades of the KPD were right and we were wrong, I believe to this day that their tactics at the time of the first council republic were tragically mistaken. I also believe to this day that if the KPD had supported the revolutionary elements in the council government early on, the revolution would have taken a much more encouraging course (even if it might nonetheless have been defeated).

The support we received from the party communists in Northern Bavaria proves that by no means all KPD comrades saw our actions as a farce. The confusion, however, that was created by the orders of the party leadership in Munich is to a large extent the reason why the counterrevolution was able to strike back so quickly and without much resistance. The participation of the KPD in the first council government (even if they had voiced criticism) would have allowed the revolutionary proletariat to passionately rise up in unity. The social democrats would have been removed from all posts on the third day, when Hoffmann formed the countergovernment in Bamberg, and they would have been treated like the bourgeoisie. In short, the uncertainty among the workers and soldiers that made the Palm Sunday Coup possible would not have arisen.

To end this, I want to draw attention to the following: the heroic struggle that Munich's workers engaged in during the first days in May in defense of the council republic—a struggle in which the proletarians who had supported us during the first week of the council republic participated alongside the supporters of the KPD; the terrible blood sacrifices that the proletariat made for the communist idea; and the graves of those murdered, with the names of Gustav Landauer and Eugen Leviné remaining engraved in the hearts of Munich's proletariat.

1. See "1918–1919: Munich III, Revolution and Council Republic" in the Introduction.
2. Similar bias is expressed in the major English work on the Bavarian Revolution: Allan Mitchell, *Revolution in Bavaria, 1918–1919: The Eisner Regime and the Soviet Republic* (Princeton, NJ: Princeton University Press, 1965).
3. Mühsam refers to the SDP-led government in Berlin that lost all trust of radical leftists after its collaboration with the bourgeoisie and the Kaiserreich's army in crushing communist rebellions.
4. "Palm Sunday Coup" refers to first the attempt of social democrats to overthrow the Bavarian Council Republic by force on April 13, which happened to be Palm Sunday.
5. Biggest Bavarian town in the vicinity of Munich, about sixty kilometers northwest.
6. Refers to dual power agreements between the SPD and council communists in Bavaria.
7. On March 21, 1919, a council republic was established in Hungary; it was crushed by Romanian forces on August 6.
8. Otto Bauer (1881–1938), Viktor Adler (1852–1918), prominent Austrian social democrats.
9. Gustav Noske (1868–1946), Friedrich Ebert (1871–1925), Philipp Scheidemann (1865–1939), leading SPD members.
10. The Revolutionary Workers' Council was founded to push for a radical council-based course for the Bavarian Revolution after Bavaria was proclaimed a republic by Kurt Eisner on November 7, 1918.
11. Towia Axelrod, KPD member of Russian descent.
12. Bavarian parliament; in general, *Landtag* indicates a provincial parliament as opposed to the *Reichstag*, the German parliament.
13. Reference to the SPD whose members, with few exceptions, supported the war to the end.
14. Johannes Hoffmann (1867–1930) was the prime minister of the SPD government in Bamberg.
15. Fritz Soldmann (1878–1945), USPD member.
16. The Wittelsbach dynasty effectively ruled Bavaria from 1180 to 1918.
17. Arnold Wadler (1882–?), lawyer.

"GUSTAV LANDAUER'S DEATH"

Erich Mühsam, imprisoned after his arrest during the first social democratic attempt to crush the council republic on April 13, reacts to Gustav Landauer's death in diary entries from early May 1919.

Ebrach Prison, Monday, May 5, 1919

EVER SINCE I HEARD ABOUT THE APPARENT KILLING OF HOSTAGES, I cannot shed my fear for Landauer.[1] Hardly anyone could have been more opposed to such an action than he! If this happened, it was criminal madness! You take hostages to prevent the enemy from doing harm to the prisoners they have taken. At the very moment you start killing them, you sacrifice the lives of your own comrades. It is senseless and foolish!

Unfortunately, I can see certain leaders of Munich's Communist Party engaging in such dastardly stupidity. However, the claim that the victims' bodies were mutilated makes me very suspicious. This part sounds so exaggerated that it all might be a shameless lie.

How dreadful it would be if they killed Landauer of all people! What do these barbarians know about his great, clear, and strong spirit? What do they know about his teachings, principles, realizations, and achievements? What do they know about his gifts to the people as a philosopher and as a socialist? I refuse to speak about how deeply this would affect me. I will not do this now, because I do not believe it. I do not want to believe it!

Ebrach Prison, Tuesday, May 6, 1919

Landauer is dead. I refuse to accept it. I cannot accept it—although it seems that I will have to. There is only a glimmer of hope left that the news is not true, and I try to cling to it.

The note in the *Bamberger Volksblatt*[2] says: "Landauer was captured by government troops in Pasing.[3] According to a reliable source, he was killed by a mob when being escorted to prison."[4]

This means lynching. Landauer was killed like Rosa Luxemburg: by disdainful soldiers who had been turned into fanatics and bloodthirsty murderers because of lies, defamation, and smear campaigns. It is so terrible! So gruesome! My friend and guide, my teacher and comrade! And here I sit, incarcerated by the same criminals who have caused his death, and I cannot help, cannot comfort anyone, cannot go to his funeral, cannot say a word in his honor. Nobody—not even those who now condemn his murderers—truly knows what kind of spirit has been extinguished.

1. See footnote 110 in the Introduction.
2. Local Bamberg newspaper.
3. Munich suburb.
4. Rudolf Rocker described Landauer's final days thus: "After the end of the first council republic, which he had dedicated his rich knowledge and abilities to wholeheartedly, Landauer lived with the widow of his good friend Kurt Eisner. He was arrested in her house on the afternoon of May 1. Close friends had urged him to escape a few days earlier. Then it would have still been a fairly easy thing to do. But Landauer decided to stay. Together with other prisoners, he was loaded on a truck and taken to the jail in Starnberg. From there, he and some others were driven to Stadelheim a day later. On the way he was horribly mistreated by dehumanized military pawns on the orders of their superiors. One of them, Freiherr von Gagern, hit Landauer over the head with a whip handle. This was the signal to kill the defenseless victim. An eyewitness later said that Landauer used his last strength to shout at his murderers: 'Finish me off—to be human!' He was literally kicked to death. When he still showed signs of life, one of the callous torturers shot a bullet into his head. This was the gruesome end of Gustav Landauer—one of Germany's greatest spirits and finest men" (Rudolf Rocker, "Das Ende Gustav Landauers" [The End of Gustav Landauer], in Erich Mühsam et al., *Gustav Landauer–Worte der Würdigung* [Gustav Landauer–Words of Appreciation], Darmstadt: Die freie Gesellschaft, 195, 38–39). Starnberg is a town near Munich. Stadelheim is Munich's most notorious prison. Heinrich Freiherr von Gagern (1878–1964) received a nominal fine for assaulting Landauer; no one was charged with Landauer's murder.

"Zenzl"

Erich Mühsam reacts to news from Zenzl after the crushing of the Bavarian Council Republic in diary entries from early May 1919.

Ebrach Prison, Friday, May 16, 1919

FINALLY A MESSAGE! THANK GOD! A LETTER AND A PACKAGE from Zenzl! She is in the countryside with her son. She says that she went there to be safe. Apparently, the police suggested that she should not show herself anywhere I had been active. In other words, she has to flee the threatening kindness of our neighbors!

Anyway, thank God! After the warden had opened and checked the packages, and handed me the letter, and I saw butter, bacon, and eggs, and Zenzl's handwriting, I devoured the kind, hastily written, brief sentences and the faulty orthography as soon as the man was out the door. When I was done, I felt dizzy and had to hold on to the bedpost before starting to cry like a little boy, in complete shock. An egg helped restore my energy, and right now I feel happier than I have felt in weeks. Zenzl is alive, free, and healthy! I could not care less what the police and the military do with my things! So, they took everything. Whatever. I doubt that they will destroy my diaries and my notebooks.[1]

Ebrach Prison, Monday, May 19, 1919

Zenzl sent me a huge loaf of bread, a coupon for another pound, which can also be used to buy a piece of cake, and a few sugar cubes. The cubes arrived a bit damp and I gave them to the prisoner who had told me that a package had arrived for me. I can do without the sugar, especially since I was able to buy a package of artificial honey for 68 pfennige today from a warden.

Zenzl's letter is terribly sad, and my heart is aching. Heaven itself has sent me this woman. If she only knew how convinced I am of this!

Her intelligence, naturalness, kindness, directness, honesty, strength, motherly humor, grace, and beauty, her unwavering dedication to supporting the arts by supporting the artist, her clear understanding of my ideas, and her beautiful, pure, and strong love—what a pearl I have for a wife!

The one fault that Zenzl has is understandable—and should actually flatter me: it is the jealousy which she does not want to admit. My gracious, dear Zenzl! I am simply not made to be faithful. If there were nights that I did not spend in the marital bed but with Mila, why should I have told lies?[2] Why could we not have done without the silent (or not so silent) accusations?

Now that we are apart, however, she seems to have forgotten all of this. Well, these episodes had already been forgotten when I was still at home. How wonderful she is! She writes of an "excruciating longing for all the happy moments we have had." Me too! Me too!

Other than that, she writes hardly a word about her feelings: "It would be silly to write that I love you. You know that…"

So the rest of the letter is all very much matter-of-fact. And what terrible facts! "I cannot go to Georgenstraße. People are so brainwashed—as your wife I cannot go anywhere."[3] This is what you get when you want the best for the people! Zenzl, however, closes with enviable dignity: "However, all of this can be endured, my dear husband. You know that I did not expect anything different."

Oh, what the poor woman has been through during recent weeks! She was arrested, but the policemen treated her fairly. All of our acquaintances seem to have disappeared. "I have basically been abandoned," she writes. "The friends who were good to me cannot be found, and the others are afraid to host Frau Mühsam." This seems not to perturb her all that much, as she writes the words with lead on crumpled old paper.

1. They were returned to Mühsam after several months.
2. Mila Deutsch, a lover of Mühsam's in early 1919.
3. The Mühsams had lived in an apartment on Georgenstraße since 1915.

Final Court Statement

On July 11, 1919, Mühsam presented his final statement at the high treason trial that followed the defeat of the Bavarian Council Republic. It was first printed on July 12 in the popular daily *Münchner Neueste Nachrichten* [Munich's Latest News].

R EVOLUTIONS CANNOT BE STOPPED AT RANDOM. THIS WOULD always lead to new revolutions; it would mean the opposite of peace and order. We all want peace and order. But there is no place for this in the revolution.

I see all those in power as counterrevolutionaries, even if they call themselves socialists. When I speak of those in power, I mean everyone at work in Weimar, Berlin, and Bamberg.[1] These individuals act as if no revolution has ever occurred—and they demand that we do the same. They want to reestablish a system of peace and order, which is responsible for the turmoil and disorder we are experiencing today. It was not we who set this world in motion. It was not we who have made this revolution—a revolution which is already taking shape in each and every country and which will inevitably develop into a world revolution. It all began on August 1, 1914—the day capitalism defeated itself. Capitalism has rendered itself obsolete through the World War. All we have to do now is to create a society that prevents war and that makes further revolutions unnecessary.

The state prosecutor contradicts himself when he suggests that by proclaiming the dictatorship of the proletariat I disregard the people.[2] The people are, in fact, disregarded by the dictatorship of the democrats in Bamberg, by the dictatorship of the bourgeoisie, or, to put it simply, by the dictatorship of indifferent over active folks, a dictatorship of passiveness over activeness. Besides, the dictatorship of the proletariat has never been our goal. It is only a *means*: it has to be put in place until the revolution has achieved its purpose, namely the abolition of exploitation.

I do not believe the violence of the drumhead court-martial used to suppress us has been effective. I believe that everything that gets in our way from now on only serves to interrupt an inevitable process. It will not prevent the revolution.

I am the opposite of a putschist; I am a revolutionary, which means that I do not believe in coups, but in revolutions. If the state prosecutor cites my role in the events of November 7, 1918,[3] as proof that I am a putschist, then many more will end up in this court accused of high treason. I can already see the Hoffmann cabinet and the prime minister himself[4] defending their actions in front of a drumhead court-martial summoned by officers of the Wittelsbach kind.[5]

The *Münchener Post*,[6] the mouthpiece of the party that still calls itself "socialist," published a statement in November 1918, claiming that the party had nothing to do with the revolution. That is right. And it remains the case. The only contribution that the party made to the revolution was first to exploit and then to sabotage it. So when the honorable state prosecutor cites the events of November 7 to prove that I was involved in a coup, then I say, "Yes, in such coups I will always be involved!"

The same kind of coup occurred on April 4.[7] There was no Hoffmann government at the time; at least we were not aware of one. Hence, we cannot have committed high treason, as there was no one to betray. Perhaps there were two governments in Bavaria when the rest of Hoffmann's cabinet escaped to Bamberg and acted as a parallel government—but this means that I can just as easily claim that it was Hoffmann and his ministers who committed high treason.

In any case, if those who came after us[8] committed high treason, the only ones they could have betrayed were we. However, we did not see it that way. The bloodshed that haunts Munich is not the fault of the Communist Party, but of the Bamberg government alone. Without the attempted Palm Sunday Coup,[9] things would have developed very differently in Munich. But that attack forced the Communist Party to make quick decisions, causing the confusion that we now all deeply regret.

The state prosecutor also said that I would never be satisfied with a revolution, because none could ever go far enough for me. If I understand the honorable state prosecutor right, then he understands me wrong. You cannot choose between different kinds of revolutions. The revolution will take as long as it has to for the socialist and communist goals necessary to eliminate the causes of revolution to be achieved. A few revolutionaries being sentenced to prison, put up against the wall, or beaten to death, is of no significance; it will not change the course of the revolution.

The communists had nothing to do with the proclamation of the council republic. They are not responsible for the consequences. Those who have brought civil war to Munich are responsible.

In short, I strongly object to the claim that I was involved in any form of high treason. These are fantasies of the state prosecutor. High treason against the

Hoffmann government was not possible. And if it had been, then only I, not the communists, would have committed it.[10]

I do not feel the need to justify my actions to you, *meine Herren*. I need to justify my actions to the people for whom I live and work, and who alone must judge me. I dispute that any high treason has occurred, and I more forcibly dispute that those who came after us betrayed the Hoffmann government in any way; they replaced *us* and no one else.

Judgment is yours. I do not ask you to consider mitigating circumstances or to show any kindness. I have no reason to plead—I only have reasons to demand. And I demand acquittal, because nothing else makes sense.

If you arrive at a different judgment, I must accept it, but I doubt that it will be considered fair by the people. The people see the drumhead court-martial as an institution of the counterrevolution, whose main function it is to use prerevolutionary laws during revolutionary times. This is one way in which the Hoffmann government proves to be a counterrevolutionary body.

How long I will be in prison will not be determined by you—it will be determined by the development of the revolution and by the will of the proletariat.

1. Berlin was the German capital, but due to the radical socialist opposition there, many government meetings took place in the small town of Weimar in Thuringia, which later gave the Weimar Republic its name. Bamberg was the northern Bavarian town where the SPD-led government had fled to after the proclamation of the council republic.
2. See *Liberating Society from the State* in this volume for Mühsam's understanding of the "dictatorship of the proletariat."
3. The day when Bavaria was declared a republic.
4. Johannes Hoffmann (1867–1930) was the prime minister of the SPD government in Bamberg.
5. The Wittelsbach dynasty effectively ruled Bavaria from 1180 to 1918.
6. A social democratic daily from 1888 to 1933.
7. The day the proclamation of the Bavarian Council Republic was conceived—the actual proclamation was issued on April 7.
8. Reference to the KPD, which took charge of the council republic after the government's first attack on April 13.
9. See footnote 4 in "Excerpts from 'From Eisner to Leviné.'"
10. The KPD was not involved in the original proclamation of the Bavarian Council Republic on April 7.

"Sentenced"

Diary entry after Mühsam's sentencing: Ebrach Prison, July 12, 1919.

S O NOW WE KNOW. IF THE DRUMHEAD COURT-MARTIAL GETS ITS WAY, I will spend the next fifteen years of my life confined in a fortress. I assume that the duration will be more like fifteen weeks, maybe fifteen months—in any case, closer to fifteen days than to fifteen years.

The verdict was that I was the driving force behind the "high treason" that was apparently committed and that I could not just be sentenced for aiding and abetting, as requested by the state prosecutor. I did not receive a death sentence because mitigating circumstances were taken into account, namely my "fanaticism bordering on psychosis." I received the verdict without any particular emotion, and I know that my Zenzl will not be devastated by it either.

1919–1924: IMPRISONMENT

"The Ebrach Prison Commune"

In a diary entry from the Ebrach Prison, July 29, 1919, Mühsam comments on the development of a "prisoners' commune," founded by the fortress's inmates, many of whom were incarcerated for their involvement in the Bavarian Council Republic.

M Y HAPPINESS TODAY RECEIVED A SOFT BLOW AFTER OUR commune met to discuss its constitution. We can already see, after just a few tiny steps, the instinctive human resistance against anything that might compromise individual comfort for the benefit of all.

I spoke against the gambling habits that some comrades have developed. It has troubling consequences. We have some among us with no means at all. They are supported by others who do not have much either. It is already the case that they receive money and lose it instantly to better-off comrades in a card game. I suggested that we should no longer use any money in the commune, but some alternative kind of currency that was distributed equally, so that everyone could visit the canteen and the shop with the same means. Card games should not involve any money on principle. This caused great outrage. People talked about restrictions on their individual freedom, and all commitment to social responsibility was gone with the wind.

There are still many obstacles to overcome if we want to prove to the world that communists are able to form a commune. It will require a strong effort. Education is the key. During the embarrassing discussion today, when the primitive egotism of the comrades ran rampant, I wanted to lead by example. When we discussed the options we had for raising collective funds, I declared that I would offer the rights of my "Räte-Marsellaise"[1] to the Ebrach Prison Commune, i.e., that the lyrics should be reproduced and sold for the benefit of the commune. People cheered—but tomorrow they will be as stubborn as today when it comes to protecting the tiniest aspect of their own habits and imagined needs.

Eighteen years ago in the Neue Gemeinschaft, it was exactly the same, it was the same among the comrades of the Socialist Bund and of the group *Tat*,[2] and it has always been the same among the anarchists: the ideas are understood and welcomed, but when they take on a concrete form and can be turned into practice, the human being gets in the way. In other words, humanness fails humanity.

However, my faith is strong enough to move mountains. These obstacles must be overcome. These obstacles *will* be overcome.

1.   Mühsam wrote German lyrics to the tune of the famous French "Marseillaise" in early 1919.
2.   See "1909–1914: Munich I, Socialist Bund and *Kain*" in the Introduction.

ON THE JEWISH QUESTION

Mühsam very rarely wrote about Judaism. One exception, a short commentary on the case of Mendel Beilis, a Jew accused of ritual murder in Kiev, has been included above in this volume. Another exception is a short paragraph–doused in early-twentieth-century race rhetoric–included in the pamphlet "Die Jagd auf Harden" [The Campaign against Harden], published in 1908:

> The idea of solving a racial problem by dissolving one race within another seems absurd to me–not to mention the technical impossibility. Harden completely overlooks the value of the Jewish race in the sourdough of all nationalities and cultures. He overlooks the qualities that have allowed Jews to preserve their race despite all obstacles; he denies the creative principle and the aesthetic drive that lies in preserving valuable races, such as the Jews and the Gypsies overall. This is why Zionism, especially the cultural Zionism championed by Martin Buber, seems to be much more apt for us Jews than Harden's ideas of amalgamation, even if I feel no kinship at all to ordinary Zionism and its desire to establish states.[1]

The longest text that Mühsam ever dedicated to questions of Judaism and Jewish identity was published as "Zur Judenfrage" in *Die Weltbühne*, December 1920. It is translated here.

I**N GENERAL, I DO NOT REALLY LIKE TO ADDRESS A QUESTION** that has long been the monopoly of anti-Semites and of Zionists. It seems to me that the rest of us Europeans, whether of Aryan or Semitic origin, agree that the "Jewish Question" is at best a question of race psychology or of biology. Perhaps it is of some cultural and historical interest, but it is hardly relevant for the present, other than it being exploited by anti-Semites who prove the decadence of contemporary culture. Zionism could only be seen as relevant if it did not present itself as an answer to the "Jewish" question. If Jews from all over the world came together to build a society–in Palestine or wherever else–based on socialist and communist principles, ignoring the capitalist world market and developing new forms of community, they would do a tremendous service to the global proletariat. It would be a service only rivaled by what the Russians have done. Zionism could give Bolshevism a stronghold in the orient, which would also strengthen the efforts in Russia. The achievement would be glorious, and if it were the work of Jews it would add enormously to Judaism's historical legacy. However, no "Jewish" question could be solved that way.

Zionism becomes completely uninteresting if it means nothing more than Jews from all the countries beset by anti-Semitism uniting in order to create a new state that will be just like any other state: with a capitalist economy, exploitation, private ownership of the means of production, bourgeois parliamentarian blabber, and proletarian misery. If this is what Zionism means, then its politics are as trivial as those of reformist welfare clubs. In the best case, they can lead to a charitable ease of private misery; but no question of any significance for the world can ever be solved.

So why am I joining the discussion of the Jewish Question at all? It would have never happened had I not been attacked personally. It is common knowledge that anti-Semites blame Jews for everything that public opinion considers a problem at any given time. It is also clear that there are always honorable Jews who strengthen this anti-Semitic habit by distancing themselves from all tribe members whose conduct or appearance might offend "public opinion." As if it were of any concern to a Jew what another Jew thinks or does! I have been active in the proletarian struggle as a communist revolutionary for twenty years. I have always voiced my opposition to social democratic reformism. My being Jewish has played no role in this. I have held no posts and presided over no bureaus. All I have earned is hostility, persecution, and poverty. I have supported the class struggle without compromise in articles and speeches, and in the reactionary courts. The class struggle divides the propertied, exploitative minority from the dispossessed, exploited, and working majority. Jews and Aryans are found on both sides. Society is not organized according to races, faiths, or biological heritage. Every individual—Christian, Jew, or heathen—joins one of the two sides depending on opportunity, lifestyle, interest, or conscience. We hear the warnings of rich Jews to other Jews who side with the poor: "Hello! You are one of us! We Jews must unite! You will compromise our situation!" This is ridiculous. "We Jews" have as much—or as little—in common as "we Germans," "we French," "we the passengers on the same bus." In society, there are only two groups: the capitalists and the parties working in their interest; and the proletarians, who are joined by those who have made a commitment to supporting them and to upholding the revolutionary ideal. So much for an introduction.

One day, I received a copy of the *Münchner Neueste Nachrichten* from September 14, 1920.[2] The sender had marked an article entitled "The Jewish Question." I do not subscribe to this particular paper, and so it was only as a result of this article that I learned that in its pages there has been a discussion about how rich Jews should respond to the "subversive revolutionary propaganda of communists and Bolsheviks of Jewish descent." One contribution to the debate was a letter written by the Councilor for Commerce, Sigmund Fränkel.[3] The letter was written before April 6, 1919. At the time, the author hoped that it would discourage Jews from proclaiming the Bavarian Council Republic. Why? I suppose because another Jew had decided to write a letter to them. In any case, the effort came too late. When

Fränkel took his letter to the journal's office in the morning of April 7, the Red Guards had already stopped the advertising plantations and sent their editors on vacation (without asking them for their tribal membership). The Councilor for Commerce, Sigmund Fränkel, however, still believes his text to be important one and a half years later. He has handed the "Open Letter to the Herren Erich Mühsam, Dr. Wadler, Dr. Otto Neurath, Ernst Toller, and Gustav Landauer"[4] to the *Münchner Neueste Nachrichten*, apparently for the benefit of the Jewish community, even though one of his addressees has been expelled from the country, two are confined in fortresses, one is languishing in prison, and one—the best of them—was murdered.[5]

I do not think that there is any point in reproducing the letter here. My response will reveal its contents. I will only quote the last sentences of this text by a modern-day Isaiah:

> If my warning goes unheeded, then I can only do one final thing in the interest of my religious community: Jewish religious law teaches that when a murder victim is found on a field, the elders of the nation must gather at his side and ceremonially confirm: *It was not by our hands that this has been done!* In a similar way, I, in the name of the Bavarian Jewish community, say to the Bavarian people today: our hands have nothing to do with the horror, the chaos, and the misery that the politics of these people will cause for the future of this country. They alone, and no one else, bear this responsibility. Munich, April 6, 1919, 11 p.m., the evening before Pesach 5679.

Our politics never came to fruition. Armed forces, called in from northern Germany, were responsible for a bloodbath in Munich; not among the peers of Herr Fränkel, of course, but among the proletariat. It is well known how Gustav Landauer, one of the addressees of Fränkel's letter, died.[6] Herr Fränkel must also know. However, I am not in the habit of holding individuals responsible for the horror that occurs. Hence, I do not say, "You, Councilor for Commerce Fränkel, have been hostile to our politics and carry full responsibility for the chaos and the misery that your politics have brought on Bavaria." Instead, I have sent him the following response on September 24 from the Ansbach Fortress, where I am currently detained:

> I am a Jew and I will be a Jew as long as I live. I have never denied my Jewish identity, nor have I ever officially left the religious Jewish community (because I would still be a Jew, and it does not matter to me how I am categorized by the state). I see being a Jew neither as a virtue nor as a flaw. It is simply part of who I am, like my red beard, my weight, and my personal interests. Consequently, I think we need not discuss Jewish "pride," a notion exploited by the anti-Semites as a justification for their hatred. Similarly, we need not

discuss people's beliefs, i.e., their private relationship to metaphysics. So let us discuss only the following: must Jews, as members of a minority that is disdained in many ways, abstain from political commitment and activity in the name of solidarity with their tribal members, at least as long as these commitments and activities are not officially approved? I think the question already implies the answer: I do not think that membership in the Jewish community demands spinelessness. Spinoza did not think so, and neither did Karl Marx or Heinrich Heine.[7]

I was surprised, honorable Councilor for Commerce, to find the word "*landfremd*"[8] in your attempt to deny us the right to participate in the social liberation of the people. This word belongs to the terminology of the *Deutschvölkischen Schutz- und Trutzbund*.[9] In fact, I am not sure who exactly you are calling "*landfremd*": is it every European Jew, or only every non-Bavarian Jew in Bavaria? I assume you mean the latter. But how does this fit in with the notion of undivided Germanness, embraced by all of Germany's Jewry since at least 1914? During the war, even Jews celebrated the anti-Semitic tune "Deutschland, Deutschland über alles,"[10] and they stood united from Helgoland to Bavaria and from Mecklenburg to Ostelbien[11] (via Bavaria of course) until the war's disastrous end. (With a few exceptions, among which can I count myself; in this case, admittedly, with pride.)

Is it not peculiar that the accusation of being *landfremd* is only ever raised in connection with contentious political convictions? Have you ever seen a speaker's commitment to monarchism challenged because he was from Karlsruhe, Lübeck, or Posen?[12] Even Austrian monarchists are welcome in Germany! Such people are left in peace, even in the current Bavarian republic. But let us look at those you call *landfremd* in more detail: Landauer (whose assassination does not seem reason enough for you to revoke your accusations, even seventeen months later) was from Karlsruhe. I am from Lübeck, but have been living in Munich for twelve years and am married to the daughter of a Lower Bavarian Catholic peasant. For all I know, Wadler is a Munich native. Could it be that, in accordance with the anti-Semites, you perceive every single Jew in Germany as *landfremd*?

It would probably be fruitless to discuss our ideals, let alone our revolutionary convictions with you. Of course you deny attacking us as an economist, as an industrialist, and as a capitalist. However—and please do not be offended—all your arguments reveal the Councilor for Commerce. You will never understand why we reject all of your declarations, no matter how insistent: our plans were not "ominous and against human nature," our path was not destined to lead to "chaos, destruction, and devastation," and our ideas were not going to cause starvation in Southern Bavaria.

My dear Councilor for Commerce! I do not know you, and you do not know me. This is why I cannot accuse you of egotism, although you accuse us of personal ambition. However, all your arguments indicate to me that you can only assess the well-being of the world and its people from the perspective of a capitalist. You are fully convinced of your righteousness. You cite Jewish doctrine (in my opinion incorrectly, because the Jubilee was a communist effort, which renders your argument pointless[13]) when proclaiming that "the differences between the rich and the poor will never disappear from the world." This is *your* credo. The "dedicated and eager contribution to Bavaria's economic life," which has made your hair turn grey (and bestowed upon you the title of "Councilor for Commerce"), is *your* contribution to an economy that condemns the poor to be poor and that gives the rich the right to turn the poor's sweat into champagne for themselves.

You also cite Mosaic Law. I know it well. I find it audacious of you to list the tenth commandment as proof that Judaism does not need our "confused and convoluted fantasies" to realize that social problems require alleviation. The tenth commandment assumes poverty by entitling the poor to the tenth part of social wealth. And what has become of the "tithe" today? I involuntarily think of stock market quotations, turning religious charity into balance sheets. Are we talking about a ten percent dividend? Who pays the tithe today, dear Councilor for Commerce, and who pockets it?

Finally, let me ask you whether what we are discussing here is a "Jewish" problem or a human, socio-ethical, and international problem? Personally, I do not follow your argument that the world revolution, the rescue from the unspeakable misery caused by a war waged in the interests of world imperialism, demands different things from us Jews than from other people. I wholeheartedly accept the Jewish postulate that you quote: "Work for peace and the benefit of the people in whose midst you reside!" This is a wonderful motto of internationalism: all socialists, communists, Bolsheviks, and anarchists agree with it, whether we are Jews or not. But that the distribution of anti-Semitic propaganda on the streets, the hate speech of barking Jew-eaters, and the pogroms of Teutonic wannabe heroes should keep us from working for peace and happiness, with the means we consider useful, this I cannot understand—although I realize that you are, unfortunately, of a different opinion.

Anti-Semitism is always a symptom of reactionary times. If we had won, we could have dealt with it. Without a doubt, this would have benefited the Jewish community (except for those individuals who might have lost some of their riches). Right now, the Bavarian economy, which you are so concerned about, can pursue its capitalist course unhindered, while, at the very same time, the swastika has turned into a respected public symbol. Do you need more proof that anti-Semitism is not dependent on what five Jews among tens of thousands do?

I believe it honors Judaism that the daily anti-Semitic attacks are not reduced to attacks on Jewish extortionists and profiteers, but also include attacks on idealists and martyrs like Rosa Luxemburg, Leo Jogiches, Gustav Landauer, and Eugen Leviné.[14]

This is what I have to say to the Councilor for Commerce who sees it as his duty to defend Judaism against its degenerate sons.

1. Erich Mühsam, "Die Jagd auf Harden," quoted from Erich Mühsam, *Prosaschriften I*, edited by Günter Emig (Berlin: Verlag europäische Ideen, 1978), 227.
2. See footnote 3 in "Riot in Berlin."
3. Sigmund Fränkel (1860–1925) was both a successful industrialist and a prominent figure in Munich's orthodox Jewish community.
4. Arnold Wadler (1882–?), lawyer; Otto Neurath (1882–1945), political economist; Ernst Toller (1893–1939), playwright–with Landauer and Mühsam prominent Jewish figures in the council republic.
5. Like Mühsam, Toller and Wadler were imprisoned. Neurath, an Austrian citizen, was expelled. Landauer was murdered.
6. See "Gustav Landauer's Death."
7. Heinrich Heine (1797–1856), libertarian German poet.
8. Literally, "foreign to the land." Common xenophobic German term.
9. Roughly "German People's Protection and Defiance Alliance;" a powerful nationalist and anti-Semitic organization in the Weimar Republic.
10. Officially called "Das Deutschlandlied" [The Song of Germany], the song, based on a 1797 tune by Joseph Haydn and an 1841 poem by Hoffmann von Fallersleben, has served as an on-and-off national anthem for Germany since 1922. Today, only the third verse is in official use, although the first one remains widely popular in right-wing circles. "Deutschland, Deutschland über alles" [Germany, Germany above all] is the first verse's opening line.
11. A vague and rarely used term for historical German territories east of the River Elbe.
12. German name for the Polish city of Poznán.
13. The original Jewish Jubilee, the year at the end of seven Sabbatical years, involved the redistribution of land.
14. Leo Jogiches (1867–1919), longtime comrade and lover of Rosa Luxemburg of Lithuanian origin, was murdered on March 10, 1919, while investigating the deaths of Luxemburg and Karl Liebknecht. For Eugen Leviné see footnote 59 in the Introduction.

THE INTELLECTUALS

Mühsam formulates a biting critique of left-wing intellectuals. Published as "Die Intellektuellen" in *Die Aktion*, January 1921.

WHO, IN FACT, ARE THESE PEOPLE? ARE THEY CHARACTERIZED by special intelligence? It appears so when you hear them talk about themselves. However, when you hear the revolutionary proletariat talk about them, you sense caution and suspicion. It is not their intellectual capacities that are questioned; it is the role that they play in the working-class struggle.

Everyone among the bourgeoisie thinks they are intellectuals. The attire seems sufficient. It is only among the proletariat that intellectuals form a more distinguished group. This has led to a rather unique species in contemporary society. One usually calls an "intellectual" a person with a background in literature, education, law, or some other academic field who has joined the ranks of the fighting workers. These individuals commonly demand a lot of respect for themselves as "educated" folks.

It is an indication of the growing revolutionary consciousness among the proletariat that it hardly matters anymore whether a comrade resists bourgeois society based on an academic education or based on his own class background. The times are gone when those with bourgeois or aristocratic background, equipped with more knowledge than the masses for no other reason than privilege of birth, automatically receive a leading position just because they have discovered their sympathies for the working class. At the same time, the blind hatred for all "academics" within some proletarian circles, which at times made it almost impossible for even the most sincere and determined educated people to fight alongside the oppressed class, has also subsided.

Much of this is based on the diverse experiences with "bourgeois refugees," on the one hand, and prominent working-class politicians, on the other. It is simply impossible for any proletarian not to count the "academics" and "people of letters," such as Lenin, Trotsky, Lunacharsky, Bukharin, Zinoviev, Liebknecht, Luxemburg, Mehring, Landauer, and so on, as revolutionaries.[1] Similarly, the bourgeois behavior of Heine, David, Landsberg, Kerensky, Kautsky, and others, cannot simply be explained by the fact that they are "intellectuals."[2] Many "proletarians" stand right next to them: Scheidemann, Noske, Ebert, Legien, Winnig[3]—there are many prominent representatives of the proletariat who have been assimilated into the bourgeoisie in the same way in which the above-mentioned revolutionaries have assimilated into the proletariat.

Whether or not an individual belongs to the working class depends neither on his origins nor on his profession. The word *proletariat* can be defined quite clearly: it is the name of the class of the oppressed, the exploited, those without rights. The word *proletarian*, on the other hand, can never be defined clearly. All references to profession or personal dependency on capitalism fail the test of reality. If it was true that everyone whose labor was exploited by capital, i.e., who does not receive the output of his labor, is a proletarian, then this would also be true for general managers or executive directors who run branches of large corporations and earn sixty thousands marks a year. They receive salaries from their bosses, just like any other employee. The salary is higher of course, but they are still being exploited. Yet, such individuals would certainly take offense to be called *proletarians*, and the proletariat would not want to count them among its ranks. Nor can police officers, prison wardens, government soldiers, or executioners be regarded as proletarians, even if they come from the ranks of the exploited masses, have not worked themselves into higher positions, and receive less for their labor (I am not sure if there is an actual "output" in this case) than what this labor is worth to the propertied class. Their activity is anti-proletarian, they are servants and aides of the privileged class, and they stand on the enemy's side in the class struggle, both objectively and in the people's perception. Who, on the other hand, would challenge Karl Liebknecht's identity as a proletarian, even if his education was bourgeois through and through and his academic profession made him an exploitative employer of secretaries?

All this proves that belonging to the proletarian class does not follow a simple formula. Proletarians are those who see themselves as proletarians and who are accepted as such by their peers based on their behavior. An individual's education can never be the criterion, and an individual's profession even less so.

Still, there is good reason for the instinctive rejection of the "intellectuals" by the masses. It has been a long time since the term only stood for educated and literary people. Today, it refers to a very particular type of people and to their special role in the revolutionary movement. Every proletarian knows who I mean when I speak of the ethical busybodies who come down from their enlightened heights to declare their heartfelt sympathy for the workers in verse and prose.

There is nothing more despicable, nothing more disdainful, nothing more hostile to the proletariat than these characters whose revolutionary commitment rests on Christian pity. They see their actions as merciful gifts to the poor, and they embrace every difficulty they encounter as a new opportunity to prove their martyrdom and their gallantry. When they share some of the wisdom they have learned from books due to their parents' wealth with proletarian listeners, then they egotistically gloat about elevating the lower people to their level. In short, the struggle of the exploited gives them the opportunity *to do* something; it is a drainpipe for a world-weary helper syndrome. They do not understand that the proletariat needs and wants mutual aid and not charity. They are not connected with the proletariat in any deep or emotional way. They do not understand that the workers neither can nor want to be freed by pitying fellow citizens. The knowledge and the intelligence of better educated people are only of use when they come from true comrades. True comrades are those who feel connected to the proletariat in indivisible unity. True comrades are those who join the workers because they feel the same desperation, the same need for support, the same urge and desire as the proletariat. True comrades are not those who come to offer "help."

Every intellectual needs to determine for himself which group he belongs to. The proletariat will always know who truly belongs to it and who it has to be wary of.

Proletarians, beware of "intellectual workers"! The worst are those who seem conscious of the mechanisms of a capitalist society and of their position within it, yet parade their "intellectualism" nonetheless. I do not want to condemn unions, alliances, and cooperatives of artists and writers; nor do I want to speak against professional associations of doctors, lawyers, or professors. Trade unions are always important! But when they try to be something special, we must be careful. In 1918, when the revolution came, when everyone—general and governor, doctor and professor—adapted to the "facts on the ground," oh my! All sorts of councils were founded (by the same people who hated Bolshevism), and look! Also the intellectuals, who understood the mood of the time and wanted to be modern human beings and socialists, instantly founded a "Council of Intellectual Workers." This allowed us to study them. We could see how, under the mantle of "class struggle," they instantly attempted to form an upper class within the proletariat: a bourgeoisie *above* the proletariat. You could see them, panic-stricken, eager to distinguish themselves by all means as "intellectual" workers, distinct from the plebs with calloused fists. You could see them gathered, the canvas blotters and clay kneaders, the sentence torturers and rhyme abusers, the law manipulators and poison mixers, the rump drummers and the bookworms—a theatre of vanity! During the entire revolution, these "intellectual councils" never showed any solidarity with the workers. Whenever the reactionary forces reared their ugly head, however, they were welcome.

Let us shine some light on the justification with which these "also-workers" claim "intellectualism." I always thought that there was no "non-intellectual" labor; it seems that all labor has–or at least can have–intellectual dimensions. At the same time, there appears to be no purely "intellectual" labor separated from physical efforts. Does a district judge who, day after day, settles divorces, separating man and wife according to §1565ff. of the civil code, really do more intellectual labor than a precision engineer who constantly works on the most diverse and subtle of machines? Is the work of a doctor who puts his fingers into the openings of human bodies not physical? Does a shoemaker's effort to produce boots that fit, are well-shaped, and can be worn comfortably, not imply an intellectual effort? Are the bad eyes and the cramps in the hands of a writer, the bad back and the hemorrhoids of a scholar, not clear proof of their physical efforts? Even those who clean our sewers can derive intellectual satisfaction from their occupation; after all, it is a challenge to prevent others from being disturbed by the smell and to protect one's own health. These workers deserve enormous gratitude from their fellow citizens. At the same time, some "intellectual workers," like priests, who never think beyond what they have learned by heart, or meat inspectors, who mechanically collect data from one ham after the other, deintellectualize their activity completely. Nonetheless, they will still be on the "Council of Intellectual Workers." After all, they need to show that they are better than shoemakers and bricklayers.

Once we have advanced to the true council system, such differences will cease to exist. Then the noble "intellectuals" will have to join truly proletarian associations. The doctors will be united with all health workers, with nurses and paramedics, with dentists and masseurs. The artistic painters will be together with the house painters, the poets with the printers, the architects with the construction workers, and the university professors with the beadles. This is what the natural interconnection of labor demands. There will be no "higher" and no "lower" form of labor, no "noble" and no "common" labor–there will only be labor that contributes to the common good, labor that everyone will do for everyone according to their interests and talents.

The intellectuals who have not yet understood this sober revolutionary truth and who think that the proletariat needs their compassionate hand to see the light of freedom need to go through the school of the proletariat before attempting to be the workers' teachers. This applies in particular to those young academics who, filled with social idealism, think that they can offer their intellectualism to the proletariat as a gift. Their intellectualism matters little. What matters is their libertarian desire; a desire that must be tested when they join the proletarian youth. The elementary school student has nothing to learn from the high school student. Reality teaches both the same thing, namely struggle, and they must embrace it hand in hand. They must not be divided by levels of intellect (*Geistigkeit*), but must stand together as comrades, united in spirit (*Geist*).

1. Anatoly Lunacharsky (1875–1933), Nikolai Bukharin (1888–1938), Grigory Zinoviev (1883–1936), Bolshevik revolutionaries; Franz Mehring (1846–1919), German socialist and member of the Spartacus League.
2. Heinrich Heine (1797–1856), libertarian German poet; Eduard David (1863–1930), Otto Landsberg (1869–1957), Karl Kautsky (1854–1938), German social democrats; Alexander Kerensky (1881–1970), second prime minister of the Russian Provisional Government in 1917.
3. Philipp Scheidemann (1865–1939), Gustav Noske (1868–1946), Friedrich Ebert (1871–1925), Carl Legien (1861–1920), August Winnig (1878–1956), German social democrats.

"Max Hoelz"

Max Hoelz was born in 1889, the son of a farmworker. He became a day laborer at a young age. Politicized as a soldier during World War I, he joined the Communist Party in 1919. In 1920, he organized groups of armed workers in the Vogtland, an area in the border region of Thuringia, Saxony, and Bavaria. This was not condoned by the Communist Party leadership, not least because Hoelz's political ideas veered toward council communism and anarchism. Hoelz was expelled from the party, and the Vogtland uprising was crushed in 1921. Hoelz was sentenced to life in prison, but freed by an amnesty in 1928. One year later, he emigrated to the Soviet Union, invited by Stalin. He achieved recognition as a speaker at workers' gatherings, but grew increasingly critical of Soviet policies. Soon, he was under surveillance by the authorities. In 1933, he drowned in the Oka River near Gorki. The exact circumstances have never been clarified.

Mühsam was a big supporter of Hoelz. In 1925, he dedicated his poetry collection *Revolution: Kampf-, Marsch- und Spottlieder* [Revolution: Songs of Struggle, Marches, and Satirical Verses] to Hoelz, "the great revolutionary, with brotherly affection." In 1926, with Mühsam free and Hoelz in prison, Mühsam published a pamphlet entitled "Gerechtigkeit für Max Hoelz!" [Justice for Max Hoelz!] with the press of the Rote Hilfe Deutschlands, the prominent communist prisoner support organization that Mühsam was heavily involved with after his release.[1] Around fifty thousand copies of the pamphlet were sold. On April 5, 1921, while incarcerated in the Niederschönenfeld Fortress, Mühsam wrote the following in his diary:

THE BANDITS' STRUGGLES (*BANDENKÄMPFE*) CONTINUE. ONE hundred thousand marks have been put on Hoelz's head. He is accused of several bombings, including the one at the Berlin Victory Column,[2] and of organizing the entire bandit movement in central Germany. What a beautiful fellow! He is the first and only one who has fully understood the necessity of a total revolution in Germany. The bourgeoisie uses intimidation and terror—this means that intimidation and terror must be used against it. Individual deeds and bandits' activities that are connected to economic struggles are the only possible revolutionary means in Germany: every single bourgeois must fear for his life and for his property; that is the only way to undermine the capitalists' morale. Hoelz knows this, and he has proven to be the man who can turn knowledge into action. His ubiquity is marvelous; he always vanishes at the right moment, and always reappears in the right place. Equally marvelous are the thoughtful execution of his plans and his boldness: he confidently invites journalists to accompany him and his men and to observe him in action as a commander and a conqueror;

then, when he no longer wishes for anyone to be aware of his whereabouts, he sends them on their way. He also proves to have a deep understanding of the proletarian psyche (apparently, he has worked as a day laborer himself), as he shrouds everything that he does in romantic haze. Yesterday, I wrote a "Max Hoelz March" to the melody of "Es blasen die Trompeten" [The Trumpets Are Blowing].[3] It would be wonderful if it reached him and if his own guards sang it during their marches. I am happy that such a man, such a proletarian Napoleon, should emerge from the German Revolution. This gives hope to the people and to their cause!

1.   See "1924–1933: Berlin" in the Introduction.
2.   The Victory Column (*Siegessäule*), a famous monument in Berlin, was inaugurated in 1873, commemorating German war victories. It has since been of symbolic political importance for the German right. A bomb attack by left-wing radicals on March 13, 1921, failed.
3.   "The Trumpets Are Blowing," traditional German song. As a punishment for writing the "Max Hoelz March," Mühsam was placed in isolation for a week.

"HITLER AND THE FLEDGLING NAZI MOVEMENT"

Observations by Mühsam on Adolf Hitler and the emerging National Socialist Movement. Diary entries from August 1922 to February 1924.

Niederschönenfeld, Monday, August 28, 1922

THERE WAS ANOTHER BIG EVENT IN MUNICH, SEEMINGLY with serious ambitions. The *völkischen* swastika buffoons, the National Socialists, the *Bund der Frontsoldaten* [League of Frontline Soldiers], nationalistic disabled war veterans, and every other group that belongs to the *Ordnungsblock*[1] called for huge demonstrations on Friday evening against the Berlin agreements and the capitulation of the Bavarian government.[2] Participants were asked to bring pistols and batons–everything was geared toward great action. The police prohibited the hullabaloo at Königsplatz, barricading the square.[3] But since Karolinenplatz is close by and also quite spacious, the demonstrators went there under the personal guidance of Herr Xylander.[4] God knows what prevented the police from joining the ranks of those they were sent to disperse, but that did not happen and much less came of the gathering than expected. Emotions ran high in the Kindlkeller, though.[5] Given the failure of the agitation on the streets, Hitler spoke with caution appropriate to an Austrian, and then let his friend Esser take over.[6] [...]

The way I see the future course of the movement is based on my own experiences in the winter and early spring of 1919. At that time, we, the *Vereinigung Revolutionärer Internationalisten* [Alliance of Revolutionary Internationalists][7] and the communists, who in practice held power and controlled the Revolutionary Workers' Council, related to the republican governments of Eisner and, particularly, Hoffmann in very much the same way as Hitler and his comrades relate to the current government.[8] We conducted our politics on the streets and at our meetings. Whenever the government tried to silence us, the masses were there and their will protected us. However, the masses' excitement proved to be fleeting, while we had thought that we were witnessing a process of ever-increasing, permanent radicalization. This was simply an error of judgment. We took the noise of crowds agitated by revolutionary slogans for actual power, and we eventually did what the crowds seemed to demand of us: we made the decisive move and toppled the system. Then, when the counterrevolution struck back, posing a serious danger to all of us, the masses disappeared. We were betrayed by those who had shouted the loudest. We realized too late how many had rallied to our side for as long as they thought that we would win—as soon as we were under serious attack, these opportunists disappeared and awaited the outcome in cowardly silence, with some even actively supporting the other side.[9] Even the social democrats tried to be our friends as long as we looked strong—but only because they feared being left behind.

The masses that gather and cheer under the swastika today, demanding and threatening action, are none other than those who, at the time, gathered and cheered under the red flag, also demanding and threatening action. Yes, they are literally the same people. They are the kind of people who offer little in terms of their own critique, but who find the conditions unbearable and blame those who are blamed by the most popular of the current sloganeers. They will disappoint Xylander and the others too, although these people have one great advantage: they have many followers in important posts in the state administration, especially in the police and the judiciary. Thanks to Eisner's politics of compromise, this was one of our biggest problems. Eisner did not throw out all the monarchists and even recalled some to posts they had lost. On the other hand, we had great advantages too: viable programs to alleviate the people's misery, and the Russian example. They have nothing but empty phrases.

If I had my way, the nationalists would get a chance to govern Bavaria. They would end up in the same situation as us in April 1919. They would face—all at once—the limits of their organizational abilities, strong resistance both from within the country and from the outside (we were mainly attacked by the peasants; they would be attacked by the workers even more ferociously), and the defection and betrayal of those who seemingly supported them, but were in reality only looking for a springboard to better their personal situation.

If the Xylanders and Hitlers should really succeed, there will be a much greater reason to speak of a "terror regime" than during the days when we were in charge. This will only take a short time, though. Then the regime will burst like a bubble and Bavaria will continue to follow the politics of Berlin and the rest of Germany.

Niederschönenfeld, Tuesday, December 5, 1922

This morning, I wrote a letter to the fortress administration. I gave it to a warden at noon. I wrote the letter in reaction to Hitler's threats, which have been conveyed to us by mail, newspaper articles, and the report of a visitor. Apparently, Hitler declared that the revolutionaries in Niederschönenfeld must be massacred. (The sudden attention that we receive now, after having been incarcerated for four years, might be the result of Max Weber being one of Hitler's new reference points.)[10]

Now, me personally, I'm not easily worried by such threats. I know the atmosphere at mass gatherings. It is very easy to say certain things—it is much harder to do them. Nonetheless, there is reason to address this. Even if Hitler does not take such words seriously, I do know the kind of people who listen to him and get worked up by such words. To a large degree, they are the same people who followed us in 1919 and who will always follow those who promise to provide an outlet for their anger.

The problem with these naïve rebels is that they are *blind* followers and cannot comprehend the consequences of what they do. I do not deny that some of Hitler's followers are driven by strong idealism, a willingness to sacrifice, and […], yes, even revolutionary sentiments, whether they are confused proletarians, students, or army officers. This, for example, becomes obvious in the strict rejection of parliamentarism by Hitler, Xylander, Gräfe, Hergt,[11] and their cohorts, and in the understanding that struggle means putting every body, every life, on the line. This can never be replaced by voting, by elections, and by posers, with fat cats as representatives. As strongly as I fight the *Völkischen* in all matters of ideology—there is really no common ground at all—I nonetheless acknowledge their revolutionary zeal and uncompromising opposition to the existing republic. They are of the opinion that something terrible happened in 1918; something that has to be reversed by all means. I, on the other hand, am of the opinion that something great happened in 1918, but that it subsequently went off track and still awaits true completion.

Niederschönenfeld, Tuesday, August 14, 1923

Two days ago, there was another anti-Semitic demonstration in front of the fortress. Once again, it was not disrupted by the guards. Apparently, the administration appreciates the heroism of Teutons who are courageous enough to provoke men who have been unlawfully incarcerated for five years, knowing very well that they cannot defend themselves. After all, we are not even allowed to sing songs, while these half-wits are free to intone the most preposterous anti-Semitic nonsense under their swastikas. The administration tolerates all this right outside of its gates, while prohibiting our wives and children to even wave from there—recently, Sauber's children had their visiting hours reduced for having waved to their father before entering the building. If one of our wives stops for a moment at the exact same spot where the saviors of the German race rant, threaten, insult, and chant without disturbance, then the men in green[12] leap into action and chase her away. As I wrote, the songs of the protesters are never disturbed. Two days ago, singing was again their main activity. At least this allows us to get a poetic impression of the profound notions that excite German minds. In their last song they belted out: "Throw the Jewish mob out of the German fatherland—we neither need nor want a Jewish republic!"

Niederschönenfeld, Thursday, February 28, 1924

For at least fourteen days, I will not write much in my diary. All of the prisoners are devouring the newspapers. I have just read Hitler's indictment[13] and a significant part of his lengthy court statement to everyone from the *Münchner Neueste Nachrichten*.[14] Hitler spoke for four hours! I have now read an hour and a half, and in two hours, at half past four, I will begin with the second part. The indictment clarified some of the circumstances for the first time—of course, in the way that seems best for Kahr, Lossow, and Seisser.[15] The first impression is that the Nazis are basically naïve and dim-witted loudmouths. It is true that our council revolution had its share of stupidity, but compared to this beer cellar revolution it was a well-organized and levelheaded affair. It cannot, however, be denied that Hitler's speech makes an impression. In particular, it appears honest. At the same time, the man has an opinion of himself that far exceeds his actual abilities. I know how easy it is to misinterpret the strong impact that rhetorical talent has on the masses. That, however, seems to be his only strength. The success it has bestowed on him so far has clearly led him to misjudge his overall capacities.

1.   Literally, "Bloc of Order," a Bavarian alliance of right-wing forces in the early 1920s.
2.   Right-wing forces in Bavaria believed that the politics of the 1921–1922 Bavarian government led by the conservative Hugo Max Graf von und zu Lerchenfeld (1871–1944) was too accommodating to the interests of the central German government in Berlin.
3.   Square in central Munich.
4.   Oskar von Xylander (1856–1940), influential Bavarian army officer.
5.   Munich beer hall frequented by right-wing forces.
6.   Hermann Esser (1900–1981), early Hitler associate.
7.   Organization founded by Mühsam in November 1918 as a radical force within the Bavarian Revolution.
8.   See "1918–1919: Munich III, Revolution and Council Republic" in the Introduction.
9.   Referring to the events following the first government attack on the Bavarian Council Republic on April 13.
10.   The Nazis exploited some of the famed German sociologist Max Weber's (1864–1920) analyses of the nation and of political leadership for their own benefit.
11.   Albrecht von Gräfe (1868–1933), Oskar Hergt (1869–1967), conservative-nationalist politicians.

12. Green is the traditional color of police and security personnel uniforms in Germany.
13. For the "Beer Hall Putsch," see footnote 73 in the Introduction.
14. See footnote 3 in "Riot in Berlin."
15. In 1923, Gustav Ritter von Kahr (1862–1934), right-wing politician and former Bavarian Prime Minister, Otto von Lossow (1868–1938), prominent Bavarian army general, and Hans Ritter von Seisser (1874–1973), head of the Bavarian State Police, played a dubious role in Hitler's coup attempt of November 8, 1923, known as the Beer Hall Putsch.

"FREE!"

Mühsam's diary entry on the day of his release from the Niederschönenfeld Fortress after five and a half years of imprisonment.

Saturday, December 20, 1924

Morning. Half past ten. Free!

1924–1933: BERLIN

GERMANY NEEDS COLONIES

Mühsam published this comment on Germany's ongoing colonial ambitions[1] under the title "Deutschland braucht Kolonien" in the December 1926 issue of *Fanal*.

Apparently, a recent uprising in West Java rapidly became widespread.[2] We have not yet been informed of its motivations, so it is impossible for us to say whether the goal of the rebellion is revolution and the genuine liberation of the people from Dutch slavery, or whether it is first and foremost a desperate act of violent self-defense against the slaveholders' brutality. Nor do we know whether it is in any way connected to the revolutionary nationalist uprising in China.[3]

Since I do not see it as a radical journalist's task to pompously comment on each and every event without knowing anything about it, I will limit myself here to expressing my joy at the resistance of yet another oppressed people—a people whose misery under the coffee magnates has been illustrated hauntingly in Mutatuli's *Max Havelaar*.[4]

In Germany, many voices demand that the League of Nations assign colonies. Colonies for Germany? More than two million German workers are unemployed. The rest work for salaries that are about forty percent below prewar levels. What the Dutch plantation owners do in Java, the German capitalists do in their own country. Germany does not need colonies—Germany needs the people of Java!

❧

1. Germany was never a huge colonial power and, compared to other European nations, only controlled modest colonies in Africa and in the South Pacific.
2. In 1926–1927, a strong uprising against the Dutch colonizers, led by the Communist Party, occurred in the modern-day province of Banten in West Java.
3. Referring to the so-called "Northern Expedition," a 1926–1928 campaign of the nationalist Kuomintang, under Chiang Kai-shek, to unify China.
4. Mutatuli (1820–1887, born Eduard Douwes Dekker) was a Dutch socialist writer who denounced Dutch colonialism in Indonesia in his most famous novel *Max Havelaar* (1860).

BISMARXISM

"Bismarxismus" was a term Mühsam coined to indicate the intricate link he perceived between Marxist ideology and the German Kaiserreich, founded by Otto von Bismarck in 1871. This essay, using the term as a title, was published in *Fanal*, February 1927.

F REEDOM IS A RELIGIOUS TERM. REVOLUTIONARIES WHO PURSUE freedom are religious people. To be a non-religious revolutionary means to use revolutionary means to pursue goals other than freedom. In other words, when revolutionary activity derives from the necessity of the soul, from an inability to tolerate oppression, coercion, and depersonalization, then it is religious. When it derives from a clinical calculation of historical determinism, then it is positivistic. The positivist is not religious; he is a cleric, a dogmatist and a fatalist, to whom freedom is a petty bourgeois fantasy and the struggle for it an assignment.

Here we address the revolutionaries whose revolutionary goal is freedom. Freedom is a social condition whose fundamentals are the voluntary agreement of people to work communally and to share life and its goods. The social condition of freedom rests on the freedom of the individual. The freedom of the individual finds its limits where the freedom of all is threatened, because if not everyone is free, no one is.

To fight for freedom beyond any kind of authority, legal coercion, structured discipline, and state violence is the religious ideal of anarchy. Its realization requires a revolutionary transformation of society's foundations, i.e., the creation of a material basis upon which freedom is possible, namely economic equality. We anarchists are socialists, collectivists, communists. Not because we see the fair distribution of labor and goods as the ultimate criterion for human happiness, but because no struggle for spiritual values, for the deepening and the differentiation of life—and this is the meaning of free-dom!—seems possible as long as humans are born and raised under unequal conditions, as long as the wealth of spirit is drowned in material misery, and as long as spiritual poverty can be disguised by corrupt power and education.

Equality has nothing to do with what we call democracy today. The "equality" of bourgeois democracy is reduced to counting every person who is eligible to vote as an independent unit. This means that the majority of the votes always go to the class that is able to dominate the propaganda apparatus as a result of its economic privilege. Furthermore, the sole purpose of the institutions that we are allowed to vote for is to preserve and administer the status quo. Even if the majority of voters cast their ballots with revolutionary intentions, those who are voted into office are bound by the rules of their institutions, no matter which party they belong to.

Socialism and freedom cannot be won by way of parliamentary democracy. If it is to mean freedom and equality, then democracy can only exist on the grounds of realized socialism. True democracy means self-rule. The self-determination of each individual, based on an awareness of his social significance, is the basis of economic and legal equality, which in turn is the precondition for freedom.

Nowhere in this world is the religious push for freedom held in lower regard than among Germans. Positivism, as a philosophical principle established by the Frenchman Comte, has found its real turf in the country that witnessed the victory of the brutal rationalist Luther over the glowing revolutionary Thomas Müntzer.[1] This reflects Germany's entire history: diagrams and formulas always trample on the living spirit, erudition on the impulse of inner knowledge, and the church on religion. The strongest spirit of the German *Geniezeit*,[2] Goethe, impresses Germans not because of his Apollonian nature, but because of his scientific understanding of life, and they admire him because he dresses his phenomenal mind in bourgeois clothes and has provided the philistines with the observation that "where equality is in place, freedom cannot exist."

Germans know little about the deepest minds of the period–Hölderlin and Jean Paul.[3] Nor do they ask themselves why the Romantics' attempt to flee to mythology and mysticism turned into a dull sentimentality that was eventually replaced by the likes of Börne and Laube, who wrote positivistic literature with a sprinkling of Hegel.[4]

There are two schools of thought whose simultaneous appearance was necessary to destroy the best quality of the German people, namely cosmopolitanism, and to replace it, both in spirit and in politics, with centralism, national regimentation, and "state consciousness": positivism, the philosophy of clinical facts, confusing numbers with reality; and Hegelianism, the uniform "Metternichization"[5] of the spirit, whose apodictic abstractions and dialectical nonsense resulted in the ludicrousness of finding everything that was real also to be "rational."

In the second half of the nineteenth century, when capitalism began to industrialize Germany, Lutheran Prussiandom mixed the banality of the most concrete of all philosophies and the quirkiness of the most abstract. The result was a complete lack of spirit. Meanwhile, the class struggle that had broken out saw the opponents on both sides grab the same philosophical rope, only at opposite ends: Bismarck created the central Reich, with the Prussian king at its head, and provided the foundation for the uncontrolled expansion of capitalist ownership monopoly; Karl Marx divided the International, ejected Bakunin and all revolutionaries who believed in the self-determination of the proletariat in its will to freedom and its decision-making capacities, rather than in the calculations of paid revolutionary managers, turning the religion of socialism into the church of social democracy. Bismarck started three wars to give the agrarian, industrial, and stock market capitalists the elbow room necessary for exploiting human labor; Marx wrote an excellent, if very professorial, analysis of capital for its time, garnished with abstract philosophy drawn from Hegel (under the influence of the latter, capitalism was portrayed as a necessary stage of human development, following the logic of historical dialectics, while historical materialism guaranteed its eventual demise under the pressure of the inevitable proletarian revolution). Bismarck implemented the authoritarian state, whose power structures build on the power of the "corporal" over the "recruit" and so forth; Marx adopted the discipline, the drill, the subordination, and the authoritarianism of the military state as well as the infallibility of the pope and the hierarchies of submissive piety as guidelines for parties and trade unions. Bismarck, following the wishes of the bourgeoisie, organized his state according to the principle of authoritarian centralism, while Marx proclaimed the same form of organization to be the most appropriate for the proletariat and the "workers' state."

In the new Reich, these two branches became opponents, but they stem from the same roots: dull and unimaginative authoritarian doctrine, strict discipline that prohibits both critical thought and passion, and an all-encompassing, sterile bureaucracy. Their similarities continued to be apparent, especially when it came to crushing their opponents (or at least trying to) using raw power: in Bismarck's case, the capitalists of other countries; in Marx's case, the revolutionary socialists who neither believe in fatalism nor in universal suffrage, who want to destroy states, not conquer them, and who want all workers, no longer divided by state borders, to produce and consume in a self-determined way.

Both Bismarck's capitalist state and the dogmatic Marxist workers' movement reach for stars that have never been theirs. The most embarrassing similarity between the two is the complete lack of creative originality, the complete absence of religious enthusiasm, the complete abdication of freedom on all levels. All of this, combined with pretentiousness, pedantry, bureaucracy, legality, and philistinism, created the villainous German spirit that allowed the ruling class to become an international financial powerhouse, all the while leading the German workers' movement further and further away from socialism and toward a path of resignation, internal decay, and the loss of any fighting spirit. This is what I, summarizing all the misery of our times, call *Bismarxism*.

The parallels between Bismarck's non-theoretical praxis and Marx's non-practical theory were already noted by Mikhail Bakunin five and a half decades ago. In very superficial analyses, Bakunin has been called both anti-Semitic and a Germanophobe.

He was neither, and he always objected to these characterizations. It is true that his polemics are dotted with spiteful references to "the Germans" and "the Jews." However, our swastika-bearing Teutons must understand that he meant one and the same thing with these words: *Bismarxism*. Bakunin railed against the German Jews and the Jewish Germans because of their spirit of despotism and centralized authority, propagated both by the German Bismarck and by the Jew Marx, in common disregard for human dignity and freedom. This is why Bakunin saw Germanness and Jewishness as one, fully conscious that he highlighted a characteristic that only seemed appropriate for a *certain* kind of German and for a *certain* kind of Jew.

Mikhail Bakunin died over fifty years ago. He saw the proletarian revolution in danger because of Bismarck's influence on Europe and because of Marx's influence on the workers' movement. We are witnessing the grim results of these influences today. However, both of these legacies are under threat!

Once in this journal, I referred to the "death crisis of capitalism" and was criticized by a comrade.[6] However, the comrade was wrong in thinking that I had now accepted Marxism's fatalistic ideology, according to which world history develops in a "natural" manner, based on solid and eternal laws, independent of humans' active will. Nothing could be further from the truth. I completely agree with Gustav Landauer that the abolition of capitalism, and the establishment of socialism, is only possible when human beings create revolutionary conditions. I do not see the "death crisis" of capitalism as a result of a divine providence that tells us to sit back and watch the economic system crumble, before—inevitably and determined by divine will—a new socialist phase replaces one of the other "phases" in Marxism's historical materialism.

This, however, does not mean that capitalism is not in crisis. I can see clear indications that it is. The first, and most obvious, is that the damage caused by the World War cannot be repaired by capitalism. Again, recognizing this crisis has nothing to do with fatalism, but it forces us to intervene so that the dying beast does not take the seeds from which revolution, socialism, and freedom shall grow with it. The end of capitalism in its current form does not mean that socialism will arise automatically. A different capitalism, possibly organized more effectively, can certainly create new and even expanded options for exploitation in different forms, if the revolutionary socialists do not definitively eradicate the roots of capitalism. If the state continues to exist in any form, then capitalism—and with it positivism, the clerical order of life, in one word: *Bismarxism*—will reign freely!

The terminal illness of capitalism and the terminal illness of Marxism are identical. Today, especially in Germany, the workers' movement rests entirely on these fatalistic doctrines. Social democrats of the SPD and of the USPD, right and left Bolshevik communists, members of the *Kommunistische Arbeiterpartei Deutschland* [Communist Workers' Party of Germany] (KAPD),[7] and unionists of all shades fight viciously over the right interpretation of the bible of "scientific socialism" or, in other words, Marxist dogma. None of them dares to challenge the word of the bible or the Marxist promise of salvation. To them, it would be as much a crime as it is for Bismarck's heirs to deny the necessity of the German Reich under Prussian rule. It is telling that no one has confirmed this necessity as strongly as the social democratic and communist Marxists: the former in 1918–1919, the latter in 1923.[8] *Bismarxism everywhere!*

Should we be surprised? In *Aufruf zum Sozialismus*, Landauer brilliantly demonstrated how, in all of its theoretical writings, Marxism never addresses socialism; it only develops an analysis and critique of capitalism.[9] As such, it bases itself on the Hegelian doctrine that all being is "rational" and that the capitalist period is inevitable—and this means not only the emergence of capitalism, but its expansion until it bursts somewhere in an undefined future. This is the foundation of Marxism's revolutionary teachings. As a consequence, Marxism affirms all the preconditions of capitalism, i.e., it accepts the state, centralism, authoritarianism—everything that capitalism is based on.

The proletariat cannot gain freedom and socialism without rejecting the state. But it cannot reject the state if, in its own struggle, it does not reject the doctrines that serve as the state's pillars: authority and discipline, centralism and bureaucracy, positivism and fatalism.

Science, says Bakunin, must enlighten life, not rule it. The beacon in the struggle of the revolutionary proletariat must not be the refutable science of Marxism, which is nothing but *Bis*marxism, but the irrefutable religious belief in the proletariat's righteousness and power, hatred against exploitation, and the will to freedom!

1.   Auguste Comte (1798–1857); Thomas Müntzer (1488–1525), peasant rebel leader
2.   Literally, "time of the genius;" refers to German arts and literature of the late eighteenth century.
3.   Friedrich Hölderlin (1770–1843), Jean Paul (1763–1824; born Johann Paul Friedrich Richter), German writers.
4.   Ludwig Börne (1786–1837), Heinrich Laube (1806–1884), German writers.
5.   Klemens von Metternich (1773–1859) was a famous Austrian diplomat and a pioneer of modern-day *realpolitik*.
6.   Mühsam is probably referring to the article "Wetterleuchten" [Sheet Lightning] in *Fanal*, October 1926, in which he speaks of "the agony of the capitalist system."
7.   The KAPD was founded in 1920 by former members of the KPD who had been expelled at the 1919 party convention. Strongly leaning toward council communism, the KAPD existed throughout the 1920s. Max Hoelz (see "Max Hoelz" in this book) was one of its most prominent members.
8.   Referring to the social democrats' actions during the German Revolution of 1918–1919, and to the centralization of the KPD after a failed independent rebellion by KPD members in Hamburg in October 1923.
9.   Published in English as *For Socialism* by Telos Press in 1978, trans. Michael J. Parent.

THE ANARCHISTS

Published as "Die Anarchisten" in *Fanal*, no. 7, April 1927, the text reveals some of the differences between Mühsam and the broader anarchist movement in Germany at the time. The latter was mainly represented by the Föderation Kommunistischer Anarchisten Deutschlands. The main points of contention were Mühsam's relative openness to non-anarchist leftists and his advocacy of both a "dictatorship of the proletariat" and revolutionary violence.[1] The article was written in response to harsh criticism levied against Mühsam by FKAD members. It also confirms that Mühsam was adamant in his rejection of portraying Gustav Landauer as a pacifist.

I HAVE TO SPEAK HERE WITH THE DIRECTNESS THAT ANY MATTER deserves when it provides reason for serious concern. I cannot consider certain people's sensitivities in this case, no matter how convinced they are of their own righteousness. I am talking about people who have transformed a set of convictions they considered true decades ago into an unalterable list of theses. Today, they guard this list with a snarl, acting like policemen protecting a dried-up virtue. My own passion for the idea of anarchy requires me to examine–dispassionately–why the German anarchists are unsuccessful in spreading the anarchist idea among the proletariat; an idea that is the most promising and clearest of all revolutionary ideas and that, more than any other, should be better protected from trivialization and corruption by intellectual purity.

The ridicule with which the party communists comment on the lack of unity among anarchist groups and the splintering of the movement into innumerable tiny factions with special agendas is, as such, unjustified. Differences within a movement that pursues a common goal save the movement from stagnation and fossilization, and the question of whether differences in organizational and tactical matters must be bridged in pursuit of collective strength is of technical nature. If anarchist groups often opt for autonomous organizing, then this simply expresses the conviction that it does not advance libertarian aspirations if we have to work in groups with people whom we have no desire to work with.

Besides, factionalism among anarchists is not as widespread as party communists claim. In fact, I doubt that the number of anarchist groups can compete with the various open or hidden factions within the Communist Party, with its right-wing, left-wing, centrist, opportunist, Menshevist, Trotskyist, Zinovievist,[2] Luxemburgist, KAP-ist, ultra-leftist, reformist, Meyerologist, Scholemanic, and Urbahnausic[3] "deviations" from the "truth," as defined by the recently catechized and untouchable "platform" of Bolshevik Leninism. Essentially, the decentralization of the anarchist movement helps avoid the ugly internal struggles that are destroying the KPD from the inside. The anarchist movement allows for comradely collaboration between groups while respecting the special characteristics of each; it allows for paths that might otherwise run parallel to merge into a single wide road. However, this is only true if the different anarchist groups themselves grasp the advantages of decentralization. This is not the case in Germany. Instead, the organizational divisions become—apparently with the party communists serving as role models—the cause for bitter hostility, with some factions with centralist and authoritarian ambitions trying to play a leading role.

Let us not waste much time on the "individualist anarchists." Since they not only believe that their individual liberation from oppression, law, and the state can occur without a mass movement, but also that this individual liberation is the precondition of social liberation, they can play no role in the proletarian revolution, which is our sole interest. Individual anarchists deny the class-based foundation of our enslavement by the state, consider the personal egotism of internally free human beings as a social virtue regardless of the actual social conditions, and fear that the abolition of economic competition by communism means the suppression of all intellectual and individual freedom. After the revolutionary overthrow of the capitalist system, individual anarchists might help strengthen the notion of individual freedom in the minds of the people used to conformity; until then, however, their aspirations for freedom will remain a bourgeois-philosophical affair, separate from any proletarian-revolutionary endeavor. (On a side note, I consider their frequent references to Stirner unjustified. Stirner was connected to the masses.)

The teachings of Silvio Gesell have to be taken much more seriously.[4] They are very important for the revolutionary transition period. Yet, they are irrelevant to this text, because, despite their roots in Proudhon, they cannot really be considered anarchist, and because we are not concerned with scientific theories here, but with the practical behavior of revolutionary comrades. Hence, we will not examine the FFF movement (*Freiland–Freigeld–Freiwirtschaft*[5]) of the physiocrats.[6]

The history of the German communist anarchist movement has not yet been written. Its outline has been sketched in Rudolf Rocker's excellent biography of Johann Most. Rocker, who has all the qualities that are needed—broad knowledge, power of judgment, philological dependability, and revolutionary passion for the anarchist cause—will hopefully not let us wait too long for an anarchist equivalent to Franz Mehring's history of German social democracy.[7] Rocker's book about Most has already demonstrated how a movement emerged and grew that brought us not only Most, but also people like Neve and Reinsdorf[8] and the wonderful spirit of Gustav Landauer. It is a movement that has contributed significantly to the body of revolutionary world literature, and yet it was not able to defend itself against the brutal persecution of the reactionaries and the unscrupulous intrigues of authoritarian social democrats; in short, against what I call *Bismarxism*.[9]

In his book, Rocker does not conceal the shortcomings of the anarchist comrades. Monomaniacal confusion, personal jealousy, disappointed impatience causing dejection and bitterness, many petty and all-too-human problems undermined passion, energy, and appeal. An examination of the movement's history that goes beyond the lifetime and influence of Johann Most will need to address the most disappointing development: the confusion of autonomy with isolation and sectarianism. *Leave the sects! Join the masses!* Rudolf Lange has said this repeatedly. He was wise enough to leave this world on July 31, 1914.[10] As a result, he was not forced to witness how, beginning the very next day, the lack of revolutionary preparation spoiled the good seeds that had been sown.

In November 1918, the revolution found nearly all anarchists at their posts. Our comrades were in Berlin, occupied the *Vorwärts* offices, fought for the *Marstall* and at *Büxenstein*,[11] and, instinctively and enthusiastically, did their duty everywhere, in the Ruhr Valley, in Saxony, in Bavaria. What duty am I talking about? Joining the masses, weapon in hand! Fighting and bleeding with the revolutionary proletariat that united spontaneously to attack and to defend! What were the common demands of all the fighting workers at the time, regardless of the doctrines they followed and the final goals they had? *Remember them, anarchist comrades!* They were: Fight the counterrevolution! Realize socialism! Overcome parliamentarism! Leave behind social democracy and trade unionism! Socialize production! Expropriate privileged property! Put public administration in the hands of the workers' and peasants' councils! Show solidarity with revolutionary Russia! All power to the councils! Replace the class struggle by the dictatorship of the proletariat! Yes, you heard correctly: *dictatorship of the proletariat!* In late 1918 and early 1919, this was self-evident to all revolutionaries. Of course there might have been some pseudo-anarchists, in Klosterneuburg or elsewhere,[12] who turned old books upside down in order to prove that anarchist theorists have always condemned dictatorships, that to condemn oppression means to condemn violence, and that it was forbidden for anarchists to join a revolution of the class-conscious proletariat. However, this amounted to little more than an annoying little dog barking while you oiled your rifle.

The German Revolution drowned in proletarian blood. Many revolutionaries, at the time united with the proletariat—people who had always embraced Karl Liebknecht not as a party representative, but as an admirable rock in the struggle—slowly retreated and, once again, lost connection with the working class. They withdrew into the safe confines of the Social Democratic Party, hiding behind the thrones of their well-paid leaders, the program, the declaration of principles, the administrative regulations, the teachings of the party clerics, and the Torah arks of true faith decorated with party emblems, from where they kicked dirt at each other.

And the anarchists? What did they learn from an experience that finally put them in the middle of the masses? Apparently, not much. Today, they have nothing better to do than to accuse comrades who want to leave their sectarian groups of treason. I will not dwell on my own experiences here, but all the old prejudices and doctrines have returned, and whoever calls for a "dictatorship of the proletariat" is a renegade and no longer recognized as an anarchist—no matter that the Russian anarchists were clearly committed to a revolutionary proletarian dictatorship and that the meaning of the term has been clarified by the council movement (which I consider clearly anarchist).

It does the anarchists no good to hysterically shy away from everything considered Marxist. Bakunin opposed the notion of the dictatorship of the proletariat, because he rightfully assumed that Marx meant the domination of the party—of course the dictatorship of a party can never be a dictatorship of the working class, but only cliquish despotism, reproducing state government. Russia proves this today. However, in the very first issue of this journal, I defined the dictatorship of the proletariat as "a dictatorship of the working class as long as the enemy is still breathing; a dictatorship for the revolution and against the counterrevolution."[12] Bakunin never objected to such a notion. We can quote numerous passages in his writings and reference numerous of his actions. Let us, for example, look at the decrees that proclaimed the Lyon Commune,[14] which he helped distribute: if these decrees did not call for a dictatorship, then what is a dictatorship?

Would you, honorable enemies of all dictatorships, not use coercive means in a revolutionary situation? Would you instead allow the reactionary press to spread its poison? Would you allow the self-determination of the proletariat to be sabotaged and destroyed by its enemies? Do you really believe that it will be enough to say, *The people are free!* Will this suffice to erase all coercion? Is this your revolution? You cannot seriously believe that, yet you are so afraid of the word *dictatorship* that you instantly rail against anyone who dares to mention it!

Here is the problem: proletarians who are influenced neither by doctrines nor by paranoia are used to calling things by their common name. Today's meaning of the "dictatorship of the proletariat," however, is exclusively determined by the Marxists, who use the term constantly. In other words, it is you, the anarchists, who are allowing the dictatorship of the proletariat to turn into the dictatorship of the party! It is you, the anarchists, who have abandoned all proletarian symbols, simply because the Bolsheviks claim them. Thereby, you have allowed these symbols to be monopolized by parties. Take, for example, the old workers' symbol of the hammer and sickle that the party communists have chosen as their emblem. Today, whenever an anarchist uses it, he hears from his own comrades that it belongs to the party communists. Likewise, what has been achieved by using a black flag instead of the red one that has always indicated the unification of the proletariat? Nothing but the exclusive association of the red flag with the Communist Party.

And what about the symbols that the anarchists embrace? Apparently, it is okay if they are shared with people who have no revolutionary ambitions at all. Apparently, it is also okay if they are not at all related to anarchism or the negation of the state. Let us look at one example: as long as there was compulsory military service in Germany, the most important struggle against the state was the anti-military struggle. At the time, the symbol of the broken rifle meant the will to destroy the state's weapons and the refusal to carry them. Since the old German military state has collapsed, the anti-military cause, once reserved for the most radical groups among the proletariat, has become a playground for bourgeois pacifists. They yell *War–Never Again!* and preach gallantly against bloodshed. None of them wants to admit that their beautiful vision can never become reality unless a revolutionary struggle destroys capitalism. They are not accustomed to getting to the roots of social problems. They are happy to reform; touching the system itself scares them. So they took the old anti-military symbol and made it theirs. Did the anarchists notice? No. Caught in noble childhood dreams and displaying staunch conservatism, they not only forgot to take off their pins, but they also forgot the original meaning of the symbol and simply embraced its current implications. This is the reason why anarchist ranks are filled today with sentimental pacifists denying the reality of violence. One of Germany's best anarchists, August Reinsdorf, ended up on the scaffold.[15] Today, German anarchists are non-violent kohlrabi apostles and have turned into objects of scorn among revolutionary workers.

It is true, the most ludicrous forms of this confusion seem to have been overcome almost everywhere outside of Klosterneuburg, but it is sad that such developments were possible at all. Besides, many ridiculous and embarrassing tendencies remain widespread. Worst are the anarchist cabbage settlers who are impudent enough to justify their peaceloving existence by evoking the spirit of Gustav Landauer. My dear friends, Gustav Landauer never mistook the breeding of bunnies in allotment gardens for revolutionary activity! His revolutionary settlement idea built on a militant boycott of capitalist production and consumption. He knew that it could only be realized if the land was taken "by means other than purchase."[16]

How was it possible that the anarchist movement in Germany could so completely lose the identity it developed at the time of the *Sozialistengesetze*, at least for a certain period?[17] Trying to find an answer would certainly make an interesting study. One aspect that must not be underestimated is the influence of syndicalism on anarchist groups. When the localist movement[18] spread from France to Germany at the beginning of the century and a network of syndicalist *Arbeiterbörsen* was formed,[19] it attracted many anarchists due to its strong federalist principles. Anarchism was generally accepted as the ideological foundation of the *Freie Vereinigung deutscher Gewerkschaften* [Free Association of German Trade Unions], established in 1897.[20] In turn, workers who had never heard of anarchism were exposed to its ideas. It is understandable that for many of them the daily struggle for survival, and the political compromises it demanded, took priority. This contributed to an association of anarchism with a merely economic struggle. Armed resistance seemed utopian and was rejected.

Only recently have anarchists—among them many syndicalists—begun to free themselves from the paralyzing influence of exclusive trade unionism! The spirit of Bakunin and Most is returning. Comrades resist the distortions of anarchism's revolutionary ideas, the exploitation and centralization of the movement by bureaucrats, the zealous and debilitating dogmatism of the keepers of outdated beliefs, and the complacency of the anarchist pagodas, where eggheads, convinced they possess the truth, sit on piles of books and shake their heads, because the ignorant masses do not share their belief that humankind's salvation will come from endlessly reciting the same old lines.

We will have to speak about the anarchist youth some other time. We rely on them to give the movement vision and direction. If Germany's anarchist movement cannot shed the dominance of the dinosaurs—in other words, if the youth cannot take the lead and cannot find the courage to act, to set an example, to criticize, to make decisions, to transform, and to rebuilt, then I do not know how the anarchist movement can be saved from turning into a study group of bitter grouches. It is mandatory to change the course that the movement has followed for the past twenty years and to return to the traditions that once made anarchism the horror of bourgeois respectability. Of course anarchists must guard their independence in the areas of deliberation and decision-making. Yet it is equally important to overcome self-imposed isolation and to join all groups among the proletariat that are ready for revolutionary struggle!

1. See "1924–1933: Berlin" in the Introduction.
2. Grigory Zinoviev (1883–1936), Bolshevik revolutionary.
3. Ernst Meyer (1887–1930), Werner Scholem (1895–1940), Johann Urbahns (1890–1946), prominent KPD members.
4. The German economist Silvio Gesell (1862–1930) developed the concept of *Freiwirtschaft* [Free Economy], based on the principles of *Freiland* [Free Land], *Freigeld* [Free Money—a demurrage currency], and *Freihandel* [Free Trade]. He was a "People's Delegate for Finances" during the Bavarian Council Republic.

5. *Freihandel* [Free Trade] was usually used as the third F; *Freiwirtschaft* was usually used to refer to the concept in its entirety.

6. The term dates back to French economist François Quesnay (1694–1774), whose theories focused on the "physiological" relationships between production, distribution, and consumption. Gesell embraced the term for his own theories. In the 1910s, he published a journal entitled *Der Physiokrat* together with Georg Blumenthal (1872–1929).

7. Franz Mehring (1846–1919) was a German historian and socialist. His *Geschichte der deutschen Sozialdemokratie* [History of German Social Democracy] was published in two volumes in 1897–1898.

8. John Neve (1844–1896), August Reinsdorf (1849–1885), prominent German anarchists.

9. See the essay of the same name in this volume.

10. Rudolf Lange (?–1914) was a prominent member of the *Anarchistische Föderation Deutschlands* who committed suicide at the outbreak of World War I.

11. *Vorwärts*–social democratic journal founded in 1876, serving as the journal for the SPD, Germany's Social Democratic Party since 1891; *Marstall*–royal stable; *Büxenstein*–royal printing house.

12. Klosterneuburg, a small town near Vienna, was the home of the Austrian anarchist Pierre Ramus (1882–1942, born Rudolf Grossmann), a personal adversary of Mühsam.

13. See also *Liberating Society from the State* in this volume.

14. The short-lived Commune of Lyon was proclaimed in 1870.

15. August Reinsdorf was executed in February 1885, following a failed assassination attempt on Kaiser Wilhelm I.

16. Mühsam is quoting Landauer here, but provides no reference–I have not been able to find an appropriate passage in Landauer's writings.

17. Literally, "Socialist Laws;" the *Sozialistengesetze* outlawed socialist activities in Germany from 1878 to 1890.

18. *Lokalismus* was a common German term for local workers' organizing in the late nineteenth and early twentieth centuries; often seen as a predecessor to syndicalism.

19. *Arbeiterbörsen*, in French *bourses du travail* [literally, "Labor Exchanges"], were labor councils established in France in the late nineteenth century; they were of great importance for the development of syndicalism.

20. The *Freie Vereinigung deutscher Gewerkschaften* was a radical trade union association and a driving force behind the foundation of the *Freie Arbeiter-Union Deutschlands* (FAUD; see footnote 94 in the Introduction) in 1919.

SACCO AND VANZETTI

Mühsam followed the Sacco and Vanzetti case very attentively. He published three articles in *Fanal* in 1927, the year of their execution: "Sacco and Vanzetti" (May 1927), "Amerika-Import" [American Import] (July 1927), and "Die Lehren von Boston" [The Lessons of Boston] (September 1927). The essays, as well as a call for boycotting American imports, published in *Fanal*'s June 1927 issue under the header "Rettet Sacco und Vanzetti!" [Save Sacco and Vanzetti!], are translated here. A Chris Edmonston translation of the play *Staatsräson. Ein Denkmal für Sacco and Vanzetti* [The Reasoning of the State: A Memorial for Sacco and Vanzetti], one of Mühsam's most popular, is accessible on the websites *saccoandvanzetti.org* and *erichinenglish.org*. Mühsam also published several poems about Sacco and Vanzetti.

Sacco and Vanzetti (May 1927)

IN GERMANY, THE JUDGES ARE CALLED JÜRGENS, NIEDER, OR Vogt.[1] In the USA, these men have equivalents, which are, for example, called Thayer. In both countries, such people are feared by the proletariat. Mr. Thayer wants blood—or rather, electricity. After all, unlike us, modern America no longer simply cuts off heads filled with unwanted thoughts—they have more advanced methods.

For seven years now, the two anarchist workers Sacco and Vanzetti have been in prison, sentenced to death for robbery-homicide. For seven years, they have been waiting every day for either the suspension or the execution of their sentence. For seven years, proof has been collected that has long shown that the two strike leaders had nothing to do with the robbery-homicide they are accused of. The man who committed the murder has been found and has confessed. Still, Mr. Thayer has confirmed the death sentences by rejecting the last possible appeal, and every morning we must wonder whether our comrades Sacco and Vanzetti are still alive.

In November, it will be forty years since the comrades Parsons, Spies, Schwab, Fischer, and Lingg were led to the gallows.[2] Those responsible for the sentencing and the execution at the time knew very well that these anarchists had nothing to do with the deed they were accused of, namely throwing a bomb at Chicago's Haymarket. We are facing the same situation today. Mr. Thayer also knows that Sacco and Vanzetti will be paying for a crime that they did not commit. There is still a chance for clemency. If it is denied, history will repeat itself: as in the case of Chicago, the innocence of the executed will be proven after the fact, and the authorities will bemoan that the art of bringing the dead back to life has yet to be mastered. The augurs,[3] of course, will still be content, because the murdered anarchists will no longer be able to organize strikes.

The representative of the "land of the brave and free" in Berlin, Ambassador Schurman,[4] refused to receive a delegation of the *Deutsche Friedenskartell* [German Peace Association],[5] comprised of the pacifists Ludwig Quidde, Hellmut von Gerlach, and Jelena Stöcker,[6] who meant to inform the ambassador that the execution of Sacco and Vanzetti will be seen as an immoral judicial murder by morally upright human beings all over the world. Mr. Schurman preferred to instead show solidarity with Mr. Thayer. Let us show solidarity with Sacco and Vanzetti!

Save Sacco and Vanzetti! (June 1927)

The lives of our comrades Sacco and Vanzetti, sentenced to death seven years ago, are in immediate danger! If the global revolutionary proletariat fails to prevent it, they will be executed in early July! Workers! Fight with whatever means you have against the intended crime of American capital! Boycott the United States! Do not buy goods imported from North America!

American Import (July 1927)

In 1917, the royal Prussian Minister of Finance Oskar Hergt, currently Minister of Justice of the German Republic, stated, "The Americans cannot swim, they cannot fly, they will not come!" Now, two American adventurers have proven Hergt wrong on all accounts. In the next war, the Americans will not only come swimming, as they did in the last, they will also come flying. German cities will be destroyed and fumigated by American bombs and American poison gas.

Everyone was cheering when Chamberlin and Levine landed in Berlin after their journey across the ocean.[7] They were showered with gifts, and in Hanover Herr Noske himself showed his admiration.[8] From what we hear, they also want to visit Munich. In that case, the enterprise's financier and passenger might want to use a pseudonym. He will certainly not have a street named after him otherwise. Although, one day there will be a Leviné Street in Munich! One day there will be an enduring Bavarian Council Republic that will remember deeds and heroes that are more important than any airplane journeys, pilots, and passengers could ever be, no matter how impressive the achievement. (By the way, do people in the German Republic know who paid for the shooting of comrade Eugen Leviné, ordered by the Social Democratic government of Hoffmann, Schneppenhorst, and Segitz?[9]

The money was taken from the victim's widow; she had to pay for the bullets that killed her husband!) Sometimes, a random similarity of names evokes all sorts of associations. Mr. Chamberlin, for example, is only an "a" short of the famous family whose members have successfully turned technological inventions in the transport business into a tool of mass murder.[10]

On a side note: the Norwegian workers have initiated a boycott of American imports in protest of the judicial crime committed against the comrades Sacco and Vanzetti. They hope to prevent their murder by the state.

According to the last news we received from America, a special commission will investigate the case anew. This will probably prolong the lives of the two comrades, but they are not saved. We have to fear that this commission will listen to the same bought-off witnesses and snitches, and that it will be nothing but a charade to appease critical souls. It seems very likely that the anarchists will once more be "proven" to be robbers and murderers, especially given what is known about political justice in general, and about American justice in particular.

The boycott of American imports is now more urgent than ever. And it should not be reduced to goods; it should be extended to people. When Chamberlin and Levine arrived, the excitement of Berlin's proletariat, fired up by the *Vorwärts* propaganda,[11] competed with that of the military, the petty bourgeoisie, and the industrialists. Since the workers took the time to watch the plane arrive, they should have at least greeted the compatriots of Judge Thayer with cheers for Sacco and Vanzetti! Wherever Chamberlin and Levine go, wherever they breakfast, attend festivities, and receive honors, the names of Sacco and Vanzetti, the two men sentenced to death as a result of infamous political slander, must ring in their ears!

Let those who love records and wars celebrate Chamberlin and Levine! The working class must celebrate Sacco and Vanzetti—and the bourgeoisie must take notice!

The Lessons of Boston (September 1927)

Sacco and Vanzetti have died for the proletariat. Their names live on. The seeds that they have sown will bear fruit. Beware, you murderers!

The worldwide revolutionary movement triggered by the Vienna Ultimatum to Belgrade's government thirteen years ago[12] has since undergone many significant changes. Today, it has entered a new phase characterized by brutal reactionary repression, on the one hand, and a new wave of revolutionary activities, on the other. We, eyewitnesses of events that will shape the history of the coming centuries, tend to believe that any success on either side means everlasting victory or defeat. We are too busy with the here and now to really understand these events in historical perspective. Once we do, certain theses will instantly prove ridiculous: for example, that Mussolini's shameful five-year reign in Italy proves fascism to be a lasting phenomenon. Look at the French Revolution: it appears to have happened with a bang; yet, it still took three years from the Storming of the Bastille on July 14, 1789, to the proclamation of the republic on September 21, 1792. And this was only meant to dispose of a symbol of a feudal order that had already collapsed. Fascism is much more ambitious. It is a pretentious attempt to save a struggling capitalist system by blending antique tyranny with modern technology.

For seven years, the pawns of the American justice system denounced two anarchists as robbers and murderers and tortured them in prison. For six years, death sentences hung over their heads like the Sword of Damocles. Now, they have been executed.

So far, America has not seen much of the world revolution that has been set into motion. But in this case, the protests of the worldwide proletariat challenged the brutality, unscrupulousness, and pretentiousness of "democratic" millionaire bureaucrats even there. Time after time, they were forced to delay their gruesome deed. Do these seven years not prove that nothing can be taken for granted? That nothing that moves, excites, frustrates, or inspires us today, nothing that is current history, is unchangeable? The case of Sacco and Vanzetti goes back longer than fascism!

Sacco and Vanzetti earned the trust of the Massachusetts proletariat as strike organizers. They revealed the shameful conditions in the New York prison system and the scandalous torture and murder of their comrade Salsedo,[13] triggering numerous revolutionary protests. Since their beliefs have caused heinous men to call them street criminals and to sentence them to death in the electric chair, the social conditions have changed dramatically on all continents and in all countries. Wars have taken place in Russia and in the Balkans. Revolutions have occurred in Poland, in Syria, and in Morocco. Colonized peoples have risen up. The effects of the World War have taken unexpected forms: currencies have crashed; entire nations, especially Germany, allow a few individual profiteers to exploit them down to their bones; corporations run by mad despots using extortion schemes have emerged and subsequently collapsed; corruption, murder, and an unleashing of barbarism have illustrated the dire social and political problems everywhere.

Oblivious to reality, people celebrate a constitution that has been drafted in blank fear of revolutionary uprisings and is hardly worth the paper it is written on. Its paragraphs do nothing but cover up the outrageous exploitation of the proletariat by capital. In fact, we are heading back to *vormärzliche* conditions:[14] jury courts are abolished, censorship is reestablished, the youth are stripped of their rights, the schools are handed over to the church, the right to strike and the right to form associations are both in danger, the military has an impact on educational facilities, and fear and panic are spread among the population to serve the reactionaries' interests. This has been going on for some time, and it was going on while Sacco and Vanzetti were waiting for the execution of their verdict. As a result, the world believes that the struggle is resolved, that the League of Nations[15] will eternally define the relationships between the states, that the storm is over, and that God has made the day after tomorrow the same as the day before last. Even Bucharin[16] gave up fatalistically two years ago and ordered communist parties around the world to accept capitalism as a contemporary reality and to adapt their policies accordingly–which they will probably do with much success. This error in judgment, bordering on insanity, has allowed a shaken capitalism to recuperate, supported by Russia and its communist lackeys, who throw new paint on old structures.

In the context of global revolutionary fermentation, the tragedy in Boston is of enormous significance. The American rulers have proven innumerable times–whenever they sensed the slightest resistance by the proletariat–that they recognize no moral restrictions. You learn a lot about these people by reading Upton Sinclair's *The Jungle, Jimmie Higgins*, and *100% - The Story of a Patriot*, and Jack London's *The Iron Heel*. The murder of five anarchists in Chicago on November 11, 1987 (despite protests around the world), the use of torture during court cases, the shameless violence against foreign populations resisting exploitation by dollar capital (the bombings and mass killings in Nicaragua provide a recent example[17]), and the infamous treatment of Sacco and Vanzetti (who, for seven years, never knew whether they would still be alive a week later) prove that the land with the most advanced technology is also the land with the least developed ethics.

Luckily, this extraordinary case of immorality, exercised in its ugliest possible form, incited a humanitarian triumph that has no example in modern history. The workers of all countries, no matter their political convictions, and even wide circles of the bourgeoisie and the intelligentsia, joined in protests against a barbaric act that human beings who have any heart and conscience simply cannot endure. The worldwide solidarity with these two revolutionary proletarians is an enormous consolation at a time when the workers' liberation movement is hopelessly divided and has gone off its natural track. The vast majority of revolutionaries has fallen victim to a wrong and fatal theory that has replaced solidarity with discipline, self-determination with centralism, free will with coercion. In the support for Sacco and Vanzetti, however, we have for the first time seen true unity among those who usually romanticize their separateness. This unity derived from the only possible source: not from science, whose findings will always be contentious, but from a common human experience of outrage and desperation.

The American rulers have not listened to the united voice of humanity. We can safely assume that they were already determined to murder Sacco and Vanzetti on August 10.[18] If the last postponement indeed would have indicated a capitulation of barbarism before humanity, then the victims would have not been prepared for death only to be led back to the dungeon forty minutes before the scheduled hour of execution. No, the henchmen of the land of the brave and free have never allowed pleas and protests to deter them from their crimes. I am convinced that the last postponement was a simple matter of fear: the fear of the rich American bourgeoisie for their safety and their lives. After all, when the fate of Sacco and Vanzetti seemed sealed, their comrades reverted to the final available means, those of organized terror: bombs in subway stations, bombs in churches, bombs in courthouses. It was the explosion of these bombs, together with the angry voices of humanity, that prolonged the life of the two anarchists for a few days.

It is an old social democratic custom to portray every act of individual terror as the act of an agent provocateur. In this case, the party communists followed their social democratic teachers. They mixed contradictory reports in their journals: on the one hand, they accused the police of staging bombings in order to turn public opinion against Sacco and Vanzetti; on the other hand, they claimed that the members of the propertied class across America were running around with pale, fearful faces, smelling dynamite everywhere.

The purpose of the attacks is so self-evident that it almost feels embarrassing to offer an explanation. The comrades who were responsible for them meant to strike fear into the authorities and into the passive public. A bomb, thrown in a moment of extreme tension, speaks so clearly that it does not need interpretation. It says: *The comrades Sacco and Vanzetti are still alive, so they can still be saved! Listen to how I thunder! Look at how I destroy! Beware! If you kill these anarchists, you will realize that there are much worse weapons, much more destructive means, to blow apart your foul order! This is a revolutionary warning! Abstain from deeds that demand revolutionary vengeance!* Now the bombs say: *The murders have happened. Murderers, beware!*

While the entire proletarian world understands the bombs correctly, the German Marxists remain skeptical, raise their index fingers pedantically, and say, "Agents provocateurs or madmen!" Then they argue against individual terror, because only the "red terror of the masses" is justified. It is hardly worth the time to show how ridiculous such arguments are. How do you even distinguish "individual" from "mass" terror? What kind of terror is the killing of Sacco and Vanzetti? Individual or mass? Representatives of the ruling class conduct it in the name of the ruling class. It is no different with the bombs of New York and Philadelphia, only that they come from the proletariat.

Supporters of the Russian Revolution also question the effectiveness of "individual" acts of terror. This is no less absurd! The Russian Revolution would never have occurred without the terrorist activities that date back to the 1870s. Likewise, the reactionary nationalist forces in Germany could have never returned to power after the 1918 Revolution had not the *Organisation Consul*[19] and other terror organizations intimidated the proletariat, and eventually all republicans, with individual assassinations, which, as they were committed in the name of their class, were simultaneously acts of mass terror.

When the United States of North America entered the World War, they opened the last valve needed for the world revolution to take the shape of open civil war. The case of Sacco and Vanzetti has drawn the United States right into it, and the bombs of their anarchist friends demonstrate a refusal to allow the counterrevolutionaries to be its sole active force. As in all countries, the Yankees' first reaction was to use the justice system as a weapon in this war fought by the exploited for their right to freedom and to a life with dignity. This time, though, the reactionaries went too far. The case of Sacco and Vanzetti opened the eyes of the exploited masses throughout the world, and a counterattack began with a global cry for justice, accompanied by the thunder of exploding bombs.

On July 15, the abused and deceived proletariat in Vienna, its belief in the justice system shattered and its very survival threatened, took to the streets and set the Palace of Justice (*Justizpalast*) aflame.[20] The blaze was a warning to the thrones of the powerful: *You disgrace the law to protect your slave holding powers! Now you can see that it is not hunger alone that causes revolution! You call on the courts to fight us—we call on justice and enter the battle under its banner!*

The Austrian proletariat is heading toward bitter days. The treason that the German workers experienced in 1919 has only now arrived in Austria. But the bitter days will not last. The signal of July 15 can no longer be silenced, and history is rapidly unfolding.

The struggle in Vienna and the eyes focused on Boston prove that, despite everything, the proletarian revolution is on the offensive. The demand is for neither bread nor money. *It is for justice!* Let us hope that the bourgeoisie, the powerful, the exploiters, the rulers, and the judges see the writing on the wall!

1. I have not been able to establish which judges Mühsam is referring to here—if any specifically.
2. Reference to the Haymarket martyrs. Albert R. Parsons (1848–1887), August Spies (1855–1887), and Adolph Fischer (1858–1887) were, in fact, led to the gallows. Michael Schwab (1853–1898) appealed to the governor and had his sentence commuted to life imprisonment. Louis Lingg (1864–1887) committed suicide the night before the execution. Mühsam probably confused Schwab with Georg Engel (1836–1887), who was the fourth person hanged on November 11, 1887.
3. The augurs were Roman religious officials whose duty it was to predict the future.
4. Jacob Gould Schurman (1854–1942), U.S. ambassador to Germany from 1925 to 1929.
5. An umbrella organization for peace activists during the Weimar Republic.
6. Ludwig Quidde (1858–1941), historian and liberal politician; Hellmut von Gerlach (1866–1935), publicist; Jelena Stöcker (1869–1943), publicist and women's rights activist.
7. Clarence Duncan Chamberlin (1893–1976), pilot, and Charles Albert Levine (1897–1991), plane owner, completed the first transatlantic air passenger flight on June 5, 1927. They first arrived in Eisleben in Saxony-Anhalt, and then visited several German cities.
8. Gustav Noske (1868–1946), prominent German social democrat, Federal Minister of Defense in 1919–1920, responsible for the violent oppression of several radical socialist

endeavors, including the Spartacus Uprising and the council republics in Bremen and Bavaria.

9. For Eugen Leviné see footnote 59 in the Introduction. Johannes Hoffmann (1867–1930), Ernst Schneppenhorst (1881–1945), and Martin Segitz (1853–1927) were leading social democrats in the Bavarian government at the time.

10. Reference to the involvement of the British Chamberlain dynasty of businessmen and politicians in the Kynoch company that provided the British Army with ammunition during World War I.

11. The social democratic journal *Vorwärts* [Forward] was founded in 1876 and has served as the journal of the SPD, Germany's Social Democratic Party since 1891.

12. Reference to the events triggering World War I. The Vienna Ultimatum (or: July Ultimatum) was a set of ten deliberately unacceptable demands delivered to the Serbian government by the Austrian-Hungarian Empire. War was declared on July 28.

13. In May 1920, Andrea Salsedo (1884–1920), arrested for distributing anarchist literature, plunged to his death from a window while in police custody.

14. *Vormärz* [literally, "Pre-March"] refers to the time between the Vienna Congress of 1814–1815 and the European Revolutions of 1848, erupting in the spring. During the *Vormärz*, European monarchs tried to reestablish the political order prior to the Napoleonic Wars from 1803 to 1815. The period is also known as the "European Restoration."

15. The League of Nations was founded after World War I; it turned into the United Nations after World War II.

16. Nikolai Bukharin (1888–1938), leading Soviet politician and main theoretical voice behind the Stalinist "Socialism In One Country."

17. Reference to U.S. government reactions to the emergence of a Nicaraguan resistance movement under Augusto César Sandino (1895–1934) in 1927.

18. Sacco and Vanzetti were scheduled to be executed on said date, but there was a last minute suspension.

19. A reactionary death squad formed by former Free Corps soldiers that killed several hundred political opponents in 1921–1922.

20. In January 1927, three right-wing militia members murdered two people during clashes with social democrats in the small town of Schattendorf, Burgenland. When they were acquitted in court in July, a crowd of demonstrators set fire to the Vienna Palace of Justice. The police responded with arms, killing 89 protesters and wounding hundreds.

Leaving the Rote Hilfe

Throughout the 1920s, there were many discussions within the German left about the disproportionate influence of the Communist Party on the Rote Hilfe Deutschlands [Red Aid Germany], the solidarity organization that Mühsam was heavily involved with after his release from prison in 1924. It was seen by many as a mere front organization. Mühsam was strongly criticized for his involvement by other anarchists, especially members of the Föderation Kommunistischer Anarchisten Deutschlands.[1] The Rote Hilfe, which existed from 1924 to 1936, was part of the International Red Aid (Russian acronym: MORP), founded in Moscow in 1922 and dissolved in the 1940s. Mühsam finally left the Rote Hilfe in 1929. He sent the following letter on January 15, 1929; it was published in the February 1929 issue of Fanal under the title "Absage an die Rote Hilfe."

DEAR COMRADES!

I hereby declare the end of my membership in the Rote Hilfe Deutschlands.

The crucial factor behind this decision—which was not an easy one—was the announcement in the *Rote Fahne* [Red Flag][2] that the Rote Hilfe intends to promote the journal of the Communist Party.

This means that it has become utterly impossible to see the Rote Hilfe as a non-party organization and to explain to my left-revolutionary comrades how being active in the organization does not imply working for a specific political party.

When I was released from Bavarian captivity four years ago, I decided to dedicate most of my energy as a speaker and organizer to the Rote Hilfe. I won many members and active supporters. I made it a condition for my involvement that I would never have to deny being an anarchist. This has always been clear. Nonetheless, I was met with a lack of understanding and even with hostility in revolutionary circles because of my work with the organization. I tolerated all of this, because I wanted to support the comrades who languish in jails and prisons as victims of class justice and who expect all proletarian organizations to unite in supporting them. I tolerated the organization's rigid bureaucratic structure for the same reason, and I never criticized the many actions that had little to do with supporting prisoners and the victims of the revolution, namely the agitation for KPD candidates during the consumers' cooperatives' elections, etc.

Even when the Rote Hilfe denied aid to left-revolutionary prisoners and persecuted comrades in Russia, I did not object, but simply limited my focus within the organization to the domestic struggle against class justice. Once again, it was the consideration for the imprisoned comrades that kept me from breaking with the Rote Hilfe altogether; after all, it was still officially an independent proletarian organization, i.e., an organization without party affiliation.

I attended the regional Rote Hilfe conference for Berlin-Brandenburg in 1927 as a delegate and formulated some of my critique. In particular, I stressed the need to demand an amnesty for the left-wing revolutionaries who have been imprisoned or exiled in Russia. As a consequence, I was no longer asked to act as a speaker. I have since continued to work for the prisoners, but I had to find ways other than those previously available to me to educate the public.

Some of my friends and I continuously tried to convince ourselves that the Rote Hilfe Deutschlands was indeed independent. It has become impossible now to maintain this illusion. To tie itself exclusively to the *Rote Fahne* means to abandon the last pretense of being a non-party organization and is an insult to all members who are involved in non-parliamentarian groups, who are critical of trade unionism, who have an alternative understanding of communism, or who belong to the independent social democratic movement. By explicitly favoring the *Rote Fahne* over other proletarian journals, Rote Hilfe chooses one out of many, one that does not even represent the Communist Party as a whole, but only its current dominant faction, and one that all left-revolutionary groups and parties within the organization detest. The only decision that could have been accepted and understood by everyone, including the prisoners, would have been to promote *all* left-leaning proletarian journals and newspapers, without regard for the particular factions that the organization itself is divided into, whether its representatives admit it or not.

If I remained involved with the Rote Hilfe, my political credibility would once again be questioned, and this time I would not know what to say in my defense. This is what forces me to leave the organization. I will have to find other ways to fight for the victims of state justice. By no means, though, do I intend to sabotage the work of the Rote Hilfe. Whenever fruitful and comradely cooperation is possible, I will cooperate. But I can no longer be a member of an organization that forces me to support a party whose politics I neither agree with nor consider beneficial to the revolutionary workers' movement.

With revolutionary greetings,
Erich Mühsam

1. See "1924–1933: Berlin" in the Introduction.
2. Founded by Karl Liebknecht and Rosa Luxemburg in November 1918, the journal served as the KPD's publishing organ until 1945.

LIBERATING SOCIETY FROM THE STATE: WHAT IS COMMUNIST ANARCHISM?

PREFACE

In July 1931, Berlin's Chief of Police, the social democrat Grzesinski, banned the anarchist journal *Fanal* for a period of four months. It was the time of the bank failures, when financial capital was at its wit's end and the federal government suspended the circulation of currency. The entire industrial economy was shaken in a way that rendered the usual political methods of ensuring capitalist hegemony no longer sufficient. The path toward fascist dictatorship was spread out, smoothed over, and set out upon. The suffering of the masses increased, and with it the helplessness of the public authorities, while the demands of the industrialists and great landholders were simultaneously growing higher. The crisis was fought through heightened pressure on workers and the unemployed, its victims pacified with elections, elections, and more elections. The parties tried to turn the suffering of their followers to the benefit of their leaders. A new government assembled from the remnants of bankrupt feudal times launched a series of constitutional disputes. A threatening air of civil war descended upon Germany. All attempts to dispel stress and despair, all remedies imploringly suggested by fascists and democrats, ecclesiastics and right-wing as well as left-wing socialists, came straight from the pharmacy of authority. Each one praised *his* state, *his* claim to power, *his* authoritarian system.

The fight of the anarchist monthly *Fanal* against centralism and authoritarianism and for freedom and renewal was interrupted. Only occasional newsletters could assure the paper's readers that the blow struck against it after nearly five years of regular publication had not been fatal—even if it has not yet been overcome. The general state of affairs could only be mentioned in passing in these newsletters; their main purpose was to ask people for donations in order to keep the publication from dying. One way of proving our determination to keep *Fanal* alive was the announcement of this pamphlet, which shall in part compensate for the suspension of the newspaper and which is hereby presented to the public.

The publication appears as a special edition of *Fanal*, in order to declare the continuing existence of our journal; at the same time, it has the format of an independent publication in order to achieve distribution beyond the circle of the journal's readers and friends. As a substitute, this pamphlet cannot focus on daily events in the same way the journal did. It has to outlive the moment and must concern itself with the general principles and convictions that carried the journal's contents—and always will. In other words, anarchists were challenged to outline the fundamental features of their anarchist beliefs. This is what I have attempted to do.

We are repeatedly asked the following by those who are unacquainted with the world of anarchist thought: "What do you actually want? How do you imagine a society without the state and authority? Is there not an internal contradiction in the term *communist anarchism?*" I want to answer these questions here; comprehensively, on the one hand, yet accessibly, on the other. As far as my comrades are concerned, they are invited to compare their views to mine, to test and to sharpen them, and to expand or qualify the outline I am presenting here based on their own beliefs.

I have dispensed with historical arguments and scientific bases in this text, along with citing older anarchist writings to support or illustrate my thoughts. Thoughts do not become more correct because someone else has previously formulated them. Furthermore, I believe that I can present my ideas in the liveliest way if I do so exclusively in my own words. Therefore, there will not be a single quote in this text, except for the quote by Wieland at the very beginning: 150 years old, these lines shall prove that anarchist thought has always come naturally to the greatest spirits of all eras.

Those who have already studied the basic ideas of anarchism will be familiar with the contents. If anything, I could possibly claim the incorporation of the council system into anarchist concepts of administration as an original contribution to the theory of libertarian socialism. No one has previously attempted anything of the kind. In general, though, my aim was a well-structured summary of the logic and coherence of anarchist thought. Such a summary is still missing from the extraordinarily rich body of anarchist literature. However, the text will also address specific questions of history, philosophy, economics, natural rights, and political struggle from an anti-authoritarian perspective. For those readers who want to investigate further, I have compiled a bibliography as an appendix.[1]

Berlin-Britz, November 1932

> To know nothing of sultans, viziers, governors, qadis, treasurers, customs officials, fakirs, and fat cats is a pleasure which the majority of humankind does not know.
>
> (C.M. Wieland, *Geschichte des weisen Danischmend*[2])

I. THE WORLDVIEW OF ANARCHISM

ANARCHISM IS THE TEACHING OF FREEDOM AS THE FOUNDATION OF HUMAN society. Anarchy—in our language: without oppression, without authority, without state—signifies the social order that anarchists aspire to, namely the freedom of each individual through the freedom of all. It is this ambition, *and nothing else*, that connects all anarchists and that distinguishes anarchism fundamentally from all other social and moral theories.

Anyone who makes the freedom of the individual a principle for all of human-kind and anyone who sees the freedom of society as the freedom of all individuals, united in community, can call himself an anarchist. Anyone who allows individuals to be oppressed in the name of society or society to be oppressed in the name of individual freedom has no such right. There are different opinions about how to achieve freedom, about the means that need to be employed against its enemies, and about the exact shape and administration of the free society. These different opinions constitute nothing more than different currents within a common *Weltanschauung*.[3] To compare and evaluate these different opinions is not the purpose of this text. This pamphlet limits itself to presenting and promoting the principles of *communist anarchism* as the writer and his closest comrades understand them.

I will not engage in a scientific interpretation of the term communism either. Communist anarchists have little interest in a dogmatic definition of how the distribution and consumption of goods should be regulated in a society freed from the state and from capital. Their interest lies in creating a libertarian socialism—a socialism different to the authoritarian and centralist socialism of the state social-ists, especially the Marxists.

We understand by communism simply a social relationship that builds on common access to society's goods, allowing all to work according to their abilities and to take according to their needs. We believe that the basic socialist demand for equal rights for everyone would be more secure with this economic form than with collectivism or mutualism, both of which seek to make access to society's goods dependent on individual labor. However, all of these theories have found followers among anarchists, and there is enough room for them within libertarian socialism. Some questions can only be resolved in the future. For example, the level of personal property that is necessary to guarantee an individual satisfaction of needs. Yet, a clear line has to be drawn when anarchism is interpreted in a purely individualistic sense, and when egotism and individual interests alone determine the negation of the state and of authority. Followers of such beliefs see any form of general social organization, socialism included, as oppressive to an isolated I. They deny the natural facts that human beings are social creatures and that humans are a species in which each individual depends on society and society on each individual.

We maintain that it is neither possible nor desirable to separate the individual from society. The supposed freedom of such an individual is nothing but isolation, and the consequence will inevitably be his dissolution in a social vacuum. We assert that no one will be free until *everyone* is free! Everyone will only be free, however, once people are united in socialism.

Economically speaking, socialism means a classless society in which the land and the means of production are no longer under private control, and where economic rent, business profit, and wage labor will no longer rob the producers' hands and minds of the result of their efforts. Private—or state—exploitation will be replaced by coordinated productive use of what is commonly owned. The privileged minority of landowners will be replaced by people united in community.

Beyond economic terms, socialism is a moral and a spiritual value. Socialism does not only mean the sensible organization of labor, distribution, and consumption, and the satisfaction of everyone's natural material needs. Socialism also means the satisfaction of everyone's moral requirements, whose habitual neglect has done more damage to humankind than hunger or any other form of physical deprivation. In other words, socialism means the demand for equal rights.

Material hardship of any kind and labor under the most strenuous of circumstances can be borne when the burden is distributed equally among all, when the misery is shared in spiritual community, and when there is a common will to eradicate the causes of misery based on a universal feeling of connectedness. What can never be accepted is misery as a result of social injustice. Look at the society we live in: it is a society that lets children go hungry, that denies the majority of people enough sunlight, clean air, healthy food, rest, hygiene, sanitation, and spiritual development throughout the entire course of their lives; a society that reserves wealth and riches for a minority; a society in which the comfort and affluence of some rest on the sacrifice and the toil of many; a society that does not allow everyone to work or only allows them to do so under the worst conditions and for pitiful pay; a society that puts the burden of caring for those who have nothing on those who have too little; a society where the latter are also required to sustain the apparatus administering this insanity, only to perpetuate social inequality for the benefit of a capitalist economy. Such a society cannot be changed into a socialist society by merely modifying its material framework. Marxists err in the assumption that the spiritual and moral qualities of humans derive mechanically from the economic modes of production, and that the religious, legal, and scientific realities are nothing but the ideological superstructure of the material base. The influences go both ways, neither side is more important than the other.

Capitalist oppression rests both on material and spiritual pillars. It requires an infiltration of the people's spirit through education; otherwise, the people would never accept social inequality as their inevitable fate. In turn, socialism requires spiritual preparation. Its justification comes not only from the material advantages it will bring to the majority of the people, but also from its spiritual values. This means that socialism will allow spiritual values to prosper; but it also means that socialism is a spiritual value in itself! The transformation of economic relations in socialism, and the equal rights it will bring, can only become effective if the spiritual relations between the people are renewed. Only new forms of spiritual relations make an economic transformation from individualism and inequality to socialism and solidarity possible.

Communist anarchism agrees with the socialist teaching that economic equality is the basis for communal social relationships. It disagrees with the materialism of the Marxists, which makes the economic conditions the only concern. The economic conditions are but one of the necessary requirements for a radical social transformation that touches on *all* aspects of life. *Equality* must not be confused with *conformity*. The demand for equality means nothing but the demand for *equal rights*, i.e., equal conditions for all to develop their talents in the best possible way. Economic equality means eradicating all obstacles to the free development of the personality, obstacles that arise as a result of difficult social circumstances, in particular poverty. Equality in the sense of equal rights does not hinder individual development, but rather renders it possible. Capitalist society beds the children of the rich in silk, raises them physically and spiritually in the most refined of ways, provides them with quality education and knowledge, and hands them the professions of the powerful without regard for talent or character. At the same time, also without regard for talent or character, the children of the poor grow up in dreary holes with little light and bad air, exposed to a sad environment and under the influence and the weight of misery from an early age, without any education that would allow them to challenge the intentions of the powerful, and forced into obedience and labor that kills their individuality. Under the equality of socialism, every child will have light, air, joy, and the opportunity to develop a unique personality based on what nature and consciousness can provide, always connected to those who share their times, their fate, and their humanity.

Capitalism causes the worst kind of conformity, both for the exploiters and for the exploited. Classless socialism creates equal conditions for everyone, conditions in which all can develop their own values and make use of the common good according to their needs, their uniqueness, and their individuality, while always remaining connected to everyone else.

Only when the principle of equality receives such spiritual meaning and such moral strength can we speak of equality from a socialist and anarchist perspective. What is important is not the mere transformation of unbalanced external relationships; what is important is to reach a balance based on inner necessity. In other words, the problem is not inequality itself; the problem is the injustice it is based upon. If morality was only an ideological coating on utilitarian calculations, and if it were only material considerations that determined the best way to live, then arguing with capitalists would be entirely pointless. References to starving children and other expressions of working-class misery and squalor could never convince them to change the mode of production if human thought, will, and consciousness were completely dependent on material conditions.

The current mode of production is the capitalist mode. It goes without saying that this has implications for the material life of both capitalists and proletarians.

However, the Marxist formula, according to which *being* determines *consciousness*—thereby reducing being to a merely economic condition—is highly questionable. The consciousness of human beings is determined by many things besides those that are material, and the vitality of the soul can be at its strongest in the very midst of capitalism. It is true that our behavior is determined by social conditions, but social conditions cannot be reduced to *economic* conditions. They include emotional aspects, spiritual connections to other people, as well as climatic and astrological aspects. Furthermore, our behavior might also be determined by deeply-rooted moral convictions that are entirely independent of all forms of production.

Capitalism rests entirely on material thought. If we mount the logical argument that people who are living in misery and are excluded from the common good pose a threat to social well-being, capitalists can always claim that the accumulation of property in the hands of a small number of consumers is the most effective way of using the labor force—regardless of whether or not the measurement of effectiveness is entirely bereft of all moral considerations and only relates to the material needs of the capitalists, which are protected by the dominant political order. The point is: the capitalist system cannot be challenged (let alone overthrown) by mere logic, especially not in the name of a pseudo-scientific theory like that of "historical materialism." You cannot deal with things rationally that affect people in emotional ways and that are, for this very reason, experienced as unbearable. The replacement of capitalism with a socialist society can only derive from an innate social ethic, even if the most tangible result of society's complete transformation will be the newly established economic forms. This conviction marks one of the crucial differences between the anarchist and the Marxist understanding of socialism.

The capitalists have never attempted to turn the principles of their behavior into eternal law for everyone. They simply make use of capitalism because it ensures them power over the proletariat and it protects their privileges. Not even they take seriously the pathetic accounting tricks that claim that the earth can only produce enough wealth for a selected minority, while the great majority is condemned to privation and slavery. Marxism appeared as a savior in the moment of need, with the bold theory of determined thought and action, which so far only capitalism had consistently implemented in social life. Materialism—i.e., the understanding of the world in terms of pure mathematics and strict metabolism; a mindless denigration of all the questions of humankind to mere affairs of production and distribution—was presented as an immutable, eternally valid institution of nature, ordained by fate. We anarchists oppose capitalism because it subordinates the spiritual and moral values of humanity to the profits and the power of an unscrupulous class of masters who think in purely materialistic terms. We believe that the class character of society—developed by capitalism to a degree where we see two different species facing each other—was only possible because all life came to be occupied by materialist thought and interest, which inevitably led to social divisions and, in turn, to the enslavement of one part and to the complete domination of the other. We further believe that the most important cause for the decay of capitalist society, for its helpless tottering about in its own mismanagement, and for its resort to wars and increasingly brutal oppression of the dispossessed and disenfranchised masses is the unnaturalness of purely materialistic feeling, thinking, and acting. In the long run, nature does not allow itself to be abused in such a way that the satisfaction of the most basic material needs becomes life's goal rather than life's basis.

Greed, dishonesty, and power—which always implies the abuse of power—are the inevitable consequences of this. We strive for socialism, because we see in it the guarantee that people's basic material needs and comforts will be provided for, i.e., the guarantee for a basis on which social life can rise to the highest levels of a unified soul and a unified spirit. Today, Marxism offers a theory to socialists explaining splendidly the nature of capitalism, as well as its expressions and its effects. However, capitalism has turned into a natural law that allegedly determines all of the social forms that have, in fact, been established by human beings. Marxist theory is embellished by philosophical words of wisdom and supposedly rock-solid science. The message for those who want to replace capitalism with socialism is: socialism must have the same basis; materialism is the foundation of capitalism, but it has to be understood as "historical materialism," i.e., as the foundation of all social forms. The materialist perspective teaches us that capitalism could only become what it is—an expression of modern slavery, of the depersonalization of human beings, of the subjugation of the will under the mechanism of the economic apparatus—because it declared material efficiency to be the lever of all social forces (maybe not theoretically, but practically). The only difference between the socialists and the capitalists is, so the Marxists conclude, that the socialists understand all of this theoretically. In any case, materialism remains the foundation of everything.

Could you do the capitalist power-holders any bigger favor than to present such a theory? Are they not morally justified in what they do when socialists base their worldview on the same foundation that supports their damned system? The means to destroy a bad system might be forced upon its opponents by those who defend it. People with arms can hardly be fought with nice words. However, those who want to use the bricks of the old society to build the new one will inevitably build gates though which the old spirit can return.

Socialism has nothing in common with capitalism, neither economically nor ideologically. That socialism must replace capitalism is not based on the practical logic of utilitarian economics, but on the moral conscience of the just mind. We despise the hunger of the poor—for the sake of justice!

To explain the meaning of justice is unnecessary. Human beings have always been able to distinguish between right and wrong; this is an innate gift, much like the gift of being able to feel lust and pain. The only difference is that lust and pain are already apparent in the first hour of life, while the capacity to distinguish between right and wrong takes some time to develop. However, this does not jeopardize the theory of an innate and instinctive ability to differentiate between the two. There are a number of innate qualities that need time to develop: walking, speaking, the perception of different colors, or the assessment of beauty and ugliness all take time to develop, yet no one would doubt that they are abilities provided by nature. Knowing right from wrong is part of human social consciousness. If humans did not possess this quality, the misery of strangers could never touch us in any way. Lust and pain come from sensations of body and soul that–unlike emotions–can be influenced by human will. The same goes for social consciousness. The will for justice is a part of our spiritual nature. Whether it is satisfied or not depends on whether certain basic demands of conscience are fulfilled. The first such demand is equal rights.

Equal rights means justice through equality. The requirement for the realization of equal rights is the principle of *mutuality*. The life of humans, animals, and plants depends on the killing of one species by another and on the transformation of the life force of the destroyed creature into the life force of the destroyer. This fight of the world's species against one another, i.e., this struggle for self-preservation, is reproduced by the organized effort to support members of the same social species in their fight for survival and perseverance. The extent to which collaboration or division within one and the same species appear in nature is of no matter here. It is certain that human beings are the only social beings who have reproduced this struggle within their own species, and not because–as it is the case among certain animals and cannibals–malnutrition forced them to, but because there was an interest in dividing the species and in giving some of its members more rights than others. At the bottom of this lies the lust for power. Mutuality is a necessary component of equal rights. Social inequality makes mutuality impossible.

Capitalist society destroys mutuality within society and replaces it by cliques of power-hungry minorities that aim at oppressing and exploiting artificially divided social groups. Many proletarians have understood that they need to unite in the spirit of mutuality in order to pursue their well-being, but so far their struggle has hardly gone beyond repelling the worst consequences of capitalist violence. Even where they are guided by socialist and communist principles, their struggle is limited to the material transformation of life. Their attack is solely directed against the expressions of capitalism and against the consequences of power and property for the life, health, and social status of the dispossessed; never, with some exceptions, is it directed against the moral principles that have made the emergence, the growth, and the effects of capitalism possible. However, if the spirit of equal rights and of mutuality–without which there will never be socialism–are ever to come to life, these principles must be overcome, alongside the abolition of the economic system.

Communist anarchism fights against two things simultaneously: the economic oppression of human beings by human beings and the moral system that distinguishes between different kinds of human beings. Capitalism could have never developed had not the abdication of controlling one's own labor force, which is the essence of economic oppression, been preceded by the abdication of *self-responsibility*. There are historical theories about the emergence and the development of capitalism and the class struggle. According to these, the earliest communist societies of farmers began to select armed men to defend their lands. Slowly, on the basis of the power of their arms, these men became the masters of the land. They developed into a privileged class that turned the output of those who had selected them as protectors into personal riches. Eventually, they became the effective owners of the land and subjugated the workers to their will. These theories are highly plausible, and they go against the Marxist doctrine, according to which the economic conditions come first, and the feelings, thoughts, and actions of human beings come second. Before arms were handed to a selected few, there must have been a sense of weakness, of a necessity for defense, of a loss of natural and original unity. The disappearance of trust in the unity of humankind, however, is an ethical process, a process of the soul—the economic manifestations follow. Here it is *consciousness* that determines *being*. Is there any possible explanation for the disappearance of self-confidence based on economics? Hardly. Every economic and social relationship is a human affair, but thought precedes action, and unconscious sensations, i.e., whatever we feel in our soul, precedes thought. Living together means sharing a common responsibility. Social fragmentation can only occur once common responsibility wanes. If society ascribes a task that concerns everyone to a particular group of people, then these people are released from responsibility for everyone; at the same time, society releases itself from the task it has ascribed to that particular group.

In the context of economic production, it makes sense to divide tasks. Defending the land from attack and working the land are not the same thing. The division of tasks does not in itself harm the principle of community. However, leaving work exclusively to one group, while turning over defense exclusively to another, inevitably undermines social unity. It eradicates common responsibility and creates inequality, which inevitably leads to oppression. Common responsibility is the real meaning of communism. Common responsibility, i.e., responsibility of all for all, means the individual responsibility of each for the whole of society—which is the real meaning of anarchism.

This raises the question of the mutual relationship between *the society and the individual*. Marxism intends to create social equality by forcing individuals into the straightjacket of a society that allegedly creates equality by means of rational economic balance. Individualism makes the self-fulfillment of the individual the measure for social existence, without regard for equality and the well-being of all. Both perspectives assume a contradiction between the society and the individual. They only differ in championing opposite ends.

Communist anarchism rejects the distinction between the society and the individual. It sees society as a sum of individuals and individuals as intrinsically linked to—and *within*—society. A social equality that inhibits the activity of the individual who is conscious of his own value and a social equality that contents itself with leveling the control of material goods can never by itself create social equality, i.e., an equality that fulfills the demand for justice, an equality that rests on mutuality (in everything, not only material things), and an equality that builds on a shared feeling of responsibility as well as on the self-responsibility of each and every individual. To establish equality in the sense of equal rights is not a mere mathematical exercise.

Marxism knows that this is its weakness. Therefore, it escapes into philo-sophical consolations and trivializes the role of individual responsibility in social interaction by referring to antiquated theories of predetermination and a restricted will. It does not help Marxism's esoteric aberrations that it replaces the notion of God's will with the notion of historical materialism, i.e., the dependency of human action on the current forms of production. Economic conditions certainly influence human decisions, but so do many other things: geographical and biological, genetic and social aspects, as well as all sorts of peculiarities that merge within our soul, in what we call "personality." Even if the development of consciousness is affected by many social aspects, it does not take away the individual's ability to make deci-sions and to have a direct impact on these conditions. Within the confines of one's personality, the will always remains free.

The intent here is not to recommend making the individual will the center of everything, to consider the interests of society less important, or to presume that the sole purpose of society consists of satisfying the material and spiritual needs of the individuals who are conscious of their unique I. This would be nothing but escape from reality into an imagined world of isolated beings lacking social bonds. The unity between the individual human being and humankind is insepa-rable, and it is felt by every individual. For example, we can point to the desire of all human beings to leave a record of their lives for the rest of humankind. For the individual, the world only exists as long as he perceives it with his senses. If individual and social life were not completely intertwined, death—erasing both an individual's consciousness and an individual's perception—would be the end of all things. Mutuality is no whim. The instinctive human desire to contribute to the benefit of humankind, to enrich the material, spiritual, and moral treasures of society by one's own abilities, could not exist if the individual was a discrete aspect of the whole. All individual activity is motivated by an awareness of community. Society is simultaneously the origin of life and the purpose of life. Since it consists of individual beings united in community, its active qualities are no different from those of the humans, animals, and plants that build community together, that come from community and that create community anew. The society and the individual have to be seen as *one*, and every problem between individuals constitutes a social problem, while every social problem impacts upon every individual. The whole is inseparable from its parts, and the parts, of which each constitutes an organism containing the qualities of the whole, are all connected. It is the togetherness and the interwovenness of the individual with the whole that is the characteristic of *organic being* in the world and in every natural relationship. A forest consists of trees, which have their own individual life and their own roots. They nourish themselves, they cast off dead branches, they develop new shoots, and they make space for new life by losing leaves and by producing new ones, by spreading seeds and by slowly losing strength. At the same time, the entire forest has the character of an individual being that lives, dies, and constantly regenerates itself, based on the coming and going of the individual trees and their mutual transfers of vital force. In the same way, every community is an organism made up of organisms, an alliance of alliances, a multiplicity of unities that has itself become a unity.

Communist anarchism aims to reestablish these natural social connections and the individual—including equal rights, mutuality, and self-responsibility—as the framework of social life. Its goal is to have social life rest on consciousness, commitment, and common responsibility of and for all. For this to happen, the complete transformation of the organizational principles of economic and social exchange is necessary. *Federalism* is the form of organization that expresses a union deriving from individual parts that (naturally) unite to form a whole, and from a whole that supports the individual parts as its life force. The opposite is *centralism*, the artificial form of organization adopted by the powerful and by the state, reared by capitalism, and leading to the complete annihilation of individuality, equality, self-determination, self-responsibility, and mutuality.

Federalism relates to centralism in the same way that organism relates to mechanism. On the one side, we have something that has grown and flowered from nature, something original; on the other side, we have something that has been molded and shaped, an imitation. Federalism is the community of living parts that form a living whole. Centralism is a row of chained parts lacking will and controlled by a mechanism without a soul. Federalism is driven by the agreement of the individuals to unite their wills to produce, distribute, and consume fairly, and to create justice in all other areas of life as well, understanding both their individual advantage and that of society as one and the same. Centralism is driven by an external power, by laws and by institutions that subjugate the will of the masses. Federalism builds the social body from below; it allows the creative forces to make their own decisions based on mutual exchange, and hence guarantees the well-being of both the individual and society, seeing no difference between the two. Centralism directs the individuals from above; with centralism individuals are tied together superficially, but have no intimate contact, since their individual will has been crippled and replaced by an external will, alienated and removed from the community. Federalism is organization based on the natural order of things. Centralism replaces this order (*Ordnung*) by authority (*Überordnung*) and collocation (*Anordnung*). Federalism corresponds to the demands for justice, mutuality, equality, self-responsibility, and community (a community of individuals). Centralism corresponds to the needs for power, authority, exploitation, class division, and privilege. Federalism is an expression of society. Centralism is an expression of the state.

The *state* and *society* are two different things. Society is not a conglomeration of different organizations and associations, in which men administer their common affairs, the state being one of them, and the state is not just one of society's organizational forms. Rather, where there is society, there cannot be a state. The state only relates to society as a spear in its side, not allowing people to develop and breathe. The state divides people into classes and keeps them from truly becoming society. A centralist entity cannot be federalist at the same time. An authoritarian administrative system means government, bureaucracy, domination–the characteristics of the state. A community based on equal rights and mutuality within certain geographical confines constitutes a people; as a general form of communal living it constitutes society. The state and society are contradictions. They are mutually exclusive.

To speak of a "state composed of classes" is the same as to speak of "wood composed of wood." The state can never be anything but the centralized executive body of a class that is removed from the people. The state exists to dominate and control the disenfranchised people of the oppressed class. The administrative system of the state divides human society into social classes by preserving the land and the means of production as the property of the privileged class, and by regulating the use of property by the dispossessed–meaning the vast majority of people–according to the untouchable privilege of property and an understanding of labor output as the reification of labor force.

The state has been created solely to serve this purpose and no other, and it will never serve any other purpose. The state only has a function where masters stand against slaves. Only with the emergence of private property as a means of exploitation could the state emerge. Then, with the evolution of capitalism, it constantly expanded and tightened the net of laws, surveillance, and control mechanisms that keep the proletariat under the power of the privileged class, which made the material principles of exploitation of the property owners the center of all human life. Along with the materialist worldview, Marxists also want to adopt a centralized form of organization, this most essential characteristic of the capitalist state, as the foundation for a society freed from capitalism.

I have shown that social conditions determine the behavior of people, but that these conditions are to a significant degree determined by the willful actions of the people themselves; meaning that the people's behavior shapes the social conditions. In general, we can say that particular social conditions lead to certain kinds of behavior, just as certain kinds of behavior lead to particular social conditions.

Capitalism has installed a centralist state administration to strengthen its domination over people. With the increase of authoritarian pressure, the power of capital increased as well. This, in turn, caused even stronger state oppression, hurting the workers and serving the privileged. This means that the state, controlled from above, is the sole form of organization for maintaining and advancing the capitalist economy. It also means that capitalism and the centralist state are inevitably connected and that every centralist state must develop capitalism—or recreate it wherever it disappears. This drastically challenges Marxist assumptions that socialism can be established even if the means of production are still owned by private exploiters, as long as production itself is controlled by the state. This is nothing but a distortion and inversion of the basic socialist idea. *State capitalism*, or, if you prefer, *state socialism*, has absolutely nothing to do with true socialism. To the contrary, it is a form of capitalist oppression that is hostile to the spirit of community, mutuality, and self-responsibility, without which no socialism can exist.

It does not matter at all whether the proletariat conquers the capitalist state in order to prepare it for a slow transformation toward socialism or whether it establishes a new state, in which institutions determine the duties of the working people who, once again, are deprived of controlling and using the products of their labor. The explanation that the state will wither away once it has implemented socialist economic structures to the degree that no residues of capitalism remain is unhelpful. It is a meaningless concession to the natural socialist insight that there cannot be social equality within a state. The state will never wither away, nor will it ever allow people who desire equal rights and a federation to realize socialism. The state will only become stronger as it expands its foundations. The basis of the state is the capitalist class society. It makes no difference whether the class divisions derive from the private control of a few over the earth and the means of labor or from delegating this control to a selected clique of power mongers sanctioned by the state. Even if there is a certain moral satisfaction in knowing that the right to exploitation has been removed from greedy private hands, *all* exploitation must end; to depersonalize it is not enough. For the worker, it is of no relevance whether his labor serves the interests of a joint stock company that pays dividends to people who have nothing whatsoever to do with his work and who might not even know what is being produced, or whether the state collects the product of his labor. The personal effect is the same: the product is not his, it is removed from his control, and the only compensation he receives is a wage.

The wage labor system, the key characteristic of exploitation, does not change a bit when private capitalism is turned into state capitalism. Some Marxists claim that although the control of the labor force by the state appears to have exploitative dimensions, this is not the case, since the products of individual labor serve the interests of society. But, once again, this distorts the basic socialist idea. First of all, the capitalists make the same claim: they produce things that serve the common good, and more profit means more production, and hence more products for the common good. More importantly, though, both overlook the meaning of workers' self-determination. Capitalist labor, whether it is demanded by a private person or by a state, never serves the common good. No common good can be served where there is a distinction between those who define it and those who fulfill it. In fact, in state capitalism, the state acquires more power over the workforce than private capitalists ever could, since the state has a monopoly on all work-related decisions. In any kind of capitalist economy, supplying the market with the most basic goods only serves the position of those in power. Wherever there is a conflict between the privilege of control and the needs of the people, the people lose out—in state capitalism as much as in private capitalism.

Privilege must be eradicated. This can only happen if *self-management* of the workers replaces control of labor from above. Self-management is nothing but the self-responsibility of people with equal rights, following the principles of mutuality. It is federative organization instead of centralist organization. I will show in the second part of this text how the *council system*, the only true form of economic self-management, can realize the organization of labor and distribution in communist anarchy in a federative manner. At this point, the following statement suffices: a society in which the relationship between labor and consumption and between humans themselves, materially as well as spiritually, is regulated by the principles of equal rights, self-responsibility, and mutuality, demands a federative administration, i.e., direct communication among all those concerned.

Central communication facilities must only serve the purpose of bookkeeping and the distribution of tasks, never the power of bureaus or privileged administrative units; as long as these are not wiped out, no self-determination can exist. The attempt to create socialism out of capitalism by the means of a transitional state is doomed to fail given the centralist nature of the state. The statist order rests on the transfer of public services to an exclusive group of magistrates selected for this purpose. If, after the collapse of the capitalist social order, one attempts to build socialism without shunning this pattern, the historical division between workers of the land and defenders of the land will be repeated, leading to class division, the expropriation of many by a powerful minority, exploitation, and capitalism. The administrative class will have the same function that the warrior class once had: it will become an aristocracy and will force a system of bondage upon the people who put their trust in it. It would only take a very short time for it to become an end in itself.

Currently, the magistrates are entirely dependent on the power of the landowners and the owners of the means of production. The state diligently attempts to constrain the competition of the capitalists within administrative confines. At the same time, capitalists unite in a transnational federation in order to free themselves from the regulations of the centralist state. The greater their power to oppress the working class, the more determined the state's legislative and executive bodies are to limit their focus to the justice system, the police force, and tax collection, as well as to safeguarding their own domination of the dispossessed. The expropriation of private owners would channel the labor output in ways beneficial to the state, but it would not diminish the dependency of the workforce on the exploiting powers. It would do nothing more than eliminate the dependency of the state on anything but its own power interests. State administration, the magistrate, and the governing apparatus in general would become bigger and bigger and—since any form of domination has the tendency to become static, frozen, and permanent—would direct all activity of both its means of propaganda and of violence toward the goal of making authority appear as the true benefactor of society. At the end of this path lies the heredity of bureaucracy that inevitably implies the reproduction of exploitative relationships for the benefit of an upper class, i.e., the complete restoration of private capitalism, only with a new group of owners and a different face for deceiving the masses. Marxism represents, both in the state structure and in its own organizations, the strictest form of centralism. It fights against the authority of the current state not because the current state denies people self-determination, but because its authority does not encompass the ruling class as well.

We are faced with the following facts: capitalism needs the state only insofar as the state undermines self-determined decisions on the part of the workers. In order to fulfill this role, the state has been equipped with far-reaching powers. The laws of the state serve to protect the capitalist institutions and are formulated in a way that, on paper, applies to the members of both social classes. With the development from individualistic capitalism to corporate forms of exploitation that reach far beyond state borders, some of these laws have become too narrow for the members of the propertied class. This is why the propertied class demands a liberalization of state laws with respect to themselves, but a strengthening of state laws with respect to the members of the dispossessed class, which can be more effectively controlled as a result of recent technological developments. As far as the increase of its powers over the majority is concerned, the state is content; however, it will resist losing power with respect to the privileges of the ruling class, as long as the entire state structure has not been adapted to the needs of transnational and corporate capitalism. It is this transformation that establishes the fascist state.

The centralist socialists take the state's side in its efforts not to relinquish any of its powers. At the same time, they attack it, because it gives in to the demands of the propertied class every step of the way. Since we are looking at a model case of capitalist expression here, the economic conditions really do determine consciousness. The socialists believe that the ruthless expansion of authoritarian power over the poor has its origin in the state's weakness toward the rich, not in the nature of state authority itself. They turn against authority not because it is authority, but because they want a different kind of authority—one made up of people who share their opinion, of people who, as leaders of parties or trade unions, have become accustomed to governing in centralist ways, to giving orders, to demanding discipline and obedience, to oppressing people while convincing them that they are being oppressed for their own good. Since the state socialists are used to authority and discipline, to centralist control, and to the abdication of individual will, and since they have been trained to believe in the state and in leaders, they will be model citizens for state capitalism.

State capitalism lacks all of the qualities of socialism; there will be neither equality nor justice, neither self-responsibility nor mutuality. A generalized bureaucracy will oppress all human activity from above. A state will be established that has nothing more in common with true community than any other state that has ever existed. It will carry all the seeds necessary for an economy based on class division and exploitation.

What makes the state a state and what essentially makes all states the same, regardless of any superficial differences, remains in any socialist state as well: the replacement of the immediate connection between people by the transfer of power to some so that they can rule over others. The absence of power in social organization is the crucial criterion of anarchy, or, to put this negative explanation in positive form: anarchism does not fight for a certain kind of power—it fights for human self-determination and self-management. By "power" we understand any kind of authoritarian claim or capacity that divides humans into those who govern and those who are governed. The exact form of government is irrelevant. Monarchy, democracy, and dictatorship are only different forms of centralized oppression of people. They all establish states. Democracy claims that it allows everyone to participate in public administration by casting a vote. However, we have to remind ourselves that universal suffrage has nothing to do with equal rights. The selection of representatives implies that voters *do not* participate in the administration, but that they delegate a circle of rotating rulers. Where there are privileges of property, universal suffrage can never create true equality. Nor can true equality be created where self-determination is replaced by awarding privileges of power. Power always rests on economic dominance. If economic dominance is abolished without power being simultaneously abolished, those in power will soon seek to again defend their position by means of economic domination.

Lawmakers, no matter how temporary their position, feel elevated above those who have to accept their decisions. This applies to presidents, ministers, and parliamentarians alike. Even if they do not come from an upper class (with different needs and goals), their administrative role will separate them from the people they administer. We can observe this in the centralized workers' associations. A bureaucratic leadership receives the privilege of determining the guidelines for the behavior and the obligations of the rest. The result is power and authority. The interests of the leaders of the organization become very different from the interests of the rank and file. The administration of the organization becomes an end in itself. The needs of the organization will always be more highly valued than the tasks for which the organization was originally founded.

It lies in the nature of power not only to defend itself by any means, but also to materially and ideologically strengthen itself; indeed, to make its expansion and consolidation the only purpose of its activities. There is no innate lust for power in human beings or social animals. The belief that natural law condemns humans to compete for a place on the bright side of life is nothing but the result of thousands of years of privilege and disenfranchisement. Only humans have developed this belief. They forget that there was no bright side and no dark side of life before humankind was divided into two classes. There can be no power (*Macht*) where there is no lack of power (*Ohnmacht*). Those who desire power can only attain their goal if they take away power from others. The greatest power in history up to this point is the power developed by capitalism. However, it is not the purpose of boundless and uncontrolled accumulation of capital to provide a comfortable life for the capitalist. People can live in wealth and indulge in luxury without individuals taking possession of enormous assets, of vast lands, of mines, of entire industries. The big capitalist gathers his goods not for a comfortable life; to the contrary, a lot of painful work goes into the maintenance and expansion of his capital, although he knows that his lifestyle will not change a bit if he gets even richer, and although every augmentation of his riches demands even more effort.

The capitalist also knows that if the land is worked in a just and natural way in socialism, with the consumptive needs of all taken into account, no one will experience a lack of goods or of pleasure, including himself. If it is worked in a socialist way, the land can provide riches for everyone. We are fighting for communist anarchy to abolish poverty, not wealth. The capitalist makes himself rich by making others poor. His motivation for accumulating capital is not greediness; it is the lust for power. The greater the number of people he impoverishes, the greater the number of people who will have to obey him. The poorer someone is, the more dependent he is; and the more dependent he is, the easier it is to oppress him. This is why it makes no difference for the worker whether his labor is purchased by a private entrepreneur, by a corporation, or by the state. By denying him the product of his labor, power is created, making him dependent. In order to exercise power, the state requires his poverty in the same way as did the private entrepreneur. The power of the state, however, is the most dangerous of all, because it claims to be the expression of the common will and to use the products of the workers' labor for the common good. The truth is that these riches only serve to perpetuate the state, i.e., the power of authority that requires the powerlessness of the masses. Anarchism has realized that power, no matter who it is exercised by and no matter for what genuine or alleged purpose, implies exploitation, and that the state and centralism, even if defended by socialist rhetoric, are institutions of power, and hence also imply exploitation. Therefore, it is anarchism's objective to destroy power as a part of social life, which means radically destroying any state, no matter its form, and replacing it with a federative community of human beings with equal rights.

We often hear the objection that the destruction of power itself requires authority and hence the exercise of power. Those who raise this objection confuse things. The terms *power, coercion,* and *violence* mean very different things. Equating and mixing them has led to fatal consequences even within anarchist ranks. Violence is a means of struggle, and does, in its essence, not differ from other such means, for example persuasion, deception, or civil disobedience. The claim that the anarchist idea is irreconcilable with a struggle that implies the use of physical force or its technical enhancement by weaponry is a random distortion of the anarchist idea. Those who do not feel comfortable using violence in a struggle do not have to use it. However, this is a question of personal taste; it has nothing to do with anarchism. Since anarchism calls for struggle, it cannot create a hierarchy of the forms that the struggle might take, nor can it draw a line beyond which it refuses to struggle. The same goes for coercion. The use of coercion does not pose a general contradiction to the anarchist idea. Once an opponent has been forced to the ground in a struggle, he must not be allowed to get back up. Asocial elements have to be forced to adapt to the necessities of communal life. This, however, requires coercion. Violence and coercion only become unacceptable from an anarchist perspective when they serve authority. This is from where the superficial equation of "power," "coercion," and "violence" derives. The state claims a monopoly on violence by virtue of its power. Anarchism is against state violence and state coercion, because it is against state power. However, in order to think clearly, we have to distinguish: *violence* is an act of struggle, a mere means to achieve a purpose; *coercion* is control as a means of struggle and as a means of securing the struggle's objective; *power* is a permanent condition of violence and coercion for oppressing the desire for equality, it is the oppressive monopoly of coercion and violence implemented from above. Hence, power signifies the actual reality that comes with any centralist, authoritarian, legislative, and statist relationship.

Power uses the internalized human belief in the necessity of *authority* as its moral justification. Authority is the surrender of one's own decision-making abilities to someone else. The claim to authority therefore demands of people to give up their own opinions and to blindly follow a ready-made package of ideas, rules, and principles. By accepting authority, one abandons critical thought and individual will and subjugates oneself to external doctrines and regulations.

It is self-evident that power would never be tolerated if the human spirit had not already been made susceptible to the impact of authority. Wherever authority appears, power can be established. Once power is established, authority finds it easy to emerge everywhere. The lust for power is what distinguishes humans most clearly from animals, whose communal organization follows nature and not power relations they themselves have established. Ever since some human beings first handed power over to others and granted them the right to be rulers, i.e., ever since privilege entered human communities and the craving for power became the most important factor in the formation of social relationships, the belief in authority has been instilled in those who are to be ruled. Authority rests on the infiltration of the soul, on the manipulation of the spirit, which chooses belief and trust over reflection and judgment. Once people make this choice and no longer question even that which is most improbable and irrational, they will obey without resistance, even if ordered to do things that are directly opposed to their own interests.

The oldest and most tested way to induce a belief in authority is to cite metaphysical, divine powers whose orders humans have to follow and whose judgment they must accept. The original sense of right and wrong would never allow an attack against human self-determination. The consciousness that true social law can only be built on equality and mutuality would render any exercise of power by some humans over others impossible. To cite supernatural, heavenly creatures as creators and masters of all things was therefore the only way to insert notions of authority, privilege, and obedience into the natural minds of the people. They were told that their actions did not need to be justified in their own eyes, but only in the eyes of these gods. Once a belief in divine power was established, a belief in worldly power could also be established. All that was required was the claim that the gods had transferred some of their authority to earthly representatives, blessed with special privileges and the duty to watch over other people's behavior. This established the authority of the priests and opened the door to all other forms of authority.

Priests understood the human soul. They knew that the reason for the natural rejection of authority lies in genuine self-esteem requiring self-determination and equal rights. They knew that self-esteem could only be broken by fear. Hence, fear, usually seen as a weakness, became a virtue with respect to the invisible gods. Once people learned to fear gods, they also learned to fear priests, kings, laws, and property; they allowed others to rule them.

Apart from self-esteem, humans' innate sense of justice also needed to be broken in order to establish authority and power. The sense of justice was broken by rejecting equal rights and mutuality in social life. Since authority requires inequality and dependency, the original meaning of right and wrong needed to be distorted. This is the origin of sin, a notion detached from society and solely connected to divinity. *To do wrong* means to violate the human community; *to sin* means to violate the divine and the priestly authority. While violating the human community actually threatens its existence, the concept of sin is nothing but a means to justify the authority of those who want to control human souls. They need to instill a sense of guilt in the believers, because only terrified souls submit to heavenly claims of power. The priesthood depends on humans' guilty consciences. The threat of punishment after death and the surveillance of the most secret of thoughts and desires guarantee that people will always fear to disappoint divine expectations even when their social conduct is at its most righteous. It is inherent in authority to disregard all moral duties demanded by social conscience. Authority needs to bring human conduct entirely under the control of principles that lie outside of personal convictions. Otherwise, no authority could ever morally justify its violation of the principle of equality.

It is social conscience that distinguishes between right and wrong. The criterion is the regard or disregard for equal rights. Authority, on the other hand, distinguishes between what is allowed and what is forbidden. There is no criterion for this distinction available to the oppressed. It is the gods and the priests—and the dukes, the princes, the aristocrats, the leaders of all kinds—who decide. It is they who command, forbid, blame, punish, tax, and abuse. Law replaces self-determination, belief replaces judgment, obedience replaces responsibility, meekness replaces courage, and the fear of the afterworld replaces the struggle in this world. Social community vanishes, and people accumulate guilt, repent, and make amends, worship and desire power, kill both individuality and society, and betray worldly life in the name of heavenly life. Those who long for heaven after death long for power in life, and those who have power in life refer their victims to the afterlife. As long as people felt related to nature, as long as they created and enjoyed life communally, they knew no central divinity with unlimited authority.

The childish need for adoration gave divine names to stars and natural forces, but the heathens divided the qualities they ascribed to spooks, and hence the authority of the priests was limited to the particular field in which their particular God was worshiped. It was Judaism that centralized divinity. It was Judeo-Christian religion that established power over humankind, that invented the term *Gottesknechtschaft*,[4] and that subjugated thought, feeling, and action to the articles of an authority beyond all doubt or question. This gave the priests representing the all-powerful, all-knowing, and omnipresent God limitless power over the souls of the believers; a power that was completely centralized with the establishment of the church.

It seems unnecessary to explain why anarchism and the belief in a conscious and willful force outside of the individual cannot coexist. The only understanding of religion that could fit into the anarchist worldview is one of individual devotion and submission with respect to humankind and the universe.

When, as sometimes happens, people speak of Christian anarchism, it seems that they mean a rejection of the state and of worldly authority. Yet, they mistrust their own souls enough that they leave open a gateway that allows them to submit themselves to a divine creator and a controlling authority. However, every real or imagined authority implies the abdication of self-responsibility to a power that exercises control, authority, and judgment. It is no surprise that the authority of the state always and everywhere uses the structures of the church to gain moral legitimacy. In turn, the church seeks the protection of its divine authority by the power of the state. Today, there exists freedom of religion as a result of hundreds of years of struggle by people who rebelled against the oppression of their conscience. Still, freedom of religion does not keep the lawmakers from assuming the authority of Judeo-Christian monotheism and from providing it with special protection. Even in the countries where technology and science have made the greatest advances, the libertarian struggle against clerical doctrine is met with more repression than the libertarian struggle against the state, its laws, and its institutions. Angry accusations, as well as satirical criticism, are met by God and his worldly representatives with state repression and punishment of the most severe kind. Religion claims responsibility for *Seelsorge*,[5] which relates earthly well-being to devotion, to the observance of emotional and behavioral commands, and to the preparation for eternal life after death. By doing so, religion provides the state with the moral foundation that allows it to count on people submitting themselves to its government. It is therefore no contradiction that the state—contrary to the claims of strict materialists—does not exclusively base its laws on the immediate needs of the capitalists. The right to exploitation on the part of the owners of land, estates, and machines is hardly dependent on the punishing of extramarital sex, certain sexual practices, or abortions. In these and similar cases, the state laws simply serve the ambition of the church to control people's most private affairs and to prevent individual independence.

The state strengthens the power of the church by punishing what it calls sins. By doing so, the state expands its own power beyond the borders of public control, the sphere of influence originally assigned to it. The church benefits from the increase of state power in two ways: first, it can rely on the state's physical force when its own apparatus of control does not suffice; second, no power can remain for long if it does not combine the *exercise* of power with the *conferment* of power.

The power of the church allows the power of the state to enter its precincts in order to assert power over the precincts of the state. It thus supplements the power over the souls, which is based on religious influence on the people, with political power, becoming indispensable for the holders of economic power, who open new avenues for the expansion of church authority. For example, they allow the church to take charge of schools, where the youth are educated in the spirit of authority and trained in obedience. This creates a new generation ready to be exploited, while simultaneously being instilled with the lust for power. The state knows that only those who can be masters themselves make good servants; the church, for its part, knows that only those who have a master above them want to be masters.

With the awaking of the lust for power, people created divinity. They submitted themselves to divine domination in order to submit other people to their own domination. In order to keep people submissive, you hand them power over others. This is the most effective way. Submission and domination both lead to material exploitation, and exploitation leads to authority, centralism, and the state. God and the state are the two poles of the power structure that rest on the negation of equal rights, mutuality, and self-responsibility. God and the state—with all their expressions: church, government, judiciary, military, police, bureaucracy, sultans, viziers, governors, qadis, treasurers, custom officials, fakirs, and fat cats—are embodiments of centralized authority. All elements of the federative society of anarchy are directly opposed to these two basic poles of power. The structure of a federative society is entirely and fundamentally different from the structure of authoritarian organization, beginning at the roots.

What are the roots of the state? What is the smallest unit of its authority? It is the family. The family, protected by authority and controlled by a set of general rules, is both the prototype and the symbol of centralism; it is the embodiment of the notion of power, and the immediate model for the church and the state, the original form and epitome of exercised and received authority. The qualities of the family created, maintained, and controlled by the church and the state are upheld by the institution of marriage (certified by the state and blessed by the church), and by patriarchy,[6] which defines the relationship of the family to society, as well as the relationship between family members. Patriarchy is formally sanctioned by a priestly or bureaucratic wedding of two people who have agreed to live together and to have children together. The wedding, no matter whether it is a church wedding or a civil one, introduces public power into the private decision of two people having a sexual relationship. In order to make such an infiltration into the most personal and intimate human desires by authoritarian power acceptable and justifiable, a complete distortion of the natural inclination of self-determination and self-perception was needed. This was achieved by turning morality from a social measure of justice and decent human interaction into a guideline for negotiating power and dependency. Originally, the relationship between the genders, the very beginning of life itself, allowed for no interference of third parties. In order for power to control it, it had to be associated with guilt. So it became a requirement for the priest, the *Seelsorger*, to formulate prescriptions for love. It became possible for the priesthood—and hence the church, the state, and any form of authority—to extend power into spheres where it can never have any meaning for healthy souls. Therefore, sexual desire was linked to guilty pleasure and a guilty conscience. This was needed to ensure that the satisfaction of sexual desire was considered "dirty," unless exercised exactly according to the prescriptions of the religious and worldly authorities.

Life, in its natural course, dispenses pain and pleasure on the basis of the individual's character. The effort and the risk required to secure one's material existence is juxtaposed to the joy derived from creating social values and by the pleasure derived from observing and breathing nature, from absorbing artistic creation, and from the sensual encounter with the opposite sex. Human institutions of power and exploitation have transferred the efforts and dangers implied in the production of goods to the oppressed class—a class whose creative pleasure has been destroyed by the capitalist mode of production, since the worker can neither determine what he produces nor see a final product in his hands due to the division of labor. He does not benefit from his labor in any way and has no influence on the way its products will be used. The joyful experience of nature is markedly diminished for him as a result of unhealthy living conditions, a lack of control over his free time, insufficient nutrition, and the desperate circumstances of life in general. Artistic creations are hardly accessible to him. First, admission to art institutions costs money that the worker does not have. Second, the ruling class has ensured that the best art and the best poetry cater entirely to their own aesthetic demands, which means that they remain alien to the masses. The only human joys that cannot be restricted by the rule of some people over others are love and sex. Natural pleasure remains unaffected by legal division. This is why the soul itself needs to be infiltrated and beset by a guilty conscience. This is the only means for eradicating self-determination and implementing bureaucratic control, power, and authority in the only area of life where the poor can feel happiness and bliss.

With the help of the unquestionable and inescapable authority of God, people were told that the satisfaction of their sexual desire was only acceptable if it was performed by two married partners for the purpose of procreation. Any other sexual activity was considered illicit. The marital bond is for life and requires the assent and the stamp of the church or the state. Any sexual encounter of men and women outside of wedlock is a punishable act and, should one of the partners be married, sinful adultery. The guarantee of this bond is based on the unnatural elevation of *fatherhood* to a legally protected right. This right is unnatural, because the begetter of a child can only be known to the mother and can never be determined by a third party. Physical similarity or supposed hereditary traits can never count as evidence. The patriarchal family could only be established by granting unrestricted authority to the husband and by keeping the wife and the children in servile dependency. They are forced under a control that renders self-determination disobedient and the pursuit of one's own path dangerous. In order to bring sexual activity under the control of central state administration, the begetter of the children has been equipped with central authority within the family. Mutual surveillance of sexual conduct has become a moral duty for both husband and wife, while children are forced into obedience from the beginning of their lives. With their powerful father as the only role model, they develop the desire to acquire power themselves at an early age.

In no other area of life has the deadening of natural instincts succeeded to the degree it has in the realm of sexuality. Even among adherents of anti-authoritarian doctrines, one frequently encounters the tendency to deny self-determination, individual responsibility, and equality within the family. Jealousy is regarded as an inborn emotion, and therefore vindicated; it is said to be naturally tied to love, hence providing a moral justification for the husband's exclusive sexual demands. Such claims express nothing but complete entanglement in the authoritarian notions that have been used by the church, by the state, and by educational institutions for thousands of years to control people's minds. Those who claim an exclusive sexual right over another person demand the surrender of that person's sovereignty; they want to be slaveholders, possessors of another human being. Those who accept another's exclusive claim over one's body, surrender their sovereignty in all fields of life, and become slaves of another person. However, if you can be a slaveholder or a slave in one area of life, you can be a slaveholder or a slave in any area of life.

Jealousy is the envy of property directed at another person's feelings of love. Envy is usually declared the most pathetic of human qualities, insofar as it applies to goods which wealth denies to poverty. When it threatens the inequality in the distribution of material property, envy is considered a disgrace. The envy, however, which selfishly begrudges another person's self-determination in the most private affairs, is crowned with the halo of love and revered everywhere; even the most oppressed, with their desire to rule and to gain power, cling to it.

There was a time when the patriarchal family was unknown. Before there was a state, before the priesthood and the warrior class established privilege and power, there were matriarchal rights. Women could choose the father of their children. In those times, sexual jealousy was obviously not considered a good enough reason to take possession of another person. Very gradually—in long transitional phases and out of the unconstrained community of men and women, in which the number of partners and the duration of their relationships was left to the discretion of everyone involved—the family arose. At first, the mother admitted the father of her children into the household. Then, clan marriages were arranged, in which men and women of one kin were available to one another. Finally, patriarchy appeared, closely connected to the rise of property privileges. With the spread of the Jewish religion, which so clearly expresses patriarchal authority, the institution of patriarchal marriage, so well suited to the centralist notions of the church and the state, attained the consecration of sanctity.

Communist anarchism is utterly inconceivable as a social reality unless the authoritarian power relations of the family are shunned and removed as the foundation of the state and of any kind of centralism and exploitation. If two people want to share their lives, then it is a matter of their own agreement. As soon as this agreement spawns a mutual, unilateral, or entirely exclusive property right, an intimate power relationship is established that will inevitably affect others negatively; first and foremost, those who are sexually desired by one of the partners. Power is a plague that affects everything it touches, that creates dependency, which, in turn, creates inequality and, finally, authority and exploitation. Anarchist morality must therefore rest on the uncompromising acceptance of all sexual conduct, without external influence, between responsible adults. What two people do to please one another can never be immoral. Only the interference of a third person in their agreement can.

No human being, man or woman, is constituted by nature to be sexually attracted to only one individual throughout their lifetime. Sexual desire cannot be controlled without becoming tainted, and it cannot be prohibited or limited without becoming stunted. Jealousy ensures sexual exclusivity only among people under the spell of power. Among independent people who are not susceptible to authority, it destroys the freedom of conduct and usually causes the opposite of what is intended. All love rests on mutuality. Mutuality is not threatened by those who have multiple sexual partners; mutuality is threatened by those who make claims to exclusivity. General rules and moral laws cannot be deduced from relationships between humans that are based on desire, no matter whether they intend to satisfy a common momentary urge or to share a common household.

Issues of sexuality have not the slightest thing to do with morality, as long as neither violence nor abuse, neither economic dependency nor the seduction of children or of people deprived of their free will reduces the sexual act to a mere act of power, destroying the mutuality of partners with equal rights and affecting society in negative ways. The religious commandments and, following in their tracks, the state laws have made sexual behavior, which from a social perspective seems an unlikely means of power, the foundation of public morality. They have accustomed the people to understand morality as a process of submitting one's sensual needs to prescribed limitations. Only thus was it possible to establish the authoritarian marriage, i.e., the forced lifelong commitment to the family, as the undisputed model for the organization of private life. Patriarchal power in the home gave moral consecration to priestly power in the church, governmental power in the state, and capitalist power in the economy. It cannot, therefore, be protected enough. The difference between the right of oriental men to marry as many women as they please and the Christian and European principle of monogamy is one of degree only, not one of essence. Polygamy is only allowed to the man. It is the most blatant expression of unlimited patriarchal authority in the family and protects the man in his sexual life from any interference within his domain. In monogamy, the woman is just as subjugated to the man's command, though. Both state law and church law assign the wife the role of obedient servant and willing satisfier of sexual needs. This continues to this day. The difference is that the prohibition from keeping more than one marital slave also places the husband under sensual restrictions. His godliness within the family is limited in this one area, and, more importantly, the wife acquires a fraction of power herself and indulges in the pride of at least be allowed to exercise some authority. This helps to ensure that she will raise her children in the spirit of authority, while submitting herself to the authority of the husband, the church, and the state.

Not officially marrying changes the character of a family only if the traditional morality of a mutual power relationship is not perpetuated in other ways. Every relationship based on dutiful obedience, on the denial of self-determination, and on the prohibition of extramarital affairs, carries all the essential characteristics of centralist, authoritarian organization. The husband, the father of the family, possesses almost unlimited authority, which is bestowed upon him by the public authorities. He has the right of corporal punishment over wife and children, he represents them before the agencies of the state, he oversees the property, and he determines the place of residence. No law stands in his way if he exploits his wife and his children economically. The only thing that he must not do is to extinguish his family members' lives. The state reserves that right for itself. After all, it needs a workforce to be able to oppress the masses. Family law ensures that the man who is bound everywhere can bind others in his most immediate surroundings. This helps to distract him from his own submission, which he is sometimes not even conscious of. He gains a taste for centralism, since he himself exercises central power. Since the human desires for self-responsibility and mutuality can never be entirely extinguished, the man is granted a small sphere, in his home, where he can act out these desires—even if the mutuality that is possible in this sphere is nothing more than the mutual policing of husband and wife. The godliness of the parents with respect to their children is anchored in the morality prescribed by the church and the state. It becomes useful to capitalism thanks to inheritance law.

The close-knit family unit also breeds a pride of kin, which causes this miniature model of the state to compare itself with other family units and to enter into economic competition with them. Thus, the development of any federative community is prevented at the roots; the striving for equal rights is undermined by the competition for dominance; the borders between the common victims of a greater power are reinforced; the idea of hostile segregation, without which no centralist power can exist, becomes rooted in the private power interests of the individual. By self-righteously and jealously retreating with one's clan members to an enclosed fortress, from where one fights against other clans, the authoritarian family fulfills its true function, namely to instill in the youth the principle of the state, its will to power, its enmity toward other states, and its desire for conquest, suppression, and exploitation of the peoples beyond the state borders; in other words, *nationalism*.

A nation is *Völkerschaft*,[7] a spatially connected community of human beings who belong together by virtue of common living conditions, language, and customs. The concepts of a "nation" and of a "people" are approximately equivalent, insofar as they are simply used for distinguishing groups of humanity gathered in different lands. "Nationality" means "belonging to a people." None of these words contain anything more than a distinguishing characteristic, none express any measurable quality. Only with the division of the people into classes, with their subjugation to the estates of warriors, priests, landowners, and capitalists, did the nation become an oppressive structure with a supposed moral value. Today, "nation" mainly serves as the ceremonial label for the state—a term of pure power. Nationalism is the ideology that holds one's own state above all others. The alleged moral superiority of its people allows the state to expand its borders, to impose its laws and moral doctrines upon other people, and to exploit their labor. Nationalism is the romanticization of the state, the transference of authoritarian family morality onto the peoples.

In the patriarchal family, elevated to a legally protected social institution, power hides behind sentimental concepts such as chastity, love of one's own, and bonds of blood—all things, which may or may not exist, but which never derive from legal prescription. Along the same lines, nationalism declares power to be a moral principle and elevates the authoritarian apparatus of those who control the means of labor, namely the state, to its mighty carrier. For the sake of the state—whether labeled "nation" or "people"—the notion of humankind is eradicated from people's consciousness, and the priority of the interests of a people united in state borders and ruled by a centralized regime replaces the demand for equal rights for all.

Subsequently, the claim to subordinate, to dominate, and to enslave the other peoples is proclaimed; violence, war, even the extermination of populations outside of the national borders become an obligation; cruelty, malice, slander, arson, the betrayal of all inborn social sentiments are passed off as bravery and national rights; finally, every power advantage favoring one's own state is consecrated.

It is certainly true that all wars, all expansions of state borders, and all national claims are aimed at material benefits. But here, as everywhere else, the objective of power takes precedence over all material objectives, and the domination of people by people is the motivating factor of all oppression, even if economic superiority remains an indispensable means for attaining power. Proof of the priority of the lust for power—compared to the mere lust for enrichment—is the fact that one can *always* appeal to the national sentiment in times of a weakened power structure or of an alleged insult to "national honor" (which stands for nothing but prestige, control, and authority) and be successful. The masses ready to battle for the nation can hardly ever expect any material gains, and the promise of a profitable reward is only a small factor in recruiting them. It is the spiritual value of their membership in the nation that is stressed. The authoritarian principle they know so well from the family and the church is elevated to a frenzy of national power. Each individual's pride is enhanced, since each individual can see himself as a part of an all-important authority. Thus, the lust for power is reduced to an ideal common denominator for exploited people, the spatially demarcated state territory elevated to a religious value in their imagination, the centralized government dressed in priestly clothes, as if it were not the executive organ of capitalist power, but instead the symbol of an awe-inspiring creative power. At the same time, the exploitative upper classes have an agreement beyond all national boundaries to preserve their property. They make agreements that consolidate their power by means of profit and wealth, uninhibited by any nationalism. Theirs is *pure* power. The upper classes' power agreements extend over all economic spheres, including the manufacture of the weapons of war, which keep alive the national lust for power among the people when they are busy killing each other. The idea is to make the people comply to real authority by providing them with imagined authority. Nationalism, i.e., the arrogance that rests on belonging to a certain people or state, has the same source as any feeling of self-worth that derives from external circumstances rather than from personal achievement and social conduct: authority demands unquestioned recognition in order to exercise power and to bestow authority and apparent power upon others to prevent the notion of power itself being questioned.

The Jewish doctrine of "God the Father" places the solitary, just, all-powerful, omnipresent, and menacing God over humankind. He is beseeched in endless prayer, honored, and assured of adoration and gratitude, even in times of torment and humiliation. For Western peoples this doctrine provided the prerequisite for accepting the patriarchal family with the godlike position of the master ruling over his own. The same authoritarian model has secured the people's subjugation to a centralist governing power, their renunciation of individual responsibility, self-determination, and equal rights for the state with its nationalist ideology. God-father, father, fatherland–people are made to comply. Natural social connection, which neither ends at the door of someone's house nor at the borders of a country, is disregarded. Instead, arrogance is groomed by ridiculing all religious teachings other than your own, by deifying your family with all its ancestors and idiosyncrasies, by sanctifying your own nation, and by displaying hostility toward other peoples in the name of moral obligation.

It is the predicament of the Jews that they, who have introduced authority as the highest form of life over humankind, must feel the effects of their doctrines in the harshest ways. They have brought monotheism, the belief in *only one* God, into this world, the God-given authority of the father, and, as a logical consequence, the nationalist formula of "God's chosen people." Whoever speaks of a fatherland, speaks in a Jewish manner, for he embraces the glorification of one nation, namely his own. He counts himself among the chosen people. From this, he derives the right to hate, to despise, and to assault other peoples. The Jews, themselves formerly a centrally-organized nation with a confined territory and now scattered across all countries, are pursued, insulted, slandered, and abused as intruders, enemies, and foreigners by nationalists, i.e., by fanatical descendants of their spirit, though of a different stock. The natural conscience of justice is destroyed by alleged national and racial superiority. To have the same ancestry, the same family tree, the same place of residence, and the same master suffices to form a community that despises the descendants of other ancestors and the slaves of other masters.

After everything that has been said so far, there is no need for further explanations of why anarchism is incompatible with national or racial hierarchies. Anarchy means a human society with a federative structure that brings with it the international extension of all connections, including emotional ones. The organization of labor and of communal living from the bottom up rests on the cultivation of the individual who unites with other individuals who share the same ambition. Within a single language group, this implies camaraderie, community, economic alliance, and intellectual exchange. Within the world community, it implies scientific, artistic, technical, athletic, and international associations. The individual derives his values from within himself in order to be judged according to the quality of his character and his work in the social context.

The color of the ancestors' hair, eyes, and skin; the question whether someone was born on this or that side of the river; the question whether his language and his customs were shaped by these or those historical, geographic, and climatic circumstances–all these aspects can only be used as standards of judgment of human values by those who crave and obey power. Here, the urge to establish boundaries prevails, in order to give all human organizations a pyramidal form, with everything coming together at a peak. This ensures centralization and command from above, connected to hostile competition with neighborly organizations and their centralist peaks.

Naturally, there exists an intimate connection of humans with the earth in spirit and soul, but only where labor and life grow directly from the soil. Only the peasant still maintains an intimate contact with the land that makes the land a part of him, while he, in turn, feels himself to be a part of the land he works. Therefore, the peasant has a love of home (*Heimatliebe*)—but no consciousness of the state (*Staatsbewusstsein*). The conflation of the terms *home* and *fatherland* belongs to the deceptive tricks that the centralists use to confuse all natural thought. The "fatherland" is an imagined ideal without spiritual substance, rationally applied to a demarcated territory whose unity rests solely on common laws proclaimed by a centralist government—maybe dictatorially, maybe democratically, but in any case tailored to the prevalent power relations and property rights. The borders of this territory can change, and the powerful constantly want to expand them to expand their power. The idea of the fatherland advances this purpose. This is why it has been instilled in the minds of people prepared for the reception of authoritarian ideas by the traditions of religion and the family. There is no natural attachment to a fatherland. It has been artificially produced, expressing a craving for recognition. The same is true for developing a consciousness of the state. It instills the alleged necessity of the state and helps those who control it. There can be no attachment to a fatherland that is not nourished by hostility toward other fatherlands.

The education of the youth is shaped from an early age by the alleged superiority of their own nation. One's own country is presented as the only fatherland that is historically destined to sway power. The spirit of submission to authority, cultivated by the church and the family, is supplemented by the illusion that belonging to a certain people, citizenship in a certain nation, justifies ruling over other people. Such national arrogance becomes a moral duty. Every state tries to use it to solidify its own power; every race presents itself as the chosen one, worthy of privilege, and nobody is allowed to choose another nation over his own. This causes hostility between peoples, benefitting the maintenance of the state and the notion of authority itself. People do not believe what they understand to be right on the basis of independent judgment, but what they have been told to believe.

Love of home has nothing to do with the worshiping of a fatherland. The preachers of the fatherland evoke the "love of home," because humans connected to nature need such phrases to be seduced into embracing unnatural concepts. Every human being who has been shaped by his natural environment and its climate feels a love of home. Every animal that has not been torn from its natural surroundings feels a love of home, without it ever turning into some kind of feeling for a "fatherland" or wishing for its expansion or for fenced and protected borders. An animal without a home will have no love of home, only a *longing* for a home. It is no different among humans. Can a child who grows up poorly nourished in an airless basement cherish his childhood home? Can he long for these conditions once he is removed from them? Is not this the true criterion for "love of home"? Those who had no home in their youth, or whose home did not bring them joy, have no home they can feel love for either.

You cannot oblige people to love, and hence you cannot oblige people to love a home. Still, there is an effort to convince people who have never developed any true feeling for a home that there exists a "fatherland" that deserves devotion, love, heroism, and blood sacrifice. This shows the degree to which the distortions of authoritarian mania have been able to deform the human soul.

The peasant has love of home because he has a real home—at least as long as he has not been alienated from his natural senses by being exploited and indebted by large landowners and the state. A specific piece of land enfolds him, nourishes him, and is familiar to him—in times of trouble, as much as in times of happiness. His work is one with his personal life, his piece of land is his nest; nature, expressed in the particular landscape of the region, is his estate. The success or the failure of his existence depends on it. The peasant does not see himself as the owner of his land, but rather as its keeper. He takes care of it with people who are not his subordinate family, but helpers connected to him by mutual commitment. Unfortunately, the priesthood has been able to instill the spirit of authority in the peasantry. Since peasants are stubborn, the principles of marital bondage and patriarchy are strong. Furthermore, they have been tied cunningly with family and inheritance law. In other words, the renewal of the world will meet with substantial resistance among the peasantry. Still, it is not the least approachable terrain for communist anarchism, but rather its most fertile ground!

With the exception of brief periods, during which the peasantry was exposed to heavy political propaganda, it was never susceptible to nationalist poison. And even during those times, when it was demanded that they cast their votes for one party or the other, only a relatively small number of peasants were open to influence. It is indeed the deeply rooted connection with their home that saves them from the embrace of the fatherland. Those in power try to convince them that their home expands over the entire territory that is under the state's control and that they have to love this territory as much as they love their own land. The geographical range of this love, of course, has to change according to the borders drawn up after the end of a war. However, the peasants do not feel any particular connection to people who might live within the same nation-state borders, but with whom they have no daily contact. Consequently, they do not hate or have contempt for strangers either, as long as the latter do not insinuate themselves into their lives in harmful ways; whether these strangers live on this side of a mountain chain or on the other matters as little as their color of skin, the shape of their heads, or their ancestry.

The peasants' nature rebels against anything that threatens their self-determination in the sphere of work, everything that tries to replace their mutual communication with authoritarian orders. They rebel against the interference of central powers in their affairs, against bureaucracy and officialdom. They choose the village over the state and contracts over law. Every peasant is an anarchist without knowing it, and hence communist anarchism is most likely to be realized by the peasants. The peasants of all countries and regions keep their natural will alive, despite all attempts by the powerful to eradicate it. This natural will includes the conviction that everyone shall work on the basis of equal rights according to his abilities and that everyone shall consume according to his needs. The peasantry has no consciousness of the state and will never have one either, because it has the consciousness of its own power, i.e., the consciousness of individuality and of a federative, cooperative community of individuals managing their own social affairs. Anarchy will find its place in the countryside first, because the countryside has never stopped living and producing in anarchy.

To live and to produce in anarchy means to create an *order of freedom*. Thus is the realization of the anarchist idea: there is no order without freedom; state, centralism, authority, and power are not only incompatible with freedom, they are also incompatible with all true order based in lively social *Geschehen*.[8]

What we have tried to define as the essence of federalism above can be considered to be the organization of libertarian order in general. In daily life, we understand by order the maintenance of common principles in social interaction. Where centralism, i.e., the regulation of things according to authoritarian orders, reigns, the principles of social interaction are subjugated to the fluctuating interests of power; there is nothing "common" about them. The interaction of creative forces, the only characteristic of lively order, is replaced by mechanical business and degenerates into duties of forced labor without any sense of social connection. Lack of social connection is the opposite of order. It means subjugation, discipline, chastity, lack of freedom, and servitude. An ordered society is based on a united human will to fulfill communal tasks. It requires equality, mutual commitment, and everyone's individual responsibility. In brief, order in the anarchist sense can only derive from the self-determination of those who want to keep order. Self-determined order is the same as social freedom.

Freedom is the epitome of all anarchist thought and will. We are anarchists for freedom's sake, we are socialists and communists for freedom's sake, we fight for equality, mutuality, and self-responsibility for freedom's sake, and we are internationalists and federalists for freedom's sake. Still, so far I have consciously avoided speaking of freedom in this sketch of the anarchist worldview. The reason is that the will to freedom is so genuine and so deeply rooted in the human soul that no political doctrine, no matter how authoritarian, can operate without evoking the idea and without claiming to establish it. All states, democratic as well as fascist and bureaucratic ones, claim freedom when they implement laws, go to war, or repress ideas. All revolutions happen because people feel that the lack of freedom has become unbearable. Their rebel yells are always for freedom. But so far all revolutions have been lost, or have lost their way, because the desire for freedom has remained unfulfilled. No party that has ever led a revolution, that has placed itself at the forefront of the revolution and above the people, went further than to promise the eradication of the current restrictions on freedom. Its followers never get to know in any concrete terms what the trumpeted freedom will look like. In the best case, certain freedoms will lead to improvements in certain areas of life—but this is different from a completely free society.

Freedom cannot be granted. Freedom has to be taken and lived. Nor is freedom a sum of freedoms, but a universal social order that has eradicated authority. There cannot be a free society if each individual is not free. Likewise, individuals cannot be free if society is not free, if there is centralization, a state, and power. The freedom of anarchy is the free association of free individuals to form a free society. Free is the individual who acts freely, who does everything that he does because he considers it necessary or desirable. The requirement to allow each individual to do that is a society without privilege of power or property. All property and all power create dependency and hence render free decisions and free actions impossible. In short, they are incompatible with true freedom. Hence, the individualists are wrong when they say that every human being has the right to be free, but that this right ends when it clashes with that of another person. As long as the right to individual freedom is in any way limited, there is no social freedom. If we equate the terms "free" (*frei*) and "voluntary" (*freiwillig*[9]), the freedom of one human being cannot be restricted by the freedom of another. Otherwise, the act that restricted the freedom of a fellow human being would constitute privilege and there would be power and subjugation. Those who want to exercise privilege and power are dependent on the obedience of others; in other words, they do not act independently. This also confirms the complete unity of society and the individual, and the legitimacy of the claim that no one can be free without everyone being free.

What remains is the objection that human beings cannot be free, because most of them are unable to take matters into their own hands and need a *leader*. To begin with, if certain human beings lack the ability to take matters into their own hands, then this is the result of authoritarian indoctrination, of power exploiting both the human soul and human labor. Aside from that, it is self-evident that people have different talents and that everyone needs advice from others in certain areas of life. To interpret this as proof for a natural restriction of freedom only shows that under the influence of authoritarian education, people have lost all belief in freedom. Their only desire is power.

We anarchists despise leadership that is based on institutionalized authority; this means every form of state government, bureaucracy, and party administration, every dictatorship, and every oligarchy. We do not, however, deny the usefulness of a stage director, a chairperson at a meeting, or a captain on a ship. In all these cases, certain tasks are assigned to certain people on the basis of their individual qualities. The same applies to political struggles, to uprisings, or to the defense against armed attacks. Every group of wandering animals follows one animal that takes the lead—not because it was elected to do so, but because it takes that position confidently and is trusted by others. As soon as it is worn out, it will be replaced. It is the same with humans. There are talented speakers and agitators, and people will listen to them because they are able to formulate the will of the people in particularly apt ways or because they are the most determined in action. Leaders are those who set examples, not those who implement laws or who pull others around on a leash.

Leadership is a question of the moment and has no claim to permanency. The momentary abdication of decision-making and self-determination does not exclude freedom, as long as it is a voluntary decision and does not imply general servitude.

To act freely and voluntarily is the foundation of all anarchist values. There is no freedom without equality, and there are no equal rights without freedom. Voluntary action in all regards is only possible on the basis of constant awareness and self-responsibility, as well as a constant dedication to mutuality. Mutuality, self-responsibility, self-confidence, and self-determination all require that voluntary decisions be the driving force of life.

Anarchism is the idea of freedom. There can be no freedom where there is exploitation, power, authority, and centralism, where some humans control and command while others obey. The destruction of all authority, of all privilege, of all property institutions and enslavement can only derive from a libertarian common spirit. The stateless community of free human beings—that is communism. The free association of equal human beings—that is anarchy!

II. The Way of Anarchism

The most important objection to anarchism as a social ideal is the skepticism about it ever being more than an idea, about it being realizable. The purpose of this text is to present the convictions and the demands of anarchists to people who experience lack of freedom as an affliction. It is impossible to foresee how far the anarchist idea will spread and how much ground libertarians will be able to defend against the forces of authority, centralism, and the state. It all depends on whose will is strongest and who has the best means—it has always been like that. It is not numbers that are important, but perseverance, unity, and truthfulness. The means must be tied to the ultimate goal, and they must not lose sight of it.

Communist anarchism is revolutionary in its theory and in its objective. The principles of social freedom cannot be realized on the basis of legal and economic inequality. Anarchy requires the complete transformation of land ownership, social relations, and the administration of work and consumption. Such a complete transformation cannot be achieved gradually. At best, such an attempt will lead to certain improvements within the current social system. Mountains and islands are created by sudden explosions after a long process of restratification underground. Eventually, the obstacles in the way of a landmass at the bottom of the sea or within the earth are pushed aside. Likewise, every new human life begins with a living creature violently demanding exit from his mother's womb, in which he has prepared for his independent existence. In the same vein, a new social order can only become reality through a revolutionary outburst that follows proper prenatal preparation. However, this is not enough under dreadful, miserable, and unbearable conditions. In that case, two steps are necessary: first, the seed of the new society has to be freed from the enclosure of the dominant system, with revolutionaries acting as obstetricians; then, the revolution must be kept alive, must repel all the germs of the old system, and must guarantee the creation of the imagined ideal—this is the much more demanding task.

In the beginning, the way of anarchy is therefore a way of *revolutionary preparation*. Preparing the revolution implies three main elements: 1. Agitation: the rottenness of the current system must be exposed, its overthrow demanded, and the creation of a better system announced. 2. Self-education: after rejecting the current conditions, the determination to change them must be developed. 3. Struggle.

Nothing in anarchist teachings excludes any human being from helping in the preparation of the revolution. People exclude themselves by their behavior. Communist anarchists—and I think I can speak for all of them here—do not believe that a fundamental social transformation can come from those who have established the current system and who benefit from it. It can only come from those who are chained and robbed of their freedom. The struggle against property rights has to be led by those who have no property; the struggle against exploitation and oppression has to be led by those who are exploited and oppressed; the struggle against the privileges of the masters has to be led by the slaves and the underprivileged. Equal rights, mutuality, and self-determination can only be attained in a struggle led by those who suffer as a result of the privileges of others, as a result of authority and as a result of asocial egotism. Liberating society from the state is primarily the task of the class that is suppressed by the capitalist system and its aide, the state; by the class that has been rendered obedient by the authority of the church and school, by social institutions of power like the patriarchal family and monogamy, by becoming accustomed to the centralist organization that produces hostile divisions in all areas of life, by national and racial supremacy, by laws, punishment, taxes, unemployment, hunger, misery, bad air, arrogance, and defamation. Liberation from the state means liberation from class oppression—hence it is the oppressed class that must carry out this struggle. In other words, during the phase of revolutionary preparation, the struggle for communist anarchy must be conducted as a *class struggle*.

The affirmation of the class struggle by communist anarchists is a necessary consequence of the ideals of self-determination and individual responsibility. Dividing society into two classes is a statist and capitalist means of oppressing those who must sell their labor force, i.e., the workers. By taking the struggle into their own hands, the workers affirm their natural right to determine their own lives. The realization that the borders of the state are expressions of the class system was a guiding principle behind the foundation of the First International. State borders breed national prejudices, create artificial hostility between the workers of different countries, and prevent the unity of the exploited. The basic principle of the internationalist proletariat is the commitment to the self-determination of the proletariat in all matters of opinion and decision!

The liberation of the working class must be the task of the workers themselves. Implied in this statement is the commitment to self-responsibility, to equal rights, to mutuality, and to voluntary action. International unity implies the rejection of the state, of centralism, of oppression, and of authoritarian power. It was the infiltration of Marxist doctrines into the class struggle that jeopardized class unity and proletarian internationalism. Under the influence of Marxism, the workers established centralist party and trade union organizations, appointed bureaucrats as workers' representatives, handed the liberation struggle over to higher officials, participated in elections for state parliaments, granted nation-state borders meaning, and even fell for the trap of state socialism. As a result, the worker has become a citizen and his struggle against exploitation has become meaningless, since he supports and strengthens the public apparatus that maintains his exploitation.

This text is not the place for a detailed explanation of the differences between anarchist tactics and Marxist tactics. The task of this text is to provide a general outline of anarchism. In order for the class struggle to be successful, Marxism and anarchism must not be confused. It is the anarchist path that promises success.

Communist anarchists are in no way obliged to organize, but founding an organization is in no way contradictory to anarchism either. Only the foundation of centralist and bureaucratic organizations would pose such a contradiction. It is the most crucial anarchist principle that social life exists only where each individual is entitled to participate in all resolutions and actions. For example, the foundation of self-determined trade unions in order to strengthen the class struggle—the means used by the anarcho-syndicalist movement—must not be questioned. It is not those who join with like-minded comrades in militant economic associations who violate anarchist principles, but those who attack federative workers' organizations because they themselves, for whatever great reason, do not want to join. Indeed, the power of the federative idea is based on the fact that no one has to submit to a program that he has not helped to formulate or that he does not wholeheartedly agree with. The common Marxist accusation that anarchism is split into dozens of different currents and perspectives is not only ludicrous because Marxism is split in at least as many currents, but also—and especially—because comradely unity only becomes possible when the way in which every perspective is presented is as open as the means it employs for its struggle. Quarrels or breaches of contract are by no means necessary consequences. The centralist bureaucracies of the Marxist groups always fight one another bitterly, despite their common ideological foundations, because mutual acceptance would undermine the principle of authority that is so crucial for them. Divisions based on a desire to dominate are always hostile divisions. Federalism stresses neighborly unity. It encourages division with a positive spirit whenever people have different perspectives on specific issues—which only strengthens collaboration in all other areas. True, dispute and conflict can also occur between anarchist groups. But this does not refute federalism. It is simply proof that the legacy of centralism, of lust for power, and of intolerance still besets even the minds of those who, intellectually, have grasped federalism's advantages.

An organization that is built from the bottom up creates various alliances between people. It is an organization that rests on a feeling of togetherness. Alliances form according to perspectives, tasks, and places: houses, streets, municipalities, towns. All of them are completely independent in their decisions, remaining in close contact with similar alliances. There is constant communication regarding the workplace, profession, and ideology among the organization's members, and each member is always available to provide advice to others. The principle of mutuality is the basis of all common action, without ever jeopardizing the self-responsibility of each individual and each group. This creates a web of completely independent, yet intimately intertwined alliances of people united at their workplace, in their neighborhood, or on the basis of shared principles. Mutual influence extends from house to house, from village to village, from precinct to precinct, from province to province, from country to country, from workshop to workshop, from factory to factory, from industry to industry; in short, it is present in all economic and spiritual relationships between the individual and the society, and it brings all participants together in a spirit of comradeship. The anarchist organization must always present a small-scale representation of the libertarian order aspired to.

The following rule applies to all anarchist behavior, not only to anarchist organizing: the way to our goal must lead straight ahead—we must not take any detours
that will cause us to lose sight of our goal. Anarchists have to follow the guiding
principles of equal rights, self-responsibility, social justice, federalism, and complete
independence of will and thought. This applies to all phases of the revolutionary
process and to all stages in the creation of a free communist society. In everything
they do, anarchists keep both the final goal and all of society in mind; every decision
is based on the understanding that the individual and society are materially and
morally united; the individual anarchist, the anarchist alliance, and the association
of anarchist alliances all direct their will toward agitation, education, struggle, and
conduct leading to the realization of stateless socialist freedom; they eliminate
secondary goals and live with the consciousness and the commitment to prove, by
their own example, that a free and just life is possible for future generations.

The anarchist relationship to politics can be deduced from this general principle. To say that anarchists categorically reject the political struggle is a foolish
and malicious allegation. Politics means dealing with public affairs. This means
that the intention to change public affairs, especially if connected with coordinated
efforts to put this intention into practice, is itself politics. Marxists like to portray
anarchists as apolitical, because anarchists reject politics that attempt to introduce
socialism through state administration. Marxists want it to appear that anarchists
are unwilling or unable to struggle. But the anarchist formula for political struggle
has always been the rejection of all politics whose goal is not the immediate and
direct liberation of the working class. This clearly indicates that it is *parliamentary*
politics within the context of the state power structures installed by capital that
are seen as counterproductive by the anarchists, not only because they divide the
representatives from the working class and transform them into a class of their
own, but also because they bolster the state's democratic image by integrating the
opposition. From a socialist perspective, parliamentarism brings no improvement
for the working people; instead, it feeds the proletarian masses the illusion that the
transfer of their own initiative to powerful representatives can replace the necessity
for an independent and responsible struggle—not to mention the fact that the
appointment of parliamentarians, government officials, city councilors, and public
servants solidifies the power of central authority and the proletariat's dependency
on the power structures. The Marxists endorse such politics. Anarchists reject
them, refusing to support the state in any way. Their politics focus on immediate
and determined struggle against the state, the state's institutions, and all forms of
centralist power. This is true for all anti-authoritarian alliances, as well as for all
individual anarchists.

This is not to say that anarchism's means of struggle are limited. It only dispenses with the tools that it has identified as dull. The means that derive directly

from the anarchist worldview are the means of *direct action*. Since capitalist power peaks in the mode of production and in the property rights of the current social order, anarchism favors giving an economic form to the political struggle. The united will of the people, whose hands move the levers of the machines, can bring the entire capitalist apparatus to a halt. There are various ways for this to occur: strike, sabotage that renders labor impossible, boycotts of certain goods, passive resistance of many kinds, such as the exaggerated observance of workplace regulations, exclusion of strikebreakers, intentional bricolage. All these are means that demand sacrifice and dedication. Anarchism does not exclude any means that allow the individual to directly interfere with or to refuse to participate in work that is asocial, that harms society, or that compromises the individual himself. No anarchist should participate in the state's wars, which always pit workers against workers to advance capitalist interests. These wars deride all principles of equal rights, mutuality, and voluntary decision-making; they violate the most basic human feelings and all moral decency; they betray the international unity of the exploited in the name of national interests advanced by exploiters united in international cartels. Even worse, these wars, more than anything else, help to instill the notion of power, the belief in both heavenly and earthly authority, and the instincts of both master and slave into the desires of a degraded humanity.

It is unnecessary to offer a detailed list of all the possible ways of interfering in public affairs based on the principles of self-responsibility and mutuality in the pursuit of freedom. Some examples are the refusal of labor in the barracks, in the prisons, and in the courthouses; in the production of ships and weapons for war, of ammunition for the police force, of journals that spread hostile lies about workers. These are but some of the thousands of ways in which self-help in the political struggle can be exercised when the determination of the individual to take matters into his own hands and the willingness to sacrifice are as strong as his insight and will. If we employ the means of personal intervention in our struggle, the question of whether anarchists should participate in everyday struggles for an improvement of their working conditions within capitalism becomes entirely irrelevant.

The writer of this text shares with a great number of anarchists the opinion that there is no contradiction between a worker using his own power to fight for better pay and shorter working hours, on the one hand, and the demand that he engage in struggles that directly aim at liberation, on the other. The capitalist economy is not strengthened by workers' struggles directed at improving the system and securing their "daily bread." Such struggles are not the same thing as workers' parties entering parliamentary politics. Every strike increases workers' self-esteem, deepens their feelings of unity with their comrades in struggle, and, when successful, eases the material hardships of their lives. Such a success only stops weaklings from continuing to struggle. Free and strong natures will be inspired!

Capitalism is the source of class struggle. If workers refused to struggle because the revolution did not seem immediately attainable, the enemy would be able to go about his business free of any resistance. This would prove fatal, as the enemy would be alone in continuing the class struggle, and the workers would be unprepared when the opportunity to topple the system arose.

Anarchism prescribes no particular method of struggle and rejects none, as long as it accords with self-determination and voluntary decision-making. During violent uprisings, the will of the individual alone determines the quality of his participation. He is free to join groups whose means might be criticized by other libertarians. There are human beings who prefer to stand aside and do nothing but judge and complain during important phases of the struggle, if everything does not go their way. But not everyone is like that. So far, anarchists have almost without exception supported the workers during revolutionary struggles, even if the latter were under the influence of centralist powers and misled by authoritarian promises. In such cases, we could witness the feeling of connectedness, the conscious solidarity among the exploited, the untamable will to fight, the refusal to abandon those who are facing the enemy, and, above all, the desire to instill a libertarian moment into the courage, the sacrifice, and the passion, which achieved wonderful things, even if it the ultimate objective was distorted. Anarchists might "veer from their path" during such times, but they only "betray" the anarchist idea if they hinder the struggle by self-important calls for order. There is no patent on the idea of freedom, and its expression cannot be categorically defined. Freedom is a spiritual value that can be realized whenever force is set in motion. It is the task of anarchists to introduce freedom into every struggle.

The same people who believe that they can accuse anarchists of one-dimensional political activism, because anarchists call electoral politics a waste of time for proletarians and the class struggle, also want to deny anarchists a means that many of them have used in the past: the *violent individual deed*. Marxists condemn it, because it supposedly interferes with the organized revolutionary action of the masses, and because it supposedly provides justification for the counterrevolutionary forces to retaliate, making the entire class pay for the actions of a single individual. It is evident, however, that this is not the true reason for the condemnation of individual assassination, arson, expropriation, and so on. This condemnation is not based on moral concerns: moral concerns play no important role in Marxist considerations. Mass terror as a political means is explicitly sanctioned by these opponents of individual terror. It is the individual initiative of a person who thinks and decides for himself that troubles these authoritarian centralists! They even condemn the self-sacrifice of revolutionaries if their actions were not conceived, ordered, and controlled by a central authority. Our take is this: whenever an individual becomes active in the struggle, he threatens the centralist power of the master, of the priest, and of the father. He proves that effective acts are possible, even if they are not planned and directed from above.

It is dumb to maintain that individual violence is an exclusively anarchist means of agitation—recently, almost all political murders have been committed by nationalists. However, it is equally dumb to believe that individual violence cannot have a place in the class struggle, or that anarchists have reason to distance themselves from violent militants within their own ranks. It is solely the individual who decides what means to employ, and if, on the basis of anarchist conviction, an individual arrives at the conclusion that a violent deed will be beneficial, he ought to be free to commit it. Of course it can subsequently be assessed in terms of effectiveness and success, but it can never be condemned on the basis of class struggle principles.

Anarchism and its doctrine of freedom value the right of the individual too much to deny an aggrieved soul its lust for revenge or a libertarian spirit the belief that an act of agitation, of warning, of intimidation, of defiance, of inspiration is worth confronting the world with a startling deed. The strong anarchist belief in the right of the individual also refutes the Marxist assertion that violence is justified only when it is committed upon central orders. It is exactly this kind of violence that is mechanical, that reduces the hand that commits it to a mere tool and the person who was sent to carry it out to a mere pawn. From an anarchist perspective, only deeds that are committed on the basis of the perpetrators' free will and that have been conceived in their own minds can be morally justified; deeds that have been reflected upon by those who commit them, risking their lives because they are convinced that they act in the spirit of mutuality and brotherly commitment, serving both the idea and the class. It makes no difference whether these deeds are committed by an individual, a group of conspirators, or the masses. The only thing that matters is that each individual remains in control of his own actions and only acts on the basis of decisions rooted in his own reflections and social conscience, not on the basis of obedience or fear of power.

Individual commitment is the anarchist way to the revolution and, at a later stage, the requirement for its victory, and finally the means of establishing the stateless society and the essence of life in communism. The meaning of direct action, of strike, of sabotage, of resistance, of refusal, of individual or conspiratorial deeds is that each individual is involved with body and soul, that everything that happens is based on the free agreement of the actors, that no one follows central orders but only the principle of self-responsibility and individual commitment informed by social spirit. Where the masses are in motion, they have to be *masses of individuals*; otherwise, their motion cannot lead to freedom but only to power for those who lead them.

To hold individuality in high regard does not mean to celebrate leaders; to the contrary, it is the only protection against being misled by them. The centralist workers' parties, like all authoritarian organizations, do not cherish individuality, neither in their leaders nor in the leaders' followers. They try to secure blind adherence. Individuality contradicts this. Individuality means freedom of spirit—this is incompatible with centralism. The authoritarian leaders elevate themselves above the masses not because of superiority in character and spirit, but only because they know how to command; a quality that can only be nursed in people lacking strong individuality. Usually, the leaders of centralist organizations do not become leaders by their own initiative. They are appointed—not even elected—to be leaders, because they have proven capable of uncritically passing on orders from above to those below and of protecting those above from criticism using authoritarian methods. Once they are leaders, they are presented as glorious and impeccable human beings. This is only possible because individuality as a value is completely disregarded.

There is a correlation between the disregard for individuality and the cult of personality. Anarchism rejects any cult of personality, resisting it by stressing individuality. Mutual respect among all people exists where all qualities that are socially useful and that strengthen the individual life force can develop freely and without restriction, and where no individual has to be ashamed of his idiosyncrasies and desires, as long as they do no harm to society. This guarantees mutual esteem—leaving no place for power, deification, servility, personality cults, and domination.

The anarchist struggle can only be a movement of individuals who associate voluntarily. This also answers the question of whether or not the idea of freedom requires a *mass organization* to grow strong. The idea of freedom needs the alliance of all men and women who have recognized the necessity for anarchy as the foundation for social life, and who are determined to realize it in a federation in which the values of individuality, equal rights, and voluntary decision-making are one. The more people unite to pursue this task, the sooner society will be liberated from the state. When all people become anarchists, anarchy will be a reality. A struggle that aims at abolishing the current power structures without establishing new ones must rest on the self-responsibility of every militant, on the mutuality of libertarian ideas, and on the free decisions of each individual.

It is therefore unnecessary to gather as many people as possible into an organization, regardless of whether or not they share the organization's principles. Such an organization is not the means to wage a struggle that rests on the above principles. Centralist parties do not care whether or not members share their convictions; they are only interested in numbers. Their membership is supposed to follow, nothing more. Their leaders would be finished if free-thinking individuals started to examine their orders before obeying them. For these organizations, power lies in numbers alone. This is why they focus on gathering numbers, trying to woo people into the organization by promising them rewards if they follow the orders of the leaders and help solidify their power over the organization. Conviction plays no role for these organizations. This becomes particularly obvious when we consider that they mainly agitate among the ranks of hostile organizations in order to win people over to their side with enticing promises. A change in views and principles is neither demanded nor expected—all that matters is adding the name of another member. Centralist organizations are even willing to change their programs and tactics to gain more members. Every revolutionary party has been forced to make concessions to fear—concessions that consist of promises to improve certain aspects of the capitalist state system, because its expansion is dependent on membership among the non-revolutionary masses. Every revolutionary party has also made concessions to clerical and nationalist prejudices in education. In short, the attempt to establish themselves as centralist mass organizations has forced all of them to abandon their revolutionary, and even their socialist, goals.

The creation of anarchist groups and alliances must be based solely on the need felt by anarchists to work with other anarchists toward anarchy. The federative character of all anarchist alliances allows no place for the idea of combining masses of members into one organization. Anarchists' political alliances always permit enough space for each individual to express himself fully. Since there is no central bureau and no institutionalized leadership whose power depends on the number of obedient adherents, no anarchist alliance would benefit from including wavering, unconvinced, skeptical people who unite with a herdlike mentality. People who want to join an upper class on the shoulders of the proletariat will naturally refrain from joining the anarchist movement, since it has no place for the desire to dominate and for personal ambition. In non-revolutionary times, anarchist organizations have, as a result, little room for growth. Their role simply lies in keeping the idea alive, in providing an example of comradeship and federative organization, and in discussing questions related to the proletariat, the revolution, and the libertarian preparation of the socialist future.

There lies a danger in this that must not be denied; namely, the danger of ending up with unproductive, cliquish blabber, of settling for one's own little scene, and of losing touch with the everyday life of the working class. However, this danger can easily be avoided if the comrades understand that the struggle for the idea can never happen outside of its proper domain. This does not mean that anarchism has to buy into mass demonstrations and mass pledges. It must, however, be present whenever the masses gather and pledge. It is the task of the anarchists to invigorate all mass events, to actively support all public uprisings, and to instill the spirit of freedom in all revolutionary tendencies—all this has to be done without regard for the benefit of their own organizations.

Anarchists are not the ones who put the stamps of some anarchist club into their little book; they are those for whom the unity of the individual and the society, the social consciousness of individual responsibility, equal rights, voluntary mutual commitment, and the rejection of power, capitalism, the state, and authority have become ideological convictions and ethical directives.

If, and to what degree, anarchists organize in alliances is secondary, as long as the general principles are upheld and as long as the emergence of authority within their own ranks is prevented. The question of how the economic transformation of society can be prepared by anarchist activity is urgent. The political workers' parties accuse anarchists of being caught up in petty-bourgeois ideology and of being incapable of grasping the wisdom of dialectical materialism, i.e., the concept of a unification of opposed principles that elevates both to a higher level, in the context of a social history solely driven by economic forces. Anarchists, so the Marxist argument continues, want first to change the human being, and then, based on mere idealism, to establish a more just economic system in the form of social-ism and communism. The opposite is true. In strict opposition to the Marxists, anarchists reject any ambition of uniting workers in anything *but organizations based on economics*. Dialectical thought may be good or bad—we can let the philosophers determine that. For the struggles of the workers, abstract theories of this or any other kind are completely irrelevant. The demand that workers always consider the historical *reactions* to their actions will defuse their activity rather than advancing it. The participation in lawmaking and the attempt to influence the governmental affairs of the capitalist state create the deception that the transformation of society could be brought about by forces other than workers and peasants, who are united as classes by economic considerations.

The influence of the anarchists on the unification of workers and peasants can only be secured by anarchists being active. Anarchist tactics everywhere have to be determined by the desire to turn the moral and practical principles of the libertarian idea into praxis. In the same vein, they have to create groups that can, even now, present plans for a federative economic order in a society ready for revolution.

Agitation among the masses mainly serves the purpose of accelerating the overthrow of the current system by drawing attention to its injustices and to the madness of the capitalist system. The work in trade unions and education is an attempt to keep a militant spirit alive, both economically and ideologically, under the given circumstances. Yet, we must never lose sight of the goal of communist anarchy. The bridge to this goal is the *social revolution* that follows the political.

The outrage, the uprising, the decisive struggle against the old violence, the overthrow of the old system, the creation of revolutionary councils, the protection of what has been achieved, the suppression of opposing and counterrevolutionary forces, all that belongs to the political part of the revolution. Where, in which way, and with which means he will join this struggle is dependent on the individual anarchist's conscience. The decision will be based on a number of considerations: the obligation to support the struggle of the exploited class, of which they are members; the necessity that the struggle remains internationalist in nature, a struggle of the world proletariat; the defense of the struggle against cooptation by ambitious, egotistical, authoritarian defenders of the state, both individuals and parties wanting to govern the revolution; and the preservation of passion's fiery and creative lust, which, fed by ideas, is the moral motivation of all revolutions. During the revolution, the anarchists have to be the guardians of freedom.

The social revolution is a time-consuming process, which begins with the overthrow of the current power structures and does not end until freedom permeates all economic and social relationships. What is required from the very first hour is to safeguard the trust of the entire working people in the active carriers of the revolutionary will. Whether the masses, without conviction, vote for the parliamentary parties depends on all sorts of circumstances: economic influence, social mood, schmaltzy propaganda, and defamation. Even if on occasion a party claiming to have socialist politics wins an election, this does not mean that the passive masses voting for it have now joined the struggle. It only means that this party can now suppress all others. Numerical democracy means nothing but the oppression of active people by passive ones. The proclamation that the workers are already an active social force, that they already have enough socialist education, socialist will, self-confidence, and critical judgment to make the right decision when voting, is a deceiving lie. The vast majority of the workers and the dispossessed lack trust in themselves, but also have very little trust in those who they give power to only because they think that they cannot take care of things themselves. Due to authoritarian indoctrination, they have lost the courage to engage in liberating ventures directly. At the same time, the authoritarian powers have taught them not to accept the liberating ventures of others. This is why the enormous number of passive observers of the struggle poses an incredible danger for the victory of the social revolution. Against the will of this majority, ultimate victory is impossible. The revolution depends on this majority supporting it, at least in spirit. This is why it is mandatory to make the people understand that the revolution will not make their situation worse. And this alone will still not be enough. In the long run, the people's active support needs to be ensured. The people must realize that by voting certain individuals into power, they are expressing no conviction, but are only turning their lack of conviction into a ladder to power for the ones they vote for, namely their oppressors. The people must understand that the activity of an individual in public life serves that individual's interests. As long as those in power are asked by the powerless to govern them, the revolution has failed to create the requirements for victory.

The power of the exploiters is crushed by the political revolution. The general strike, the most effective means available to revolutionaries, brings the economy to a complete standstill and proves to the masses that the capitalist powers cannot provide any bread if the hands of the proletariat do not produce it. As soon as the revolution is victorious, i.e., as soon as it has taken control of the public apparatus, its duty is to demonstrate to the watching masses that the working people are indeed capable of producing everything they need, without the capitalists. The duty of the anarchists is to be prepared for that moment, no matter how small the groups. When the red flag of the proletariat[10] flies on top of state buildings, the revolution has to take on the responsibility of providing for the masses. Everything has to be in place: as soon as the general strike ends, bread, meat, vegetables, and milk have to be available for every table; there has to be food for children and medicine for the sick. The distribution of all basic goods must not be delayed a single hour. If this cannot be achieved, the masses cannot be won over to the revolution; instead, they will heed the calls of the counterrevolution or fall victim to centralist powers attempting to take control.

The revolution can succeed if it encompasses the entire country and if agreements have been made with the peasants about how to provide the townspeople with all they need, depending on local circumstances. This requires a few things: the peasantry and the rural proletariat must be convinced of the honesty of the revolutionaries; the peasants must not be concerned with townspeople seeing them as a necessary evil or as people who have to be tricked into forming alliances; the peasants must understand that proletarians do not want to take their land, but that they want to ensure that the peasants control it; it must be clear to everyone that no new authoritarian state institutions will replace the old and that all questions of land distribution and cultivation will be decided independently, without central legislative powers. In opposition to Marxists, anarchists see the agrarian revolution as a precondition for the industrial and social revolution.

Anarchism accords with the peasant sentiment in many ways: in the rejection of authoritarian orders, of permanent leadership ambitions, and of all forms of centralism. In short, the countryside is a very productive terrain for anarchist agitation. It is up to the anarchists to win the peasants over to the revolution and to make them dedicated supporters of the libertarian cause. It is the anarchists' task to establish comradeship between the towns and the villages, to secure mutuality during the decisive revolutionary moment. This will create the best possible conditions for securing the belief of the masses in the social justice of the revolution and, hence, for securing their support.

Just as the anarchists must be prepared to secure the provision of the people with all basic goods during the revolutionary days of the struggle, they must also develop ideas about how to *transform the capitalist economy into a socialist* one. The childish belief that socialism can be achieved by occupying the factories and by establishing self-management without changing the production process is as silly as it is dangerous. The occupation of factories is certainly a great means of direct action, but it is only a means to prepare and to defend the revolution—once the revolution is completed, an all-inclusive transformation of the economic structures is required.

In capitalism, all factories are modeled and organized exclusively according to the capitalists' profit calculations. There is no consideration for the needs of the masses, the demands of justice and reason, the life and health of workers and consumers. Demand is only of concern insofar as it secures the sale of goods and gain for the invested capital. The mode of production depends on stock market agreements; these concern the acquisition of raw materials as much as the mass production and the assembly of individual parts, the transport of goods, etc. What eventually happens to the goods does not depend on the needs of the consumers, but on the speculations of factory owners, tradesmen, and moneylenders. In short, we are facing an economic system that denies the majority of the people an adequate and healthy life, while the storerooms burst from the pressure of goods that cannot be sold; we are facing an economic system where millions without work are literally starving, while staple foods are being burnt, dumped in the sea, left to rot, or used as fertilizer. Such an economic system cannot be adopted and continued. It needs to undergo a radical transformation. To prepare this transformation is among the most concrete tasks of libertarian revolutionaries.

A model for how to do this cannot be provided in this text, which is but a general introduction to anarchism. However, one needs statistics and calculations to determine the supply needed in different areas, depending on landscape and population density. This concerns food, clothing, shelter, hygiene and health, transport, and leisure. According to these calculations, an economic plan must be established that guarantees the most effective distribution of labor in the towns and in the countryside, the safest and most productive means of labor, and the most reasonable organization for delivering the goods to the consumers.

Eventually, it can be decided which factories to keep, which ones to close, which ones to downsize or to expand, which industries to create anew or to revive, and in which way to organize the acquisition of raw materials and the exchange of money and goods, both for the transitional period and for socialism. The final answers to these questions will be provided by life itself. However, they still require serious investigation now. Otherwise, the workers will never escape the wage system and the assembly line, work will never be enjoyable, people will never find occupations that suit them, and the storerooms will continue to burst while people are starving, no matter how many revolutionary victories they enjoy.

There are thousands of open questions for the future. The centralist parties are busy with reforms of the capitalist system and compete with the fascists over the state's funds. Let us anarchists use this time to investigate the socialist usage of railway tracks and river beds, and to examine the possibilities of providing healthy living conditions for all working, elderly, and ailing people, as well as for all children and all women. We also need to develop plans for dealing with the oppressive state regime's fortresses, palaces, prisons, courthouses, and government buildings, for transforming arts and educational institutions into general facilities of learning, and churches into meeting halls, places of true community, schools of enlightenment against authority and family—in short, exemplary spaces of freedom. The foundation of socialism can be laid now, but only in voluntary devotion of individuals who are filled by social spirit, who are connected as comrades, and who are committed to the revolution.

The anarchist idea can only benefit from such preparatory work. The example of an effort that serves society and is not steered from above will give people the courage to rely on themselves in all things, rather than on a higher class of bureaucrats. Anarchists hand their proposals, the result of much investigation and reflection, not to some government office, but to the self-responsible working class that must test, improve, and oversee the implementation of the plans. This will happen through councils created for these specific purposes. Their members will never be released from the working community, not even temporarily. These councils will be the social driving force of the revolution. They will, from the moment of victory, have control over the economy and the administration of communities; they will safeguard the order of freedom both during the transitional period and in the following socialist economy and socialist administration; they will establish communist anarchy, and they will organize the federation of all economic and social alliances in the anarchist community. They will be the *free workers' and peasants' councils.*

There exist many false perceptions as far as the essence, meaning, and organization of the council system are concerned. Even within the libertarian workers' associations there are many conflicting opinions about the council system. "Shall councils be created? If so, how? And what shall be their tasks?" The confusion is deepened further by the fact that state laws and capitalist modes of production adopt the term. Apparently to appease the demand of the workers for control over the administration and the organization of labor at the workplace, boards of workers have been introduced and called "factory councils" (*Betriebsräte*[11]). This means that the basic form of a revolutionary society has been incorporated into the lift pump of capitalist exploitation. The system of numerical parliamentary democracy, directly opposed to the council idea, is being used to control these "councils" from central party offices and to ensure their dependency. Unsurprisingly, these boards have barely any power at all.

Even where the German Revolution brought true victory for the workers and the peasants under the motto *All Power to the Councils!*, the councils were submitted to the party and the state. Instead of administering public life in a socialist spirit, they were reduced to mere tools of authority.[12] However, when anarchists, as it sometimes happens, draw the conclusion that the entire council idea goes against libertarian principles, they make the same mistake as those who conclude from the current reality of state justice that there can never be any kind of justice. The distortion of an idea can never discredit the idea.

Councils, as the pillars of the socialist community, are appointed by all human beings involved in building this community. They allow each and every person to participate in the social process. In a time without exploitation, every single human being will fulfill council functions, if he does not consciously place himself outside of all social affairs. It is only during the transitional period that some will have to be excluded from the councils, namely those who the revolution was directed against. It is the primary duty of the councils to abolish capitalist exploitation and to realize socialism. This means that people who do not want socialism cannot be included in its creation. Hence, during the transitional period, the councils will also have to ensure the coercive measures of the proletarian class that are necessary to break the counterrevolutionary forces. They have to prevent new power structures, even if they claim to be necessary to defend the revolution. There will always be those who speak of the "power of councils" to strengthen their own power, and of the "dictatorship of the proletariat" to be dictators themselves.

It is beneficial for anarchists to use the phrase *dictatorship of the proletariat* as rarely as possible, even though, if we understand the council idea correctly and have no malicious intentions, the phrase can only mean the repulsion of attacks against the proletarian revolution. The coercive suppression of counterrevolutionary conspiracies by means of arms, revolutionary courts, and all other appropriate security measures is necessary as long as the former upper class still has means of power and as long as attacks on the revolutionary rights of the working class are to be feared. A revolutionary dictatorship of class against class is indispensable in times of struggle. Such a dictatorship is nothing but the revolution itself. No revolutionary individual, group, or party can be granted the right to oppress and persecute revolutionary proletarians, no matter the pretext. By the dictatorship of the proletariat, Marxists understand the dictatorship of a Marxist party committee that has governmental authority over the councils, legislative powers, the rights to collect taxes and to represent the revolution—which might even include declaring war against foreign state governments or signing contracts with their leaders.

Supposedly, the party will only remain in power until the realization of socialism. However, every centralist government implies a state structure, and hence authority, privilege, and inequality. Hence, such a dictatorship cuts nothing but the path to a new oppressed class, to new oppression, and to the return of all of the ills that were eradicated by the revolution. Socialism can never be implemented under a proletarian dictatorship that is not really one, and the new power will not abdicate before a new revolution abolishes it in the name of the councils.

If properly implemented, the council system produces no bureaucracy, no special privileges for certain individuals, no totalitarian power. In this, we can see a correspondence to anarchist principles: an assignment given by councils does not affect the relationship between those who determine the task and those who execute it. The council organization is the federative unity of all workers and consumers, from the smallest groups of people sharing the same interests to the broadest economic alliances.

Each individual is a part of the council organization. Councils select delegates to provide a certain service, to conceive a certain plan, to discuss a certain question with delegates from other councils, to execute or oversee a project deemed necessary and decided upon by the community, to present a perspective, to test a proposal by others. None of this grants the delegates any privilege over those who have selected them. Nor does it relieve those who have selected them from their responsibility. All tasks remain tied to the will of those who have appointed the delegates. The delegates are only executive organs of the councils that have selected them to fulfill a certain task that they were deemed suitable for. They execute the will of a community that they belong to, and they only have this role in this specific case. The diversity of social life demands innumerable social services, in the smallest and in the largest circles, so that the division and constant rotation of social duties demands the use of all social forces. Everyone is under the permanent control of the entire community, guaranteeing the unity of the individual and the society in both self-responsibility and responsibility for others. This, in turn, guarantees equal rights and mutuality in all common affairs.

Delegates can be removed from their appointed position at any time. The acceptance of an appointment is voluntary. If delegates realize that they cannot fulfill the appointment they have accepted, they can remove themselves. They can do the same, if they think that someone else is more suitable. This implies that parliamentary elections that equip some people with special privileges over an extended period of time have nothing to do with the council system; the same applies to all bodies that are not under full control of the workers themselves. Councils cannot exist within capitalism. Councils are based on the revolutionary will to focus on what is politically and economically necessary in the workplace—without the interference of governing public servants and through voluntary mutual cooperation on the part of the revolutionaries instead. After the revolution, councils are the executive and administrative organs of the entire society, and they will encompass all of society, forming its framework.

The *creation of the council system* has nothing to do with questions of active or passive franchise or with questions of direct, indirect, or proportional voting. However, as long as the revolution has to defend itself, the participation in administering social affairs remains restricted to the socialists who are determined to push the revolution forward under all circumstances until the ultimate goal is reached: a classless society and an order of freedom maintained by the councils.

Revolutionary socialists must unite in their workplaces and in their neighborhoods, based on their common areas of influence and activity. They have to overcome all former ideological quarrels and strictly prevent all interference by professional politicians and authoritarian know-it-alls. They have to discuss and determine the tasks necessary to guard the new spirit and the introduction of the new economic and social structures. Part of this is the interweaving of workers' and peasants' councils in order to secure the general provision of goods, as producers and consumers have to aspire to common economic activity. In the countryside, there has to be agitation for the council idea, but under no circumstances its violent implementation by townspeople! It must also be ensured that the peasants' councils cannot be coopted by the economically more powerful landowners before socialism is fully established and secured. Where exploitation still exists, the councils must be uniquely the tools of the exploited and underprivileged. In the countryside, this means that they must consist of poor peasants, farmworkers, and impoverished country folk. The urban workers must pay particular attention to securing the federative character of social organization from the very beginning. A "council state" that imposes central regulation on the councils in certain regions abuses the councils, disenfranchising and destroying them. A council society, a council economy, and a council republic must have federative character and can never be a state or find its place within a state. We must not misunderstand the term "republic"! It does not necessarily refer to a particular form of the state; it can, as in this case, mean nothing but the self-determination of a people.

The council republic is built from the bottom up. Its bases are the village and town councils. In these councils, the actions of the factory or neighborhood councils are discussed, can be criticized, expanded upon, and proposals can be presented. The village and town councils can meet occasionally or regularly, depending on need and possibility. They can also form committees for special purposes and appoint individuals, who remain under the constant observation of all, to take care of special tasks. The village and town councils will decide on matters of health, housing, transport, justice, and social services. They will protect the social institutions. In short, they will take care of everything that people naturally take care of when they control their living conditions.

For example, the legal structure of the state can never create justice, because central institutions decide individual cases based on central orders. Justice can only be done when the accused person is interrogated, found guilty, and, if necessary, prevented from doing further damage to the public; this process must be handled by a group of peers, familiar with the material and psychological circumstances of the deed and without obligation to one-dimensional legal codes. In the council republic, the perpetrator is dealt with by people who are his equals, by his neighbors and comrades. The council system spreads from the municipality through neighboring regions, provinces, and countries to the entire earth. It knows no national borders. District councils and workplace councils, regional councils and world councils guided by particular aspirations can make any agreements they deem necessary—the council idea receives its justification from the fact that each delegate is nothing but the representative of the will of the neighborhood, trade, or ideology that he shares with those who sent him. He always remains accountable to them, they can revoke his delegation and replace him at any time. During the transitional period, it will be difficult for the councils to avoid granting a special representative role to the most talented agitators, speakers, and organizers. Many men and women, left by the state system without self-esteem, will not want to play a special role. It will be the task of the anarchists to ensure that this challenge will not cause the return of authority, power, and abuse, and that the revolutionary spirit never loses sight of its mission: to be the spirit of freedom.

It would make no sense to present a detailed blueprint for the future council society. The final realization of an idea will always be different from the way it was imagined by those who formulated it. To be conscious of the most basic principles of the council system must suffice in order to understand the libertarian order of communist anarchy. The formation of the councils depends on the natural relations of labor and of the community.

The workers' council of an industrial factory, which includes the entire workforce, determines the distribution of duties within the factory itself based on trade. However, when deciding on an expansion, the wishes and concerns of all people who are directly or indirectly related to the factory will have to be considered. A council will have to be formed that includes representatives of all factory departments, all manual workers and accountants, the gatekeepers, janitors, and window cleaners, the engineers and bricklayers, all outside workers who are in regular contact with the factory, health counselors, women and girls who might have a special interest in an issue related to the factory, the municipality, and anyone else who might be affected by the factory or who simply shows an interest in it. In the case of a hospital, doctors and nurses will make all decisions together with custodians and coroners, with the sick and their relatives, with architects and builders. When building a road, the people living next to it will be just as involved as those in neighboring towns, technicians, workers, surveyors, electricians, hydraulic engineers, and anyone who was part of the planning, who knows the local conditions, or who will use the road. All these parties will form a council of confidants for the sole purpose of this one project. Its members will work under permanent supervision and can at any time be recalled or replaced—individually, in groups, or completely.

It does not seem necessary to list further examples. The reader can apply this principle to all imaginable social scenarios, and he will realize that, from a libertarian perspective, this is indeed the best system to make all affairs the affairs of interconnected individuals, from the smallest social circle to the world federation. This applies to agriculture and the exchange of goods, to transport and intellectual matters. Each is accountable to all, and all are accountable to each in a spirit of equal rights and voluntary decision-making, without privilege or power.

Once the councils are understood in this way, i.e., as the epitome of the living harmony of individuality and society, then it seems absurd to question the anarchist connotations of the slogan *All Power to the Councils!* Maybe it is ill-advised to ever use the word "power." However, this particular slogan has emerged from a decided rejection of state power and from the conviction that all legislative and executive power must be seized by the revolution, i.e., by the revolutionary class, by the workers, the peasants, and their revolutionary bodies, the councils, which, in turn, embody all proletarians. Once socialism is realized, once it is alive, the classes will disappear, and the revolutionary coercion executed against the counterrevolution-aries of the former ruling class will fade away, with everyone working together in the councils with equal rights. The power of everyone involved in creating the stateless communist society—in other words, the power of the councils—will then no longer be real power, as there will be no one left to be oppressed by it. In any case, this slogan is better than that of the "proletarian dictatorship," although the latter can also be interpreted in a way that indicates only the workers' necessary defense of the revolution against capitalist forces and their influence.

All Power to the Councils! should also work as a slogan because it is only used by anti-authoritarian socialists. Hence, no one needs be concerned that it will be used to replace the power structure that has been overthrown by a new one. The idea of the dictatorship of the proletariat, on the other hand, is today mainly entertained by the state socialists, who have used it as a justification for party domination in a very concrete sense. It is therefore unlikely that these slogans will be confused and misunderstood. Still, in order to avoid any possible misunderstanding, it might be best for anarchists to speak of *All Rights to the Councils!* or *All to the Councils!* or *All by the Councils!* or simply *All for All by All!*

The *way to anarchy* leads via anarchist behavior. Reality comes only from realization. This applies to intellectual and manual labor in the preparation of the economy, and it applies, to an even higher degree, to the preparation of the spirit. If human beings are to be ready for councils, if they are to be able to seek and give advice in mutual trust and with equal rights, if they are to be ready and united for action, then the revolution must be built on more than the mere belief that capitalism will, in the long run, crumble because of the hunger and the misery of humankind. This is not guaranteed. Capitalism will prevail as long as it does not meet resistance directed against its moral foundations, against authority and its expressions, namely the state, the church, the law, and the family.

Such a resistance does not come from agreements, from scientific teachings, or from wise tactics. It can only come from the conscience of the social human being. It is hence one of the anarchists' tasks to awaken feelings of justice and freedom, innate in every human being, but pushed into the subconscious by the authoritarian education of the church, the school, the military, and especially the patriarchal family. It is the anarchists' task to make people understand that the worst is not the misery itself, but the fact that it is borne! To accept poverty when others live in wealth is spiritual defeat; it is an indication that the soul has become insensitive to the insult of the propagation of joyless values. No one must be forced to beg those in power to be allowed to work for peanuts because it is the only way to avoid starvation! The crucial requirement for the struggle against denying the majority the control over the means of production and against state-sanctioned slavery—a true insult to humankind—is not the knowledge of historical laws and economic circumstances; it is the *pride of freedom*, the *anarchists' sense of honor*.

Only when pride, inner freedom, and exemplary righteousness express themselves in the conduct of anarchists, among themselves and in relation to others, do we have hope that society can be liberated from the state and that a federative, non-authoritarian council republic can be created.

Anarchy can only be created by anarchists; contemporary anarchists, may they be many or few, must express the basic principles of anarchy every day and every hour, if there is to be anarchy in the future and if the coming generations are to be anarchists. This is why the communication and the alliance of anarchists in the preparation for new social conditions must be strictly guided by justice. No talented speaker, teacher, organizer, or agitator should ever be tempted to take everything into his own hands, and no majority should ever disregard the rights of a minority. The goal must be a community that knows neither majorities nor minorities, and nor foul compromises that fail to satisfy anyone from either the majority or the minority. The goal must be a community that makes consensus possible in all decisions, because it allows each individual to be an active part of society. Voluntary connection by contract and comradeship allows for such accords. Human beings unite in will and action and form associations and cooperatives. The cooperative spirit that guides the interaction of anarchists will prepare and show the cooperatives and the voluntary alliances in culture and the economy the way to the future.

Especially important is exemplary anarchist conduct in the fight against other opinions and ideologies. Dirty tricks, accusations, defamation, deceptions to mislead both comrades and foes will always hurt an idea whose strength lies in its purity. The authoritarian Marxist parties do not care about ethics in their struggle.

They give orders from the top, expect compliance and obedience from their follow-ers, and call this "proletarian discipline." The orders can be changed at will, and any sign of individual resistance is denounced as "bourgeois prejudice." The distinction between *proletarian* and *bourgeois morality* has caused much confusion. "Bourgeois" signifies the ideas of the social structure that has historically been created by the capitalist mode of production. By exaggerating the capitalist forms of exploitation and by the increased importance of imperialism, i.e., the exploitation of dependent foreign territories for the profit of the imperialist states' capitalists, the current social structure has lost all morality. There only remains the natural morality of the revolutionaries who demand the transformation of the social structure in the name of an innate feeling of social justice.

If proletarian morality means a morality of equality and mutuality that opposes the asocial power structure with the revolutionary rage of the insulted and disen-franchised, then it can be distinguished from a bourgeois ideology that believes it has the right to defend its selfish means of servitude with all of the brutality, perfidy, and psychological abuse it deems necessary. If, however, the workers are told that they are allowed to employ lies, defamation, deceit, and betrayal in their struggle against oppression and cruelty, or if these means are praised as "class tools" in internal disputes, then we cannot stress enough that these are reflections of degenerate bourgeois morality, which is what makes the revolution necessary in the first place. In violent confrontations, it is the enemy that determines the weapons. But the weapons will be carried openly, and morality is on the side of those who fight for the just cause.

In the struggle of ideas, morality is on the side of those who are honest and genuine, and who carry the flag of pure conviction. Anarchists strictly reject any morality that denies the original notions of right and wrong, since this has noth-ing to do with proletarian morality. It is merely guile and perfidy. It is not even a characteristic of the bourgeoisie, but rather the expression of the bourgeoisie's decay in a world that is merely materialistic. If the proletariat is to renew human justice, then it must express its calling in its moral conduct.

The centralist parties gather workers around them, making fine promises. But behind their words, there is nothing but lust for power. This lust for power sends proletarians into the struggle under false pretexts. The parties justify deceit and betrayal. By seducing the workers to means of betrayal, they betray them too. If one expresses disgust at the practice of turning defeats into rhetorical victories, one is ridiculed as being bourgeois. However, there are still many members of the bourgeoisie for whom the natural feeling of justice remains alive and who could therefore easily be won over to the revolutionary cause. This means that the moral untrustworthiness among proletarians strengthens the ruling class, repels pure souls from joining the proletarian struggle, and divides the working class through mistrust and miserable infighting. Lying is a natural means of powerless people to limit power's might and to evade authority. Children lie to their parents, husbands lie to their wives and vice versa, students, recruits, subordinates, and believers lie to teachers, sergeants, superiors, and clerics, because a healthy sense of freedom resists the obligation to account for something that only concerns oneself. Here it is not the liar who sins against the truth, but the one who is lied to. Where there is power, truth finds no breathing room. But where people lie to gain power, the lie becomes an attack on freedom. The revolution demands of socialists not only that they chase away the old regime's powerful, but also that they hold the proletariat's leaders accountable for what they have done. If any of them have ever deceived people who put their trust in them when they spoke of freedom, or if any of them ever claimed to be nothing more than messengers, while effectively striving for power, then they must play no role in the creation of a new society.

Restraint within one's own ranks and truthfulness toward everyone is the requirement for victory. The order of freedom depends on the righteousness of all who strive for freedom. Lip service does not create a new world. The anarchists who want to create a new world of freedom, equality, mutuality, justice, truthfulness, and the interconnection of all must express their beliefs in action. This means that they have to lead their lives in a way that anticipates the communism of the stateless society. The demand is not that someone should or could individually leave capitalism behind. The yoke of the state can only be broken in a collective struggle. This is why there is little point in demanding the violation of the laws of the state in daily life. But there is no holiness to the laws, just like there is no holiness to property. No one can be expected to hold the laws and the powers of the state in high esteem. For the anarchist, the books of law are like train schedules—they help navigate the society in which he has to live until the revolution comes—nothing more.

The anarchist accepts no obligations that threaten his self-determination or that might subjugate him to an authority. There is no place for him in the church and he accepts no honorary posts within the state. If he is forced to play judge over others as a juror, he evaluates the case based on his social conscience and challenges the right of the state to punish the victims of capitalism. If he is forced to go to war in order to kill his peers in the interest of strangers, he refuses and would rather die for his conviction than for the profit of his torturers. In his home, he exercises no authority and tolerates none. In sexual matters, he follows the paths he deems right for himself and does not care which paths others are following. No woman belongs to a man, and no man to a woman. What two adults do in private to please one another is no third party's business, not that of the husband or the wife, of the neighbor or of the comrade, of the church or of the state. Anarchists are not the masters of their children but their comrades and helpers. Those who beat their children abuse their physical dominance in order to establish a relationship of power; thereby they cement the power and the authority of the state and capital. They beat the delusion of power into their child and into the next generation. The anarchist does not believe in gods or spooks, nor in priestly dictums or scientific proclamations that he cannot test himself. He is not interested in the gossip of the street or the latest fad in the world of arts or ideology. He follows his path unwaveringly, accountable only to himself and his conscience and to a humankind he feels united with. He does the right thing because he knows righteousness, since righteousness and freedom are the same, just like individuality and society. Righteousness spawns the equality of communism, and the equality of communism spawns the freedom of anarchy!

1. The bibliography was an extensive overview of anarchist literature available in German at the time. Numerous works by Mikhail Bakunin, Peter Kropotkin, Gustav Landauer, Johann Most, Max Nettlau, Pierre-Joseph Proudhon, and Rudolf Rocker were listed.
2. Christoph Martin Wieland (1733–1813), German poet and writer; the *Geschichte des weisen Danischmend* [The Story of the Wise Danischmend] was published in 1775.
3. Literally, "perception/view of life."
4. Literally, "servitude under God."
5. Literally, "care for the soul;" in its German usage closer to "soul counseling."
6. Mühsam uses the term *Vaterrecht* [literally, "Father Right"]. Since this is in clear reference to the concept of *Mutterrecht* [literally, "Mother Right"], developed by Johann Jakob Bachofen (1815–1887) in his 1861 book of the same name (see footnote 5 in "Women's Rights") and most regularly translated as "matriarchy", the term "patriarchy" seems appropriate for a modern-day English translation. The German term *Mutterrecht* has also been largely replaced by *Matriarchat*.
7. Roughly, "a coming together of people."
8. The German verb *geschehen* means "to happen," "to occur." In its substantive, mostly philosophical, usage, it roughly means "everything that happens."
9. *Freiwillig*, the German term for "voluntary," literally means "of free will."
10. Mühsam was opposed to anarchists adopting a black flag instead of a red one—see also "The Anarchists."
11. *Betriebsräte* remain an integral part of institutionalized trade unionism in the German-speaking world.
12. Reference to the policies of social democratic governments during the German Revolution: while they encouraged the formation of councils, the councils were kept under strict government control and had very limited executive power. This was also the case in Bavaria under Kurt Eisner.

APPENDIX I

ADDITIONAL DIARY ENTRIES

Mühsam kept a regular diary from 1910 until his release from the Niederschönefeld Fortress in 1924. Today, over thirty notebooks are stored at the International Institute for Social History (IISH) in Amsterdam. Some, covering the period from November 1916 to April 1919, went missing while Mühsam's papers were being kept in Moscow. Chris Hirte has edited an excellent selection of the remaining journals in German.[1]

Some of Mühsam's diary entries were included in previous chapters. The additional entries included here shed further light on three important aspects of Mühsam's life: the complicated relationship with his father; his financial woes; and his love life.

The excerpts do not necessarily cover the entire entry for the day listed. Omissions within the selected parts are marked in the text.

Munich, Monday, October 3, 1910

SINCE LAST NIGHT, I AM HAVING A PROPER AFFAIR WITH THE maid. Before that, we had only kissed. Yesterday she had a night off and I took her to the Oktoberfest, which ended today. Afterwards, she followed me to my room. There I found out that this twenty-year-old was still a virgin. I remain surprised. For the first time in my life, I have deflowered a woman.

Equally strange is that the good child is crazy in love with me—she even said that she fell in love with me the first time she saw me. As far as I am concerned—and I think I can speak with certainty—I am not even remotely in love. The girl touches me with her wild tenderness; this is something I have not experienced much. It is special to me, since I always assumed that women like that were not attracted to me. I lived under the impression that it would be very difficult to find someone who would show me this kind of love and affection.

The girl is cute but in no way beautiful. She kisses magnificently and sneaks into my room whenever she can. For me, the relationship has mainly the attraction of novelty—and some others. […] I am happy that my sex life is at last provided for—I hope it will remain that way for several weeks.[2]

Munich, Sunday, May 7, 1911

This dreadful gonorrhea! I can feel it constantly, it bothers me in everything I do, it slows me down, it spoils my mood. I have had it for three weeks now, and there hasn't been any improvement. I will go to Hauschild again tomorrow.[3] I finally have to deal with this disaster properly!

Last night was terrible. Emmy was in the café.[4] I had met Eduard Joël and his wife in the Luitpold earlier.[5] Emmy was obviously horny and asked me to accompany her home on my way to the Torggelstube.[6] I did. I went with her to her studio, and her kisses excited me a good deal. Then she went to change her clothes, and when I saw her naked, I got so aroused that I could have screamed from both pain and desire! The jockstrap I was wearing almost tore under the pressure of my extremely hard member. We were very unhappy that we couldn't do what we both wanted to do desperately.

It was the exact same story five years ago in Vienna, when I lay naked next to Irma Karczewska,[7] who also suffered from a venereal disease. We kissed like crazy and tried to satisfy each other at least with our mouths and fingers, but eventually pain got the better of me. That story was very tragic. We had only met and we were to part soon. We never got to engage in proper intercourse.

I had already visited Emmy in the afternoon. Morax and Fräulein Vital[8] were there, and I drew a few pictures for a ballad that Emmy and Morax wanted to recite together at Kathi's.[9] The pictures turned out to be very funny. Emmy inked them very discreetly and nicely.

Eduard Joël is a good fellow. But our interests are becoming increasingly different, and I have to admit that when we meet, I am most interested in getting money for *Kain* out of him. I have already tried. This afternoon I will meet him and his wife again. Will there be any results?

After the intermezzo in Emmy's studio, I accompanied her to the Simpl.[10] The sweet thing carried candles and a candle holder the entire way, so she would be able to find her way up the stairs when she returned home, especially since she had promised the night to Engert.[11] She told me this very nonchalantly, regretting that I wasn't able to do my duty. After all, it'd be impossible for her to sleep alone for that long. But Engert of all people? I didn't like the idea at all. But who can tell women who to sleep with?

Munich, Saturday, July 15, 1911

The "Mühsam Family" sends me yet another invitation for a family day with a detailed "agenda": a feast and a "meeting regarding finances." This kind of gathering is to become a regular affair. What nonsense!

Munich, Friday, July 21, 1911

This morning (I am writing this at night), Lotte[12] came and picked me up, just when I was on my way to go swimming. Of course I went with her to the café. I like her a lot, and every time she tells me with her sinful smile about her upcoming journey, I am so happy I could eat her!

I have thought a lot about my love for her these days, and about my love for Frieda.[13] How narrow-minded are the people who think that a heart cannot be pulled in several directions at once! My love for Frieda does not suffer a bit from my infatuation with Lotte. When I think of Frieda, my heart is filled with longing and tenderness, yet I never doubt the truthfulness and the value of the feeling that connects me with Puma.[14] I can sit next to her, wish to kiss her passionately, and yet think of Frieda, wishing for her. I catch myself grabbing thin air in the illusion that it is her hand. And then Uli[15] can appear, and a word, a motion, or a look can make me feel burning love for her, and five minutes later I might see Vallière[16] and drown her hands in kisses, hoping to see her breath fog up my watch—and the next second I might rush to meet Lotte again.

Maybe it is stupid of me not to hide any of this. Maybe it makes things more complicated. But I couldn't do it differently. I can lie in bed with Lotte, love her madly, and still rave about Moggerl.[17]

How is it possible that I, a man who—and I am fairly convinced of this—is an eroticist of a special kind, has so little luck with women? Nature doesn't seem to know what it is doing. [...]

Last night in the Torggelstube, I flirted with Frau Mewes, the former Grete Gräf.[18] She even let me kiss her on the mouth. Then I kissed the hands of Vallière and Frau Weigert, who both have very beautiful hands.[19] And then all three of them went home with their husbands. It is crazy! I more or less have to rely on masturbating, which seems to be one of the most ludicrous jokes that fate has ever come up with.

If only Strich was gone![20] Then I could travel with Puma. The thought of it is so joyful like the heavenly daily baths out in the Ungererbad.[21] Puma, sweet Puma! Women, sweet women! Love, sweet love!

Munich, Thursday, November 2, 1911

The new *Pan*, in which Kerr[22] continues his outrageous attacks against Harden, has arrived.[23] In a small resort at the Baltic Sea, Harden has been observed going down on a whore. He had a room on the first floor, and the window was open. Apparently, he had brought the lady from Berlin. Since the local farmers made a big deal out of it, Paul Cassirer,[24] who was at the resort at the time, offered Harden use of his apartment for such purposes.

Cassirer spread the story fast—I first heard it months ago from Heinrich Mann.[25] Wedekind[26] also knows about it, and now Kerr has been castigating Harden in every issue of *Pan* for two months. "Gross acts of perverse weakness."

How mean and cheap! Has Kerr never gone down on a woman? I do not deny that I enjoy it very much. The highest sexual pleasure lies in observing the pleasure we can give to our partners, and women like a man's tongue down there. We must also not forget that the tongue is a very sensitive sexual organ in itself!

I hope that Harden is secure enough not to feel compromised by Kerr's stupidity.

Munich, Wednesday, November 29, 1911

When I came home this afternoon, I found a letter from Lübeck. It was my father's response to a request for three thousand marks. He refuses to give them to me. He says that he has no liquid capital at the moment. He doesn't get much money from the houses, since they need to be repaired all the time; the rest of his money is in mortgages, and the *Reichsbank*[27] charges six percent in interest because of Charlotte's dowry—if I understand it all correctly.

The bottom line is that he paid sixty thousand marks each for my sisters' dowries, and he paid for their weddings (expensive affairs!), and for Hans's laboratory,[28] which certainly cost several thousand marks—but to loan me three thousand marks, with good interest, in order to secure my life as a writer, he cannot do. At least the letter eventually reveals the real reason: "Your endeavors have always been characterized by a lack of maturity and have only brought me grief. My health is declining, but I do not want to talk about this. I would instead be happy about you coming to understand that we only want the best for you. I no longer think anything of *Kain*. Nor does Hans, Grethe, Charlotte, Julius, or Leo.[29] It is a bad journal that will never have any influence—and never can!" And so on. Then the old story: I have to find "a steady job with a steady salary in a respectable store." What is there left for me to do?

My father is very happy that I receive a steady income from the journal *Komet*. Great! Yet he knows that I'm using it all for my work. He knows that I will not obey his will and give up *Kain*. He says that he does not want to talk about his health, which I have apparently ruined. Yet, by mentioning it, he talks about it anyway. What does he expect from this? He has reached the age of seventy-three despite this supposedly ruined health, and he is in better shape than I am. Now, who has ruined my health? Who has brought me "unspeakable grief"?

"Until now, you have followed the wrong path." And he has followed the right path? For example, by completely disregarding the special needs of his own child? By repeatedly demanding things that go against my nature?

I told him about my wish to finally move out of the furnished room in which I have to sleep, eat, and work. I told him that I was dreaming of having my own house. He writes that he is hoping with all his heart that I would find one. Yet, he refuses to give me the help that I need! Instead he writes, "Maybe one day I will receive good news, then everything will be forgotten!" Fine. For me, however, there won't be any good news as long as my father lives. And if I forgot everything that *he* has done, wouldn't that be pathetic? How could that even be possible? How can a father be so stubborn? I offered him the opportunity to finally establish a good, decent relationship with me. Is he interested? No!

He knows that there is nothing I can do but wait for him to die. And I have to hope that he will die soon, so that I can live—and with me my ambitions, my pride, my consciousness, and my values. He forces me to hope for his death. Does he not realize this at all? I would so much like to be able to love him! But his behavior forces me to hate him. It reveals that there is not a spark of love in him for me. All that is in him is the principle: *I, the father, am right!* Hence, everything will go the way it has always gone: I am expecting more years of sorrow, discomfort, deprivation, sacrifice, loneliness, bitterness, depression, discontent, downheartedness—this will continue until he dies or until I break.

Munich, Saturday, December 2, 1911

The meeting on Thursday night went well. To my surprise, the great hall of the Schwabinger Brauerei was packed.[30] I had reserved the small *Galeriesaal*, which has space for about three hundred people, but we had to move to the great hall, because there were over a thousand attendees. It was an uncommon mixture of folks: many writers [...], artists, anarchists of all kinds, and the rest students. I spoke for an hour and a half, but I was not very happy with my talk. It wasn't well structured. At least I spoke fluently and, judging from the many interruptions of applause and shouts of approval, spiritedly. The end was way too short. I had intended to speak about "possibilities of change," but could only give vague hints at what the Socialist Bund wants. Still, people cheered and clapped heartily.

In the discussion, the dryness and the lack of vision of some of the students irritated me. The best contributions came from Sirch, the woodworker, who was tipsy. It was distasteful how the students mocked him for his unrefined speech. They became increasingly drunk and noisy. It was very sad to see their lack both of kindness and of political passion. While one young man spoke, they even started to play the piano. I had to call them "silly school boys" to make them stop. In my closing words, I mentioned the cold hearts of the spoilt sons of rich people. I was very angry about their behavior.

Munich, Thursday, January 18, 1912

Finally, the January issue of *Kain* has arrived and things will be a little more relaxed for a while. The *Komet*, however, demands a lot of my time.[31] In fact, I am really tired of the "comedy" I am supposed to deliver, but I need the two hundred marks they give me every month. I am really worried that I won't be able to finance *Kain* much longer.

Fuhrmann is still optimistic.[32] He claims to have a great prospective investor. But what are prospects? My entire life has been built on "prospects," and the results so far have been a disgrace. Right now, it's once again the prospect of my father's death that occupies me. Hans writes that father's nervous depression is getting better, but I think that a seventy-three-year-old man can die at any time if the will to live leaves him. I have to admit that I get anxious every time I see a telegram delivered. At any time, I could get a message that will completely alter my fate. It is very bad for a human being of my age to be so dependent on external circumstances. But I need financial security to produce good work. My ongoing financial problems absorb too much of my energy. And I do not believe in the bourgeois notion that people only deserve a good life when they can take care of life's necessities themselves. Food, clothes, shelter, and certain luxuries should be guaranteed for everyone, since only a strong spirit can produce things that everyone will benefit from. I am still a long way from that. My suit is in tatters, but I cannot afford to buy a new one. My money is almost gone, especially since I had to pay five marks and forty pfennige to the shoemaker today. The thought that I will have to go on borrowing money tortures me terribly. In addition to this, people ask me for money all the time! No day passes when I don't give away some. People follow me on the streets and hope for help from my side, and I always tell myself that the really poor have it much worse than I do, and so I share with them what I have—and find myself in even more trouble than before.

Munich, Friday, February 9, 1912

In the evening, there was a party at Uli's.[33] Early on, I got upset with Lotte.[34] She made out with Cronos on the sofa.[35] I wanted to say hello to her, and she kicked me in the chest—so hard that I almost lost my breath. I was very angry. She apologized right away and said that she had only meant to fool around. But the pain spoiled my mood. Uli noticed and tried to cheer me up. She was extremely kind, kissed me gently, and said, "But Mühsam, you know how much we all love you!" Then she fetched Lotte, who tried to appease me by shoving her tongue as far down my throat as possible. I lack character, and so this really cheered me up. I continued to kiss many others: the Kündinger, Emmy, a homosexual young Italian, Strich, and even the ugly Frau Kutscher.[36] Finally, the Götzen couple arrived, and I got busy with Fanny.[37] The woman is very much in love with me. "Don't make me crazy!" she begged, and when I insisted on her finally visiting me, she said, "I'll come if you are ready to watch me die!"

Later, she followed me to the room where we had left our coats, and in the dim light I put my hand under her skirt to make her come. We got interrupted by the short Hoerschelmann,[38] who brought Fanny a glass of punch. We flinched when he also said hello to someone else: Cronos was pretending to sleep right next to, or rather, under us. To make things worse, some Russian fellow emerged from underneath a bunch of sheets. Both had probably observed Fanny's adultery. It was all very uncomfortable. But I assume that they saw it as drunken foolishness and did not understand that there is deep love—in me too!

The orgy ended with Luitpold and Stefanie...[39]

Munich, Whit Monday, May 24, 1915

My financial situation worries me. I would really like to get everything that I need so I can live with Zenzl permanently. I no longer receive news from Lübeck. I must assume this means that my father is again well and will not die anytime soon.

I do not know how I can earn any money, and so I am considering becoming an inventor. I had the idea of constructing a machine that allows you to easily eat asparagus in an appetizing way. It is horrifying to watch the whole world grab asparagus from the plate and suck it dry.

I also want to have celluloid tongues in the shape of oyster shells constructed and patented. But who will pay me for these ideas?

Zenzl is coming soon. She must help me.[40]

Lübeck, Sunday, July 25, 1915

Father died on Tuesday, the twentieth. [...] Uncle Leopold[41] explained to me how my father had changed his will to my disadvantage: I will only get the legal portion. The rest of my inheritance will be bound, collecting interest until I will either become a pharmacist or marry a Jewish woman (one *born* Jewish—very funny) or turn sixty. Then, I will get it all.

On the same day, my siblings and I sat together in the house of the deceased, and Leo read the will. Father made plans for everything. His foresight is unparalleled. [...]

I was very surprised, and disappointed, when I learned how much my father has left in total. The "multi-millionaire" only left 235,000 marks. Ninety thousand are a part of my sisters' dowries. Twelve thousand marks will have to be paid in taxes. This means that I will be left with thirty-five to forty thousand marks for the next twenty-three years. I have to immediately use fifteen thousand marks to repay debts and to buy some modest furniture for my apartment (alternatively, I can take furniture from my father's home). In the end, I will be left with no more than twenty thousand marks, from which I cannot even access enough to pay the Bern debt.[42] [...]

This is a very painful experience. Now that my wishes have finally come true, I find myself back where I started: financial worries and fears. My consolation is that, from now on, I can put no more hope in death and inheritance, but only in life and work!

Munich, Saturday, January 1, 1916

I will long remember New Year's Eve 1916. We had a big party, with eighteen people, plus those who fled other events. It was very loud and jolly. Most of it was drowned in alcohol and gaudiness. Zenzl had worked very hard and provided a lot of food and drink. The strong punch soon freed me of all restraint, and I lay in the arms and on the mouth of a professor Frau Aenny v. Aster. Since Frau Ehrengard became very jealous, I had to turn my attention to her as well.[43] So-called "Schwabing bundels" had formed everywhere, and no one but Zenzl had a problem with them. Unfortunately, in my drunkenness, I realized this too late.

When the guests left between half past six and half past seven in the morning, Ehrengard made such a scene that I accompanied her home to calm her down. But she was back at our apartment right away, apparently because the door to hers was locked. I got very angry and explained to her that she was causing me a lot of problems. She could not think of anything better to do than to challenge Zenzl. Afterwards, in the bedroom, Zenzl was very upset with me and said that she wanted to leave me, since I continuously put her in such ugly situations. The worst thing for me was when she said that she regretted leaving Ludwig Engler.[44] She said that she was thinking about returning to him.

I am not sure what will come of this. I am afraid. Zenzl does not believe me when I say that I cannot live without her and that she is closer to my heart than any other person.

1. Erich Mühsam, *Tagebücher 1910–1924* (München: dtv, 1994).
2. The relationship ended fairly soon.
3. Presumably, Mühsam's doctor at the time.
4. Emmy Hennings (1885–1948), writer and artist, one of Mühsam's lovers, later married to the Dadaist Hugo Ball (1886-1927).
5. Friends of Mühsam.
6. Munich wine tavern and restaurant frequented by artists and intellectuals.
7. Actress and long-time lover of Karl Kraus (1874-1936) and of the psychoanalyst Fritz Wittels (1880–1950).
8. Morax was a nickname for Karl Schultze (1882–1916), pianist and comrade of Mühsam's; Fräulein Vital remains unidentified.
9. Kathi Kobus (1854–1929), proprietor of the bohemian bar *Simplicissimus*.
10. Short for *Simplicissimus*–see the previous footnote.
11. Ernst Moritz Engert (1892–1987), artist.
12. Lotte Pritzel (1887–1952), artist and lover of Mühsam's.
13. Frieda Gross-Schloffer (1876–1950), lover of Mühsam's in 1908.

14. Nickname for Lotte Pritzel (1887–1952), artist and lover of Mühsam's.
15. Uli Trolsch, lover of Mühsam's.
16. Jenny Vallière, actress.
17. Nickname for Johanna Terwin (1884–1962), actress.
18. Presumably, the wife of Ernst Mewes (1884–1918), actor.
19. Presumably, the wife of August Weigert (1877–?), actor.
20. Fritz Strich (1883–1963), philologist, partner of Lotte Pritzel.
21. Public pool in Schwabing, Munich.
22. Alfred Kerr (1867–1948), theater critic, editor of the journal *Pan* from 1911 to 1914.
23. Maximilian Harden (1861–1927), popular German journalist and editor. In 1906, he was involved in a controversy after accusing the Emperor of hypocrisy by revealing that one of his closest advisers, Philipp zu Eulenburg (1847–1921), was gay. Harden's conflation of political critique and of disclosing intimate information was heatedly discussed within radical circles in the German-speaking world. While some, most notably Karl Kraus in *The Fackel* [The Torch], criticized Harden harshly, Mühsam came to Harden's defense, publishing the pamphlet "Die Jagd auf Harden" [The Campaign against Harden] in 1908.
24. Paul Cassirer (1871–1926), publisher and gallery owner.
25. Heinrich Mann (1871–1950), novelist, elder brother of Thomas Mann (1875–1955).
26. Frank Wedekind (1864–1918), renowned German libertarian playwright.
27. Central bank of Germany from 1876 until 1945.
28. Mühsam's brother.
29. Siblings and other relatives of Mühsam's.
30. Brewery in Schwabing.
31. The *Komet* was founded in 1883 as a journal for county fairs, festivals, circuses, etc.
32. Paul L. Fuhrmann, editor of the satirical journal *Komet*, which Mühsam contributed to.
33. See footnote 15.
34. Lotte Pritzel (1887–1952), artist and lover of Mühsam's.
35. Cronos cannot be identified.
36. "The Kündninger" cannot be identified; Frau Kutscher is presumably the wife of Artur Kutscher (1878–1960), literature and theater scholar.
37. The Götzen couple cannot be identified.
38. Rolf von Hoerschelmann (1885–1947), illustrator.
39. Luitpold and Stefanie cannot be identified.
40. The plans were never realized.
41. Leopold Cohn was Erich's mother's brother, who often functioned as a mediator between Erich and his father.
42. Mühsam owed money to Margarethe Faas-Hardegger—see the letter from July 28, 1914 in "Additional Letters."
43. The identities of Aenny v. Aster and Frau Ehrengard could not be established.
44. Ludwig Engler (1875–?), painter, partner of Zenzl when she met Erich.

ADDITIONAL LETTERS

This additional selection of letters by Mühsam is intended to illustrate his personal struggles, the correspondence he maintained with notable anarchists of his era, and the desperate months in Nazi prisons and concentration camps.

A significant number of Mühsam's letters have been published in two superb volumes edited by Gerd W. Jungblut.[1] A number of letters remain unpublished, in particular those to family members. Many letters have disappeared, some dramatically. Egon Friedell and John Henry Mackay ordered that all their personal correspondence be burnt after their death.[2] Bruno Vogel, pursued by Nazi troops, dumped all of the letters that Mühsam had sent to him into a Norwegian fjord.[3] As German troops advanced on Savoy, Friedrich Wilhelm Foerster charred all his personal correspondence.[4] Finally, the papers buried in the garden of Antonie Pannekoek's[5] Amsterdam home during World War II were destroyed during a bombing raid.[6]

To Margarethe Faas-Hardegger, Munich, July 28, 1914

MY DEAREST MARGRIT,

As you can imagine, I am terribly sorry that I have put you in this position! I will of course make every effort to return to you at least the few hundred francs that you really need right now!

If only my father would finally die! It is probably not kind to wish for something like this, but even if I love the old man, I must hope for his end, since it will also mean the end of my troubles. His heart is weak. It was already weak when we made this deal. Otherwise, I would not have dared to take on the debt. I never expected this resilience. He is almost seventy-six years old! [...][7]

> I kiss your forehead and your children,
> Yours,
> Erich Mühsam

To Alexander Berkman, Charlottenburg, December 26, 1924

DEAR COMRADE BERKMAN!

People constantly demand things from me, and I have not yet had a quiet moment to respond to your letter.

It will be a pleasure to meet you and to shake your hand! I am also looking forward to an account on the situation of our comrades in Russia. I still do not have a clear picture, and I want to hear all sides before taking a position.

Right now, I am focusing my energies on winning the freedom of the Bavarian comrades who are still in prison. I will speak in Hamburg, Essen, and Chemnitz next week on behalf of the Rote Hilfe, campaigning for amnesty. Tomorrow, I will meet anarchist youths at the Town Hall. Can you possibly come there, dear comrade? We can then either discuss things immediately (maybe in a coffeehouse) or arrange a meeting.

I thank you for your friendly greetings! You have gone through even harder times than I have, and this is why I feel a particularly strong bond to you.[8] I hope to see you tomorrow!

Your comrade,
Erich Mühsam

To John Henry Mackay, Berlin-Britz, February 6, 1929

The two of us hardly ever agreed,
but were united by the longing for anarchy,
and any proclaimer of freedom,
despite all differences in theory,
is related to all other proclaimers of freedom.

To the poet and confessor John Henry Mackay,
Neighborly greetings in struggle!

Erich Mühsam

To Carl Georg von Maasen,[9] Berlin-Britz, June 2, 1929

MY DEAR C.G.!

[…] I am still not making any money off my journal. To the contrary, I am losing money. *Fanal*, no matter how highly respected and lauded, is once again close to folding. On top of that, I give a lot of talks, for which I don't even receive travel expenses if they take place in the greater Berlin area. Furthermore, in the prisons of the German model republic, I have acquired the reputation of being someone who is willing to help, and so dozens of poor devils petition me constantly. As you can imagine, I can hardly ever really help any of them. But you cannot disappoint the trust that people put in you. Since I have no secretary, I have to do every single damn thing myself. My personal life suffers the most. I have no distractions.

The worst thing is that in order to have food on the table, I need to do work that is entirely pointless. The only steady income I have right now is the twenty-five marks I get every Monday for a poem in the *Welt am Montag* [The World on Monday].[10] But this is forced poetry, and it ruins all true lyrical instinct.

I want to write a political comedy against the ideology pushers of all colors (it will be as bad under the swastika as it is under the Soviet star). But I would need three months of vacation to do it; I would need to be spared domestic worries, telephone calls, visits, etc. At the same time, I would need to be able to keep the house. With an advance of one thousand marks, I could do it. But who will give me one thousand marks?

One tries to get by and it does not lead anywhere, and one's only hope—namely, that the proletarians will rectify the situation with bombs and hand grenades—increasingly disappears, because the worse the situation gets, the more passive the proletarians become, leaving everything in the hands of their corrupt and rich leaders. [...]

Yours truly,
Erich Mühsam

To Rudolf Rocker, Berlin-Britz, September 8, 1929

DEAR RUDOLF,
Your letter from the beautiful region of the *mittägliche Provinzen* has surprised me very much.[11] I am very happy that you and Milly are finally getting the rest that you deserve, particularly under the care of our dear Emma.

I must ask you to apologize to Emma that I find so little time to write. You know how many duties I have. I hardly find the time to do the work required for us to survive. I once again spent all day yesterday at the prison in Brandenburg an der Havel,[12] where I was confronted with so much misery that I have been unable to do anything for twenty-four hours.

I am very grateful for your efforts in helping *Fanal* to carry on! We have rented a room in Berlin, where we will establish an office for the journal. We have done this mainly to relieve Zenzl, who basically broke down. The room is very central, near Lützowplatz. I pay only twenty marks per month, because the apartment (a modest studio on the fifth floor of a building facing the yard) belongs to a woman with whom I had a liaison twenty years ago in Munich. For Zenzl, the office makes things much easier, and for me too, because I can now stay in Berlin overnight as I please. However, we have new financial worries. We need to pay travel costs for

Hellmuth and to buy several pieces of furniture.[13] So we can't be overly optimistic. What bothers me particularly is that we won't be able to do an index for the issues of the past year, including all of the covers and listing all of the printing mistakes. Well, the necessary dollars might still arrive. For now, I struggle on and won't give in until the very last option has been exhausted.

Now on to Emma's memoirs. I strongly encourage her to keep the rights for foreign publication. Since she already has a German publisher, the biggest step has been taken. Had you asked me to recommend a publisher, I wouldn't have had any idea: I can't even find a publisher for my own books these days! I assume that Erich Reiß, who hasn't been able to edit anything in two years, has sorted out his financial problems.[14]

Emma should in any case insist on an advance of at least one thousand marks. Apart from that, I would demand the following: 15 percent of the cover price of the paperback, with 10 percent going to her and 5 percent to the translator, and prepayment for at least three thousand copies—but, again, not less than one thousand marks!

I am ready to negotiate for Emma with Reiß if she gives me a mandate. I would consult with the *Schutzverband Deutscher Schriftsteller* [Association for the Protection of German Writers], just to be clear about the legal issues.[15] One again, though, I would like to emphasize that Emma should keep her rights for Germany, France, etc. With respect to America, it is hard for me to give advice. I think that Karin Michaelis[16] would say the same thing if Emma decided to leave the decision to the American publisher.[17]

You did not mention how long you intended to stay. If you return in the fall, I hope that you will bring Emma with you.

I greet all three of you very dearly—in Zenzl's name as well—and assure you with all my friendship and love that I will not tell anyone about your disappearance.

Yours,

Erich M.

To Karin Michaelis,[18] Berlin-Britz, May 5, 1932

DEAR COMRADE!

My best wishes for your sixtieth birthday come very late! But I offer you a gift, rather than an excuse: yesterday, we founded a "Committee for the Rescue of Mooney and Billings."[19] I know that this will add to your happiness, since it was one of your wishes!

About ten organizations were present at the meeting. Apart from founding the committee, we agreed to organize a big demonstration at the end of the month.

By then, we hope to have won over a number of additional organizations and individuals; we also hope that all (or at least almost all) revolutionary proletarian associations will be united in this fight against the brutal and biased reactionary legal system of America and of all countries.

Unfortunately, at least in Germany, this has to happen without the two great workers' parties. They like to speak of a "United Front," but what they mean is a front that is entirely under their control. To them, the interests of the party are more important than the interests of the class. They insult, defame, sabotage, and destroy all common action.

I have to ask you something in the name of the committee. We want you to take part in our demonstration! Ideally, you would come here yourself to speak to the workers of Berlin. If you cannot make the journey, I would ask you to send me a short text that we could read—a passionate call to the world to defend our comrades Mooney and Billings in the same way that Sacco and Vanzetti were defended.

You have probably been updated on Sascha Berkman's situation.[20] Your wonderful appeal to the humanity of the French government has met with the support of many important figures, but has only led to formal niceties among those in power. The thread holding the Sword of Damocles over Sascha's head has become a little stronger. But it can still tear. Sascha has to continue renewing his residency every three months.

Some time ago, we had the pleasure of our comrade Emma Goldman visiting Berlin. Angelica Balabanoff was also here, about half a year earlier.[21] It seems to me that it is your turn now—you should come to visit Berlin again! If you do, you must see our house in Britz! Spring is beginning. In our little garden, many flowers, especially roses, await you![22]

With the most sincere greetings, I am your dearly devoted
Erich Mühsam

To the State Prosecutor Dr. Mittelbach

Political prisoner Mühsam

Sonnenburg, April 16, 1933, Police Prison

Mr. State Prosecutor Dr. Mittelbach
Police Headquarters
Berlin

Political Division

My health is deteriorating daily, and I am again asking to be sent to a hospital to have my fitness for imprisonment assessed.[23]

The damage to my left ear causes me great difficulty. Abrupt movements, physical strain, bending, etc. cause piercing pain in the auditory canal. My head buzzes constantly. Even worse than these physical symptoms are the consequences for my soul and for my nerves. Often, I cannot hear orders at all; at other times, I do not understand them or at least not properly. I wince whenever there is a loud noise, and I am not able to locate it. In addition, there are the social challenges that come with the loss of hearing. I cannot speak with the other prisoners, since I am unable to follow their conversations. This means that I am completely isolated and alone all day. As a consequence, I am terribly anxious and unable to do what is expected of me.

The absence of a dentist further contributes to the deterioration of my health. I cannot bite properly and cannot eat the bread we receive. My nourishment is reduced to soups and to soft foods in my own possession. My intestines are suffering terribly.

My heart does not work properly either. The prison doctor cites nervousness as the cause. However, I do have a dilation of the heart, confirmed by X-rays. All the symptoms I have now—from congestion and exhaustion to nightmares and body aches—are the same as I had before, only that they have become worse.

I am fifty-five years old, and I do not feel that I am fit for imprisonment under these conditions. I get worse every day. This is why I am asking that my situation be changed as quickly as possible by a transfer from Sonnenburg to a place where my fitness for imprisonment can be assessed.[24]

Concerning the political reasons for my imprisonment, I would like to state the following: I have never held nor wanted to hold a leading position. My journal *Fanal* has not released an issue since July 1931. In the special editions that have appeared since, I did not comment on current political affairs. They were of a purely rhetorical nature.[25] I was never able to support myself by the political work I did, only by my literary work.

Should my imprisonment be lifted, I will diligently follow the regulations that the police deem necessary.

Erich Mühsam
Writer

To Kreszentia Mühsam, Concentration Camp Oranienburg, 1934

[…] Recently, quite a few comrades have been released, and I am happy for everyone who can go home—especially for those who I will miss most. It will take some time before I myself can go home. I have no illusions. […]

To Kreszentia Mühsam, Concentration Camp Oranienburg, May 30, 1934

[...] Your last letter, which arrived yesterday, made me very happy! I wonder whether animals remember the past in the same way we do. I believe that Nicky thinks that I am actually present when he smells my laundry.[26] He would probably recognize me right away without the beard and not even remember what I looked like before. Friends and acquaintances, on the other hand, would probably not think that I was Mühsam, but rather someone else [...]

To Kreszentia Mühsam, Concentration Camp Oranienburg, June 20, 1934

Mühsam No. 2651
Prisoners' Company, 2nd Unit

MY BELOVED ZENZL!
Sunday is visitors' day. Until then, what shall I write? I don't have much to say. As you know, that is usually a good sign. Everything is the same. The weather provides the only change. Otherwise, I pass the days and the long nights thinking about you, the animals, the past, the future. What I need, I have, thanks to your care. The only thing that I have to report is that I am using my last stamp for this letter. Oh, and my spectacle case broke. I will need a new one, but there is no particular hurry. Sunday's package was very beautiful, as always! You know better than I what you should bring this time, both with respect to food and clothes (no napkins, I have plenty).

I was very happy to receive greetings from old grandma.[27] If she is still around, I return them sincerely! I am curious whether Peps will join you again next Sunday.[28] In any case, I am happy that he got some distraction and relaxation in Munich.

This is all I have to write right now. It is no news that I love you. Many greetings to Ernst, Grete,[29] to all the good and loyal people, and to Morly and Nicky.[30]

Goodbye,
Heartfelt kisses,
Your Erich

To Kreszentia Mühsam [final note sent by Erich]

Mühsam
Oranienburg
Konzentrationslager
6th Company, 2nd Unit
No. 2651

Oranienburg, June 22, 1934

DEAREST ZENZL!
Unfortunately, I have to inform you that I am not allowed to receive visitors or carry on correspondence for four weeks.

Stay healthy and be kissed!
Your Erich

1. Erich Mühsam, *In meiner Posaune muss ein Sandkorn sein. Briefe 1900-1934* (Vaduz: Topos, 1984).
2. Egon Friedell (1878-1938), Austrian philosopher, writer, and artist; John Henry Mackay (1864-1933), Scottish-born German individualist anarchist and poet.
3. Bruno Vogel (1898-1987), German writer.
4. Friedrich Wilhelm Foerster (1869-1966), German philosopher.
5. Antonie Pannekoek (1873-1960), renowned Dutch council communist.
6. Gerd W. Jungblut, Einleitung in *Mühsam, In meiner Posaune muss ein Sandkorn sein. Briefe 1900-1934*, 1: XVII-XIX.
7. Margarethe Faas-Hardegger had previously helped Mühsam financially. She was able to resolve the 1914 crisis as a letter sent to Mühsam on July 25 confirms (Erich Mühsam, *In meiner Posaune muss ein Sandkorn sein. Briefe 1900-1934*, 2:754-756).
8. Reference to Berkman's fourteen years in prison (1892-1906), following the failed assassination attempt against the industrialist Henry Clay Frick (1849-1919).
9. Carl Georg von Maasen (1880-1940), German literary critic and historian.
10. *Die Welt am Montag* was a liberal weekly published in Berlin from 1896 to 1933.
11. Literally, "noon provinces." *Mittägliche Provinzen* is an antiquated German term that has been used to describe various regions. Rocker and Milly Witkop were in Scandinavia.
12. German town about seventy kilometers from Berlin.
13. Hellmuth Loßner delivered copies of *Fanal*.
14. Publisher in Berlin.
15. Goldman's autobiography was only published in German in 1978 with Karin Kramer Verlag as *Gelebtes Leben*.
16. Karin Michaelis (1872-1950), Danish feminist writer and activist.
17. Alfred A. Knopf (New York).
18. See footnote 16.
19. The labor organizers Thomas Mooney (1882-1942) and Warren Billings (1893-1973) were found guilty of the Preparedness Day Bombing in San Francisco on July 22, 1916, which killed ten people and wounded forty. The bomb was detonated to protest the United States'

imminent entry into World War I. Mooney and Billings, whose convictions were based on very weak evidence, spent over twenty years in prison before being pardoned in 1939.

20. Berkman was in France with uncertain immigration status.
21. Angelica Balabanoff (1878-965), Italian socialist activist.
22. It does not appear that Michaelis came to Berlin.
23. Mühsam's health had been severely damaged during his five years of imprisonment following the overthrow of the Bavarian Council Republic.
24. This never happened.
25. Mühsam had sent occasional newsletters to *Fanal* subscribers to confirm his intention to resume publication.
26. Nicky was one of the Mühsams' dogs.
27. Presumably, Meta Kraus-Fessel, a close friend of the Mühsams, who also escaped the Nazi regime and spent time in Prague, where Zenzl broke off contact with her over personal disagreements.
28. Zenzl's nephew Joseph "Peps" Elfinger.
29. Ernst Simmerling and Grete Dettmer, comrades.
30. The Mühsams' dogs.

APPENDIX II

THE FATE OF ZENZL MÜHSAM,
INCLUDING RUDOLF ROCKER'S "APPEAL TO THE CONSCIENCE OF THE WORLD" AND LETTERS BY ZENZL MÜHSAM

Background

KRESZENTIA "ZENZL" MÜHSAM WAS BORN ON JULY 28, 1884, THE FIFTH child of Augustin and Kreszentia Elfinger in Haslach, Lower Bavaria. Zenzl's mother died when Zenzl was eight years old. The family was poor. In 1900, Zenzl moved to Munich. In 1902, she gave birth to her son Siegfried outside of wedlock. Zenzl could not provide for Siegfried, who mainly grew up with foster families and relatives.

From 1909 until 1915, Zenzl lived with the painter and sculptor Ludwig Engler in Munich. She met Erich Mühsam in 1913. Mühsam, who had many romantic and sexual relationships, felt particularly drawn to Zenzl, who eventually left Engler to move in with Erich. They married on September 15, 1915.

Siegfried briefly moved in with the couple in 1917, before leaving home at a young age. He lived in Germany's southwest, became a painter, and emigrated to the United States in the 1950s. For long periods, he had no contact with Zenzl at all. In a letter to a comrade, one year after Erich's death, Zenzl wrote: "My son abandoned me when I was the most miserable. Not even once did he come with me to the camp to see his stepfather. He simply refused, even though he could have gotten permission to visit."[1] After Zenzl returned to Germany in 1955, Siegfried did come to Berlin at least once, but closer contact did not seem to be reestablished.

Zenzl Mühsam and the Soviet Union

Zenzl left Berlin on July 14, 1934, four days after Erich's death. Friends had advised her not to attend the funeral for security reasons. After a short stop in Dresden, Zenzl traveled on to Prague. She was accompanied by her nineteen-year old nephew Joseph "Peps" Elfinger, whom she had been looking after since his father Joseph had been sent to the Dachau Concentration Camp in 1936.[2]

In September, the Czechoslovakian press attaché Camill Hofmann managed to bring Erich's papers to Prague and to deliver them to Zenzl. At the same time, the first invitation to the Soviet Union reached Zenzl, but she declined, although her situation in Prague was far from perfect. "Her financial situation was disastrous. Mühsam's siblings, who had fled to Palestine, could not support her. The refugee committees in Prague were overwhelmed, and the donations from anarchists around the world did not amount to much and did not come regularly."[3]

In January 1935, Zenzl's pamphlet about her husband's tragic end, entitled "Der Leidensweg Erich Mühsams" [The Ordeal of Erich Mühsam], was published by the MOPR press in Moscow.[4]

On June 11 of the same year, Zenzl was stripped of her German citizenship for "spreading infamous propaganda." Her life in Prague continued to leave her penniless, she did not have many friends, and her safety was threatened by the rise of the local fascist movement. The Soviet government continued sending invitations. It secured the help of Jelena Stassowa, the chairwoman of the Soviet section of the MOPR, a sister organization of the Rote Hilfe, which had led to Erich and Zenzl developing a friendship with Stassowa in the 1920s. Zenzl finally decided to make the trip in July 1935, not least because she was unable to get a visa to visit Emma Goldman on the Riviera in France.

Zenzl arrived in Moscow on August 8, together with her nephew Joseph Elfinger, who she wanted to send to his brother Ludwig "Luggi" Elfinger, an engineer who had found work in Chelyabinsk.

During her first months in the Soviet Union, Zenzl gave several talks about Mühsam and participated in events dedicated to his memory. She was promised publications of Mühsam's work if she could get his papers, which she had purposefully left in Prague with Ruth Österreich,[5] to Moscow. Increasingly convinced of the government's good intentions, she asked for the papers to be sent to her in early 1936. They arrived in February and were stored in the Maxim Gorky Institute.[6] Zenzl retained the publication rights and decided to stay in Russia for another year.

On April 8, 1936, she was arrested as a "Trotskyist spy" in the wake of Sergey Kirov's murder.[7] The accusation was officially based on contacts with Erich Wollenberg[8] and on correspondence with foreign anarchists. She spent four months incarcerated in the prisons of Ljubjanka and Butyrka,[9] before being released on October 8, at least partly because of an international anarcho-syndicalist campaign on her behalf, supported by prominent figures like Ruth Österreich, Harry Wilde, André Gide, Thomas Mann, and Rudolf Rocker.

Despite being officially prohibited from residing in Leningrad or Moscow, Zenzl returned to Moscow. On June 13, 1937, she sold Mühsam's papers to the

Maxim Gorky Institute, probably out of desperation. During the course of 1937, her nephew Joseph disappeared. His fate remains unknown.

In the summer of 1938, Zenzl applied for a visa to the United States. On November 16 of the same year, she was arrested again and returned to Butyrka Prison. Her arrest may have been triggered by the visa application. Some historians, however, have suggested that it had always been the intention to rearrest Zenzl once international attention had subsided.

On September 16, 1939, Zenzl was sentenced to eight years of hard labor for "abusing the Soviet Union's hospitality, and for participating in a counterrevolutionary organization and agitation." She was transported to Camp No. XV in Potma in the Mordovian Autonomous Soviet Socialist Republic (ASSR). On December 1, she was returned to Moscow and imprisoned with other German anti-fascists, who were to be handed over to the Gestapo on the basis of the Molotov-Ribbentrop Pact signed in August 1939.[10] For unknown reasons, Zenzl was never delivered to the Gestapo; instead, she was sent to Camp No. III in Yavas in the Mordovian ASSR. She celebrated Erich Mühsam commemoration days there, reciting his poems to other inmates and telling them about his activities.[11] In November 1946, she was released from the camp and exiled to the Novosibirsk district in Siberia.

In March 1947, a railway worker recognized her at the Novosibirsk Railway Station. It appears that she was homeless at the time. The worker organized transport for her to Moscow, from where she was immediately banned. Her request to move to the German Democratic Republic (GDR) was declined. Zenzl found work at a children's home in Ivanovo, about 250 kilometers northeast of Moscow.

In February 1949, the NKVD arrested her again.[12] In October, she was returned to the Novosibirsk district, accused of belonging to an "anti-Soviet Trotskyist organization." She moved in with the Göttings, a Volga German family,[13] at a kolkhoz[14] in Yelanka in the region of Omsk, two thousand kilometers east of Moscow. The same year, Rudolf Rocker published the pamphlet "Der Leidensweg der Zensl [sic] Mühsam" [The Ordeal of Zenzl Mühsam] (a reference to Zenzl's pamphlet "Der Leidensweg Erich Mühsams") to put pressure on the Soviet government, which kept Zenzl's whereabouts hidden. Despite inspiring some international protests and an early Spanish translation, the pamphlet's release had no substantial consequences.

On August 16, 1954, seventeen months after Stalin's death, Zenzl was allowed to return to the children's home in Ivanovo. On March 13, 1955, she received an East German passport.

On June 27, 1955, she arrived in East Berlin, where she was provided with an apartment and a pension under the condition that she not speak about her experiences in the Soviet Union. On July 21, 1956, microfilm copies of Erich's papers arrived at Berlin's Akademie der Künste.[15] Once again, Zenzl tried to get them published. Her efforts did not achieve the desired results but a selection of poetry was published by the press Volk und Welt.[16]

On July 22, 1959, the military tribunal of the Moscow military district declared the 1936 and 1938 accusations levied against Zenzl unjust. The GDR government bestowed official honors upon her for her work against fascism.

On March 10, 1962, Zenzl died of lung cancer. She bequeathed all the rights to Mühsam's papers to the Akademie der Künste.

In 1991, she was posthumously exonerated with respect to the accusations of 1949.

In 1992, her urn was transferred to Erich's grave at Berlin's Waldfriedhof Dahlem.

Rudolf Rocker: "Appeal to the Conscience of the World"[17]

Why Zenzl Mühsam has been kept in Russian captivity for thirteen years—a time that not even eternity can give back to her—remains incomprehensible. It is possible that she was only used as a propaganda tool from the beginning; as a mere means of taking possession of Erich Mühsam's papers. It is also possible that she got to know too much about the inner workings of the NKVD and that the government considered it dangerous to let her return to Prague. Shortly after her arrival in Moscow, the era of terror began. If this was the case, then she was neutralized to protect the interests of the state—a purpose for which no means are despicable enough. A human life counts for nothing in a totalitarian police state like Russia.[18]

It is pointless to engage in speculation, especially since the exact circumstances are not very important. The fact is that a disgraceful crime has been committed. Even the most unscrupulous criminal would hardly dare to touch this woman, who has already experienced so much suffering.

It is in doubt whether we can win her freedom and help her settle in a neutral country to live the rest of her abused life in peace. Maybe it would be possible if we were dealing with a different state. In my long life, I have participated in a number of international protest movements, and I recall with deep satisfaction powerful campaigns like the one to liberate the victims of Montjuïch.[19] At the time, the outrage in all countries was strong enough to force the Spanish inquisitors to let their innocent victims go free. But people still had a feeling of personal dignity and a respect for human life then, something that the blind masses have lost today.

Still, now that the case of Zenzl Mühsam has finally entered public consciousness,[20] we must use all the means we have to stir up the conscience of the world once again. This is one of the most ruthless crimes that have ever been committed by those in power against a human being who has already been kicked to the ground.

Zenzl Mühsam has become the symbol of abused humanity. This simple woman, a woman from the midst of the people, personifies the gruesome fate of hundreds of thousands of hapless human beings who slowly go under in the NKVD's dungeons and labor camps, and whose cries fade away in a world that does not care—like cries in the desert…

The terrible crime that was committed by the hangmen of the Third Reich against Erich Mühsam was an act of brutal rawness and of unspeakable barbarism. But I dare say that the outrageous treatment that his unfortunate wife has been experiencing in Russia for the last thirteen years is even worse, because it has been covered up by bottomless hypocrisy and infamous lies, intentionally misleading the public. While commemorative plaques are erected for Erich Mühsam in Germany's Russian sector and streets and squares are named after him,[21] his widow is slowly tortured to death. It would be hard to take hypocrisy and mendacity any further.

After the murder of her husband, Zenzl wrote in a letter, "I know that Erich would bless anyone who is good to me." Likewise, Erich Mühsam, this poet and righteous man who carried his terrible fate with such heroic strength, would curse everyone mocking his name by allowing his courageous wife, who loyally stood by him during the most terrible of times, rot in misery, with cold-heartedness beyond belief.

I have long hesitated to make this material available.[22] The main reason was the fear of making Zenzl's situation even worse. It is often easier to speak out for someone you do not know than for a friend you feel close to and do not want to push into deeper misery. But since the struggle for Zenzl's liberation has now begun, I could no longer remain silent, especially since I am in the possession of material that no one else has access to.

I hereby declare that my entire correspondence with Zenzl, as well as all the other documents that are included in this publication for the first time, can be viewed by anyone, no matter their political orientation or party affiliation. It cannot be ruled out that the communist press in Germany and in other countries will, upon orders of the NKVD, start to publish yet another series of supposed letters by Zenzl Mühsam to mislead its readers.[23] But anyone who knows the truth will easily understand that all this hypocrisy is not worth a penny if Zenzl is not at a neutral place where she herself can say openly and without fear what has happened to her. As long as this is not the case, all such attempts are but callous lies.

What we demand is the liberation of Zenzl from the agonizing imprisonment that has been imposed on her without reason or right by barbaric men representing a new form of absolutism. We demand that Zenzl be allowed to return to the world, which she was violently removed from thirteen years ago, and where she has enough friends to take care of her and to make the rest of her difficult life a little easier. We owe this not least to a dead poet and revolutionary who has been insulted, abused, and killed by dehumanized barbarians, and who could not foresee during his last gruesome hours the terrible fate that would come upon his courageous partner.

We do not appeal only to those who share Erich Mühsam's convictions, but to all righteous people of good will who have not yet lost their sense of human dignity and human suffering, and who do not want the dark vision of George Orwell to become reality. We cannot permit a boot to keep on kicking the face of a human being who can no longer move.

Simple newspaper articles, no matter how well intended, will not get us anywhere. What we need is a powerful international protest movement that, like in earlier times, fights with all available means for the life of an innocent woman who grew up in misery, who had to watch her husband being tortured to death, and who now experiences the same as a punishment for her loyalty to him—of all places, in the "land of socialism," in the "red fatherland of the proletariat."

We have to make sure that the call *Free Zenzl!* is heard in all countries and that it will not fall silent until Zenzl has been torn from the claws of the NKVD!

Crompond, N.Y., August 1949
Rudolf Rocker

Letters by Zenzl Mühsam

Letter from Zenzl Mühsam to Milly Wittkop and Rudolf Rocker

Prague, July 31, 1934

MY DEAR MILLY AND RUDOLF!
I have to talk to you. On July 16, my Erich was buried at Waldfriedhof Dahlem. I was not allowed to go to the funeral, because my relatives were afraid. I was the only living witness, apart from his comrades in prison, who saw him being tortured.

I have seen Erich dead, my dear. He looked so beautiful. There was no fear on his face; his cold hands were so gorgeous when I kissed them goodbye. Every day it becomes clearer to me that I will never talk to Erich again. Never. I wonder if anyone in this world can comprehend this?

I am in Prague with friends now. I have not found real peace yet, although I am tired, very tired. Money is a problem. For now, I must remain here. The authorities, the police etc. are very good to me.

I kiss you,
Your Zenzl

Letter from Zenzl Mühsam to Milly Wittkop and Rudolf Rocker

Prague, August 21, 1934

XVII., Arbesova, Pension Arosa

My dear Milly and Rudolf!

On July 8, I saw Erich for the last time. On June 22, he was abused by Deputy Commander Stahlkopf. We were denied contact from June 22 to July 22. On July 6, the SA commando was called away due to the events of June 30.[24] They were replaced by an SS unit from Württemberg.[25]

A prisoner who was freed on Friday, July 6, came to me, bringing greetings from Erich, and said that Stahlkopf, who had imposed the communication ban, had been discharged, and that I should try to see Erich on Sunday, July 8. I went to Oranienburg with the little Gretl.[26] All the wives were there, even though the communication ban was still officially in place. It was explained to us that the ban was not punishment, but a necessary precaution due to camp reorganization. We refused to leave. When an SS leader appeared in a vehicle, I went to the car and said that they should have at least allowed our men to write and inform us about the ongoing ban. Now there were at least 150 women, who had come with their children and other relatives, standing there, none of them with the money to pay for a journey in vain. The SS commander allowed each wife to see her husband for ten minutes in the yard.

All of the prisoners, Erich included, had a soldier with a steel helmet guarding them, and it was not possible to talk much. The last words that I heard Erich say were, "I thank you, Zenzl, for coming. It is Arthur's birthday today. Get off at Waidmannslust[27] and bring him my best regards. Then please don't forget that Hans's birthday is on the fifteenth. Go see him and congratulate him, for me as well, and ask him to give you some money so that you can celebrate your birthday on the twenty-eighth with a few friends. You sent me plenty of food yesterday. All I need now are some fresh clothes and a few marks of pocket money. Other than that, Zenzl, believe me, I will endure this change with the same stoicism as all the others. Stay strong!"

Then the visit was over, and Erich kissed my hand, hugged me, and whispered in my ear: "Mobilize other countries! We are all in danger!" A commander with a terrible voice yelled "Get out!," and to the prisoners, "Get back!" The prisoners did not walk, they ran like madmen. I went home with the little Gretl. On Monday, I sent Erich some pocket money.

According to a trustworthy report, Erich's death occurred in the night of July 9 to 10. On Monday morning [July 9], *Rottenführer*[28] Eradt asked Erich, "How much longer do you plan on being around?" Erich replied, "For quite some time."

Rottenführer Eradt said, "We recommend you hang yourself within three days, otherwise we will have to do it." Erich went downstairs and told this to his comrades. He gave all his food away and said, "Comrades, I will not be my own executioner." Then he was called to clean SS uniforms for the rest of the day.

At 7 p.m. he was ordered to come to the yard. The other prisoners, including the five or six helpers who were usually busy cleaning, were sent to bed early. The prisoners were not counted before going to sleep, as was usually the case. The comrades knew that Mühsam was missing. Many tried to listen to determine what was happening, but they could not hear anything.

In the morning, at a quarter to five, the SA man Himmelstoß–at least that's what the prisoners called him–came to count the prisoners. One of them said, "Mühsam is missing." Himmelstoß went outside without saying a word. When the first prisoners went to the toilet, they found Erich dangling from a clothesline. It was attached at a spot that Erich, in his clumsiness, could have never reached. His face was calm and beautiful, and his fists were not clenched. There were rumors that Erich had been drugged and poisoned first, and then, when he was already dead, hanged in the toilet by the two Eradts and Gerhardt Werner.[29] I have asked journalists to demand an autopsy of the body.

Such, dear Rudolf, were Erich's last days. You will receive information from me about further developments. For now, I basically have no money.

Meta is with me.[30] Yesterday, one of Erich's fellow prisoners came to visit and confirmed the story I told you.

[…] My dear, I still cannot quite grasp it all. To watch a human slowly tortured to death for seventeen months! Please think of me with a lot of love, as I do when I think of you. I will write again soon. I have to take care of a few things first.

I kiss you both,

Your Zenzl

Letter from Zenzl Mühsam to Milly Wittkop and Rudolf Rocker

August 1, 1935

Pension Arosa, Prague XVII, Arbesova 500

My dear Rudolf and Milly!
Ruth Österreich will keep all of Erich's works that I have saved until I return from my journey. In Russia, the first Mühsam volume will be printed by the Workers' Press;[31] selected poems from *Revolution, Gefangenschaft* [Imprisonment],[32] and so forth.

Rudolf, the main reason that I want to go to Russia with Peps is so that he can find work with his brother Ludwig.[33] I do not require anything from the Russian government. I have been invited by Ludwig and will live off the money from the publications. I already have the Russian passport in my pocket, and I am only waiting for the travel money to arrive. Furthermore, Rudolf and Milly, you need to understand that I need some rest and people whose eyes light up when they see me—almost as much as Erich's eyes did in the concentration camp when I arrived...

[...] A thousand things are happening in my heart, Rudolf and Milly. I hear these devils say, "She has sold Erich to Russia!" I want to be really honest: in this first year since Erich died—in other words, since I became a widow, as they say—except for you, Rudolf and Milly, and Emma Goldman, not one of Erich's comrades has shown any concern for me or seemed to care whether or not I was about to die or to kill myself. The Dutch comrades have sent me exactly five author copies for the pamphlet that was translated into Dutch.[34] I was told that a second edition was on its way. I know nothing about the print run of either the first or the second edition. It was agreed upon that I would get a third of the earnings, that a third would go to prisoners in Germany, and a third to the emigrants. My dear Rudolf and my dear Milly, I received neither notice nor money. I specifically requested that none of the money be used for their own organization. I requested the same of the Rote Hilfe, and they gave me the money that I was supposed to get—otherwise, I could have hardly survived! I crossed the border into Czechoslovakia with nothing but my backpack.

[...] Dear Rudolf and Milly, in three months I will be back in Prague. In the meantime, Ruth will look after Erich's papers. Please send the monthly rates to the named address. I will try to live with mother Kropotkin in Russia, if she is still alive, and with Vera Figner.[35] You will receive news.

Otherwise, my dears, I am very exhausted; I no longer sleep. I know that Erich would bless anyone who is good to me. I have not been able to speak to a syndicalist or to an anarchist since Erich died. Sometimes, I have the feeling that they are as dogmatic as the others. Well, the dogmatists have to forgive me when I try to help a young man who no longer has a fatherland.[36]

I want to do the following things: work against the concentration camps in Germany, where people continue to be tortured and abused, just like they were two years ago (and possibly it has gotten worse); work against the persecution of Jews in Germany, which makes me insane—how can you blame people for what they are?; work for the wonderful boys who rot and lose hope in exile.

Wendelin Thomas sent me a letter implying that I am only in contact with intellectuals.[37] I am only in contact with proletarians! Namely, proletarians who I know from the *Rotfront* circle[38] in Berlin. I have visited their quarters. Fifty of them share a single apartment with eight or nine beds in each room. They receive a very modest lunch and in the evening a piece of bread and a tiny piece of sausage. These men come to me. They motivate me to go where I can maybe do something for them, because they are filled with both hate and love, just as I am. [...]

The political situation here is like this: the effect of the election results among the *Sudetendeutschen* is that the Czechs turn toward fascism.[39] No one knows what will happen when Masaryk dies.[40]

My next address is: Frau Jelena Stassowa, General Secretary of the MOPR, Moscow, Soviet Union. Two envelopes. You can write whatever you want.

I greet and kiss you,

Your Zenzl

Letter from Zenzl Mühsam to Milly Wittkop and Rudolf Rocker

Moscow, November 25, 1935

Zenzl Mühsam, Nowo-Moskowskaja

MY DEAR MILLY, AND MY DEAR RUDOLF!

[…] Rudolf, the German Workers' Press in Moscow will publish a selection of Erich's revolutionary poems and prison poems. The contract is already drawn up. The book shall appear on January 1.[41]

The Russian Young Guards Press will translate my pamphlet.[42] Ernst Ottwalt will write a preface.[43] Anti-war songs, poems, and ballads by Erich will be added. Young Russians shall see what kind of people they torture to death in Germany.

After Sonnenburg, when Erich was in Plötzensee in solitary confinement, he made me a beautiful picture book with fable animals. It included thirty images and thirty-two verses—both the front and the back cover also had verses. This picture book will also be printed by the Young Guards Press in facsimile, a luxury print. I believe it will come out at the end of February.[44]

Furthermore, Rudolf, they want to do a movie based on my pamphlet. It will be called *Erich Mühsam*. In the movie, in which I am asked to appear, Erich's convictions will not be distorted. It will be a movie against the barbarism of fascism; a movie that shows how a Jewish poet was tortured to death, not least for being a Jew. The project was Alexander Granach's idea. Bredel has been asked to write the screenplay, and it has to be delivered by January 15. The main people involved are Granach (the director), Bredel, I, Budich, and Werner Hirsch, who was with Erich in the concentration camp during the worst time and who was himself tortured for being half-Jewish.[45] Comrades from the Bavarian Council Republic will serve as actors. Very few of them are professionals. I have to play the part of Frau Mühsam myself. We will see how that goes…[46]

You will be interested in how I live here and how I get by. I was invited personally by Jelena Stassowa (the general secretary of the MOPR), who Erich knew well and liked very much. The MOPR has put me up in a hotel. I have a room and so does Bepp.[47] We have full board, and I live here in peace and quiet. So far, I have spoken at different meetings organized for the comrades in Germany in the concentration camps and especially for the wives of the political prisoners and their children.

The last meeting was on November 17, with about 1,500 Russians who go to school here in Moscow. They come from all parts of Russia, from Tartary and Kyrgyzstan and all the other Russian regions. All of them are factory workers who have been sent to school to learn different languages. Right now they are learning German, and so the meeting was held in German.

Budich, a comrade of Erich's during the Bavarian Council Republic, gave a very good introductory speech. He stressed that Erich Mühsam was an anarchist. All in all, dear Rudolf, his words were really fine. Then I had to speak about concentration camps in Germany, and I can tell you, the comrades were not only shaken, they were outraged. Alexander Granach recited a few revolutionary poems that the teachers had already practiced with the students, who ranged in age from twenty-two to forty-five. Carola Neher, the former wife of the poet Klabund,[48] recited a few of Erich's *Soldatenlieder*[49] and some poems and ballads. The Russians liked Erich's poetry and satire the most. Carola could have continued for hours. At the end of the night, Ernst Busch sang a few songs.[50]

This was the first meeting in Moscow. The students had prepared a little surprise for us. In a lovely small room, tea was waiting with wonderful cakes and vodka. The atmosphere was intimate, politics seemed far away, and a Tatar comrade gave a speech in the German he could muster. He said to me, "*Tovarisch* Mühsam, we grieve with you, but I tell you, you must live on! And in order to do this, you must eat! So if you have nothing to eat, let us know! We are many, and we will provide for you to eat!"

Now, Rudolf, I shall go to the faraway lands of Siberia, first to Vyatka, then to Chelyabinsk to Ludwig's factory.[51] I shall have no other task here in Russia than to tell the Russian workers what fascism really is and to encourage them to show solidarity, not only in spirit, but also materially, with our prisoners in Germany. I hope that I will be able to fulfill this task and that it will be received by the comrades around the world with the same pure heart with which I execute it.

I hope most of all that Milly is healthy, and I hope especially that we will finally meet again next year, no matter where in the world!

With greetings and kisses,
Always, your loyal Zenzl

Letter from Zenzl Mühsam to Milly Wittkop and Rudolf Rocker

Moscow, January 9, 1936

Hotel Nowo-Moskowskaja

MY BELOVED MILLY AND RUDOLF,

[…] There are many comrades here who were with Erich in Niederschönenfeld,[52] as well as some who were in the concentration camps. I can talk to them about Erich. I could not do that in Prague.

[…] I don't know whether I have already written to you about my room; it is on the fifth floor, at the corner, and I see the sun rise and set. At this time of the year, when it rises, it is a fiery red ball. I have never seen the sun like that. It looks the same when it sets. Mostly, though, the sky is heavy and grey, like today. We will probably have snow.

Moscow looks beautiful all in white. I live near the Kremlin. When I eat, upstairs in the restaurant, the Kremlin lies in front of me in its barbaric beauty. Milly, to see the cathedral on the Red Square, the domes covered in snow–oh, if I could paint! How sad I become when I think of Siegfried, who has abandoned me during the most difficult time of my life; how he could work and paint here!

A few days ago, I was in the studio of Heinrich Vogeler.[53] He painted a few workers who have spent time in concentration camps. Milly, their eyes are an eternal accusation against the death of humanity in Germany. Vogeler also wants to paint me. In any case, there are a few people here who like me, who I can visit regularly, and who feel what I feel.

I hope that this year I will be able to see you again. […]

To you in love and loyalty,

Kisses,

Your Zenzl

Letter from Zenzl Mühsam to Erich's siblings

Moscow, March 16, 1937

MY DEAR SIBLINGS,

Charlotte, I received your letter some time ago. I should have answered it some time ago too, but I simply couldn't. I can't tell you why.

I still haven't written to Melanie and Senja, but I will.[54] Jelena [Stassowa] has written to Senja, and he said that I should not come, because there was no space for me, and because Melanie was sick; apparently, she had to undergo a very serious operation.

I now live in a house of the MOPR. I will send you the exact address. I have everything that I need, but I feel very lonely, and I have big problems with the language. I also want to write to Grethe.[55] On April 6, it will be the third time that I cannot celebrate Erich's birthday. I live with his memory, and it is my fault that I am often alone, but I don't want to go anywhere. I have never been to the theatre; somehow, I can't make it there. Should some of Erich's writings finally be published, you will be the first to know. Keep the picture books with you. Should the last one be printed, I will send it.[56]

For me, the winter here is very cold; the windows were frosted until a few days ago, all the way to the top. They are thawing now, but it can still be freezing.

A young girl just brought me a small bunch of snowdrops, which made me very happy. On the streets you can buy mimosas, probably from the Caucasus.

Tomorrow I have to go to the dental clinic. They have to pull fourteen teeth. I will get new ones, and I was told that it won't hurt, but I'm a little afraid.

When will we see each other again?

It really fills me with joy that Minna and Hans are doing well.[57] If you have the chance to tell them that I am doing well, please do so. They will worry otherwise.

I have received all I need, and if something finally gets published, I will be a bit more independent. Until then I have to be patient. I will write Grethe for her birthday![58]

I also intend to write every fourteen days from now on. I wish you all the best, and I wish you health!

Charlotte, write to me. Don't be angry that I haven't written for so long; it is neither lack of love nor loyalty, I simply couldn't!

Healthwise I am doing a bit better. The doctor says that I have menopausal symptoms.

I have nothing else to say. Write to me soon!

Always,
Your Zenzl

Letter from Zenzl Mühsam to family friends

Ivanovo, January 3, 1949

MY TRUE, BELOVED HEDWIG, AND KÄTHE, AND PAPA DUNCKER![59]
The year 1949 brings great joy for me! Husch-Nusch[60] has come to visit me from Moscow, together with Jelena Stassowa and my best friends.

I have been bothering Husch-Nusch for a year to find out where you are, Hedwig. She has searched for you and found you. As soon as I have word from you and Käthe and Papa, I will write a very long letter, and I will also send you a photograph.

Greetings to your husband! Do you have children?

Hedwig, I kiss you hard in love and loyalty,
Your Zenzl Mühsam

Letter from Zenzl Mühsam to Erich Mühsam's siblings

Berlin-Pankow, January 11, 1956

My dear siblings!
I have been in Berlin since June 25, 1955, and I am doing well. For two months, I have had a nice apartment: two rooms, a kitchen, a bathroom, and a small guest room.

Erich is still honored by the workers here. In Britz, where our house was, there is a memorial stone. The house itself was destroyed by bombs during the war. On the stone it says, "Erich, we will never forget you!"

There is an Erich-Mühsam-Straße in Friedenau,[61] and the workers, who have furnished my apartment, were extremely nice to me. I have an honorary pension of one thousand marks per month, and my furniture was provided by the government. It is modern and simple, just the way I wanted it.

The grave in Dahlem is taken care of by workers. Yesterday, a comrade told me that they would erect a monument for Erich if I gave my approval.

I will send you a nice photograph of Erich tomorrow or the day after, as well as of the memorial stone and of the grave. A comrade will take the pictures especially for me and will deliver them. However, I did not want you to wait any longer for a first message. […] There is a lot still to be said. Are the picture books that Erich made for me with you?

All non-published works by Erich that the Soviet government saved in the Gorky Institute will be transferred here.

Charlotte, now you know the most important things.

With love and affection,
Your sister Zenzl

Letter from Zenzl Mühsam to Erich Mühsam's siblings

Berlin-Pankow, January 16, 1956

Dear Hans, dear Minna, dear Charlotte, dear Leo!
You cannot imagine how happy I was to hear from you again after so many years! I thank you so much for the two letters I received! I am responding to them in one, since you all live happily together in the same house.

A few days ago, I sent an airmail letter, which tells you that I am fine and that I receive an honorable pension from the government that allows me to live out my life without sorrow. I am entering my seventy-second year. As my old friends confirm, I am in good shape, both mentally and physically. "True Lower Bavarian *Friedensware*,"[62] as a Jewish Hungarian friend called me in my host country of many years. The time that I am still blessed with—I still want to add many, many years—I will use to publish Erich's works. Unfortunately, it is difficult to gather everything. A lot of what was stored at friend's places has been burnt. I am very happy, though, that the diaries from 1905 to 1924 were preserved in the Soviet Union, so those I have at my disposal.[63]

I am not isolated in my beautiful apartment. Old friends come to visit me all the time. Hedwig Duncker, who is a doctor, looks after my health. Max Schröder can no longer look after the garden, but he takes care of my balcony. The Reverend Sepp Maier, who was one of the few who went to Erich's funeral with his Annie, is my private secretary—I am dictating this letter to him.[65]

I went with father Duncker, who is a professor at the *Gewerkschaftshochschule*,[66] to the celebrations for Wilhelm Pieck's eightieth birthday.[67] There I met my old friend, the niece of the great Russian art historian Stassow. I had already said goodbye to her in my mind, because she is now eighty-two years old.[524]

Helene Weigel and Bert Brecht are especially kind to me. I will write more about this in my next letter.

For today, may I greet you all very dearly!

I wish you all the best,

Your sister Zenzl

1. Letter to Leon Hirsch, March 1, 1935, quoted from Zenzl Mühsam, *Eine Auswahl aus ihren Briefen* [A Selection from her Letters], edited by Chris Hirte and Uschi Otten (Lübeck: Schriften der Erich-Mühsam-Gesellschaft, 1995), 67.
2. The fate of Joseph, the father, remains unknown.
3. Uschi Otten, "Ein Vermächtnis und seine Erfüllung" [A Liability and Its Realization], in Zenzl Mühsam, *Eine Auswahl aus ihren Briefen*, 92.
4. MOPR: Russian acronym for the International Red Aid, founded in Moscow in 1922.
5. Ruth Österreich (1894-1943), socialist activist and close friend of Zenzl Mühsam. Killed in Plötzensee Prison, where Erich Mühsam was also incarcerated for some time in 1943.
6. Founded by Gorky in 1933, it received its current name after Gorky's death in 1936.
7. Sergey Kirov (1886-1934), high Bolshevik official, assassinated at his office in December 1934.
8. Erich Wollenberg (1892-1973), socialist writer and activist.
9. Prisons in Moscow.
10. A "Treaty of Non-Aggression" between Germany and the Soviet Union; the pact also divided up German and Soviet spheres of interest in Europe and included many other agreements, for example the extradition of political dissidents. The treaty was broken by Germany when it attacked the Soviet Union in June 1941.
11. Uschi Otten, "Ein Vermächtnis und seine Erfüllung," 97.
12. Russian acronym for "The People's Commissariat for Internal Affairs," effectively Soviet Russia's secret police from 1934 to 1946.

13. Volga Germans are the descendants of German families who settled along the Volga River in the eighteenth century, under the reign of Catherine the Great (1729-1796).

14. Collectively run farm in the Soviet Union.

15. Famous Berlin Arts Institute, founded in the late seventeenth century.

16. *Volk und Welt* [People and World] was one of the most important publishing houses in the GDR, specializing in foreign fiction.

17. From Rudolf Rocker, *Der Leidensweg der Zensl [sic] Mühsam* [The Ordeal of Zenzl Mühsam] (Frankfurt am Main: self-published, 1949).

18. Equating the "Soviet Union" with "Russia" has always been common in German. This translation follows the usage of the terms in the original.

19. A hill near Barcelona that housed a notorious prison where many political dissidents were kept, tortured, and killed. With the end of the Franco dictatorship, the prison was closed.

20. Rocker refers to a number of international articles that had recently been published, demanding information about Zenzl Mühsam's whereabouts.

21. To this day, there are streets named after Mühsam in several towns in the former GDR, including Berlin (Friedrichshain), Magdeburg, Rostock, and Chemnitz.

22. Rocker refers to letters by Zenzl Mühsam published in *Der Leidensweg der Zensl Mühsam*.

23. A common propaganda tactic used by the NKVD.

24. On June 30, 1934, the so-called "Night of the Long Knives," several prominent SA members who posed an alleged threat to Hitler's reign were killed. This marked the end of the SA as a powerful organization within the Nazi regime.

25. Region in southwestern Germany, today part of the Bundesland Baden-Württemberg.

26. Probably Grete Dettmer, a comrade.

27. Northern suburb of Berlin.

28. A low rank commonly used in the SA, SS, and other paramilitary Nazi organizations.

29. Prison wardens.

30. Meta Kraus-Fessel, friend and comrade of the Mühsams, who also escaped the Nazi regime and spent time in Prague, where Zenzl broke off contact with her over personal disagreements.

31. This is a literal translation of *Arbeiterverlag*, the German term used in the letter–it is unclear which specific publisher Zenzl was referring to.

32. *Revolution: Kampf-, Marsch- und Spottlieder* [Revolution: Songs of Struggle, Marches, and Satirical Verses] was published in 1925 (Berlin: Fer freie Arbeiter); there is no book by Mühsam entitled *Gefangenschaft*, and it is not clear which book Zenzl is referring to here.

33. Ludwig "Luggi" Elfinger was working as an engineer in Chelyabinsk.

34. Zenzl Mühsam's "Der Leidensweg des Erich Mühsam" was published in Dutch in 1935 as "De lijdensweg van Erich Mühsam" in various pamphlet editions.

35. Vera Figner (1852-1942), Russian revolutionary. It does not appear that Zenzl lived with either her or Kropotkin's mother.

36. Reference to the nephew Joseph "Peps" Elfinger.

37. Wendelin Thomas, (1884–?), communist and friend of the Mühsams; emigrated to the United States in 1933.

38. Zenzl Mühsam is probably referring to the *Rote Frontkämpferbund* [Association of Red Front Fighters], an association of militias sponsored by the Communist Party in the 1920s.

39. *Sudetendeutsche* is the term commonly used for native German-speakers in the western parts of the former Czechoslovakia; almost the entire community of three million people left after World War II. In elections in 1935-1936, the newly founded *Sudetendeutsche Partei*, with close ties to the NSDAP, won a large percentage of the vote in the region.

40. Tomáš Masaryk (1850-1937), first president of the independent Czechoslovakia.

41. Such a book never appeared. A selection of Mühsam texts in German, edited by Nina Pawlowa, appeared in 1960.

42. It seems that such a translation never appeared.

43. Ernst Ottwalt (1901-1943), KPD author, arrested 1936, died in a penal colony.

44. A book of that kind, entitled *Bilder und Verse für Zenzl* [Drawings and Poems for Zenzl], finally appeared 1974 in the GDR (Leipzig: Edition Leipzig).

45. Alexander Granach (1890-1945), actor, Willi Bredel (1902-1964), writer, Willy Budich (1890-1939), KPD politician, Werner Hirsch (?), journalist, were all in exile in the Soviet Union.

46. The film was never completed.

47. Presumably, a nickname for Joseph "Peps" Elfinger.

48. Carola Neher (1900-1942), actress; Klabund (born Alfred Henschke, 1890-1928).
49. Literally, "Soldier Songs;" a common German term for songs sung in the military, often used by Mühsam in ironic ways or adapted for Red Army units.
50. Ernst Busch (1900-1980), proletarian actor and singer.
51. Ludwig "Luggi" Elfinger, Zenzl's nephew; it does not appear that Zenzl ever made that journey.
52. The fortress where Erich Mühsam spent most of the sentence for his involvement in the Bavarian Council Republic; many political prisoners were incarcerated in the Niederschönenfeld Fortress.
53. Heinrich Vogeler (1872-1942), left-leaning expressionist artist; after 1931 permanently in the Soviet Union; starved to death in Kazkhastan.
54. Melanie and Senja (Alexander) Ginsburg; Melanie was a cousin of Erich Mühsam; the couple lived in Kharkiv in Ukraine.
55. Presumably, Erich's sister Elisabeth Margarethe.
56. It is not clear what Zenzl Mühsam is referring to here.
57. Hans Günther Mühsam, Erich's brother, and his wife Minna.
58. Presumably, Erich's sister Elisabeth Margarethe.
59. Hedwig Kaltenhäuser (1899-1990s), daughter of the KPD co-founder Hermann Duncker (1874-1960) and Käthe Duncker (1871-1953); the family had moved to the GDR in 1947, after living in exile in the USA during the war; friends of the Mühsams since the 1920s.
60. Friede Düwell (?-1962), friend of Zenzl's from the children's home Ivanovo.
61. This street no longer exists.
62. Literally, "peace commodity;" at the time, a common German term for high quality and long-lasting material that was produced before the war.
63. Some of the diaries–from 1916 to 1919–disappeared in Moscow; see "Additional Diary Entries."
64. Max Schröder and Sepp Maier, close friends of the Mühsams in the 1920s; worked in the GDR as editors.
65. Roughly, "trade union academy;" an institute of higher learning run by a trade union.
66. Wilhelm Pieck (1876-1960), German communist and the first president of the German Democratic Republic (the post was abolished after his death); acquainted with the Mühsams since the 1920s.
67. Jelena Stassow received state honors in the GDR in 1956.

BIBLIOGRAPHY

This bibliography contains the main texts by and about Mühsam available in German and English. For a more detailed bibliography, including reprints, foreign-language publications other than English, and books containing chapters and sections on Mühsam, please see the comprehensive bibliography at *erichinenglish.org*.

GERMAN

Books and pamphlets by Mühsam published in his lifetime

"Die Homosexualität. Ein Beitrag zur Sittengeschichte unserer Zeit" [Homosexuality: A Contribution to the History of Morality in Our Times]. Berlin: M. Lilienthal, 1903.

Billys Erdengang. Eine Elephantengeschichte für artige Kinder [Billy on Earth: An Elephant Story for Children Who Behave]. With Hanns Heinz Ewers and Paul Haase. Berlin: Globus, 1904. Erich Mühsam contributed the poems to the book under the pseudonym "Onkel Franz."

Die Wüste. Gedichte 1898–1903 [The Desert: Poems 1898–1903]. Berlin: Eisselt, 1904.

"Ascona." Locarno: Birger Carlson, 1905.

Die Psychologie der Erbtante. Eine Tanthologie aus 25 Einzeldarstellungen zur Lösung der Unsterblichkeits-Frage [The Psychology of the Rich Aunt: An Aunthology of Twenty-Five Portraits to Answer the Question of Immortality]. Zürich: Caesar Schmidt, 1905. Satirical short stories.

Die Hochstapler. Lustspiel in vier Aufzügen [The Impostors: Comedy in Four Acts]. Munich: R. Piper & Co., 1906.

"Die Jagd auf Harden" [The Campaign against Harden]. Berlin: NBV, 1908.

Der Krater [The Crater]. Berlin: Morgen, 1909. Poetry.

Wüste–Krater–Wolken [Desert–Crater–Clouds]. Berlin: Paul Cassirer, 1914. Poetry.

Die Freivermählten. Polemisches Schauspiel in drei Aufzügen [The Freely Married: Polemical Drama in Three Acts]. Munich: Kain-Verlag, 1914.

Im Nachthemd durchs Leben. Ein süddeutsches Weihebühnen-Festspiel [Through Life in Pajamas: A Festive Southern German Drama for a Weihebühne]. With Reinhard Koester and Carl Georg von Maasen. Munich: Verein süddeutscher Bühnenkünstler, 1914.

Brennende Erde. Verse eines Kämpfers [The Earth Aflame: Verses of a Fighter]. Munich: Kurt Wolff, 1920.

Judas. Arbeiter-Drama in fünf Akten [Judas: Workers' Drama in Five Acts]. Berlin: Malik, 1921.

"Standrecht in Bayern" [Martial Law in Bavaria]. Berlin: Vereinigung Internationaler Verlagsanstalten, 1923. Mühsam reflects on the legal situation in Bavaria following the defeat of the Bavarian Council Republic. Written while confined in a fortress for his involvement in the events.

Revolution. Kampf-, Marsch- und Spottlieder [Revolution: Songs of Struggle, Marches, and Satirical Verses]. Berlin: Der freie Arbeiter/Rudolf Oestreich, 1925.

Alarm. Manifeste aus 20 Jahren [Alarm: Twenty Years of Manifestos]. Edited by Oskar Kanehl. Berlin: Der Syndicalist, 1925. Includes poems from *Wüste, Krater, Wolken* and *Brennende Erde*, and articles from *Kain*.

Seenot [Distress at Sea]. Vienna/Ober St. Veit: Verlag der Schriften, 1925. Poetry.

"Gerechtigkeit für Max Hoelz!" [Justice for Max Hoelz!] Berlin: Verlag Rote Hilfe Deutschlands, 1926.

Sammlung 1898–1928 [Collection 1898–1928]. Berlin: J.M. Spaeth, 1928.

Staatsräson. Ein Denkmal für Sacco und Vanzetti [The Reasoning of the State: A Memorial for Sacco and Vanzetti]. Berlin: Gilde freiheitlicher Bücherfreunde, 1928.

"Von Eisner bis Leviné: Die Entstehung der bayerischen Räterepublik" [From Eisner to Leviné: The Emergence of the Bavarian Council Republic]. Berlin: Fanal, 1929

Namen und Menschen. Unpolitische Erinnerungen [Names and People: Non-political Memoirs]. Leipzig: Leipziger Bibliophilen-Abend, 1949. Incomplete book edition of the series that originally appeared from 1927 to 1929 in the *Vossische Zeitung*.

Die Befreiung der Gesellschaft vom Staat: Was ist kommunistischer Anarchismus? [Liberating Society from the State: What Is Communist Anarchism?] Berlin: Fanal, 1933.

Books by Mühsam published posthumously

Handzeichnungen und Gedichte [Drawings and Poems]. Orselina: Leon Hirsch, 1936.

Namen und Menschen. Unpolitische Erinnerungen [Names and People: Non-political Memoirs]. Edited by Fritz Adolf Hünich. Leipzig: Volk und Buch, 1949. Complete book edition of the series that originally appeared from 1927 to 1929 in the *Vossische Zeitung*.

Gedichte [Poems]. Berlin: Volk und Welt, 1958.

War einmal ein Revoluzzer. Bänkellieder und Gedichte [Once Upon a Time There Was a Revolutionary: Bänkellieder and Poems]. Edited by Helga Bemmann. Berlin: Henschelverlag, 1968.

Bilder und Verse für Zenzl [Drawings and Poems for Zenzl]. Leipzig: Edition Leipzig, 1974. West German edition: Düsseldorf, Claassen Verlag, 1975.

Fanal. Aufsätze und Gedichte 1905–1932 [Fanal: Essays and Poems 1905–1932]. Edited by Kurt Kreiler. Berlin: Wagenbach Verlag, 1977.

Alle Wetter. Volksstück mit Gesang und Tanz [Thunderation! Folk Play with Song and Dance]. Berlin: Klaus Guhl, 1977. First book edition of Mühsam's last play, written in 1930.

Briefe an Zeitgenossen [Letters to Contemporaries]. Edited by Gerd W. Jungblut. 2 volumes. Berlin: Klaus Guhl, 1978.

Scheinwerfer oder Färbt ein weißes Blütenblatt sich Schwarz. Politische Essays, Gedichte, Briefe, Flugblätter [Searchlight, or When a White Petal Turns Black: Political Essays, Poems, Letters, and Leaflets]. Edited by Fidus. Berlin: Klaus Guhl, 1978.

Der Loreleyerkasten. Eine satirische Revue [The Loreyerkasten: A Satirical Revue]. Edited by Wolfgang Teichmann, illustrated by Paul Rosié. Berlin: Eulenspiegel-Verlag, 1978.

Färbt ein weißes Blütenblatt sich rot. Ein Leben in Zeugnissen und Selbstzeugnissen [When a White Petal Turns Red: A Life in Documents and Personal Accounts]. Edited by Wolfgang Teichmann. Berlin: Der Morgen, 1978.

Ascona. Zürich: Sanssouci, 1979. Contains the original pamphlet and passages on Ascona taken from other texts.

Der Bürgergarten. Zeitgedichte [The Bourgeois Garden: Poems]. Berlin/Weimar: Aufbau-Verlag, 1982.

Zur Psychologie der Erbtante. Satirisches Lesebuch 1900–1933 [On the Psychology of the Rich Aunt: A Satirical Reader 1900–1933]. Berlin: Eulenspiegel 1984.

Ich bin verdammt zu warten in einem Bürgergarten [I Am Condemned to Wait in a Bourgeois Garden]. 2 volumes. Edited by Wolfgang Haug. Darmstadt/Neuwied: Hermann Luchterhand, 1983.

In meiner Posaune muß ein Sandkorn sein: Briefe 1900–1934 [There Must Be a Grain of Sand in My Trombone: Letters 1900–1934]. 2 volumes. Edited by Gert W. Jungblut. Liechtenstein/Vaduz: Topos Verlag, 1984.

Trotz allem Mensch sein. Gedichte und Aufsätze [Being Human Despite It All: Poems and Essays]. Edited by Jürgen Schiewe und Hanne Maußner. Stuttgart: Reclam, 1984.

Streitschriften. Literarischer Nachlass [Polemics: From Mühsam's Papers]. Edited by Christlieb Hirte. Berlin: Volk und Welt, 1984.

Gesammelte Aufsätze [Collected Essays]. Edited by Gerd W. Jungblut. Berlin: Klaus Guhl, 1989.

Wie ich Dich liebe! [How I Love You!]. Berlin: Klaus Guhl, 1990. Poetry.

Berliner Feuilleton: Ein poetischer Kommentar auf die mißratene Zähmung des Adolf Hitler [Berlin Features: Poetic Commentary on the Failed Taming of Adolf Hitler]. Edited by Heinz Hug. Munich: Klaus Boer Verlag, 1992. The first publication of a collection of Mühsam's political satire written for *Ulk*, the weekly insert in the *Berliner Tageblatt*.

Mühsam's Geschütteltes. Schüttelreime und Schüttelgedichte [Shaken by Mühsam: Spoonerisms]. Edited by Reiner Scholz. Frankfurt am Main: Stadt- und Universitäts-Bibliothek, 1994.

Tagebücher 1910–1924 [Diary 1910–1924]. Edited by Chris Hirte. Munich: dtv, 1994.

Balladen [Ballads]. Berlin: Klaus Guhl, 1996.

Der Humbug der Wahlen [The Humbug of Elections]. Edited by Jochen Knoblauch. Berlin: Klaus Guhl, 1998.

Wir geben nicht auf! Texte und Gedichte [We Will Not Give Up! Texts and Poems]. Edited by Günther Gerstenberg. Munich: Allitera, 2003.

Aus Dur wird Moll, aus Haben Soll. Gedichte und Bänkellieder von Erich Mühsam [The Major Key Turns into Minor Key and To Have Turns into To Be: Poems and Bänkellieder by Erich Mühsam]. Erftstadt: area verlag, 2005.

In addition, numerous self-published pamphlets and zines with texts by Mühsam can be found in archives and infoshops across the German-speaking world.

Editions of Collected Works

All of the following editions include comprehensive collections of Mühsam's texts, covering his political essays, as well as poetry and drama.

Ausgewählte Werke in Einzelausgaben [Selected Works in Individual Editions]. 2 volumes. Edited by Fritz Adolf Hünich. Berlin: Volk und Welt, 1958.

Auswahl: Gedichte, Dramen, Prosa [Collection: Poems, Plays, Prose]. Edited by Dieter Schiller. Berlin: Volk und Welt, 1961.

Erich Mühsam: Gesamtausgabe [Erich Mühsam: Complete Works]. 4 volumes. Edited
by Günther Emig. Berlin: Europäische Ideen, 1977–1978. The title is somewhat
misleading. Although this is the most comprehensive of all of Mühsam's Collected
Works editions, it is far from complete.

Ausgewählte Werke [Selected Works]. *3 volumes*. Edited by Christlieb Hirte. Berlin:
Volk und Welt, 1978.

Sich fügen heisst lügen. Leben und Werk in Texten und Bildern [To Obey Means to
Lie: Life and Work in Texts and Pictures]. 2 volumes. Edited by Marlies Fritzen.
Göttingen: Steidl, 2003. Also contains many texts about Mühsam.

Books about Erich Mühsam

Berg, Hubert van den. *Erich Mühsam 1878–1934. Bibliographie der Literatur zu seinem
Leben und Werk* [Erich Mühsam 1878–1934: Bibliography of His Life and Work].
Leiden: Alpha, 1992. A comprehensive bibliography of secondary literature about
Erich Mühsam available at the time.

Haug, Wolfgang. *Erich Mühsam: Schriftsteller der Revolution* [Erich Mühsam: Writer
of the Revolution]. Reutlingen: Trotzdem, 1979. Together with Heinz Hug's *Erich
Mühsam. Untersuchungen zu Leben und Werk*, the standard West German biography
of Mühsam.

Hirte, Chris. *Erich Mühsam: Ihr seht mich nicht feige!* [Erich Mühsam: You Will Not See
Me Act Like a Coward!]. Berlin: Neues Leben, 1985. The standard East German
biography of Mühsam. Very characteristic of the official Marxist GDR portrayal
of Mühsam.

Hug, Heinz. *Erich Mühsam. Untersuchungen zu Leben und Werk* [Erich Mühsam: Studies
of His Life and Work]. Vaduz: Topos, 1974. See Wolfgang Haug, *Erich Mühsam:
Schriftsteller der Revolution*.

Hug, Heinz and Gerd W. Jungblut. *Erich Mühsam (1878–1934). Bibliographie.* Vaduz/
Liechtenstein: Topos-Verlag, 1991. Comprehensive, if outdated, Mühsam bibliography.

Jungblut, Gerd W. *Erich Mühsam: Notizen eines politischen Werdegangs* [Erich Mühsam:
Notes on a Political Life]. Schlitz: Verlag der Slitese, 1984. Adds some information
to the works by Hug, Hirte, and Haug from the 1970s.

Kauffeldt, Rolf. *Erich Mühsam: Literatur und Anarchie* [Erich Mühsam: Literature
and Anarchy]. Munich: Wilhelm Fink Verlag, 1983. Focuses on Erich Mühsam
the writer.

Kauffeldt, Rolf. *Erich Mühsam zur Einführung* [Erich Mühsam: An Introduction]. Hamburg: Junius, 1989. Concise introduction to Mühsam in the popular Junius series.

Köhnen, Diana. *Das literarische Werk Erich Mühsams. Kritik und utopische Antizipation* [The Literary Work of Erich Mühsam: Critique and Utopian Anticipation]. Würzburg: Dr. Johannes Königshausen & Dr. Thomas Neumann, 1988. Another study focusing on Mühsam's role as a writer.

Mühsam, Kreszentia. *Der Leidensweg Erich Mühsams* [The Ordeal of Erich Mühsam]. Moskau: MOPR, 1935. Account of Erich's suffering and death at the hand of the Nazis, written by his wife Zenzl.

Linse, Ulrich. *Organisierter Anarchismus im deutschen Kaiserreich von 1871* [Organized Anarchism in the German Kaiserreich of 1871]. Berlin: Duncker & Humblot, 1969. An essential study on anarchism in the German Kaiserreich; contains a lot of detailed and valuable information on Erich Mühsam.

Lübeck's Erich Mühsam Society has published two series since its foundation in 1989: the *Mühsam-Magazin* [Mühsam Magazine], which appears irregularly and includes texts by and about Mühsam, as well as information on the Erich Mühsam Society; and the *Schriften der Erich-Mühsam-Gesellschaft* [Writings by the Erich Mühsam Society], which appear annually and includes formerly unpublished or out-of-print texts by Mühsam, as well as papers presented at the Society's annual *Erich-Mühsam-Tagung* [Erich Mühsam Conference]. A detailed list can be found at the Society's website, *www. erich-mühsam.de*, or in the bibliography at *erichinenglish.org*.

ENGLISH

Prose by Mühsam in print

"Freedom as a Social Principle" ("Die Freiheit als gesellschaftliches Prinzip"), *Black Flag Quarterly*, Autumn 1984.

Thunderation!/Alle Wetter!: Folk Play With Song and Dance/Volksstück Mit Gesang Und Tanz. Translated, edited, and introduced by David A. Shepherd. Lewisburg, PA: Bucknell University Press, 2001.

"The Artist in the Future State" ("Der Künstler im Zukunftsstaat"), translated by Christopher Winks, Soup 3 (1983). Reprinted in Max Blechman, ed., *Revolutionary Romanticism: A Drunken Boat Anthology*. San Francisco: City Lights Books, 1999.

Texts about Mühsam in print

Anonymous, "Erich Muehsam. Poet, Playwright, Bohemian, Anarchist Revolutionary." *Organize! for Revolutionary Anarchism*, no. 67, Autumn 2006.

Baron, Lawrence. "Erich Mühsam's Jewish Identity." *Leo Baeck Institute Yearbook*, vol. 25, no. 1, 1980.

Baron, Lawrence. *The Eclectic Anarchism of Erich Mühsam*. New York: Revisionist Press, 1976. The only general overview of Mühsam's life and work available in English.

J.T. "Erich Mühsam." *Anarchy* 54, August 1965.

Lewin, Roland. "Erich Mühsam 1878–1934." Supplement to *Le monde libertaire* 143 (June 1968). Reprinted as Roland Lewin, "Erich Muehsam, 1878–1934: The Man and His Work," *Cienfuegos Press Anarchist Review*, no. 3, 1977.

Shepherd, David A. *From Bohemia to the Barricades: Erich Mühsam and the Development of a Revolutionary Drama*. New York: Peter Lang, 1993. Comprehensive study of Erich Mühsam the dramatist.

Winks, Christopher. "Erich Mühsam: In Defense of Literary High Treason," in: Max Blechman, ed., *Revolutionary Romanticism: A Drunken Boat Anthology*. San Francisco: City Lights Books, 1999.

erichinenglish.org

The single best source for English-language texts by and about Mühsam, *erichinenglish.org* provides exclusive translations of the plays *Judas: Ein Arbeiterdrama in fünf Akten* and *Staatsräson: Ein Denkmal für Sacco und Vanzetti*, the first English translation of *Die Befreiung der Gesellschaft vom Staat*, a selection of Mühsam articles, reproductions or links to Mühsam poems translated into English, and some secondary material.

Index

A

Adler, Viktor 122, 126
Africa 80, 161
Akademie der Künste (Berlin) 269–270
America (North) 101–102, 174–180, 259
America (South) 102
America, United States of 18, 175, 180,
    263, 267, 269, 282
Amsterdam 247, 256
Anarchistische Föderation Deutschlands
    (AFD) 4, 18, 20, 173
anarcho-syndicalism 12, 223, 268
Anarchy (journal) 17
Ansbach Fortress 120, 141
anti-fascism 17, 269
anti-Semitism 95–96, 139–144, 154, 164
Aphrodite (Greek mythology) 36, 51
Arbeitertum (journal) 15
Arnim, Bettina von 89, 91
Ascona 5–6, 39–42, 43, 45–46, 50–54, 58
Augsburg 122, 125
Austria 12, 25, 42, 54, 56, 73, 122,
    125–126, 142, 144, 152, 166,
    173, 180–181, 263
Austrian-Hungarian Empire 181
Axelrod, Towia 122, 126

B

Bab, Julius 39, 42, 58
Bachlund, Gary 17
Bachofen, Johann Jakob 78–79, 243
Baden-Württemberg 282
Bakunin, Mikhail 9–10, 164–166, 170,
    172, 243
Balabanoff, Angelica 260, 264

Balkans 177
Ball, Hugo 254
Bamberg 9, 125–126, 128, 131–133
Bamberger Volksblatt (journal) 127
Banten (Indonesia) 161
Barcelona 282
Baron, Lawrence 17
Bauer, Otto 122, 126
Bavaria 7–9, 13, 16, 18, 20, 26, 67, 73,
    108, 111, 119, 121–126, 132–133,
    141–143, 150, 152–153,
    155–156, 169, 181, 182, 243,
    257, 267, 276, 281
Bavarian Council Republic 3–4, 9, 14–15,
    20, 26, 120–121, 126, 129, 131,
    133, 137, 140, 155, 172, 175,
    181, 264, 276–277, 283
Bavarian Revolution 3–4, 26, 119, 126, 155
Beer Hall Putsch 20, 156
Beilis, Mendel 95–96, 139
Belgrade 176
Berkman, Alexander 15, 256, 260,
    263–264
Berlin 1–2, 5, 7, 9–10, 12, 16–19, 21,
    22, 25, 29, 33, 36, 39–40, 42, 49,
    51–54, 58, 73, 74–75, 80, 111,
    113, 119, 126, 131, 133, 150–151,
    152–153, 155, 159, 169,
    175–176, 183, 187–188, 249,
    257–260, 263, 267, 269–270,
    275, 280, 282
Bern 5, 253
Billings, Warren 259–260, 263
Bismarck, Otto von 162–166
Blanqui, Louis Auguste/Blanquism 121
Bloch, Iwan 33

FRIENDS OF PM

These are indisputably momentous times – the financial system is melting down globally and the Empire is stumbling. Now more than ever there is a vital need for radical ideas.

In the three years since its founding – and on a mere shoestring – PM Press has risen to the formidable challenge of publishing and distributing knowledge and entertainment for the struggles ahead. With over 100 releases to date, we have published an impressive and stimulating array of literature, art, music, politics, and culture. Using every available medium, we've succeeded in connecting those hungry for ideas and information to those putting them into practice.

Friends of PM allows you to directly help impact, amplify, and revitalize the discourse and actions of radical writers, filmmakers, and artists. It provides us with a stable foundation from which we can build upon our early successes and provides a much-needed subsidy for the materials that can't necessarily pay their own way. You can help make that happen – and receive every new title automatically delivered to your door once a month – by joining as a Friend of PM Press. And, we'll throw in a free T-Shirt when you sign up.

Here are your options:

- $25 a month: Get all books and pamphlets plus 50% discount on all webstore purchases
- $25 a month: Get all CDs and DVDs plus 50% discount on all webstore purchases
- $40 a month: Get all PM Press releases plus 50% discount on all webstore purchases
- $100 a month: Superstar - Everything plus PM merchandise, free downloads, and 50% discount on all webstore purchases

For those who can't afford $25 or more a month, we're introducing **Sustainer Rates** at $15, $10 and $5. Sustainers get a free PM Press t-shirt and a 50% discount on all purchases from our website.

Your Visa or Mastercard will be billed once a month, until you tell us to stop. Or until our efforts succeed in bringing the revolution around. Or the financial meltdown of Capital makes plastic redundant. Whichever comes first.

ABOUT PM

PM Press was founded at the end of 2007 by a small collection of folks with decades of publishing, media, and organizing experience. PM Press co-conspirators have published and distributed hundreds of books, pamphlets, CDs, and DVDs. Members of PM have founded enduring book fairs, spearheaded victorious tenant organizing campaigns, and worked closely with bookstores, academic conferences, and even rock bands to deliver political and challenging ideas to all walks of life. We're old enough to know what we're doing and young enough to know what's at stake.

We seek to create radical and stimulating fiction and non-fiction books, pamphlets, t-shirts, visual and audio materials to entertain, educate, and inspire you. We aim to distribute these through every available channel with every available technology, whether that means you are seeing anarchist classics at our bookfair stalls; reading our latest vegan cookbook at the café; downloading geeky fiction e-books; or digging new music and timely videos from our website.

PM Press is always on the lookout for talented and skilled volunteers, artists, activists and writers to work with. If you have a great idea for a project or can contribute in some way, please get in touch.

PM Press
PO Box 23912
Oakland CA 94623
510-658-3906
www.pmpress.org

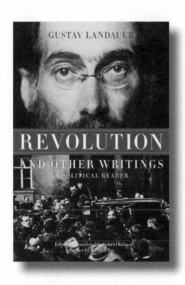

REVOLUTION AND OTHER WRITINGS:
A Political Reader

Gustav Landauer
Edited by Gabriel Kuhn
$26.95
978-1-60486-054-2

"Landauer is the most important agitator of the radical and
revolutionary movement in the
entire country." This is how Gustav Landauer is described in a
German police file from 1893. Twenty-six years later, Landauer
would die at the hands of reactionary soldiers who overthrew
the Bavarian Council Republic, a three-week attempt to realize
libertarian socialism amidst the turmoil of post-World War I
Germany. It was the last chapter in the life of an activist, writer,
and mystic who Paul Avrich calls "the most influential German
anarchist intellectual of the twentieth century."

This is the first comprehensive collection of Landauer writings
in English. It includes one of his major works, *Revolution*, 30
additional essays and articles, and a selection of correspondence. The texts cover Landauer's entire political biography,
from his early anarchism of the 1890s to his philosophical
reflections at the turn of the century, the subsequent establishment of the Socialist Bund, his tireless agitation against the
war, and the final days among the revolutionaries in Munich.
Additional chapters collect Landauer's articles on radical politics in the U.S. and Mexico, and illustrate the scope of his writing with texts on corporate capital, language, education, and
Judaism. The book includes an extensive introduction, commentary, and bibliographical information, compiled by the editor and translator Gabriel Kuhn.

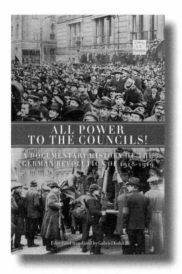

ALL POWER TO THE COUNCILS!

A Documentary History of the German Revolution of 1918–1919

Edited by Gabriel Kuhn

$26.95

978-1-60486-111-2

The defeat in World War I and the subsequent end of the Kaiserreich threw Germany into turmoil. While the Social Democrats grabbed power, radicals across the country rallied to establish a socialist society under the slogan "All Power to the Councils!" The Spartacus League staged an uprising in Berlin, council republics were proclaimed in Bremen and Bavaria, and workers' revolts shook numerous German towns. The rebellions were crushed by the Social Democratic government with the help of right-wing militias like the notorious Free Corps. This paved the way to a dysfunctional Weimar Republic that witnessed the rise of the National Socialist movement.

The documentary history presented here collects manifestos, speeches, articles, and letters from the German Revolution, introduced and annotated by the editor. Many documents, like the anarchist Erich Mühsam's comprehensive account of the Bavarian Council Republic, are made available in English for the first time. The volume also includes appendixes portraying the Red Ruhr Army that repelled the reactionary Kapp Putsch in 1920, and the communist bandits that roamed Eastern Germany until 1921.

All Power to the Councils! provides a dynamic and vivid picture of a time with long-lasting effects for world history—a time that was both encouraging and tragic.

FIRE AND FLAMES
A History of the German Autonomist Movement

Geronimo
Introduction by
George Katsiaficas
Afterword by Gabriel Kuhn
$19.95
978-1-60486-097-9

Fire and Flames was the first comprehensive study of the German autonomous movement ever published. Released in 1990, it reached its fifth edition by 1997, with the legendary German *Konkret* journal concluding that "the movement had produced its own classic." The author, writing under the pseudonym of Geronimo, has been an autonomous activist since the movement burst onto the scene in 1980-81. In this book, he traces its origins in the Italian Autonomia project and the German social movements of the 1970s, before describing the battles for squats, "free spaces," and alternative forms of living that defined the first decade of the autonomous movement. Tactics of the "Autonome" were militant, including the construction of barricades or throwing molotov cocktails at the police. Because of their outfit (heavy black clothing, ski masks, helmets), the Autonome were dubbed the "Black Bloc" by the German media, and their tactics have been successfully adopted and employed at anti-capitalist protests worldwide.

Fire and Flames is no detached academic study, but a passionate, hands-on, and engaging account of the beginnings of one of Europe's most intriguing protest movements of the last thirty years. An introduction by George Katsiaficas, author of *The Subversion of Politics* and an afterword by Gabriel Kuhn, a long-time autonomous activist and author, add historical context and an update on the current state of the Autonomen.

THE CNT IN THE SPANISH REVOLUTION VOLUME *1*

José Peirats
$28.00
978-1-60486-207-2

The CNT in the Spanish Revolution is the history of one of the most original and audacious, and arguably also the most far-reaching, of all the twentieth-century revolutions. It is the history of the giddy years of political change and hope in 1930s Spain, when the so-called 'Generation of '36', Peirats' own generation, rose up against the oppressive structures of Spanish society. It is also a history of a revolution that failed, crushed in the jaws of its enemies on both the reformist left and the reactionary right.

José Peirats' account is effectively the official CNT history of the war, passionate, partisan but, above all, intelligent. Its huge sweeping canvas covers all areas of the anarchist experience—the spontaneous militias, the revolutionary collectives, the moral dilemmas occasioned by the clash of revolutionary ideals and the stark reality of the war effort against Franco and his German Nazi and Italian Fascist allies.

This new edition is carefully indexed in a way that converts the work into a usable tool for historians and makes it much easier for the general reader to dip in with greater purpose and pleasure.

> "For those whose field of study is modern Spain, this is indeed an obligatory purchase. Given that this edition has been indexed and footnoted it may prove more useful to scholars than the original Spanish-language editions." —Kate Sharpley Library

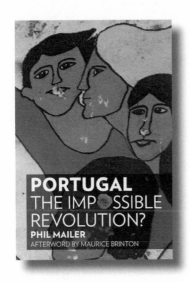

PORTUGAL
The Impossible Revolution?

Phil Mailer
Afterword by Maurice Brinton
$24.95
978-1-60486-336-9

After the military coup in Portugal on April 25, 1974, the overthrow of almost fifty years of Fascist rule, and the end of three colonial wars, there followed eighteen months of intense, democratic social transformation which challenged every aspect of Portuguese society. What started as a military coup turned into a profound attempt at social change from the bottom up and became headlines on a daily basis in the world media. This was due to the intensity of the struggle as well as the fact that in 1974–75 the right-wing moribund Francoist regime was still in power in neighboring Spain and there was huge uncertainty as to how these struggles might affect Spain and Europe at large.

This is the story of what happened in Portugal between April 25, 1974, and November 25, 1975, as seen and felt by a deeply committed participant. It depicts the hopes, the tremendous enthusiasm, the boundless energy, the total commitment, the released power, even the revolutionary innocence of thousands of ordinary people taking a hand in the remolding of their lives. And it does so against the background of an economic and social reality which placed limits on what could be done.

"Mailer portrays history with the enthusiasm of a cheerleader, the 'home team' in this case being libertarian communism. Official documents, position papers and the pronouncements of the protagonists of this drama are mostly relegated to the appendices. The text itself recounts the activities of a host of worker, tenant, soldier and student committees as well as the author's personal experiences." —Ian Wallace, *Library Journal*

REBEL VOICES
An IWW Anthology

Edited by Joyce W. Kornbluh
$27.95
978-1-60486-483-0

Welcoming women, Blacks, and immigrants long before most other unions, the Wobblies from the start were labor's outstanding pioneers and innovators, unionizing hundreds of thousands of workers previously regarded as "unorganizable." Wobblies organized the first sit-down strike (at General Electric, Schenectady, 1906), the first major auto strike (6,000 Studebaker workers, Detroit, 1911), the first strike to shut down all three coalfields in Colorado (1927), and the first "no-fare" transit-workers' job-action (Cleveland, 1944). With their imaginative, colorful, and world-famous strikes and free-speech fights, the IWW wrote many of the brightest pages in the annals of working class emancipation.

Wobblies also made immense and invaluable contributions to workers' culture. All but a few of America's most popular labor songs are Wobbly songs. IWW cartoons have long been recognized as labor's finest and funniest.

The impact of the IWW has reverberated far beyond the ranks of organized labor. An important influence on the 1960s New Left, the Wobbly theory and practice of direct action, solidarity, and "class-war" humor have inspired several generations of civil rights and antiwar activists, and are a major source of ideas and inspiration for today's radicals. Indeed, virtually every movement seeking to "make this planet a good place to live" (to quote an old Wobbly slogan), has drawn on the IWW's incomparable experience.

Originally published in 1964 and long out of print, *Rebel Voices* remains by far the biggest and best source on IWW history, fiction, songs, art, and lore. This new edition includes 40 pages of additional material from the 1998 Charles H. Kerr edition from Fred Thompson and Franklin Rosemont, and a new preface by Wobbly organizer Daniel Gross.